# FRENCH

## HOW TO SPEAK AND WRITE IT

AN EASY APPROACH TO THE LANGUAGE, WITH
THE AID OF NUMEROUS ILLUSTRATIONS AND
A NEW PHONETIC SYSTEM OF PRONUNCIATION

*By* JOSEPH LEMAÎTRE

FOREWORD BY RENÉ CASSIN, D.C.L.
*Vice-President of the Council of State in France*
*Professor of Civil and International Law*

STUDY GUIDE BY L. E. GENISSIEUX
*Director of Studies, Institut Français du*
*Royaume-Uni*

ODHAMS PRESS LIMITED · LONG ACRE · LONDON · W.C.2

# FOREWORD

IT is gratifying to a Frenchman to note that students of the French language are, in Great Britain, more numerous than ever. The language of a nation is the key to her ways of thought and her character. Through mastery of the French language, many of our British friends will realise how closely united, despite differences of manner and approach, our two nations are by their common belief in the same fundamental values.

This was never so clearly seen as in the times when those values were in danger. Two successive wars have proved to the world and to ourselves that there can be no security for either of our two nations if the other is threatened. Only through close and lasting co-operation can our common interests be served and our common ideal of freedom be maintained.

Each one of us must share in bringing out that co-operation, by trying to understand better our neighbours across the Channel. Exchanges between our respective universities and schools, and all forms of personal contact with the family, social and cultural life of the neighbour nation, will help in that great task. Whether these contacts consist of exchanges of letters or of visits ; of studies of language, literature, music or art ; or simply of a human interest in the affairs and way of life of a friendly neighbour—the gain that they will bring is twofold : the cause of mutual understanding between nations will be furthered and the personal horizon will be broadened.

For her part, France is eager to greet all her British friends coming to study her language and civilisation. Not only to these will this book be of help, but also to thousands who, though past school age, wish to have access to the study of the French language and literature. I welcome the contribution which this book brings to a new and deeper understanding between our two countries. May its readers be among the Men of Good Will through whom peace may be maintained on earth.

RENÉ CASSIN

*Vice-President of the Council of State in France*
*Professor of Civil and International Law*

# CONTENTS

*A DETAILED ALPHABETICAL GUIDE TO THE
CONTENTS IS GIVEN ON PAGE 416*

**TUNISIAN STREET SCENE**

French is spoken throughout a large part of the African continent, which also forms the background of many French literary works. This scene recalls the delightful travel memoirs of Eugène Fromentin, the nineteenth century painter-writer. An appreciation of French writers and their works is given in the Study Guide at the end of this book.

# HOW TO USE THE COURSE

THE purpose of the present French Course is to lead students easily and naturally into a real working knowledge of the French language, and also to afford them an opportunity of appreciating French literature.

This course deals more thoroughly with the elementary stage and the grading of progress is less steep than is usual in language courses. It is so designed that any intelligent person can start as an absolute beginner and finish with a practical working knowledge of French. The text must be thoroughly mastered and its correct pronunciation acquired with the aid of the translation and the imitated pronunciation. A good plan would be to study together with friends—at least one of them preferably a native speaker—who can check your pronunciation.

Grammar is conveyed throughout by practical examples which should be memorised as far as possible. This method is preferred to the mere learning of rules by rote which tends to produce a type of student who has mastered the most abstruse niceties of grammar yet is unable correctly to ask his way to a station or order a meal in a restaurant.

For those students, and we hope they will be many, who desire to utilise the knowledge gained through the Course as a stepping stone to the mastery of French Literature, a Study Guide has been provided at the end of the Course. This, written by a distinguished authority on the French language and literature, offers admirable advice in that respect.

## FRENCH PRONUNCIATION

No doubt you have heard Frenchmen speaking their language on the radio, in the cinema or elsewhere. You will have

NOTE.—In the case of certain prices quoted in the Course for meals, the reader must make allowances for varying conditions.

noticed that it sounds quite different from English ; you may even have called it a "gabble". How are you going to learn to understand that gabble, and speak the same language yourself in a way a Frenchman will understand? It is not enough to know what a French word means and how it is spelt; you must know how to pronounce it, too, and, with that, how to recognise it when spoken.

Neither this book nor any other can teach you the correct pronunciation of French. It can help you to acquire it, and can explain the difficulties, but it cannot speak French to you.

Luckily, there are other ways—the wireless, for example. Listening-in, even if you

don't at first understand, will gradually attune your ears to French sounds and intonation. On any ordinary set, you can get services in French from Paris and from other stations.

Suppose you switch on the radio and hear the French announcer introduce a programme. You don't understand him, but he says : **Poste National—Radio Paris.**

You recognise the words now that you see them. (*Poste* means a Radio-station.)

Why did you fail to recognise the words as the announcer uttered them? We use all four words in English, too, but the French pronounce them differently. If you listen very carefully you may come to the conclusion that what the announcer said was not *poste* but *boste*. You may have this idea too when you first hear a Frenchman say **pardon!** where we say "sorry!" or **une seconde** where we say "one moment please!" It may sound like *bardon, s'gonde*. To discover the reason for this, hold a lighted match in front of your mouth and say the English word "post". The match will probably go out, or certainly flicker, because so much breath is expelled before you actually make the first sound. In pronouncing the French *p* you must let out as little breath as possible before the sound; try to say *poste* in such a way that the flame of the match is disturbed as little as possible.

**National.** This is pronounced with the sounds "nah-syoh-nal", the first syllable as in "nasty" and the last rhyming with "pal". But this is still not enough to tell us what the word sounds like. Take again the corresponding English word "National". It is easy to say what sound the vowel in the first syllable is, because it bears a very heavy stress, but with the other two it is more difficult, because we pronounce them quickly and rather indistinctly. In rapid speech we may even say *nashnl*. The French will have none of this mumbling, and every syllable must be pronounced equally clearly, with an equal stress on all three.

**Radio** is pronounced *rah-dee-oh*.

**Paris** is pronounced *pah-ree*.

We must remember not to sound the *p* too sharply and not to let the *ee* at the end trail off into some other sound; it must be cut off cleanly.

Now we know that the announcer said: *post nah-syoh-nal rah-dee-oh pah-ree*.

To explain the remaining sounds of French we will take some words that are common to both French and English. The reader is almost certainly familiar with the words **charlotte russe, hors**

**d'œuvre, restaurant, liqueur, camembert,** etc. They are all French words which are often used in English, and they all have to do with eating. In the mouths of the English people these words have either an English pronunciation or a compromise between the English and the French; in either case the pronunciation of them would puzzle a Frenchman.

**Charlotte russe:** The first part of the name of this sweet is pronounced *shahr-lot*, just as in English, except that the *r* is pronounced more strongly and that we must beware of stressing the first syllable at the expense of the second. Both must have equal attention. The vowel of the second word, *russe*, meaning Russian, has no English equivalent. If you say *ee* with your lips right out, as though you were going to whistle, you will get the sound. This we represent in our imitated pronunciation by ē̃.

**Hors d'œuvre:** The first part of the word is pronounced like the underlined part of the word lo<u>r</u>d, and *œu* is pronounced like *ea* in <u>ea</u>rth. This sound is rendered as a͞y in our system of simplified pronunciation (the combination *œu* is rather unusual) so that we can render the pronunciation of *hors d'œuvre* by *or-da͞yvr*.

**Restaurant:** The first part is pronounced like 'rest'. The vowel *au* is the pure 'oh'. The only difficulty will be the sound of the last syllable. In French it is a nasal sound, and to get it right you will have to practise it a little. The term 'nasal' indicates that the sound is made through the nose. That is to say, it will bear a resemblance to the sounds a Cockney or an American makes if he has a twang. Begin by humming a long *m* on one note. Do this hard enough and you will feel a slight vibration inside the nose. Still keeping up the humming sound, suddenly open your mouth and say *ah*. The result will be the French nasal *a*, represented in the word restaurant by *an*. The *n* is not sounded; it only serves to show that the *a* is to be nasalised in the way described. Naturally you will not need to hum every time you make this sound; that is only a way the beginner may acquire it. In our system of imitated pronunciation we shall show this sound by a capital N to mark the difference between an ordinary *n* and a nasal. It is not a consonant, but merely an indication that the preceding vowel is a nasal one.

In actual French spelling the sound aN is rendered by either an, am, en or em.

| | | |
|---|---|---|
| **tante** | **gant** | **ambassade** |
| taNt | gaN | aN-ba-sahd |
| *aunt* | *glove* | *embassy* |
| | | |
| **enfant** | **vente** | **embrasser** |
| aN-faN | vaNt | aN-bra-say |
| *child* | *sale* | *to embrace* |

The French word for *long* is spelt the same as in English. To pronounce it correctly you have to let as much air as possible pass through the nose and to clip off the suspicion of *g* you can hear in the English pronunciation of the word. You also have to round your lips slightly. Now say, pronouncing *oN* in the same way:

| | | |
|---|---|---|
| **crayon** | **bon** | **réponse** |
| kray-yoN | boN | ray-poNs |
| *pencil* | *good* | *reply* |
| | | |
| **pont** | **son** | **tombeau** |
| poN | soN | toN-boh |
| *bridge* | *sound* | *tomb* |

Now say *bang* without sounding the *g*, allowing part of the air to escape through the nose. This is the way to pronounce the French word for "bath", which is spelt *bain*. In our imitated pronunciation we give it as biN, rendering the nasal by iN. In ordinary French spelling it appears as either in (im), ain (aim), or ein (eim).

| | | |
|---|---|---|
| **vin** | **pain** | **Américain** |
| viN | piN | ah-may-ree-kiN |
| *wine* | *bread* | *American* |
| | | |
| **fin** | **impoli** | **teint** |
| fiN | iN-po-lee | tiN |
| *end* | *impolite* | *complexion* |

If you pronounce *i* as in "sir" with slightly rounded lips and allow part of the air to pass through the nose you will be able to pronounce *un* or *um* and to say:

| | |
|---|---|
| **parfum** | **Verdun** |
| pahr-fuN | vair-duN |
| *perfume* | *Verdun* |
| | |
| **un**    **brun** | **lundi** |
| uN    bruN | luN-dee |
| *one*    *brown* | *Monday* |

The four nasal sounds are aN (as in *restaurant*), oN (as in *long*), iN (as in *vin*), and uN (as in *Verdun*). All the four nasals are to be found in

un bon vin blanc (*a good white wine*).
uN boN viN blaN.

## DIFFERENCE BETWEEN ENGLISH AND FRENCH PRONUNCIATION

1. *French sounds are invariably pure*

When you say "me" or "fee" in English the sound "ee" always remains the same, and so does the position of your lips. In other words: this "ee" is a pure vowel. But if you say "rate", "home", "night", watching your lips, you will notice that they gradually close, and that what you actually say is a kind of double sound (called diphthong), rather like "ray-it", "ho-em", "nigh-it", etc.

Now, in French, the vowels sound invariably pure, and the sound remains the same from beginning to end: "a" is pure *ah*, "o" is pure *oh* and "e" pure *eh*, and so on.

When you say "Paris" in English, if you hold a lighted match in front of your mouth and try to say the "p" in such a way that the flame remains undisturbed, you will say the pure French *p*. The same applies to *b*, *m*, *f* and *v* which, like the *p*, are produced by separating the lips. In French, therefore, when making these sounds, you must try to let as little air as possible come out of your mouth.

2. *The syllables of a French word are evenly pronounced*

In English it is just the opposite. There is a strong stress on one syllable—usually the first—whereas the others are muttered more or less indistinctly, and often completely slurred together.

Take, for instance, the word "generally."

This is really a word of four syllables, but in ordinary English conversation it is often reduced to "genrly". In French the corresponding word, **généralement,** is a word of five syllables, and it is pronounced with five syllables : "zhay-nay-rah-le-maN".

While English speech can be likened to a string of beads where some big beads alternate with some small ones. French

speech, on the contrary, may be likened to a string of pearls in which all are of the same size, thus:

From this we must learn that every syllable in French is to be pronounced evenly. There should be no drawling, or mumbling, as in English. This rule holds good for all words except those which end in unaccented *e,* which *e* is always silent, e.g., **table, téléphone, dame**—pronounced: "tahbl", "tay-lay-fohn", "dahm".

3. *Greater mobility of the speech organs in French*

The lips and the tongue must be more mobile in French, and the mouth must frequently be opened wider than in English:

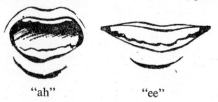

"ah"                    "ee"

e.g., when saying "pah-tees-ree" (**pâtisserie**), the mouth must be wide open for the "ah", and for the "ee" the corners of the lips have to be wide apart.

4. *When silent letters cease to be silent*

Many words are joined together in speech. Just as the English words "ham and eggs" are often pronounced as if they were one word, "hamaneggs", so, in French, words are often similarly joined together. This linking together is called liaison.

As a rule, the final consonant of a word is not pronounced in French. When, however, a word ending in a consonant is followed by a word beginning with a vowel, the final consonant is often linked with the vowel of the following word. This linking occurs especially with words which are closely connected in sense.

### EXAMPLES :

**Ils** (which means "they" and is pronounced "eel") and **ont** (which means "have" and is pronounced "oN"), when occurring together become "eel-zoN".

**Trois** (which means "three" and is pronounced "trwah") and **amis** (which means "friends" and is pronounced "ah-mee"), when coming together are said as "trwah-zah-mee".

**Mon** (which means "my" and is pronounced "moN") and **oncle** (which means "uncle" and is pronounced "oNkl") are said together as "mo-noNkl".

Note from the last example that in liaison a nasal ceases to be a nasal. The vowel loses its nasal quality and the *n* is pronounced as an ordinary "n".

*The a͡y Sound in Imitated Pronunciation*

The sound of *eu* (sometimes *œu*) in French is represented in our imitated pronunciation by a͡y, this special type indicating the sound of those letters in English, when spoken with rounded lips. There is actually a difference between the pronunciation of *eu* in French when final as in *feu* (fire) or when followed by a silent consonant as in *deux* (two); and when followed by a hard consonant, as in *fleur* (flower). In order to avoid multiplication of special characters, we indicate both by the same symbol, but students should keep their ears attuned to mark the difference in French as spoken by Frenchmen.

*et* and *est*

Our representation of both these words by "-ay" in the imitated pronunciation, is only an approximation, though it should enable you to make yourself understood by a Frenchman. But if you wish to speak correctly, you will listen carefully for the way in which these sounds really differ in French as spoken by educated persons.

*Pronunciation of -lle and -gn-*

The letters *-lle* coming after *i* in French with certain exceptions such as *ville* (town) which is pronounced "veel", are reproduced by a sound like the "y" in "yes". Examples are **fille** (fee*y*) daughter, and **tilleul** (tee-y@yl) linden-tree.

We print this *y* in italics when it comes at the end of a word, so as to avoid confusion.

We also use this italicised *y* in similar cases when representing the -gn- sounds in French, which are reproduced by a sound resembling the "ny" in "canyon".

Thus, students cannot easily fall into the error of pronouncing veen*y* (**vigne**, vine) in our imitated pronunciation, to rhyme with the infamous "Sweeney" (Todd) or kaN-pan*y* (**campagne**, countryside) to rhyme with "canny".

### PRONUNCIATION AND SPELLING

In English the same letter may be pronounced in various ways, e.g., the letter "a" is pronounced differently in the words "far", "ball", "gate", "at", "general". On the other hand, the same sound may be represented by several different spellings, as when in writing "keen", "machine", "lean", and "scene".

French has a less irregular spelling than English in so far as each letter and each combination of letters usually corresponds to one sound only. On the other hand, the same sound may be represented by several different spellings, although not quite to the same extent as in English. For instance, the sound *k*, which is usually represented by *c*, is in some words rendered by *k* or *qu*. The nasal sound "aN" will be found represented variously by *an*, *am*, *en* or *em*.

This, I fear, is rather confusing to the beginner, so in order to avoid confusion,

we have adopted a system of simplified spelling, i.e., one in which each letter and each combination of letters corresponds to one sound only. As far as possible we have rendered French sounds by their English equivalents, but in those instances where there is no English equivalent, we have rendered the French sound by the *nearest* English equivalent, together with a sign indicating how the French sound differs from the English.

As the two ways in which French vowels differ from their nearest English equivalents are either in rounding of the lips or nasalisation, we have indicated by ⊃ that the lips have to be rounded whilst producing the corresponding sound, and by "*N*" that the preceding vowel has to be nasalised in the manner described in the preceding pages.

### SOUNDS OF SPOKEN FRENCH

Tabulating the sounds of French, as represented in our system of imitated pronunciation, we have :—

ah    like a "r" in "car" cut short and without pronouncing the "r"; but when spelt "â", and in some other words, long and open as in the exclamation "ah!"

ai    as in "fair" (mouth open a little wider).

aN    nasal "a".

ay    like the "a" in "gate" (corners of the lips wide apart).

@y    the same with rounded lips—no English equivalent, but somewhat like the "ea" in "earth".

e    as in "wonder".

ee    as in "feet" (corners of the lips wide apart).

ẽe    the same with rounded lips—no English equivalent.

iN    nasal "ai" (like "an" in "bang").

o    as in "not" (lips pushed out, slightly rounded).

oh    as in "note" (lips further advanced and more rounded).

oo    as in "boot".

oN   nasal "o" (nearly as "on" in "long").
uN   like the "u" in "fur", but nasalised.
g    as in "go".
l    as in "lamp" (never as in "ball").
r    as in "rat".
s    as in "so".
zh   like the "s" in "measure".
w   as in "wise".
ŵ   the same with rounded lips (as in "sweet").
ny or ny as in "canyon".

## THE ALPHABET AS PRONOUNCED IN FRANCE

| | | | | | |
|---|---|---|---|---|---|
| A | *ah* | J | *zhee* | S | *ess* |
| B | *bay* | K | *kah* | T | *tay* |
| C | *say* | L | *ell* | U | *ee* |
| D | *day* | M | *emm* | V | *vay* |
| E | *ay* | N | *enn* | W | *doobl-vay* |
| F | *aif* | O | *oh* | X | *eex* |
| G | *zhay* | P | *pay* | Y | *ee-greck* |
| H | *ahsh* | Q | *kee* | Z | *zaid* |
| I | *ee* | R | *airr* | | |

### SIGNS AND ACCENTS

(´) **accent aigu** (ahk-saN-tay-gee) gives to the "e" the sound (ay): été (ay-tay)= summer.

(`) **accent grave** (ahk-saN grahv) gives to the "e" the sound of (ai) as in pair: père (pair)=father.

Over *a* and *u* it does not affect the sound, but distinguishes words, e.g., **la**=the **là**=there **a**=has **à**=to; **ou** (oo)=or **où**=where.

(^) **accent circonflexe** (ahk-saN seer-koN-flaix) lengthens the vowel on which it is placed; on the *e* it sounds as in the English word "there". **tête** (tait) =head; **pâte** (paht)=paste.

(ç) **la cédille** (say-deey) gives the *c* the sound of s: leçon (le-soN)=lesson.

(¨) **le tréma** (tray-mah) indicates that the vowel bearing it is pronounced separately from the preceding vowel: **Noël** (noh-ail)=Christmas.

(') **l'apostrophe** (ah-pos-troff) indicates omission of a vowel: **l'hôtel** (loh-tail) =the hotel.

### THE NUMBERS (0-20)

| | | |
|---|---|---|
| 0 | zéro | zay-roh |
| 1 | un | uN |
| 2 | deux | daÿ |
| 3 | trois | trwah[1] |
| 4 | quatre | kahtr |
| 5 | cinq | siNk |
| 6 | six | sees |
| 7 | sept | sait |
| 8 | huit | ŵeet |
| 9 | neuf | naÿf |
| 10 | dix | dees |
| 11 | onze | oNz |
| 12 | douze | dooz |
| 13 | treize | traiz |
| 14 | quatorze | kah-torz |
| 15 | quinze | kiNz |
| 16 | seize | saiz |
| 17 | dix-sept | dees-sait |
| 18 | dix-huit | deez-ŵeet |
| 19 | dix-neuf | deez-naÿf |
| 20 | vingt | viN |

[1] Many French people tend to thicken the "tr" sound, so that what is actually heard is more like "thrwah", "thraiz", etc, Students, by listening to French as spoken by Frenchmen, will gradually learn to strike a balance in the pronunciation of such words.

### VOCABULARY-BUILDING DIAGRAMS AND TEXT UNDER PHOTOGRAPHS

The most important aim of the Course is that you should complete it in possession of a proper groundwork from which you can proceed to widen your knowledge of French.

The additional vocabularies provided in the vocabulary-building diagrams, in the matter introduced for general information, and in the text under photographs contain certain words useful for background knowledge and for reading, but not necessarily heard in everyday colloquial speech.

There is no need for you to memorise all these words before working through the rest of the Course, unless you find them especially useful for your particular purpose in learning the language. You can return to them as your knowledge and vocabulary increase.

# PREMIÈRE LEÇON—*FIRST LESSON*

**Madame Roberts**
(la mère)

**Monsieur Roberts**
(le père)

### The Roberts and Lesage Families

These are the people whose adventures in Paris and in the country, at home and in public, through the myriad incidents of daily life in France, you will follow during the present Course.

The families consist of :

Mr. Roberts (English) and his wife (French); her father and mother, M. and Mme. Georges Lesage; her children Charles and Madeleine; the Paul Lesages and their children, Georges and Lucie.

They are nice people, and we hope you will like them.

**Madeleine**
(la fille)

**Charles**
(le fils)

**Monsieur Roberts est le père.  Mme Roberts est la mère.  Charles est le**
m'ss-yay[1] ro-bairts ay le pair.  mah-dahm ro-bairts ay lah mair.  shahrl ay le
*Mr. Roberts is the father.  Mrs. Roberts is the mother.  Charles is the*

**fils de Monsieur et de Madame Roberts.  Madeleine est la fille de Monsieur**
fees de m'ss-yay ay de mah-dahm ro-bairts.  mahd-lain ay lah feey de m'ss-yay
*son of Mr. and (of) Mrs. Roberts.  Madeleine is the daughter of Mr.*

**et de Madame Roberts.  Monsieur et Madame Roberts sont les parents**
ay de mah-dahm ro-bairts.  m'ss-yay ay mah-dahm ro-bairts soN lay pah-raN
*and (of) Mrs. Roberts.  Mr. and Mrs. Roberts are the parents*

---

[1]This is the pronunciation of "monsieur" in rapid speech.  Spoken slowly it is pronounced "me-ssyay"; *me* to be sounded like *le* or *de* with slightly rounded lips.

**de Charles et de Madeleine.  Charles et Madeleine sont les enfants de Monsieur et**
de shahrl ay de mahd-lain.  shahrl et mahd-lain soN lay-zaN-faN de m'ss-yāy ay
*of Charles and* (*of*) *Madeleine.  Charles and Madeleine are the children of Mr. and*

**de Madame Roberts.  Monsieur Georges Lesage est le père de Madame**
de mah-dahm ro-bairts.  m'ss-yāy zhorzh le-sahzh ay le pair de mah-dahm
(*of*) *Mrs. Roberts.  M. Georges Lesage is the father of Mrs.*

Mme Paul Lesage      Paul Lesage
(la tante)           (l'oncle)

Monsieur Lesage      Madame Lesage
(le grand-père)      (la grand'mère)

**Roberts.  Il est le grand-père de Charles et de Madeleine.  Madame Lesage**
ro-bairts.  ee-lay le graN-pair de shahrl ay de mahd-lain.  mah-dahm le-sahzh
*Roberts.  He is the grandfather of Charles and* (*of*) *Madeleine.  Mme Lesage*

**est leur grand'mère.  Monsieur Paul Lesage est le frère de Mme Roberts.**
ay lāyr graN-mair.  m'ss-yāy poll le-sahzh ay le frair de mah-dahm ro-bairts.
*is their grandmother.  M. Paul Lesage is the brother of Mrs. Roberts.*

**Il est l'oncle de Charles et de Madeleine.  Mme Paul Lesage est leur tante.**
ee-lay l'oNkl de shahrl ay de mahd-lain.  mah-dahm poll le-sahzh ay lāyr taNt.
*He is the uncle of Charles and* (*of*) *Madeleine.  Mme Paul Lesage is their aunt.*

**Monsieur et Madame Paul Lesage sont les parents de Georges et de Lucie**
m'ss-yāy ay mah-dahm poll le-sahzh soN lay pah-raN de zhorzh ay de lēē-see
*M. and Mme Paul Lesage are the parents of Georges and* (*of*) *Lucie*

**Lesage.  Georges est le frère de Lucie.  Ils sont le**
le-sahzh.  zhorzh ay le frair de lēē-see.  eel soN le
*Lesage.  Georges is the brother of Lucie.  They are the*

**cousin et la cousine de Charles et de Madeleine.  Madeleine est la**
koo-ziN ay lah koo-zeen de shahrl ay de mahd-lain.  mahd-lain ay lah
(*masculine and feminine*) *cousins of Charles and* (*of*) *Madeleine.  Madeleine is the*

**sœur de Charles.  Monsieur et Madame Roberts sont grands.  Madame Roberts**
sāyr de shahrl.  m'ss-yāy ay mah-dahm ro-bairts soN graN.  mah-dahm ro-bairts
*sister of Charles.   Mr. and Mrs. Roberts are tall.   Mrs. Roberts*

**et Mademoiselle Lesage sont grandes.**
ay mahd-mwa-zail le-sahzh soN graNd.
*and Mlle Lesage are tall.*

**Monsieur et Madame Roberts sont blonds.**
m'ss-yāy ay mah-dahm ro-bairts soN bloN.
*Mr. and Mrs. Roberts are fair.*

**Madame Roberts et Madeleine sont**
mah-dahm ro-bairts ay mahd-lain soN
*Mrs. Roberts and Madeleine are*

**blondes.  Charles et Madeleine**
bloNd.  shahrl ay mahd-lain
*fair.  Charles and Madeleine*

**sont-ils petits?  Oui, ils sont petits.**
soN-teel p'tee?  w̄ee eel soN p'tee.
*are they small?   Yes, they are small.*

Lucie       Georges
(la cousine)    (le cousin)

### HOW TO TRANSLATE "THEY"

There are two French words for the English "they": **ils** the plural of **il** (he), and **elles** of **elle** (she).  Use **ils** for masculines and **elles** for feminines.  When referring to both masculines and feminines, **ils** is used.

Examples :—
**le père** (the father) **il** (he).
**les pères** (the fathers) **ils** (they).
**la mère** (the mother) **elle** (she).

les **mères** (the mothers) **elles** (they).
les **parents** (the parents) **ils** (they).
les **enfants** (the children), **ils** when referring to boys or boys and girls.
**elles** (they) when referring to women or girls only.

In the plural both nouns and adjectives add s; this s is silent.  **Le petit garçon** (the little boy).  **Les petits garçons** (the little boys).  **La petite fille** (the little girl).  **Les petites filles** (the little girls).

**ils sont grands**
eel soN graN
*they (masc.) are tall*

**ils sont petits**
eel soN p'tee
*they (masc.) are small*

**elles sont grandes**
ail soN graNd
*they (fem.) are tall*

**elles sont petites**
ail soN p'teet
*they (fem.) are small*

| anglais (britannique)[1] | français | américain | russe | chinois |
|---|---|---|---|---|
| aN-glai (brec-ta-neek) | fraN-sai | ah-may-ree-kiN | rẽẽs | shee-nwah |
| *English (British)* | *French* | *American* | *Russian* | *Chinese* |

**Monsieur Roberts est anglais.[2]**
m'ss-yẫy ro-bairts ay-taN-glai.
*Mr. Roberts is English.*

**Madame Roberts est anglaise.**
mah-dahm ro-bairts ay-taN-glaiz.
*Mrs. Roberts is English.*

**Monsieur Lesage est français.**
m'ss-yẫy le-sahzh ay fraN-sai.
*M. Lesage is French.*

**Madame Lesage est française.**
mah-dahm le-sahzh ay fraN-saiz.
*Mme. Lesage is French.*

**Monsieur Truman est américain.**
m'ss-yẫy trẽẽ-maN ay-tah-may-ree-kiN.
*Mr. Truman is American.*

**Madame Truman est américaine.**
mah-dahm trẽẽ-maNay-tah-may-ree-kain.
*Mrs. Truman is American.*

**M. Staline est-il russe?**
m'ss-yẫy stah-leen ay-teel rẽẽs?
*M. Stalin is he Russian?*

**Madame Staline est-elle russe?**
mah-dahm stah-leen ay-tail rẽẽs?
*Mme. Stalin is she Russian?*

**Monsieur Soong est-il chinois?**
m'ss-yẫy soong ay-teel shee-nwah?
*Mr. Soong is he Chinese?*

**Madame Soong est-elle chinoise?**
mah-dahm soong ay-tail shee-nwahz?
*Mrs. Soong is she Chinese?*

**Madame Roberts et Madeleine sont-elles françaises ou anglaises?**
mah-dahm ro-bairts ay mahd-lain soN-tail fraN-saiz oo aN-glaiz?
*Mrs. Roberts and Madeleine are they French or English?*

| Elles sont anglaises | écossaises | irlandaises | galloises | australiennes |
|---|---|---|---|---|
| ail soN-taN-glaiz | ay-kos-saiz | eer-laN-daiz | gah-lwahz | oh-strah-lee-enn |
| *They are English* | *Scottish* | *Irish* | *Welsh* | *Australian* |

All the above are the plural feminine versions of the adjectives meaning English, etc.

---

[1] The word **anglais** is more frequently used in France than **britannique**, to denote the British of all races.

[2] A capital letter is used at the commencement of the word in French only when the sense involved is " a Frenchman," " an Englishman," etc., but a small letter if the sense is merely " French " or " English," used adjectivally.

## LA CATHÉDRALE DE NOTRE-DAME

Cette belle étude photographique montre la rose vitrée de la nef centrale, les contreforts et les tours encore inachevées de la Cathédrale de Paris.

| Étude (f.) | rose (f.) | vitré-e (adj.) | nef (f.) | contrefort (m.) | tour (f.) | inachevé-e (adj.) |
|---|---|---|---|---|---|---|
| Study | rose-window | glass | nave | buttress | tower | unfinished |

**n'est-elle pas jolie?**
nay-tail pah zho-lee?
*isn't she pretty?*

**il n'est pas riche**
eel nay pah reesh
*he is not rich*

### HOW TO TRANSLATE "NOT"

(1) Not is expressed by two words **ne** and **pas**. Before a vowel ne becomes **n'** e.g., **il n'est pas riche**—he is not rich. Note the position of the two words.

### Adjectives ending in -e

(2) When an adjective ends in unaccented **e** in the masculine, the feminine remains the same: **Il est riche**=he is rich; **elle est riche**=she is rich.

## MEN, WOMEN AND CHILDREN

1. **le bébé (le petit enfant)**   2. **le petit garçon**   3. **la petite fille (fillette)**   4. **le jeune homme**
   bay-bay (p'tee-taN-faN)    p'tee gahr-soN    p'teet feey (fee-yait)    zhāy-nomm
   *baby*     *small boy*     *little girl*     *young man*

5. **la jeune fille (la demoiselle)**   6. **l'homme (le monsieur)**   7. **la femme (la dame)**
   zhāyn feey (d'mwah-zail)    omm (m'ss-yāy)    famm (dahm)
   *girl (young lady)*     *man*     *woman (lady)*

8. **un homme âgé (le grand-père)**   9. **une femme âgée (la grand'mère)**   10. **grand**   11. **grande**
   omm ah-zhay (graN-pair)    famm ah-zhay (graN-mair)    graN    graNd
   *old man (grandfather)*     *old woman (grandmother)*     *tall*    *tall*
                                                               *(masc.)*   *(fem.)*

12. **petit**    13. **petite**    14. **fort**    15. **forte**    16. **mince**
    p'tee     p'teet     forr     forrt     miNs
    *short, small*    *short, small*    *strong*    *strong*    *slim*
    *(masc.)*     *(fem.)*     *(masc.)*     *(fem.)*     *(masc. and fem.)*

## MORE ABOUT THE ROBERTS FAMILY

*(Sentences using adjectives are given on pages 19 and 20)*

**Monsieur Roberts est-il riche?**    **Non, il n'est pas riche.**    **Il est très**
m'ss-yāy ro-bairts ay-teel reesh?    noN eel nay pah reesh.    eel ay tray-
*Mr. Roberts is he rich?*    *No, he is not rich.*    *He is very*

**intelligent et Madame Roberts est très charmante.**    **Charles et**
ziN-tai-lee-zhaN ay mah-dahm ro-bairts ay tray shahr-maNt.    shahrl ay
*intelligent and Mrs. Roberts is very charming.*    *Charles and*

**Madeleine sont-ils intelligents?** **Madeleine est intelligente, mais Charles**
mahd-lain soN-teel-ziN-tai-lee-zhaN?　mahd-lain ai-tiN-tai-lee-zhaNt mai shahrl
*Madeleine are they intelligent?*　*Madeleine is intelligent, but Charles*

**n'est pas très intelligent.** **Mais il est beau et charmant.** **Madame**
nay pah trai-ziN-tai-lee-zhaN.　mai ee-lai boh ay shahr-maN　mah-dahm
*is not very intelligent.*　*But he is good-looking and charming.*　*Mrs.*

**Roberts et Mademoiselle Lesage sont-elles petites?** **Non, monsieur,**
ro-bairts ay mahd-mwa-zail le-sahzh soN-tail p'teet?　noN, m'ss-yây,
*Roberts and Mlle. Lesage are they small?*　*No, sir,*

**elles sont grandes.** **Elles sont aussi toutes les deux intelligentes.**
ail soN graNd.　ail soN-toh-see toot lay dây-ziN-tai-lee-zhaNt.
*they are tall.*　*They are also both (lit. "all the two") intelligent.*

## SENTENCE BUILDING.　TABLES SUMMARISING THE FIRST LESSON

### (a) Statements

*masculine, singular (he is . . .; he is not . . .)*

| il, le père, le fils, l'oncle, le frère, le cousin, etc. | { est / n'est pas | { grand, petit, brun, blond, anglais, français, intelligent, charmant, joli, riche |

*feminine, plural (they are . . .; they are not)*

| elles, les mères, les filles, les tantes, les sœurs, les cousines, etc. | { sont / ne sont pas | { grandes, petites, brunes, blondes, anglaises, françaises, intelligentes, charmantes, jolies, riches |

*feminine, singular (she is . . .; she is not . . .)*

| elle, la mère, la fille, la tante, la sœur, la cousine, etc. | { est / n'est pas | { grande, petite, brune, blonde, anglaise, française, intelligente, charmante, jolie, riche |

### (b) Questions

*masculine, singular (is he . . .? isn't he . . .?)*

| est-il, n'est-il pas, le père, le fils, l'oncle, etc. | { est-il / n'est-il pas | { grand?, petit?, brun?, anglais?, intelligent?, etc. |

*feminine, singular (is she . . .? ; isn't she . . .?)*

| est-elle, n'est-elle pas, la mère, la fille, la tante, etc. | { est-elle / n'est-elle pas | { grande?, petite?, brune?, anglaise?, intelligente?, etc. |

*masculine, plural (they are . .; they are not . . .)*

| ils, les pères, les fils, les oncles, les frères, les cousins, etc. | { sont / ne sont pas | { grands, petits, bruns, blonds, anglais, français, intelligents, charmants, jolis, riches |

*masculine, plural (are they . . .? aren't they?)*

| sont-ils, ne sont-ils pas, les pères, les fils, les oncles, etc. | { sont-ils / ne sont-ils pas | { grands?, petits?, bruns?, anglais?, intelligents?, etc. |

*feminine, plural (are they . . .? aren't they . .?)*

| | | |
|---|---|---|
| sont-elles | | grandes? |
| ne sont-elles pas | | petites? |
| les mères | | brunes? |
| les filles | sont-elles | anglaises? |
| les tantes | ne sont- | intelligentes? |
| etc. | elles pas | etc. |

### (c) Exclamations

*masculine, singular (isn't he . . .!)*

| | | |
|---|---|---|
| n'est-il pas | | grand! |
| le père | | petit! |
| le fils | | charmant! |
| le frère | n'est-il pas | joli! |
| etc. | | etc. |

*feminine, singular (isn't she . . .!)*

| | | |
|---|---|---|
| n'est-elle pas | | grande! |
| la mère | | petite! |
| la fille | n'est-elle | charmante! |
| la sœur | pas | jolie! |
| etc. | | etc. |

*masculine, plural (aren't they . . .!)*

| | | |
|---|---|---|
| ne sont-ils pas | | grands! |
| les pères | | petits! |
| les fils | ne sont-ils | charmants! |
| les frères | pas | jolis! |
| etc. | | etc. |

*feminine, plural (aren't they . . .!)*

| | | |
|---|---|---|
| ne sont-elles pas | | grandes! |
| les mères | | petites! |
| les filles | ne sont- | charmantes! |
| les sœurs | elles pas | jolies! |

TEST IT YOURSELF.—It would be a good idea, at this stage, to practise these questions and exclamations, and so to check how many you yourself have actually learned since you started the Course.

**You now know 55 words. You can make over 800 statements, ask over 400 questions and make over 200 exclamations.**

### CHIFFONNIERS DE PARIS

Tous les matins à l'aube, les chiffonniers de Paris farfouillent dans toutes les poubelles pour y trouver des objets vendables.

| **Chiffonnier-ère** (m.f.) | **aube** (f.) | **farfouiller** | **poubelle** (f.) | **vendable** (adj.) |
|---|---|---|---|---|
| Rag-picker | dawn | to rummage | dustbin | marketable |

# DEUXIÈME LEÇON—*SECOND LESSON*

This picture shows the Roberts family packing for Paris. First read the vocabulary, then cover over the text and see if you can make a list of the objects in the picture in French. Next cover over all but the French text of the sentences below, and try to find the mistakes which the artist has deliberately introduced in the picture.

| le chapeau | la malle | le parapluie | le pardessus | les chaussures |
|---|---|---|---|---|
| shah-poh | mall | pah-rah-plẅee | pahr-de-sẽe | shoh-sẽer |
| *hat* | *trunk* | *umbrella* | *overcoat* | *shoe, boots* |

| la valise | la chaise | le sac | la table | les gants |
|---|---|---|---|---|
| vah-leez | shaiz | sak | tahbl | gaN |
| *suitcase* | *chair* | *bag* | *table* | *gloves* |

**Le chapeau est sur la chaise. Le sac est sous la chaise. Les souliers sont sur la**
le shah-poh ay sẽer lah shaiz. le sahk ay soo lah shaiz. lay sool-yay soN sẽer lah
*The hat is on the chair. The bag is under the chair. The shoes are on the*

**table. Les gants sont dans le chapeau. Le chapeau est-il sur la table? Non,**
tahbl. lay gaN soN daN le shah-poh. le shah-poh ay-teel sẽer lah tahbl? noN
*table. The gloves are in the hat. The hat is it on the table? No,*

**il n'est pas sur la table. Où est le chapeau Il est sur la chaise. Où est la**
eel nay pah sẽer lah tahbl. oo ay le shah-po? ee-lay sẽer lah shaiz. oo ay lah
*it is not on the table. Where is the hat? It is on the chair. Where is the*

**valise? Elle est sous la table. Les gants sont-ils dans la valise? Ils ne sont pas**
vah-leez? ai-lay soo lah tahbl. lay gaN soN-teel daN lah vah-leez? eel n' soN pah
*suitcase? It is under the table. The gloves are they in the suitcase? They are not*

**dans la valise. Où sont-ils? Ils sont dans le chapeau. Le chapeau est sur la table.**
daN lahvah-leez. oo soN-teel? eelsoNdaN le shah-poh. le shah-poh ay se̅er lahtahbl.
*in the suitcase. Where are they? They are in the hat. The hat is on the table.*

### GENDER

In French every noun is either masculine or feminine[1] and every thing as well as every person is spoken of as "he" or "she". From the examples given above you can see that **le chapeau, le parapluie, le manteau, le gant,** etc., are masculine, whereas **la malle, la table, la chaise, la chaussure,** etc., are feminine. Now it seems absurd to speak of a chair as feminine or of a hat as masculine. In grammar, however, the term masculine or feminine is used in an unusual sense. All French nouns are divided into two groups according to the word they use for the translation of "the". All the words which translate "the" by **le** are called masculine, because all the male beings are in this group, and all the words which translate "the" by **la** are called feminine, because all the female beings are in that group. If I say **la table** is feminine, then I use the word feminine not in the same sense as if I would speak of feminine charm or feminine beauty ; I simply mean that this word belongs to one of the two groups into which nouns are divided.

### HOW TO TRANSLATE "IT"

Special care must be taken with the translation of the words "it" and "they". Use **il** when it stands for a masculine noun in singular. Use **elle** when it stands for a feminine noun in singular. Use **ils** when it stands for a masculine noun in plural. Use **elles** when it stands for a feminine noun in plural.

For example, when translating "it is brown", "it" referring to the hat, which is **le chapeau,** i.e., masculine in French, you have to use the word **il**=he for the translation of "it": **il est brun.** But when the "it" refers to the chair, which is **la chaise,** you have to use the word for she=**elle** and so the French is: **elle est brune.**

[1] With the exception of such words as **enfant**= child, **which** is masculine when meaning a boy and feminine when meaning a girl.

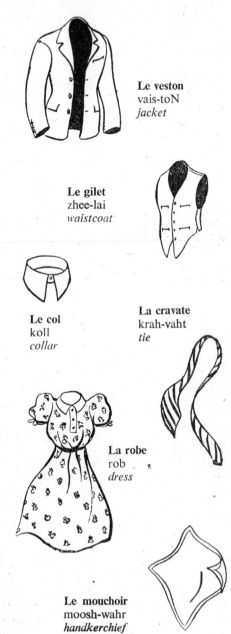

**Le veston**
vais-toN
*jacket*

**Le gilet**
zhee-lai
*waistcoat*

**Le col**
koll
*collar*

**La cravate**
krah-vaht
*tie*

**La robe**
rob
*dress*

**Le mouchoir**
moosh-wahr
*handkerchief*

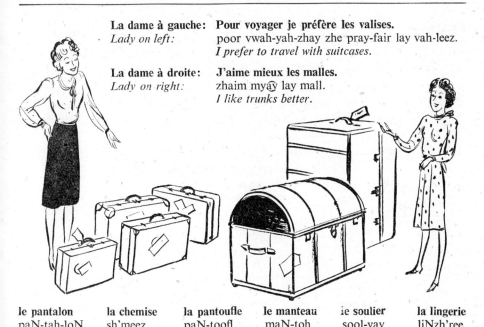

**La dame à gauche:** **Pour voyager je préfère les valises.**
*Lady on left:* poor vwah-yah-zhay zhe pray-fair lay vah-leez.
*I prefer to travel with suitcases.*

**La dame à droite:** **J'aime mieux les malles.**
*Lady on right:* zhaim myay lay mall.
*I like trunks better.*

| le pantalon | la chemise | la pantoufle | le manteau | ie soulier | la lingerie |
|---|---|---|---|---|---|
| paN-tah-loN | sh'meez | paN-toofl | maN-toh | sool-yay | liNzh'ree |
| *trousers* | *shirt* | *slipper* | *cloak* | *shoe* | *underwear* |

| la blouse | la bottine | la jaquette | la jupe | les bretelles (*f.*) | les jarretelles (*f.*) |
|---|---|---|---|---|---|
| blooz | bo-teen | zhah-kait | zheep | lay bre-tail | lay zhar'tail |
| *blouse* | *boot* | *jacket* | *skirt* | *braces* | *sock suspenders* |
| | | *(ladies' or boys')* | | | |

### COULEURS (*koo-layr*)

| masculine: | | | feminine: | |
|---|---|---|---|---|
| le . . . (*il*) est | | | la . . . (*elle*) est | |
| **rouge** | roozh | *red* | **rouge** | roozh |
| **bleu** | blay | *blue* | **bleue** | blay |
| **vert** | vair | *green* | **verte** | vair |
| **jaune** | zhohn | *yellow* | **jaune** | zhohn |
| **gris** | gree | *grey* | **grise** | greez |
| **noir** | nwahr | *black* | **noire** | nwahr |
| **blanc** | blaN | *white* | **blanche** | blaNsh |

Note from the opposite column (1) that the adjectives ending in **-e** remain the same in feminine as in masculine. (2) The irregular feminine of **blanc**—white; **blanche**. (3) That **le pantalon** the (pair) of trousers is singular in French, so that you have to say **le pantalon est gris,** when you say in English "the trousers *are* grey". (On the other hand, "news"—**les nouvelles**—is plural in French).

### TALKING OF COLOURS

**Le chapeau est brun. Le manteau est noir. Le parapluie est vert. La table est**
le shah-poh ay bruN. le maN-toh ay nwahr. le pah-rah-plwee ay vair. lah tahbl ay
*The hat is brown. The coat is black. The umbrella is green. The table is*

**brune. La valise est jaune. La malle est noire. Le col est blanc. La cravate est**
breen. lah vah-leez ay zhohn. lah mall ay nwahr. le kol ay blaN. lah krah-vatt ay
*brown. The suitcase is yellow. The trunk is black. The collar is white. The tie is*

**rouge. Le veston est bleu. La robe est blanche. Le pantalon est gris. Les gants**
roozh. le vais-ton ay blay. lah rob ay blaNsh. le paN-tah-lon ay gree. lay gaN
*red. The coat is blue. The dress is white. The trousers are grey. The gloves*

---

**sont bruns.**  **Le mouchoir est-il blanc?**  **Oui, il est blanc.**  **La cravate est-elle**
soN bruN.'  le moosh-wahr ay-teel blaN?  wee ee-lay blaN.  lah krah-vat ay-tail
*are brown.*  *The handkerchief is it white?*  *Yes, it is white.*  *The tie is it*

**blanche?**  **Non, elle n'est pas blanche.**  **De quelle couleur est la cravate?**  **Elle est**
blaNsh?  noN ail nay pah blaNch.  de kail koo-la͞yr ay lah krah-vat?  ai-lay
*white?*  *No, it is not white.*  *(Of) what colour is the tie?*  *It is*

**rouge.**  **De quelle couleur sont les gants?**  **Ils sont bruns.**
roozh.  de kail koo-la͞yr soN lay gaN?  eel soN bruN.
*red.*  *(Of) what colour are the gloves?*  *They are brown.*

### SOME QUESTIONS AND ANSWERS

**Qu'est-ce que c'est?** or **Qu'est-ce?**    **Ceci est** or **c'est**    **Cela est** or **c'est**
kaysk'-say             kay-se             se-see ay,  say      s'lah ay,  say
*What is — this? — that?*            *this is*             *that is*

uN                              ǣn                      **Ceci est la porte**
**un chapeau**  *a hat*        **une cravate**  *a tie*    se-see ay lah port
**un veston**  *a jacket*     **une robe**  *a dress*    *This is the door*
**un sac**  *a bag*          **une valise**  *a suitcase*
**un parapluie**  *an umbrella*  **une chaise**  *a chair*

**Ce sont les valises**        **Ce sont les malles**
se soN lay vah-leez         se soN lay mall
*These are the suitcases*    *Those are the trunks*

**Qu'est-ce que c'est?**    **Ce sont**
kaysk'-say?            se soN
*What are these?*       *These are . . .; those are*

lay
**les fenêtres**      **les portes**      **les mouchoirs**
*the windows*      *the doors*      *the handkerchiefs*

**les chaussures**    **les cols**        **les gants**
*the shoes*          *the collars*     *the gloves*

1) **un** and **une** are the French equivalents for *a* or *an.*
Use **un** with masculine nouns, **une** with feminine.
2) **ce** (**c'** before a vowel) is the short form for
both **ceci** and **cela.** 3) **qu'est-ce que c'est?** (kaysk'-say)
can mean (1) what is it? (2) what is this? (3) what
is that? (4) what are they? (5) what are these?
(6) what are those?

**Qu'est-ce que c'est?**     **Est-ce une valise?**
kaysk'-say?              ai-se ǣn vah-leez?

**Oui, c'est une valise.**   **Est-ce un sac?**
wee say-tǣn vah-leez.     ai-se uN sak?

**Cela est la fenêtre**
s'lah ay lah f'naitr
*That is the window*

**Mais non, monsieur, ce n'est pas un sac.**
mai non m'ss-ya͞y s'-nai-pah-zuN sak.

The Roberts family off to the station. The objects they are carrying are words you have learned. Cover over the text and see if you can name them in French.

**Monsieur Roberts a deux valises, Madame Roberts a un sac et une**
m'ssyāy ro-bairts ah dāy vah-leez, mah-dahm ro-bairts ah uN sak ay ēēn
*Mr. Roberts has two suitcases, Mrs. Roberts has a bag and a*

**couverture, Charles a une petite valise, Madeleine a un carton à chapeau.**
koo-vair-tēēr, shahrl ah ēēn p'teet vah-leez, mahd-lain ah uN kahr-toN ah shah-poh.
*rug, Charles has a small suitcase, Madeleine has a hat-box.*

### SUMMARY OF SECOND LESSON
#### (a) Statements

| | | | | | | |
|---|---|---|---|---|---|---|
| c'est | | | grand | elle | | grande |
| ce n'est pas | | | petit | la malle | | petite |
| il | | | rouge | la valise | | rouge |
| le parapluie | | | bleu | la table | | bleue |
| le sac | est | | jaune | la chaise | est | jaune |
| le veston | | | vert | la robe | | verte |
| le gilet | | | noir | la cravate | | noire |
| le pantalon | | | blanc | la porte | | blanche |
| le col | n'est pas | | brun | la fenêtre | n'est pas | brune |
| le mouchoir | | | gris | la couverture | | grise |
| le chapeau | | | joli | etc. | | jolie |
| le manteau | | | etc. | | | etc. |
| etc. | | | | | | |

### PARIS VU DE NOTRE-DAME

Une des chimères grimaçantes de Notre-Dame dans ce ciel d'orage semble menacer la
Capitale encore ensoleillée.    Au loin, la silhouette blanche de la Basilique du Sacré-Cœur
s'élève en acropole moderne au-dessus du panorama.

| **Chimère** (f.) | **grimaçant-e** (adj.) | **ciel** (m.) **d'orage** (m.) | **ensoleillé-e** (adj.) |
|---|---|---|---|
| Chimera | frowning, grimacing | stormy sky | sunlit |

| ils | | grands |
|---|---|---|
| les parapluies | | petits |
| les sacs | | rouges |
| les vestons | sont | bleus |
| les gilets | | jaunes |
| les pantalons | | verts |
| les cols | ne sont pas | noirs |
| les mouchoirs | | blancs |
| les chapeaux | | bruns |
| les manteaux | | gris |
| etc. | | jolis |
| | | etc. |

| elles | | grandes |
|---|---|---|
| les malles | | petites |
| les valises | | rouges |
| les tables | sont | bleues |
| les chaises | | jaunes |
| les robes | | vertes |
| les cravates | ne sont pas | noires |
| les portes | | blanches |
| les fenêtres | | brunes |
| les couvertures | | grises |
| etc. | | jolies |
| | | etc. |

### (b) Questions

| est-il | | grand? |
|---|---|---|
| est-ce | | petit? |
| le parapluie | est-il | rouge? |
| le sac | | bleu? |
| le veston | n'est-il pas | jaune? |
| etc. | | |

| est-elle | | grande? |
|---|---|---|
| la malle | est-elle | petite? |
| la valise | | rouge? |
| la table | n'est-elle | bleue? |
| etc. | pas | jaune? |
| | | etc. |

| sont-ils | | grands? |
|---|---|---|
| les parapluies | sont-ils | petits? |
| les sacs | | rouges? |
| les vestons | ne sont-ils | bleus? |
| etc. | pas | jaunes? |
| | | etc. |

| sont-elles | | grandes? |
|---|---|---|
| les malles | sont-elles | petites? |
| les valises | | rouges? |
| les tables | ne sont- | bleues? |
| etc. | elles pas | jaunes? |
| | | etc. |

### (c) Exclamations

| n'est-il pas | | grand! |
|---|---|---|
| n'est-ce pas | | petit! |
| le parapluie | n'est-il pas | joli! |
| le sac | | etc. |
| etc. | | |

| n'est-elle pas | | grande! |
|---|---|---|
| la table | n'est-elle | petite! |
| la fenêtre | pas | jolie! |
| etc. | | etc. |

| ne sont-ils pas | | grands! |
|---|---|---|
| les parapluies | ne sont-ils | petits! |
| les sacs | pas | jolis! |
| etc. | | etc. |

| ne sont-elles pas | | grandes! |
|---|---|---|
| les tables | ne sont- | petites! |
| les fenêtres | elles pas | jolies! |
| etc. | | etc. |

You now know 100 words. You can make over 980 statements, ask over 800 questions, and make over 400 exclamations.

## EXERCISES

**I  Answer in French**

1. Qu'est-ce que c'est?

2. Le sac est-il joli?

3. Est-ce Mademoiselle Lesage?

4. Mademoiselle Lesage est-elle jolie?

5. Qui est le cousin de Mademoiselle Lesage?

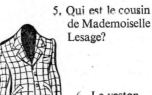 

6. Le veston est-il joli?

7. Qu'est-ce que c'est?

8. Charles est-il grand?

9. Qui est la sœur de Charles?

10. Qui sont les parents de Charles?

11. La robe est-elle élégante?

12. Les chaises sont-elles grandes?

13. Le livre est-il sur la table?

14. Où (oo=where) est le livre?

15. Le livre est-il sur la chaise?

 16. Qu'est-ce que c'est?

17. Qu'est-ce que c'est?

18. De quelle couleur sont les chaussures?

*(For Key see page* 51)

## II—Translate into French

1. The tie is white and blue. 2. The jacket is brown. 3. The dress is green. 4. The hat is not green, it is brown. 5. Is the overcoat black? 6. No sir, it is grey. 7. Is the table large? 8. Yes, it is large. 9. Is the window large? 10. No, it is small. 11. Is the handkerchief red and blue? 12. No, it is white. 13. Are the gloves brown? 14. No, madam, they are yellow. 15. Are the trunks yellow? 16. No, they are brown. 17. What is it? 18. Is it the book? 19. Yes, sir, it is the book. 20. No, sir, it is not the book, it is the bag. 21. What colour is the bag? 22. It is blue. 23. Isn't it pretty! 24. Isn't the suitcase brown? 25. Isn't the child charming! 26. Where are the children? 27. Where is George's father? 28. Where is he? 29. Where is she? 30. Where are they (the parents)?

## III—Replace the nouns by il, elle, ils or elles

1. Le mouchoir est blanc. 2. La porte est blanche. 3. La malle n'est pas grande. 4. Les livres sont rouges. 5. Les chaussures sont noires. 6. Monsieur et Madame Roberts sont les parents de Charles et Madeleine. 7. Madame Roberts et Madeleine sont blondes. 8. De quelle couleur est le veston? 9. De quelle couleur est la porte? 10. Où est Charles? 11. Où est Madeleine? 12. Où sont les enfants. 13. Où sont les livres? 14. Où sont les valises?

*(For Key see page* 52)

**Où sont les enfants?**

# TROISIÈME LEÇON—*THIRD LESSON*

When you have read the text below, cover it over and see if you can describe in French what the Roberts family are doing on the ship.

**La famille Roberts est sur le bateau. Monsieur Roberts est fatigué.**
lah fah-meey ro-bairts ay sẽr le bah-toh, m'ss-yãy robairts ay fah-tee-gay.
*The Roberts family is on the boat. Mr. Roberts is tired.*

**Il lit un roman amusant et fume sa courte pipe anglaise. Madame**
eel lee-tuN rohm-aN ah-mẽe-zaN ay fẽem sah koort peep aN-glaiz. mah-dahm
*He reads an amusing novel and smokes his short Englisn pipe. Mrs.*

**Roberts n'est pas fatiguée, elle parle avec une autre dame. Charles est**
ro-bairts nay-pah fah-tee-gay, ail pahrl ah-veck ẽen ohtr dahm. shahrl ay
*Roberts is not tired, she is speaking with another lady. Charles is*

**malade. Le jour est beau mais Charles n'aime pas la mer. Madeleine n'est pas**
mah-lahd. le zhour ay boh mai shahrl naim pah lah mair. mahd-lain nay-pah
*sick. The day is fine but Charles does not like the sea. Madeleine is not*

**malade. Elle parle avec une autre jeune fille anglaise. La mer est assez**
mah-lahd. ail pahrl ah-veck ẽen ohtr zhãyn feey aN-glaiz. lah mair ay-ta-say
*ill. She is talking with another young English girl. The sea is fairly*

**calme. Les autres passagers sont très contents.**
kalm. lay-zohtr pa-sah-zhay soN trai koN-taN.
*calm. The other passengers are very happy.*

**Ces messieurs sont sur un bateau français.**
say mais-yа̄y soN sēēr uN bah-toh fraN-sai.
*These gentlemen are on a French boat.*

**Ce monsieur est grand et fort.**
se m'ss-yа̄y ai graN tay for.
*This man is big and strong.*

**Cette dame est petite et mince.**
sait dah-mai p'tee-tay miNs.
*This lady is small and slim.*

**Cette enfant est méchante.**
sait-aN-faN ai may-shaNt.
*This child is naughty.*

## THIS, THAT, THESE, THOSE

Note from the above that there are three French equivalents for English "this" when used in connection with nouns; **ce, cette** and **cet**; **ce** is used in connection with masculine nouns.

NOTE :
**un monsieur**
m'ss-yа̄y
*a gentleman*

**Monsieur Roberts**
*Mr. Roberts*

**une dame**
dahm
*a lady*

**Madame Roberts**
*Mrs. Roberts*

**la fille**
feey
*the daughter*

**une jeune fille**
zhа̄yn feey
*a girl*

**une petite fille**
p'teet feey
*a little girl*
or
**une fillette**
fee-yait

**ce livre**=this book; **cette** is used in connection with feminine nouns, e.g., **cette table**=this table; **cet** is used with masculine nouns when they begin with a vowel or silent *h*, e.g., **cet enfant**=this child, **cet hôtel**=this hotel.

**ces** (say) is the plural of **ce, cette** or **cet**: **ces livres**=these books; **ces tables**=these tables; **ces enfants**=these children.

As we have already seen in the previous lesson the difference between "this" and "that" or "these" and "those" is not so clearly marked in French as it is in English; **ce livre** can also mean "that book", **cette table**=that table, **ces enfants**=those children etc.

If, however, the Frenchman wishes to make a clear distinction between the two he adds two little words to the noun **-ci** (pronounced see) for "this" and "these", **-là** for "that" and "those":

### THIS AND THAT

| | |
|---|---|
| ce livre-ci . . . . . . . . . . . . | *this book* |
| ce livre-là . . . . . . . . . . . . | *that book* |
| cette table-ci . . . . . . . . . | *this table* |
| cette table-là . . . . . . . . . | *that table* |
| cet enfant-ci . . . . . . . . . | *this child* |
| cet enfant-là . . . . . . . . . | *that child* |
| ces livres-ci . . . . . . . . . . | *these books* |
| ces livres-là . . . . . . . . . . | *those books* |
| ces tables-ci . . . . . . . . . | *these tables* |
| ces tables-là . . . . . . . . . | *those tables* |
| ces enfants-ci . . . . . . . . | *these children* |
| ces enfants-là . . . . . . . . | *those children* |

**ci** is the contraction of **ici**=here, of which the opposite is **là**=there.

**Cette tasse-là est pour vous.**
sait tahs lah ay poor voo.
*That cup (there) is for you.*

**Cette tasse-ci est pour moi.**
sait tahs see ay poor mwa.
*This cup (here) is for me.*

**Voici une tasse de thé.**
vwah-see een tahs de tay.
*Here is a cup of tea.*

**Voilà un verre de vin.**
vwah-lah uN vair de viN.
*There is a glass of wine.*

**Voici les tasses.**
vwah-see lay tahs.
*Here are the cups.*

**Voilà les verres.**
vwah-lah lay vair.
*There are the glasses.*

**Le café est-il bon?  Oui, il est bon.**     **La bière est-elle bonne?  Oui, elle est bonne.**

This picture illustrates two simple sentences which you can translate for yourself. Try to make up descriptive sentences from the vocabulary you have now acquired.

The feminine of **bon** (boN)—good is **bonne** (bon). Note that when the **n** is doubled the **o** loses its nasal quality, and takes on the ordinary **n** sound.

**Ces verres-ci sont**
say vair-see soN
*These glasses are*

**pour les messieurs.**
poor lay mais-yáy.
*for the gentlemen.*

**Ces verres-là sont**
say vair lah soN
*Those glasses are*

**pour les dames.**
poor lay dahm.
*for the ladies.*

### VOICI—VOILÀ

Note that **voici** can mean both "here is" and "here are", **voilà** = "there is" or "there are".

**voici la petite fille** = *here is the little girl*
**voilà la petite fille** = *there is the little girl*
**voici les petites filles** = *here are the little girls*
**voilà les petites filles** = *there are the little girls*

**voici** and **voilà** are two very useful little words; **voici** is also used in the meanings

of "here it is", "here they are" and **voilà** with the meaning of "there it is", "there they are".

**Où est la valise?** = *Where is the suitcase?*

**La voici** = *here it is*
**La voilà** = *there it is*

**Où sont les enfants?** = *Where are the children?*

**Les voici** = *here they are*
**Les voilà** = *there they are*

### MRS. ROBERTS' TALK WITH A LADY ABOARD

**La Dame :**    **Nous avons une bonne traversée, n'est-ce pas, madame?**
noo-za-voN-zéén bon trah-vair-say nais-pah mah-dahm?
*We have (are having) a good crossing, haven't we, madam?*

**Mme Roberts :** **Notre traversée n'est pas mauvaise. Le ciel est pur, la mer est**
notr trah-vair-say nay pah moh-vaiz. le syail ay péér lah mair ay
*Our crossing is not bad. The sky is bright, the sea is*

**calme, et le bateau est très confortable.**
kalm, ay le bah-toh ay trai koN-fohr-tahbl.
*calm, and the ship is very comfortable.*

**La Dame :**    **Êtes vous fatiguée, madame?**
ait voo fah-tee-gay mah-dahm?
*Are you tired, madam?*

**Mme Roberts :** **Non, madame, je ne suis pas fatiguée. Et vous, madame?**
noN mah-dahm zhe ne sŵee pah fah-tee-gay. ay voo mah-dahm?
*No, madam, I am not tired. And you, madam?*

**La Dame :**    **Je suis un peu fatiguée. J'ai mal dormi cette nuit.**
zhe sŵee-zuN páy fah-tee-gay. zhay mal dor-mee set nŵee.
*I am a little tired. I slept badly this (last) night.*

**Mme Roberts :** **Prenez un transatlantique, madame. Charles, apportez un**
pr'nay-zuN traNs-at-laN-teek, mah-dahm. shahrl ah-por-tay zuN
*Have a deck-chair, madam. Charles, bring a*

**transatlantique pour madame.**
traNs-at-laN-teek poor mah-dahm.
*deck-chair for madam.*

**Charles (qui apporte un transatlantique) : Voilà, madame.**
(kee ah-port uN traNs-at-laN-teek) : vwah-lah mah-dahm.
(*who brings a deck-chair*) : *There you are, madam.*

**La Dame :** **Merci bien. Vous êtes bien aimable.** (**à Madame R.**) **Votre**
mair-see byiN. voo-zait byain-nai-mahbl. (ah mah-dahm airr.) votr
*Thanks very much. You are very kind.* (*to Mrs. R.*) *Your*

**fils est charmant, madame. Quel âge a-t-il?**
fees ai char-maN, mah-dahm. kail ahzh ah-teel?
*son is charming, madam. How old is he?* (*lit. What age has he?*)

**Mme Roberts :** **Il a dix ans.**
ee-lah dee-zaN.
*He is* (*lit. has*) *ten years.*

**La Dame :** **Et la charmante petite fille, est-elle votre fille?**
ay lah shahr-maNt p'teet feey ai-tail votr feey?
*And the charming little girl, is she your daughter?*

**Mme Roberts :** **Oui, c'est ma fille.**
wee say mah feey.
*Yes, it's my daughter.*

**La Dame :** **Quel âge a-t-elle?**
kai-lahzh ah-tail?
*How old is she?*

**Mme Roberts :** **Elle a douze ans.**
ai-lah doo-zaN.
*She is twelve.*

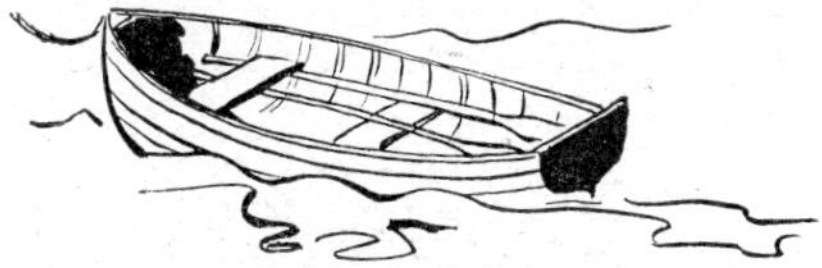

**Un bateau à rames**
uN bah-toh ah rahm
*A rowing-boat*

**La Dame :** **Vous allez à Paris, madame?**
voo-zah-lay ah pah-ree mah-dahm?
*You are going to Paris, madam?*

**Mme Roberts :** **Oui, madame, nous allons à Paris pour voir mes parents.**
wee mah-dahm noo-zah-loN-zah pah-ree poor vwahr may pah-raN.
*Yes, madam, we are going to Paris to visit my parents.*

**La Dame :** **Vos parents sont-ils français?**
voh pah-raN soN-teel fraN-sai?
*Are your parents French?*

**Mme Roberts :** **Oui, madame, ils sont français.**
wee mah-dahm eel soN fraN-sai.
*Yes, madam, they are French.*

**La Dame :** **Et vous, madame, êtes-vous Française?**
ay voo mah-dahm ait voo fraN-saiz?
*And you, madam, are you a Frenchwoman?*

This and other diagrams are provided to extend your vocabulary in a simple and interesting way. First compare the English words and their French equivalents, then

## THE MAIL STEAMER

### English

1. Anchor and anchor-chain; 2. Look-out; 3.Deck-hand; 4. Railing; 5. Forecastle; 6. Sailing boat; 7. Gangway; 8. Hatches; 9. Derricks; 10. Lifebelts; 11. Port light; 12. Mast; 13. Masthead light; 14. Halyards; 15. Bridge; 16. Captain; 17. Compass; 18. Steering-gear; 19. Engineroom telegraph; 20. Wireless cabin; 21. Siren; 22. Funnel; 23. Engineroom ventilator; 24. The ship herself (mail steamer); 25. Tarpaulin; 26, Davits; 27. Lifeboats; 28. Signal halyards; 29. Boat deck; 30. Upper deck; 31. Rafts; 32. Ship's colours; 33. Wake; 34. Stern and aft; 35. Propeller and p.-shaft; 36. Upper and lower berths; 37. Private cabin; 38. Steerage; 39. Drinking-water tank; 40. Cabins; 41. Turbines; 42. Amidships; 43. Dining-room steward; 44. 1st class dining saloon; 45. Main Boilers; 46. Saloon drawing room; 47. Starboard light; 48. Stoker; 49. Galley; 50. Freshwater tanks; 51. Galley steward; 52. Fuel tanks; 53. Officers' quarters; 54. 1st class smoking room; 55. Cargo hold; 56. Crew's quarters; 57. Portholes; 58. Bow-wave; 59. Fore and forrard; 60. Cutwater.

### French

1. Ancre (f.) et chaîne (f.) d'ancre; 2. Vigie (f.); 3. Matelot (m.) de pont; 4. Bastingages (m.pl.); 5. Gaillard (m.) d'avant; 6. Bateau (m.) à voiles (f.pl.);

cover over the letterpress and see how many French words you can attach to the numbers on the diagram. Turn back to the diagrams when you have advanced in the course.

## LE PAQUEBOT

7. Passerelle (f.); 8. Panneaux (m.pl.); 9. Mâts (m.pl.) de charge; 10. Ceintures (f.pl.) de sauvetage; 11. Feu de bâbord; 12. Mât (m.); 13. Feu (m.) de tête de mât; 14. Drisses (f.pl.); 15. Pont; 16. Capitaine; 17. Boussole (f.), compas (m.); 18. Mécanisme (m.) à gouverner; 19. Cadran (m.) de transmission d'ordres; 20. Cabine (f.) de T.S.F. (télégraphie sans fil); 21. Sirène (f.); 22. Cheminée (f.); 23. Manche (f.) à ventilation; 24. Paquebot (m.); 25. Prélart (m.); 26. Bossoirs (m.pl.); 27. Baleinières (f.pl.) de sauvetage; 28. Drisses des signaux; 29. Pont des embarcations; 30. Pont supérieur; 31. Radeaux (m.pl.); 32. Pavillon (m.); 33. Sillon, sillage (m.); 34. (De l') arrière (m.);

35. Hélice (f.) et arbre (m.) de l'hélice; 36. Couchettes (f.pl.) supérieures, inférieures; 37. Cabine privée; 38. Entrepont (m.); 39. Cales (f.pl.) à eau potable; 40. Cabines; 41. Turbines (f.pl.); 42. Par le travers; 43. Garçon de salon; 44. Salon-restaurant de 1re classe; 45. Grandes chaudières (f.pl.); 46. Salon de 1re classe; 47. Feu de tribord; 48. Chauffeur; 49. Cuisine (f.); 50. Cales à eau douce; 51. Garçon de cuisine; 52. Réservoirs (m.pl.) à essence; 53. Poste (m.) des officiers; 54. Fumoir (m.) de 1re classe; 55. Soute (f.) à marchandises; 56. Poste (m.) des matelots, hublots (m.pl.); 57. Sabords (m.pl.); 58. Lame (f.) d'étrave; 59. (De l') avant (m.); 60. Étrave (f.).

**Mme Roberts :**    **Je suis née Française, mais mon mari est Anglais.**
zhe sŵee nay fraNsaiz mai moN mah-ree ay-taN-glai.
*I was (lit. am) born a Frenchwoman, but my husband is an Englishman.*

**La Dame :**    **Vous parlez anglais comme une Anglaise.**
voo pahr-lay-zaN-glai ko-mễn aN-glaiz.
*You speak English like an Englishwoman.*

**Mme Roberts :**    **Merci, madame, vous êtes très aimable.**
mair-see, mah-dahm, voo-zait tray zai-mahbl.
*Thank you, madam, you are very kind.*

   **Êtes-vous fatigués, mes enfants?**
ait voo fah-tee-gay may-zaN-faN?
*Are you tired, my children?*

**Charles et Madeleine :**    **Non, maman, nous ne sommes pas fatigués.**
noN, mah-maN, noo n' somm pah fah-tee-gay.
*No, mummy, we are not tired.*

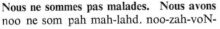

| Nous ne sommes pas malades. Nous avons | Ils sont malades. Ils ont une mauvaise |
|---|---|
| noo ne som pah mah-lahd. noo-zah-voN- | eel-soN mah-lahd. eel-zoN-tễn moh-vaiz |
| **une bonne traversée.** | **traversée.** |
| zễn bon trahvair-say. | trah-vair-say. |
| *We are not ill. We have[1] a good crossing.* | *They are ill. They have a bad crossing.* |

---

[1] It will be noted that, in early Lessons, we frequently make a literal translation of the French text, in cases where the corresponding expression in normal idiomatic English is easily guessed, as in the present case, where "we are having" would be more usual. This is in order to accustom readers to the French construction.

Ces dames sont contentes. Elles ont une
say dahm soN koN-taNt.  ail-zoN-tẽen
conversation intéressante.
koN-vair-sahs-yoN iN-tay-rai-saNt.
*These ladies are happy.  They are having an
interesting talk.*

### N'EST-CE PAS?

Vous êtes le capitaine, n'est-ce pas?
voo-zait le kah-pee-tain nais-pah?
*You are the captain, aren't you?*

Vous avez la valise, n'est-ce pas?
voo-zah-vay lah vah-leez nais-pah?
*You have the suitcase, haven't you?*

Le capitaine est content.  Il a un joli bateau.
le kah-pee-tain ay koN-taN.  ce-la uN zho-
lee bah-toh.
*The captain is happy.  He has a beautiful
ship.*

Elle est jolie, n'est-ce pas?
ail-ai zho-lee nais-pah?
*She is pretty, isn't she?*

Vous parlez français, n'est-ce pas?
voo pahr-lay fraN-sai nais-pah?
*You speak French, don't you?*

You will hear French people throw in
n'est-ce pas? after many sentences; it
corresponds to the English "isn't he?"
"isn't she?" "isn't it?" "aren't they?"
"aren't you?" "don't you?" "doesn't he?"
"haven't you?" etc. **N'est-ce pas** means
all these expressions rolled into one; it is
actually an abbreviation of **n'est-ce pas
vrai?** "is it not true?"

---

1) **Il a** means "he has", and you would
expect **a-il** for "has he?"  But this does not
sound pleasant to a Frenchman so "t" is
put in: **a-t-il** which makes the sound
pleasanter.  The same applies to **a-t-elle?**
meaning "has she?"  **parle-t-il?** "does he
speak?"  **parle-t-elle?** "does she speak?" etc.

2) The French do not say "do you?"
when asking questions.  "Do you speak?"
must be translated **parlez-vous?** = speak you.
"Does he speak?" is **parle-t-il?** = "speaks
he?"  "Do they come?" must be turned
into "come they?"  "do we start?" into
"start we?" etc.

3) There is no difference in French
between "I speak" and "I am speaking";
both are translated by **je parle.**

### ÊTRE = *to be*

| | |
|---|---|
| je suis (zhe swee) | je ne suis pas |
| *I am* | *I am not* |
| vous êtes (voo-zait) | vous n'êtes pas |
| *you are* | *you are not* |
| nous sommes | nous ne sommes pas |
| (noo somm) | *we are not* |
| *we are* | |
| il est (ee-lay) | il n'est pas |
| *he is* | *he is not* |
| elle est (ai-lay) | elle n'est pas |
| *she is* | *she is not* |
| ils sont (eel soN) | ils ne sont pas |
| *they are* (masc.) | *they are not* (masc.) |
| elles sont (ail soN) | elles ne sont pas |
| *they are* (fem.) | *they are not* (fem.) |

| | |
|---|---|
| **suis-je?** | **ne suis-je pas?** |
| *am I?* | *am I not?* |
| **êtes-vous?** | **n'êtes-vous pas?** |
| *are you?* | *are you not?* |
| **sommes-nous?** | **ne sommes-nous pas?** |
| *are we?* | *are we not?* |

### AVOIR = *to have*

| | |
|---|---|
| **j'ai** (zhay) | **je n'ai pas** |
| *I have* | *I have not* |
| **vous avez** | **vous n'avez pas** |
| (voo-zah-vay) | *you have not* |
| *you have* | |
| **nous avons** | **nous n'avons pas** |
| (noo-zah-voN) | *we have not* |
| *we have* | |
| **il a** (ee-lah) | **il n'a pas** |
| *he has* | *he has not* |
| **elle a** (ai-lah) | **elle n'a pas** |
| *she has* | *she has not* |
| **ils ont** (eel-zoN) | **ils n'ont pas** |
| *they have* (masc.) | *they have not* (masc.) |
| **elles ont** (ail-zoN) | **elles n'ont pas** |
| *they have* (fem.) | *they have not* (fem.) |
| **avez-vous** (ah-vay-voo) | **n'avez-vous pas?** |
| *have you?* | *haven't you?* |
| **a-t-il?** (ah-teel) | **n'a-t-il pas?** |
| *has he?* | *hasn't he?* |
| **a-t-elle?** (ah-tail) | **n'a-t-elle pas?** |
| *has she?* | *hasn't she?* |
| **ont-ils?** (oN-teel) | **n'ont-ils pas?** |
| *have they?* | *haven't they?* |
| **ont-elles?** (oN-tail) | **n'ont-elles pas?** |
| *have they?* | *haven't they?* |

### POSSESSIVE ADJECTIVES

| | |
|---|---|
| **mon père** | **ma mère** |
| moN pair | mah mair |
| *my father* | *my mother* |
| | **mes parents** |
| | may pah-raN |
| | *my parents* |
| **son père** | **sa mère** |
| soN pair | sah mair |
| *his or her father* | *his or her mother* |
| | **ses parents** |
| | say pah-raN |
| | *his or her parents* |
| **notre père** | **notre mère** |
| notr pair | notr mair |
| *our father* | *our mother* |

| | |
|---|---|
| | **nos parents** |
| | noh pah-raN |
| | *our parents* |
| **votre père** | **votre mère** |
| votr pair | votr mair |
| *your father* | *your mother* |
| | **vos parents** |
| | voh pah-raN |
| | *your parents* |
| **leur père** | **leur mère** |
| lãyr pair | lãyr mair |
| *their father* | *their mother* |
| | **leurs parents** |
| | lãyr pah-raN |
| | *their parents* |

| SINGULAR | | PLURAL |
|---|---|---|
| *Masc.* | *Fem.* | (*both genders*) |
| **mon** (moN) | **ma** (mah) | **mes** (may) *my* |
| **son** (soN) | **sa** (sah) | **ses** (say) *his, her, its* |
| **notre** (notr) | | **nos** (noh) *our* |
| **votre** (votr) | | **vos** (voh) *your* |
| **leur** (lãyr) | | **leurs** (lãyr) *their* |

The possessive adjectives (my, your, his, her, our, their), like any other adjectives in French, agree in gender with the thing possessed. **sa chaise** is both "his chair" and "her chair" because **chaise** is feminine in French; **son livre** is both "his" and "her book" because **livre** is masculine. When translating his or her you must keep in mind that the French **son** and **sa** are not determined by the sex of the possessor.

## EXERCISES

### I  Answer in French

1. La famille R. a-t-elle une bonne traversée?  2. La mer est-elle calme?  3. M. Roberts est-il fatigué?  4. Est-il malade?  5. Qui est malade?  6. Madeleine est-elle malade?  7. Quel âge a-t-elle?  8. Mme R. est-elle anglaise?  9. Ses parents sont-ils français?  10. Etes-vous français?  11. Êtes-vous fatigué?  12. Vos parents sont-ils anglais?

### II  Translate into English

1. Ce verre-ci est pour moi, ce verre-là est pour vous.  2. C'est une tasse de thé.

3. Ceci est un verre de bière, cela est un verre de vin. 4. Voici un joli bateau français. 5. Le capitaine est grand et mince. 6. Voici un transatlantique pour vous. 7. Merci, monsieur, vous êtes bien aimable. 8. Avez-vous mon sac? 9. Voilà votre sac. 10. Votre mari est-il français? 11. Non, madame, il est écossais. 12. N'êtes-vous pas fatigués? 13. Nous ne sommes pas fatigués. 14. Ses enfants sont charmant(e)s, n'est-ce pas? 15. Sa fille parle français, n'est-ce pas? 16. Les Françaises sont charmantes, n'est-ce pas? 17. Son fils apporte un transatlantique, n'est-ce pas?

### III   Translate into French

1. My mother is French, my father is English. 2. They have three children. 3. We are on a French boat. 4. We are not tired. 5. We are having a good (bad) crossing. 6. Is this cup for me? 7. What is this? 8. Is it a cup of tea? 9. This cup is not big. 10. Haven't you got a deck-chair? 11. Aren't you pleased? 12. You are tired, aren't you? 13. Your brother is tired, isn't he? 14. Their children are charming, aren't they? 15. Where is Charles's hat? 16. Here is his hat. 17. Where is Madeleine's bag? 18. There is her bag. 19. Have you got my gloves? 20. There are your gloves on the chair. 21. Are they brown or yellow? 22. They are not yellow. 23. They are having a good crossing, aren't they? 24. The coffee is good, isn't it? 25. Is this cup for me?

*(Key to I, II and III on page 52.)*

### DANS LE WAGON-RESTAURANT

Assis dans le wagon-restaurant d'un express continental les voyageurs attendent le déjeuner.

| **Assis-e** (adj.) | **wagon-restaurant** (m.) | **voyageurs-euses** (m.f.) | **attendre** |
|---|---|---|---|
| Seated | restaurant-car | passengers | to await |

### PARIS: LA PLACE ET LA COLONNE VENDÔME

Coulée dans le bronze des canons pris à l'ennemi, la colonne Vendôme est surmontée de la statue de Napoléon 1er, ce lieutenant corse devenu Empereur des Français.

| | | | |
|---|---|---|---|
| **Place** (f.) | **coulé-e** (m.f.) | **prendre à (quelq'un)** | **surmonté-e** (m.f.) |
| Square | cast | to take from (someone) | crowned, surmounted |

# QUATRIÈME LEÇON—*FOURTH LESSON*

In this picture are shown the notices which correspond to the English "No Smoking", "Exit", "Customs". Can you find them? Also try to make a list in French of the other objects shown in this picture of a French customs scene.

**M. Roberts:** (À sa famille.) **Maintenant nous sommes en France. Parlez français,**
ah sah fah-mee*y*. miNt-naN noo som-zaN fraNs. pahr-lay fraN-sai,
*(To his family.)* *Now we are in France.* *Speak French,*

**mes enfants. Où est la douane? La voilà à gauche (droite).**
may-zaN-faN. oo ay lah doo-ahn? lah vwa-lah ah gohsh (drwaht).
*my children.* *Where is the customs?* *There to (the) left (right).*

**M. Roberts:** (Au porteur.) **Porteur, êtes-vous libre? Prenez nos bagages,**
oh por-tāyr. por-tāyr ayt voo leebr? pr'nay noh bah-gahzh
*(To the porter.)* *Porter, are you free?* *Take our luggage,*

**s'il vous plaît. Nous avons quatre colis. Portez-les à**
see-voo-plai. noo-zah-voN kahtr ko-lee. por-tay lay ah
*please.* *We have four articles (of luggage).* *Carry them to*

**la douane, s'il vous plaît.**
lah doo-ahn see-voo-plai.
*the customs, please.*

**Le douanier: Avez-vous quelque chose à déclarer? Tabac, cigares, cigarettes?**
ah-vay voo kelk shohz ah day-klah-ray? tah-bah see-gahr see-gah-rait?
*Have you anything to declare?* *Tobacco, cigars, cigarettes?*

**M. Roberts :**   Rien, monsieur, à l'exception du tabac dans ma blague.
ryiN m'ss-yãy ah leks-aip-syoN dẽe tah-bah daN mah blahg.
*Nothing, sir, with the exception of the tobacco in my pouch.*

**Le douanier :**   Ouvrez, s'il vous plaît.   Ces bas sont-ils neufs?
oov-ray see-voo-plai.   say bah soN-teel nãyf?
*Open, please.   These stockings are they new?*

**M. Roberts :**   Non, monsieur, ils ne sont pas neufs.   Douanier : Vous pouvez fermer.
noN m'ss-yãy eel ne soN pah nãyf.          voo poo-vayfair-may.
*No sir, they are not new.*            *You can close (it).*

Le sac est fermé.             Le sac est ouvert.
le sahk ay fair-may.        le sahk ay-too-vair.
*The bag is shut.*           *The bag is open.*

### CONVERSATION AT THE STATION

**M. Roberts :**   (au porteur) Trouvez-nous un compartiment pour fumeurs,
oh port-ãyr troo-vay-noo uN koN-pahr-tee-maN poor fẽe-mãyr,
*(to the porter) Find us a smoking compartment,*

deuxième classe.   A quelle heure part le train pour Paris?
dãy-zyaim klahs.    ah kai-lãyr pahr le triN poor pah-ree?
*second class.   At what time leaves the train for Paris?*

Quelle heure est-il maintenant?
kai-lãyr ay-teel miNt-naN?
*What time is it now?*

**Le porteur :**   À trois heures vingt, monsieur.   Il est trois heures maintenant.
ah trwa-zãyr viN, m'ss-yãy.    eel ay trwa-zãyr miNt-naN.
*At three (hours) twenty, sir.   It is three (hours) now.*

**M. Roberts :**   (à sa famille) Voulez-vous manger quelque chose?   Voici le buffet.
(ah sah fa-meey) voo-lay-voo maN-zhay kailk-shohz? vwah-see le bẽe-fay.
*(to his family) Do you want to eat something?   Here is the buffet.*

**La famille R.:**   Je n'ai pas faim, mais j'ai soif. . . . . . . . . . . Une tasse de café
zh'nay pah fiN mai zhay swahf. . . . . . . . ẽen tahs de kah-fay
*I have not hunger, but I have thirst. . . . . . . . . . A cup of coffee*

pour moi. . . . . . . . **Je préfère une limonade.**
poor mwah . . . . . . zhe pray-fair ēn lee-moh-nahd.
*for me. . . . . . . . . I prefer a lemonade.*

**M. Roberts:**   **Garçon, deux cafés, une limonade et un demi**
gahr-soN dāy kah-fay ēn lee-moh-nahd ay uN d'mee
*Waiter, two coffees, a lemonade and a half (-litre)*

**de bière blonde pour moi.   Le garçon : Café nature ou au lait?**
d'byair bloNd poor mwah.     kah-fay nah-tēr oo oh lai?
*of light ale for me.          Natural (black) or with milk?*

**Mme R.**   **Café nature pour moi . . . . . . . . Café crème, s'il vous plaît.**
**et Charles:**   kah-fay nah-tēr poor mwah . . . . kah-fay kraim see voo-plai.
*Black for me . . . . . . . . . . . Coffee with cream, please.*

**La porte est fermée.**
lah port ay fairmay.
*The door is closed.*

**La porte est ouverte.**
lah port ay toovairt.
*The door is open.*

**Je ferme la porte.**
zhe fairm lah port.
*I shut the door.*

**J'ouvre la porte.**
zhoovr lah port.
*I open the door.*

Le garçon :     **Voilà les deux cafés et le sucre, la limonade et la bière.**
vwah-lah lay dāy kah-fay ay lesēēkr la lee-moh-nahd ay lah byair.
*Here are the two coffees and the sugar, the lemonade and the beer.*

Charles :     **Mais le café est dans un verre. C'est drôle, n'est-ce pas?**
mai le kah-fay ay daN-zuN vair. say drohl nais-pah?
*But the coffee is in a glass. That is funny, isn't it?*

Le garçon :     **Autre pays, autre mœurs. Évidemment, c'est votre première**
ohtr pai-ee ohtr māyrs. ay-vee-dah-maN say votr pr'm-yair
*Other country, other habits. Evidently this is your first*

**visite en France. Mais vous parlez français assez bien.**
vee-zeet aN fraNs. mai voo pahr-lay fraN-sai ah-say byiN.
*visit to France. But you speak French rather well.*

Charles :     **Je parle un peu seulement ; mais je comprends, si on ne**
zhe pahrl uN pāy sāyl'maN mai zhe coN-praN see oN ne
*I speak a little only ; but I understand if one does not*

**parle pas trop vite. Ma mère est française.**
pahrl pah troh veet. mah mair ay fraN-saiz.
*speak too fast. My mother is French.*

Le garçon :     **Alors, je comprends.**
ah-lor zhe coN-praN.
*Then, I understand.*

Mme Roberts :  **Le café est bon en France. Et la bière, aimez-vous**
le kah-fay ay bo-n aN fraNs. ay lah byair ai-may voo
*The coffee is good in France. And the beer, do you like*

**la bière française, mon mari?**
lah byair fraN-saiz moN mah-ree?
*the French beer, my husband?*

M. Roberts :     **Elle n'est pas mauvaise. Mais je préfère mon pale ale anglais.**
ail nay pah moh-vaiz. mai zh'pray-fair moN pel-el aN-glai.
*It is not bad. But I prefer my English pale ale.*

**Garçon, l'addition, s'il vous plaît.**      **Le garçon : Six francs trente.**
gahr-soN lah-dees-yoN see-voo plai.            see fraN traNt.
*Waiter, the bill, please.*                      *Six francs thirty.*

M. Roberts :     **Voilà sept francs. Gardez la monnaie.**
vwah-lah sait fraN. gahr-day lah mo-nai.
*Here's seven francs. Keep the change.*

Le garçon :     **Merci bien, monsieur. Je vous souhaite bon voyage.**
mair-see byiN m'ss-yāy. Zhe voo-swait boN vwah-yahzh.
*Thanks very much, sir. I wish you a good journey.*

This picture shows a somewhat unenthusiastic porter with the Roberts' luggage. In the list below only four of the words, which we translate, are unknown to you. Can you recognise the others from their French names?

| | | | |
|---|---|---|---|
| **Le fourreau** | **l'étiquette** (f.) | **la courroie** | **la canne** |
| foo-roh | ay-tee-ket | koo-rwah | kahn |
| Case, sheath | luggage tag | strap | (walking) stick |

**La valise**    **la malle**    **le carton à chapeaux**    **le sac de voyage**

**Le parapluie**    **la couverture de voyage**    **le porteur**    **les bagages**

## USEFUL EXPRESSIONS AT THE STATION

**De quel quai part le train pour Paris?**
d'kail kai pahr le triN poor pah-ree?
*From which platform leaves the train for Paris?*

**Quai numéro deux.**     **Les billets, s.v.p.**
kai nẽe-may-roh dãy.     lay bee-yay see-voo-plai.
*Platform number two.*     *(The) tickets please.*

**Est-ce le train pour Paris?**    **Est-ce un fumeur?**
ai-se le triN poor pah-ree?    ai-se uN fẽe-mãyr?
*Is this the train for Paris?*    *Is this a smoker?*

**(un non-fumeur)**     **Cette place est-elle libre?**
uN noN fẽe-mãyr     sait plahs ay-tail leebr?
*(a non-smoker)*     *Is this seat disengaged?*

**Est-ce que vous avez nos bagages?**    **En voiture, mesdames, messieurs!**
aisk' voo-zah-vay noh bah-gahzh?    aN vwah-tẽer may-dahm mais-yãy!
*Have you got our luggage?*    *Take your seats, ladies and gentlemen!*

**Mettez ceci dans le filet.**    **Mettez cette boîte à cette place.**
mai-tay s'see daN le fee-lay.    mai-tay sait bwat ah sait plahs.
*Put this into the (luggage) net (=rack).*    *Put this box on that seat.*

**Cela fait combien?**    **Trois francs, monsieur, c'est notre tarif[1].**
s'lah fai koN-byiN?    trwah fraN m'ss-yãy sai notr tah-reef.
*That makes how much?*    *Three francs, sir, that's our tariff.*
*How much is that?*    [1] French railway-porters have a fixed list of charges.

## A TALK IN THE TRAIN

**Mme Roberts : L'air est assez mauvais.**    **Vous permettez que je baisse la glace?**
     lair ay-tah-say moh-vay.    voo pair-mai-tay ke zhe bais lah glahs?
     *The air is rather bad.*    *You allow that I lower the window?*

**Le monsieur : Permettez-moi, madame.**    **Cette glace-là peut-être?**
     pair-mai-tay mwa mah-dahm.    sait glahs lah pãy-taitr?
     *Allow me, madam.*    *That window there perhaps?*

**Mme Roberts : Merci bien, monsieur, vous êtes bien aimable.**
     mair-see byiN m'ss-yãy voo-zait byai-nai-mahbl.
     *Thanks very much, sir.*    *You are very kind.*

**Le monsieur : Vous permettez que je fume?**
     voo pair-mai-tay k'zh'fẽem?
     *You allow that I smoke?*

**Mme Roberts : Certainement, monsieur.**    **Ça ne nous dérange pas.**
     sair-tai-n'maN m'ss-yãy.    sah ne noo day-raNzh pah.
     *Certainly, sir.*    *That us disturbs not.*

**Le monsieur (à M. Roberts)** : **Cigarette, monsieur?**
see-gah-rait m'ss-y@y?
*Cigarette, sir?*

**M. Roberts** : **Merci bien, monsieur. Mais je préfère ma pipe.**
mair-see byiN m'ss-y@y. mai zh'pray-fair mah peep.
*Thank you very much, sir. But I prefer my pipe.*

**Le monsieur** : **Est-ce que vous fumez, madame?**
ais-ke voo fée-may mah-dahm?
*Do you smoke, madam?*

**Mme Roberts** : **Merci, monsieur, je ne fume pas. Mon mari fume pour moi!**
mair-see m'ss-y@y zhe ne fēēm pah. moN mah-ree fēēm poor mwah!
*Thank you, sir, I don't smoke. My husband smokes for me!*

**HOW TO ASK QUESTIONS.** Est-ce que literally means "is it that"; placed before an ordinary statement it turns the statement into a question :

| | | |
|---|---|---|
| **Vous allez à Paris.** | | **Le chapeau est brun.** |
| *You are going to Paris.* | | *The hat is brown.* |
| | **EXAMPLES** | |
| **Est-ce que vous allez à Paris?** | | **Est-ce que le chapeau est brun?** |
| *Are you going to Paris?* | | *Is the hat brown?* |

**POSITIVE FORM**

**je fume**  (zhe fēēm)  *I smoke, I am smoking, I do smoke*

**il** ⎫
**elle** ⎬ **fume**  (eel ⎫ (ail ⎬ fēēm)  *he (it)* ⎫ *she (it)* ⎬ *smokes, is smoking, does smoke*

**nous fumons**  (noo fēē-moN)  *we smoke, are smoking, do smoke*
**vous fumez**  (voo fēē-may)  *you smoke, are smoking, do smoke*

**ils** ⎫
**elles** ⎬ **fument**  (eel ⎫ (ail ⎬ fēēm)  *they smoke, are smoking, do smoke*

**AS QUESTIONS**

**fumé-je** or **est-ce que je fume?**  *am I smoking? do I smoke?*
**fumez-vous?** or **est-ce que vous fumez?**  *are you smoking? do you smoke?*
**fume-t-il?** or **est-ce qu'il fume?**  *is he smoking? does he smoke?*
**fume-t-elle?** or **est-ce qu'elle fume?**  *is she smoking? does she smoke?*
**fumons-nous?** or **est-ce que nous fumons?**  *are we smoking? do we smoke?*
**fument-ils (elles)?** or **est-ce qu'ils (elles) fument?**  *are they smoking? do they smoke?*

**NEGATIVE FORM**

**je ne fume pas**  *I am not smoking, I don't smoke*
**il ne fume pas**  *he is not smoking, he does not smoke*
**elle ne fume pas**  *she is not smoking, she does not smoke*
**nous ne fumons pas**  *we are not smoking, we do not smoke*
**vous ne fumez pas**  *you are not smoking, you don't smoke*
**ils (elles) ne fument pas**  *they are not smoking, they don't smoke*

**AS QUESTIONS**

**ne fumez-vous pas?** or **est-ce que vous ne fumez pas?**  *are you not smoking? don't you smoke?*
**ne fume-t-il pas?** or **est-ce qu'il ne fume pas?**  *is he not smoking? doesn't he smoke?*
**ne fume-t-elle pas?** or **est-ce qu'elle ne fume pas?**  *is she not smoking? doesn't she smoke?*
**ne fument-ils (elles) pas?** or **est-ce qu'ils ne fument pas?**  *are they not smoking? don't they smoke?*

This and other diagrams are provided to extend your vocabulary in a simple and interesting way. First compare the English words and their French equivalents, then

## THE RAILWAY STATION

### English

1. Platform; 2. Engine; 3. Tender; 4. Luggage van; 5. Funnel (smoke-stack); 6. Coach (carriage); 7. Compartment; 8. Smokers' (compartment); 9. Non-smokers' (compartment); 10. Permanent way; 11. Local train (2nd and 3rd cl.); 12. Express trains (1st and 2nd cl.); 13. Station-master; 14. Buffers; 15. Engine-driver; 16. Stoker; 17. Guard; 18. Platform barrier; 19. Ticket collector; 20. Male traveller; 21. Female traveller; 22. Porter; 23. Newspaper trolley; 24. Rug and pillow trolley; 25. Luggage trolley; 26. (Carriage) window; 27. Advertisement; 28. Hanging lights; 29. Trunks; 30. Suitcases; 31. Ventilators; 32. Coal fuel; 33. Whistle; 34. Safety-valve; 35. Headlight; 36. Train-indicator.

### French

1. Quai (m.); 2. Locomotive (f.);

cover over the letterpress and see how many French words you can attach to the numbers on the diagram. Turn back to the diagrams when you have advanced in the course.

## LA GARE DE CHEMIN DE FER

3. Tender (m.); 4. Fourgon (m.) à bagages; 5. Cheminée (f.); 6. Voiture (f.); 7. Compartiment (f.); 8. (Compartiment de) fumeurs (m.pl.); 9. (Compartiment de) non-fumeurs; 10. Voie ferrée (f.); 11. Train (m.) d'interêt local, 2me et 3me cl.; 12. Trains-express; rapides (m.pl.) 1re et 2me cl.; 13. Chef (m.) de gare; 14. Heurtoirs; butoirs (m.pl.); 15. Mécanicien; 16. Chauffeur (m.); 17. Chef de train; 18. Contrôle (m.); 19. Contrôleur (m.); 20 & 21. Voyageur-euse; 22. Porteur; 23. Poussette (f.) à journaux; 24. Poussette à oreillers et couvertures, 25. Chariot (m.) à bagages; 26. Glace (f.); 27. Annonce (f.); 28. Eclairage (m.) suspendu; 29. Malles (f.pl.); 30. Valises (f.pl.); 31. Ventilateurs (m.pl.); 32. Charbon; combustible (m.); 33. Sifflet (m.) à vapeur; 34. Soupape (f.) de sûreté; 35. Phare; projecteur (m.); 36. Tableau (m.) indicateur.

If you look up "to smoke" in a dictionary you will find **fumer** (fẽ-may); to speak is **parler** (pahr-lay); to carry is **porter** (por-tay). The form of a verb[1] which you find in the dictionary is called the Infinitive[2]. The Infinitives of most French verbs end in **-er** pronounced **ay.**

All verbs ending in **-er** with the exception of **aller**=to go, have the same endings as shown above for **fumer,** i.e., they end in **-e** (which is silent) in connection with **je, il** or **elle,** in **-ez** (ay), when used with **vous,** in **-ons** (oN) with **nous** and in **-ent** (silent) when used in connection with **ils** or **elles.**

If we call the part of a verb that does not change the stem, and the part that does the ending, then **fum-, parl-, port-** are the stems of the verbs **fumer, parler** and **porter.** To say "I speak" or "I am speaking" you don't have to add anything to the stem, but in writing **-e** is added; thus you say zhe pahrl and you write **je parle.** "He (she) speaks (or: is speaking)"—**il (elle) parle** (the e remains silent). To say "you speak" or "you are speaking" you add **-ez** to the stem: **vous parlez** (voo pahr-lay); "you carry" or "you are carrying" is **vous portez**; to ask "do you smoke?" or "are you smoking?" you just reverse the order and say "smoke you?"=**fumez-vous** or

**est-ce que vous fumez?** "Do you speak English?" is: **parlez-vous anglais?** or **est-ce que vous parlez anglais?** "Are you carrying my luggage?"=**portez-vous mes bagages?** or **est-ce que vous portez mes bagages?** etc.

Study carefully the forms of the verb **fumer,** not forgetting its negative and question forms as given on page 47. If you replace the stem **fum-** by the stem of any other verbs ending in **-er** (and there are over 4,000 of them) you will be able to make hundreds and hundreds of other statements and questions. Other verbs in **-er** having occurred in this lesson besides **fumer, parler** and **porter** are **déclarer**=to declare, **fermer**=to close, **débarquer**=to land, **trouver**=to find, **apporter**=to bring and **déranger**=to disturb.

We shall deal with the verb **aller** in the following lessons, and in later lessons with those verbs which do not end in **-er.**

---

[1] A "verb" is a word used for asserting something about a person or thing.

[2] The "infinitive" is that part of a verb which names the action with no reference to who is doing it or when it takes place.

It is the part usually cited: thus one does not speak of "the verb je fume", but of "the verb **fumer, parler, porter**," etc.

## SUMMARY

*Affirmative*

| | | | | |
|---|---|---|---|---|
| je il elle $\Big\}$ -----------$e^1$ | $\Big\{$ I---------------, he (it)---------s, she (it)---------s, | I am---------ing, is ----------- ing, is ------------ ing, | I do ----------- does ----------- does----------- |
| vous --------------$ez^2$ | you -------------, | are --------- ing, | do------------- |
| nous ---------$ons^3$ | we --------------, | are --------- ing, | do------------- |
| ils elles -----------$ent^1$ $\Big\}$ | they -------------, | are --------- ing, | do-------------- |

*Interrogative*

| | | |
|---|---|---|
| -------------------- é-je? | am I -------------------- ing? | do I --------------------? |
| ------------------ e-t-il? | is he --------------------- ing? | does he -------------- ? |
| -------------- e-t-elle? | is she -------------------- ing? | does she -------------- ? |
| -------------- ez-vous? | are you ----------------- ing? | do you ---------------- ? |
| ------------- ons-nous? | are we ------------------- ing? | do we ----------------- ? |
| ----------- ent-ils?[4] ent-elles?[4] $\Big\}$ | are they ----------------- ing? | do they -------------- ? |

or : put **est-ce que (aiske)** in front of the affirmative form.

*Negative*

| | | |
|---|---|---|
| *je ne* ----------- *e¹ pas* | I am not ---------------- ing, | I don't------------------ |
| *il ne* ------------ *e¹ pas* | he is not ---------------- ing, | he does not------------- |
| *elle ne* ---------- *e¹ pas* | she is not --------------- ing, | she does not ------------ |
| *vous ne* -------- *ez² pas* | your are not ------------- ing, | you don't -------------- |
| *nous ne* ------- *ons³pas* | we are not -------------- ing, | we don't-----------------.------ |
| *ils (elles) ne* -- *ent¹ pas* | they are not ------------- ing, | they don't ------------- |

*Negative and Interrogative*

| | | |
|---|---|---|
| *ne* --------- *é-je pas?* | am I not ---------------- ing? | don't I ---------------- ? |
| *ne* -------- *e-t-il pas?* | is he not ---------------- ing? | doesn't he ------------ ? |
| *ne* ----- *e-t-elle pas?* | is she not ---------------- ing? | doesn't she ----------- ? |
| *ne* ----- *ez-vous pas?* | are you not ------------- ing? | don't you ------------ ? |
| *ne* ----- *ons-nous pas?* | are we not -------------- ing? | don't we -------------- ? |
| *ne--ent⁴ ils (elles) pas?* | are they not ------------- ing? | don't they ----------- ? |

or : put **est-ce** in front of the negative form.

¹ this ending is silent.  ² pronounced **ay.**  ³ pronounced **oN.**  ⁴ the **t** is sounded.

## EXERCISES

### I Translate into French

1. Do you smoke? 2. Is she smoking? 3. He does not smoke. 4. We are landing. 5. They keep the change. 6. I don't shut the door. 7. Haven't you got the luggage? 8. Is he not carrying our luggage? 9. We speak English. 10. We don't speak French. 11. Are we now in France? 12. Can't you find (say : find you not) your ticket? 13. Waiter, three coffees, please. 14. The bill, please. 15. Is this the train for Paris? 16. Are these stockings new? 17. You are disturbing that lady. 18. Do you mind my smoking? (translated : Do you allow that I smoke or does it disturb you that I smoke?) 19. Porter, are you not free? 20. Is it to the right or to the left?

### II Answer in French

1. Parlez-vous français? 2. Est-ce que nous sommes en France? 3. Les bas de Mme Roberts sont-ils neufs? 4. Qui porte les bagages? 5. À quelle heure part le train de la famille Roberts? 6. Qui apporte les consommations? 7. Charles a-t-il faim? 8. Est-ce que la famille Roberts va à Marseille? 9. Charles a-t-il un café nature? 10. Qu'est-ce qu'il a? 11. Le café est-il bon? 12. Est-ce que Monsieur R. fume une cigarette? 13. Qu'est-ce qu'il préfère? 14. Est-ce que vous avez une allumette? 15. Est-ce que Madame R. fume?

### III Give the correct ending and translate into English

1. Je *ferm-* la porte. 2. Il *trouv-* un billet. 3. Elles ne *fum-* pas. 4. Ne *débarqu-* -vous pas? 5. Ne *dérang-* -t-elle pas? 6. Vous *parl-* assez bien. 7. Nous *apport-* les bagages. 8. Ils ne *trouv-* pas le porteur. 9. Le garçon *n'apport -t-il* pas l'addition? 10. Est-ce qu'elles ne *ferm-* pas la porte?

*(Key to I, II and III on pages 52 and 53)*

# KEY TO THE EXERCISES
## Lesson Two

### I

1. Ce sont des gants. 2. Oui, il est joli (non, il n'est pas joli). 3. Non, ce n'est pas Mlle Lesage. 4. Oui, elle est jolie. 5. Charles est le cousin de Mlle Lesage. 6. Oui, il est joli (non, il n'est pas joli). 7. C'est un gant. 8. Non, il n'est pas grand. 9. Madeleine est la sœur de Charles. 10. M. et Mme Roberts. 11. Oui, elle est élégante. 12. Non, elles ne sont pas grandes. 13. Non, il n'est pas sur la table. 14. Il est sur la chaise. 15. Oui. 16. C'est un gilet. 17. Ce sont les chaussures. 18. Elles sont noires et blanches.

## II

1. La cravate est blanche et bleue. 2. Le veston est brun. 3. La robe est verte. 4. Le chapeau n'est pas vert, il est brun. 5. Le pardessus est-il noir? 6. Non, monsieur, il est gris. 7. La table est-elle grande? 8. Oui, elle est grande. 9. La fenêtre est-elle grande? 10. Non, elle est petite. 11. Le mouchoir est-il rouge et bleu? 12. Non, il est blanc. 13. Les gants sont-ils bruns? 14. Non, madame, ils sont jaunes. 15. Les malles sont-elles jaunes? 16. Non, elles sont brunes. 17. Qu'est ce que c'est? 18. Est-ce le livre? 19. Oui, monsieur, c'est le livre. 20. Non, monsieur, ce n'est pas le livre, c'est le sac. 21. De quelle couleur est le sac? 22. Il est bleu. 23. N'est-il pas joli! 24. La valise, n'est-elle pas brune? 25. L'enfant[1] n'est-il pas charmant! 26. Où sont les enfants? 27. Où est le père de Georges? 28. Où est-il? 29. Où est-elle? 30. Où sont-ils?

## III

1. Il est blanc. 2. Elle . . . 3. Elle . . . 4. Ils . . . 5. Elles . . . 6. Ils . . . 7 Elles . . . 8. . . . est-il? 9. . . . est-elle? 10. . . . est-il? 11. . . . est-elle? 12. . . . sont-ils? 13. . . . sont-ils? 14. . . . sont-elles?

## Lesson Three

### I

1. Oui, elle a une bonne traversée. 2. Oui, elle est calme. 3. Oui, il est fatigué. 4. Non, il n'est pas malade. 5. Charles est malade. 6. Non, elle n'est pas malade. 7. Elle a douze ans. 8. Non, elle n'est pas anglaise. 9. Oui, ils sont français. 10. Non je ne suis pas français. 11. Non, je ne suis pas fatigué. 12. Oui, ils sont anglais (Non, ils ne sont pas anglais).

### II

1. This glass is for me, that glass is for you. 2. It's a cup of tea. 3. This is a glass of beer, that is a glass of wine. 4. Here is a nice French boat. 5. The captain is tall and thin. 6. Here is a deck-chair for you. 7. Thank you, sir, you are very kind. 8. Have you got my bag? 9. There is your bag. 10. Is your husband French? 11.

No, madam, he is Scottish. 42. Aren't you tired? 13. We are not tired. 14. His (or her) children are charming, aren't they? 15. His (or her) daughter speaks French, doesn't she? 16. Frenchwomen are charming, aren't they? 17. His (or her) son is bringing a deck-chair, isn't he?

## III

1. Ma mère est française, mon père est anglais. 2. Ils ont trois enfants. 3. Nous sommes sur un bateau français. 4. Nous ne sommes pas fatigués. Nous avons une bonne (mauvaise) traversée. 6. Cette tasse est-elle pour moi? 7. Qu'est que c'est? 8. Est-ce une tasse de thé? 9. Cette tasse n'est pas grande. 10. N'avez-vous pas un transatlantique? 11. N'êtes - vous pas content(e)? 12. Vous êtes fatigué(e), n'est-ce pas? 13. Votre frère est fatigué, n'est-ce pas? 14. Leurs enfants sont charmants[2], n'est-ce pas? 15. Où est le chapeau de Charles? 16. Voici son chapeau. 17. Où est le sac de Madeleine? 18. Voilà son sac. 19. Avez-vous mes gants? 20. Voilà vos gants sur la chaise. 21. Est-ce qu'ils sont bruns ou jaunes? 22. Ils ne sont pas jaunes. 23. Ils (elles) ont une bonne traversée, n'est-ce pas? 24. Le café est bon, n'est-ce pas? 25. Ce verre est-il pour moi?

## Lesson Four

### I

1. Fumez-vous? or Est-ce que vous fumez? 2. Fume-t-elle or est-ce qu'elle fume? 3. Il ne fume pas. 4. Nous débarquons. 5. Ils (elles) gardent la monnaie. 6. Je ne ferme pas la porte. 7. N'avez-vous pas les bagages? 8. Ne porte-t-il pas nos bagages? 9. Nous parlons anglais. 10. Nous ne parlons pas français. 11. Est-ce que nous sommes (or sommes-nous) maintenant en France? 12. Ne trouvez-vous pas (est-ce que vous ne trouvez pas) votre billet? 13. Garçon, trois cafés, s'il vous plaît. 14. L'addition, s'il vous plaît. 15. Est-ce le train pour Paris? 16. Ces bas

---

[1] As mentioned in footnote to p. 22, **enfant** is masculine when meaning a boy and feminine when a girl is indicated. In this case for a girl child one would say "elle" and **charmante**.

[2] **Charmantes**, if girls are referred to.

sont-ils neufs? 17. Vous dérangez cette dame. 18. Permettez-vous que je fume? or est-ce que ça vous dérange que je fume? 19. Porteur, n'êtes-vous pas libre? 20. Est-ce à droite ou à gauche?

## II

1. Je parle français (je ne parle pas français) or : un peu seulement. 2. Nous ne sommes pas en France. 3. Non, ils ne sont pas neufs. 4. Le porteur porte les bagages. 5. Le train part à trois heures vingt. 6. Le garçon apporte les consommations. 7. Non, il n'a pas faim. 8. Elle ne va pas à Marseille. 9 and 10. Non, il a un café crème. 11. Oui, il est bon. 12. Non,

il ne fume pas une cigarette. 13. Une pipe. 14. Oui, j'ai une allumette. 15. Non, elle ne fume pas.

## III

1. *ferme* : I close the door. 2. *trouve* : He finds a ticket. 3. *fument* : They don't smoke or they are not smoking. 4. *débarquez* : Are you not going on land? 5. *dérange-t-elle* : Is she not disturbing? or Doesn't she disturb? 6. *parlez* : You speak quite well. 7. *apportons* : We bring (are bringing) the luggage. 8. *trouvent* : They don't find the porter. 9. *n'apporte-t-il pas* : Doesn't the waiter bring the bill? 10. *ferment* : Don't they shut the door?

**The Roberts family are now in France. Are you also in France? If you have studied the Lessons and listened in to French on the wireless, you should be setting your foot there already.**

### DEVANT LES BOUQUINISTES

C'est une scène familière—des passants qui s'attardent à feuilleter les livres aux étalages des bouquinistes de la rive gauche, quartier des étudiants et des professeurs.

| **Bouquiniste** (m.f.) | **s'attarder à** | **feuilleter** | **étalage** (m.) |
|---|---|---|---|
| (Second-hand) bookseller | dally over | glance through (book) | bookstall |

## LA SORBONNE (UNIVERSITÉ DE PARIS)

Héritiers d'une grande tradition, ces étudiants profitent d'un moment de liberté dans la cour d'honneur pour respirer l'air et philosopher.

| **Heritier-ère** (m.f.) | **étudiant-e** (m.f.) | **profiter de** | **cour** (f.) **d'honneur** |
|---|---|---|---|
| Heir, inheritor | student | take advantage of | grand quadrangle |

# CINQUIÈME LEÇON—*FIFTH LESSON*

Cover over the English lines of the text below, and, with the help of the picture, see if you can follow how the Roberts family are passing the time in the train.

**Il est six heures du soir. Le train n'est plus loin de Paris. La famille**
ee-lai see-zāyr dẽe swahr. le triN nay plẽe lwiN de pah-ree. lah fah-mee*y*
*It is six o'clock of the evening. The train is no longer far from Paris. The Roberts*

**Roberts ne dort plus. Charles lit un livre. Monsieur Roberts lit un**
ro-bairts ne dor plẽe. shahrl lee-tuN leevr. m'ss-yāy ro-bairts lee-tuN
*family is no more asleep. Charles is reading a book. Mr. Roberts is reading a*

**journal. Mme R. regarde par la fenêtre. Madeleine parle avec le monsieur.**
zhoor-nahl. mah-dahm R. re-gahrd pahr lah f'naitr. mahd-lain pahr ah-veck lem'ss-yāy.
*paper. Mrs. R. looks out of the window. Madeleine is talking to the gentleman.*

Madeleine : **Est-ce que nous sommes encore loin de Paris?**
aisk' noo somm-zaN-kor lwiN d'pah-ree?
*Are we still far from Paris?*

Le monsieur : **Encore une demi-heure. Nous arrivons à six heures trente.**
aN-kor ẽen d'mee āyr. noo-zah-ree-voN ah see-zāyr traNt.
*Still half an hour. We arrive at six thirty.*

Madeleine : **Est-ce que vous allez aussi à Paris, monsieur?**
aisk' voo-zah-lay oh-see ah pah-ree m'ss-yāy?
*Are you going also to Paris, sir?*

**Le monsieur :**   **Non, mademoiselle.   Je ne reste à Paris que deux heures.**
noN mahd-mwah-zail.   zhe ne raist ah pah-ree ke dâŷ-zâŷr.
*No, miss.   I am staying in Paris only for two hours.*

                      **Puis je vais en Italie.   Ma femme y est déjà.**
                      pŵee zh'vai-zah-nee-tah-lee.   mah fahm ee ay day-zhah.
                      *Then I am going to Italy.   My wife is already there.*

**Madeleine :**   **Vraiment!   Vous allez en Italie.**
vrai-maN!   voo-zah-lay-zah-nee-tah-lee.
*Really!   You are going to Italy.*

**Le monsieur :**   **Et vous, mademoiselle, est-ce que vous restez à Paris?**
ay voo mahd-mwah-zail aisk' voo rais-tay ah pah-ree?
*And you, miss, are you going to stay in Paris?*

**Madeleine :**   **J'y reste plusieurs semaines.   Puis je vais au bord de la**
zhee raist plêêz-yâŷr s'main.   pwee zhe vai zoh bor d'lah
*I stay there several weeks.   Then I am going either to the*

                  **mer ou à la campagne.**
                  mair oo ah lah kaN-pany.
                  *seaside or to the country.*

**Le monsieur :**   **Et votre frère, où va-t-il?**
ay votr frair oo vah-teel?
*And your brother, where is he going?*

**Madeleine :**   **Il va où je vais, naturellement.**
eel vah oo zhe vai nah-têê-rail-maN.
*He goes where I go, naturally.*

**Charles :**   **Non, je ne vais pas avec vous.   Je reste à Paris.**
noN zhe ne vai pah-zah-vaik voo.   zhe raist ah pah-ree.
*No, I am not going with you.   I stay in Paris.*

**Le monsieur :**   **Et vos parents, est-ce qu'ils vont aussi à la campagne?**
ay voh pah-raN aisk-eel voN-toh-see ah lah kaN-pany?
*And your parents, are they going also to the country?*

**Madeleine :**   **Oui, probablement, mais mon père va bientôt retourner**
ŵee prob-ahbl-maN mai moN pair vah byiN-toh r'toor-nay
*Yes, probably, but my father will soon return*

                  **pour quelque temps en Angleterre.**
                  poor kail-ke taN ah-naN-gl'tair.
                  *for some time to England.*

**Charles (après quelques minutes) : J'ai faim, maman.**
                  ah-prai kailk mee-nêêt : zhay fiN mah-maN.
                  *(after a few minutes) : I am hungry, mummy.*

## THE VERB ALLER = TO GO

**je vais**   zh'vai   I go, I am going

**il** } **va**   eel } **vah**   he (it) } goes,
**elle** }        ail }           she (it) } is going

**nous allons**  noo-zah-loN  we go, are going
**vous allez**   voo-zah-lay  you go, are going

**ils** } **vont**   eel } **voN**   they go,
**elles** }          ail }           are going

### NO MORE OR NO LONGER

**il ne parle plus** = he is no longer speaking
**le train n'est plus loin de Paris** = the train is no longer far from Paris
**ils ne restent plus à Londres** = they are no longer staying in London

Note that **ne** precedes the verb and **plus** follows it, the same as **ne . . . pas**

### ONLY

**il ne reste que deux heures** = he stays only (for) two hours
**Elle n'a que trois ans** = She is only three years (old)
**Qui retourne en Angleterre?   Mon père seulement** = who returns to England? Only my father

Note that **ne** precedes the verb and **que** follows it, in the same way as **ne . . . pas**, or **ne . . . plus**. But if "only" is used apart from a verb, it must be translated by **seulement** (sayl-maN).

---

**Mme R. :**   **Voici une pomme.   Donnez-en la moitié à Madeleine.**
vwah-see ĕn pom.   do-nay-zaN lah mwaht-yay ah mahd-lain.
*Here's an apple.   Give (of it the) half to Madeleine.*

**Madeleine :**   **Non, merci, je n'ai pas faim.**
noN mair-see zhe nay pah fiN.
*No, thank you, I am not hungry.*

**Charles :**   **Papa, donnez-moi votre canif, s'il vous plaît.**
Pah-pah do-nay mwah votr kah-neef see-voo-plai.
*Father, give me your (pocket-) knife, please.*

**Monsieur R.**   **(donnant son canif à Charles) :**
do-naN soN kah-neef ah shahrl
*(giving his knife to Charles) :*
**Voilà, mon fils.**
vwah-lah moN fees.
*There you are, my son.*

**Charles :**   **Merci, papa.   Voulez-vous l'autre moitié?**
mair-see pah-pah.   voo-lay voo lohtr mwaht-yay?
*Thank you, father.   Do you want the other half?*

**Monsieur R. :**   **Non, mon petit, pas pour moi.   Mais donnez-la à monsieur.**
noN moN p'tee pah poor mwah.   mai do-nay lah ah m'ss-yay.
*No, my little one, not for me.   But give it to (the) gentleman.*

**Charles :**   **Pardon, monsieur, est-ce que vous voulez la moitié de ma pomme?**
pahr-doN m'ssyay aisk voo voo-lay lah mwaht-yay d'mah pom?
*Excuse me, sir, would you like (the) half of my apple?*

**Le monsieur :**   **Merci bien, mon ami.   Vous êtes bien aimable, mais**
mair-see byiN mo-nah-mee.   voo-zait byai-nai-mahbl mai
*Thank you very much, (my friend).   You are very kind, but*
**je ne mange jamais avant le repas.**
zhe ne maNzh zhah-mai ah-vaN le re-pah.
*I eat never before the meal (meals).*

## AT A FRENCH AIRPORT

*For instructions on the method of using these*

### English

1. Wing(s) ; 2. Engine ; 3. Three-bladed airscrew ; 4. Non-smoking cabin ; 5. Smoking cabin ; 6. Aerial ; 7. Steward's galley ; 8. Direction-finder ; 9. Navigator ; 10. Mast head light ; 11. Radio cabin ; 12. Pilot ; 13. Second pilot ; 14. Landing lights ; 15. Electrically-heated speed indicator ; 16. Control tower ; 17. Wind-sock ; 18. French flag ; 19. Body of plane ; 20. Rear landing-wheel ; 21. Baggage compartment and extra passenger accommodation ; 22. Steward ; 23. Tail-plane ; 24. Rudder fin (port) ; 25. Stabiliser ; 26. Retractable under-carriage.

### French

1. Aile(s) (f.); 2. Moteur (m.); 3. Hélice

**DANS UN AÉROPORT FRANÇAIS**

*vocabulary building diagrams, see pages* **34** *and* **35.**

(f.) à trois pales ; 4. Cabine (f.) de non-
fumeurs ; 5. Cabine de fumeurs ; 6.
Antenne (f.) ; 7. Cuisine (f.) ; 8. Radio-
goniomètre (m.) ; 9. Navigateur (m.) ; 10.
Feu (m.) de tête de mât ; 11. Cabine de
T.S.F. ; 12. Pilote (m.) ; 13. Pilote en
second ; 14. Feu d'atterrissage (m.) ; 15.
Indicateur (m.) de vitesse chauffé à
l'électricité ; 16. Tour (f.) de contrôle ;
17. Sac (m.) à vent ; 18. Pavillon (m.)
national ; 19. Fuselage (m.) ; 20. Roue (f.)
de la dérive ; 21. Soute (f.) à bagages et
place supplémentaire pour passagers ;
22. Garçon de cabine, steward (m.) ;
23. Plan (m.) fixé ; 24. Gouvernail (m.) de
direction de bâbord ; 25. Stabilisateur
(m.) ; 26. Châssis (m.) d'atterrissage
relevable.

**NEVER**

**je ne mange jamais** . . . I never eat
**il ne parle jamais** . . . He never speaks
**ne** precedes the verb and **jamais** follows
it, in the same way as **ne . . . pas, ne . . .que,**
or **ne . . . plus.** If "never" is used without
a verb **jamais** only is said.

**HOW TO ASK FOR SOMETHING**
**donnez!**=give! **mangez!**=eat! **parlez!**=
speak! The imperative of a verb ends in
**-ez** (pronounced ay).

**HOW TO TRANSLATE *DON'T***
**ne parlez pas** . . . don't speak
**ne mangez pas** . . . don't eat
**ne parlez plus** . . . don't speak any more
**ne mangez plus** . . . don't eat any more
**ne parlez jamais**    don't ever speak,
                     never speak

**Lui: Embrassez-moi!**
lⓦee aN-brah-say mwah!
*He: Kiss me!*

**Elle: Jamais!**
ail zhah-mai !
*She: Never!*

---

**Charles :**    **Alors je mange l'autre moitié aussi.**
ah-lor zhe maNzh loh-tr mwaht-yay oh-see.
*Then I eat the other half too.*

**Mme R. :**    **Ne mangez pas si avidement, mon enfant!**
ne maN-zhay pah see ah-vee-d'-maN· mo-naN-faN!
*Don't eat so greedily, my child!*

**Charles :**    **Quel long voyage!**
kail loN vwah-yahzh!
*What a long journey!*

**Le monsieur :**  **N'aimez-vous pas voyager?**   **Regardez le beau village.**
nai-may voo pah vwah-yah-zhay? r'gahr-day le boh vee-lahzh.
*Don't you like to travel?*   *Look at the beautiful village.*

**Charles :**    **J'aime bien voyager.**   **Mais je n'aime pas les longs voyages**
zhaim byiN vwah-yah-zhay.  mai zh'naim pah lay loN vwa-yahzh
*I like very much to travel.*  *But I don't like the long journeys*

**en train.**   **J'aime mieux aller en auto.**
aN triN.  zhaim myⓐy ah-lay ah-noh-toh.
*by train.*  *I like better to go by car.*

**Le monsieur :**  **Ou en avion?**   **On évite tous les changements**
oo ah-nahv-yoN?  oh-nay-veet too lay shaNzh-maN
*Or by aeroplane?*  *One avoids all the changing*

**de bateau en train.**
de bah-toh aN triN.
*from boat to train.*

Charles :     **C'est ça, monsieur.**
say sah m'ss-yãy.
*That's right, sir (literally : That's it)*

Madeleine :     **Quelles jolies petites maisons! Regardez, maman!**
kail zho-lee p'teet mai-zoN! r'gahr-day mah-maN!
*What pretty little houses! Look, mother!*

Mme R. :     **Oui, elles sont très belles, ma fille.**
w͡ee ail soN trai bail mah feey.
*Yes, they are very beautiful, my daughter.*

Charles :     **Quelle heure est-il maintenant?**
kai-lãyr ay-teel miNt-naN?
*What time is it now?*

Le monsieur :     **Il est six heures et quart. Encore un quart d'heure et**
ee-lay see-zãyr ay kahr. aN-kor uN kahr dãyr ay
*It is six o'clock and quarter. Another quarter of an hour and*

**nous sommes à Paris si nous arrivons à l'heure.**
noo-som-zah pah-ree see noo-zah-ree-voN zah lãyr.
*we are in Paris if we arrive on time (literally : "to the hour.")*

### HOW TO TRANSLATE "LET US . . . "

**Allons!** *Let us go!* . . . **Parlons français!** *Let us speak French!*
Note that the ending -ons (pronounced *o*N) gives to a verb the meaning of "let us . . ."

### HOW TO TRANSLATE "BEAUTIFUL"

**Le chapeau est beau** . . . . . *The hat is beautiful*
**La maison est belle** . . . . . *The house is beautiful*
**Les chapeaux sont beaux** . . . . . *The hats are beautiful*
**Les maisons sont belles** . . . . . *The houses are beautiful*

Note (1) That the plural of words in **-eau** ends in **-x** (which is silent except in liaison, when it is sounded like *z*).
(2) The irregular feminine of **beau** : **belle.**

### HOW TO TRANSLATE WHAT A . . . . WHAT . . . . WHICH . . .

**Quel beau chapeau!.** . . . . *What a beautiful hat!*
**Quelle belle maison!** . . . . . *What a beautiful house!*
**Quels beaux chapeaux!** . . . . *What beautiful hats!*
**Quelles belles maisons!** . . . . . *What beautiful houses!*
**Quel livre avez-vous?** . . . . . *Which book have you (got)?*
**Quelle valise prenez-vous?** . . . . . *Which suitcase are you taking?*
**Quels livres avez-vous?** . . . . . *Which books have you (got)?*
**Quelles valises prenez-vous?** . . . . . *Which suitcases are you taking?*

*Note* (1) That there is no difference in French between "what a . . ., what . . ., which . . .," when used in connection with nouns, i.e., like adjectives.
(2) Like all other adjectives there is a special form for the feminine **quelle,** and in the plural **-s** is added.
(3) **quel, quelle, quels, quelles** are all pronounced the same, i.e., like **the** first syllable of the word *kel*tic.

### WHAT TIME IS IT?—IN HOURS

**De midi à minuit**
de mee-dee ah mee-nw͡ee
*From midday to midnight*

| | | | | |
|---|---|---|---|---|
| A | .. | .. | il est une heure | .. .. ee͡n-a͡yr |
| B | .. | .. | il est deux heures | .. .. da͡y-za͡yr |
| C | .. | .. | il est trois heures | .. .. trwah-za͡yr |
| D | .. | .. | il est quatre heures | .. kaht-ra͡yr |
| E | .. | .. | il est cinq heures | .. .. siN-ka͡yr |
| F | .. | .. | il est six heures | .. .. see-za͡yr |
| G | .. | .. | il est sept heures | .. .. sai-ta͡yr |
| H | .. | .. | il est huit heures | .. .. w͡ee-ta͡yr |
| I | .. | .. | il est neuf heures | .. .. na͡y-va͡yr |
| J | .. | .. | il est dix heures | .. .. dee-za͡yr |
| K | .. | .. | il est onze heures | .. .. oN-za͡yr |
| L | .. | .. | il est midi (minuit) | .. .. mee-dee (mee-nw͡ee) |

*Note.*—As the twenty-four hour clock is practically universal in France, especially in railway guides, it is wise to start now thinking in terms of **treize, quatorze heures** (1 and 2 p.m.), etc.

## WHAT TIME IS IT?—IN MINUTES

**De midi à une heure**
de mee-dee ah ēēnāyr
*From midday to one o'clock*

| | | | |
|---|---|---|---|
| A .. | .. il est midi cinq | .. .. .. | mee-dee siNk |
| B .. | .. il est midi dix .. | .. .. .. | mee-dee dees |
| C .. | .. il est midi et quart | .. .. .. | mee-dee ay kahr |
| D .. | .. il est midi vingt.. | .. .. .. | mee-dee viN |
| E .. | .. il est midi vingt cinq | .. .. .. | mee-dee viNt siNk |
| F .. | .. il est midi et demie | .. .. | mee-dee ay d'mee |
| G .. | .. il est une heure moins vingt-cinq | .. | ēēnāyr mwiN viNt siNk |
| H .. | .. il est une heure moins vingt .. | .. | mwiN viN |
| I .. | .. il est une heure moins le quart | .. | mwiN le kahr |
| J .. | .. il est une heure moins dix | .. | mwiN dees |
| K .. | .. il est une heure moins cinq | .. | mwiN siNk |
| L .. | .. il est une heure précise.. | .. | pray-sees |

*Note.*—When indicating time with precision in hours and minutes, one may also use, *e.g.*, 12·51, **midi cinquante-et-une**, 3·17, **trois heures dix-sept**, etc.

# EXERCISES

## I Translate into English

1. Aimez-vous les livres? 2. J'aime bien les livres. 3. Mon livre est très intéressant. 4. Je n'aime pas les livres de mon père; ils ne sont pas intéressants. 5. Regardez cette jolie petite fille; n'est-elle pas belle? 6. Est-ce que vous allez en France? 7. Non, monsieur, je vais en Angleterre. 8. Mes enfants y vont aussi. 9. Mon père ne va pas à la campagne. 10. Ils vont au bord de la mer.

## II Replace the dashes by quel, quelle, quels or quelles

1. — fenêtre est ouverte? 2. — portes sont fermées? 3. — livre est rouge? 4. — valises sont jaunes? 5. — monsieur est votre père? 6. — dame est votre tante? 7. Dans — train est-il? 8. Dans — valise sont les pommes? 9. — sont vos chapeaux? 10. — heure est-il?

## III Translate into French

1. What's the time, please? 2. It is four o'clock. 3. It is two-thirty. 4. It is six minutes past five. 5. It is a quarter past eleven. 6. It is twenty-five minutes past nine. 7. It is a quarter to eight. 8. It is twenty to seven. 9. It is five minutes before midnight. 10. How old is your sister? 11. She is only twelve years old. 12. Where are you going? I am going to Paris. 13. We are going to the seaside. 14. Are you going to the countryside? 15. Is your wife also there? 16. Are your children going to Italy? 17. Is your son still hungry? 18. Thank you, madam; he is no longer hungry. 19. I never speak to my brother. 20. What a beautiful bridge! 21. What a beautiful house they have! 22. What pretty girls they are! 23. Let us look at the bridge. 24. Let us get our luggage ready. 25. Please give me the half of your apple. 26. Don't speak so quickly.

*(Key to I, II and III on page 101)*

PARIS AU PRINTEMPS

Au coin du Boulevard Montmartre, un beau jour de printemps. Mais malgré le soleil, on garde toujours le pardessus. "En avril ne quitte pas un fil."

malgré              garder              "En avril ne quitte pas un fil"
in spite of         to keep (on)        "Ne'er cast a clout till May be out" (corresp. expression).

# SIXIÈME LEÇON—*SIXTH LESSON*

In this picture of the Roberts' arrival in Paris, there are at least fifteen objects you should be able to name in French. Can you do so? For key see page 92.

**M. Roberts**
**Nous avons trois gros bagages. Voici le bulletin.**
noo-zah-voN trwah groh bah-gahzh. vwah-see le bẽel-tiN.
*We have three (articles of) big luggage. Here is the receipt.*

**Laissez les bagages à main, je les prendrai moi-même.**
lai-say lay bah-gahzh ah miN zhe lay praN-drai mwah-maim.
*Leave the hand luggage, I'll take them myself.*

**Mme R. :**
**Voici l'oncle Lesage. Bonjour, Paul!    M. Lesage : Bonjour,[1]**
vwah-see loNkl l'sazh. boN-zhoor pol!          boN-zhoor,
*Here is uncle Lesage. Hallo, Paul!          Good morning,*

**ma chérie! Bonjour, Roberts! Bonjour, Madeleine!**
mah shay-ree!  boN-zhoor Ro-bairts!  boN-zhoor mahd-lain!
*my dear! Good morning, Roberts! Good morning, Madeleine!*

---

[1] **Bonjour** literally means *good day*. Note that it is also said in the morning and afternoon, as there are no French equivalents for our *good morning* and *good afternoon*. In the evening they say **bon soir** (boN swahr), even late in the night, when we would say *good night*. **Bonne nuit** (bon-nw̃ee) the French for *good night*, is used only before going to bed.

À droite: la Gare St. Lazare, terminus des lignes de Dieppe et du Havre; également la plus importante des gares de banlieue desservant Paris.

On the right: the Gare St. Lazare, terminus of the lines from Dieppe and Le Havre; also the most important of the stations serving the suburbs of Paris.

En bas: la Gare du Nord, dont la construction évoque une architecture d'ordre ionique d'un ensemble heureux.

Below: the Gare du Nord, the construction of which calls to mind the pleasing effect of architecture of the Ionic order.

PARIS : LES GRANDES GARES D'ARRIVÉE EN VENANT DE LONDRE

Bonjour Charles!  Qu'il est grand, ce fripon!  (il les embrasse
boN-zhoor shahrl!  kee-lai graN se free-poN !  (eel-lai-zaN-brahs
*Good morning, Charles!  How big he is, this rascal!  (he kisses*

tous à l'exception de Charles!)
toos ah laik-saip-syoN de shahrl!)
*them all with the exception of Charles!)*

Charles (évitant d'être embrassé) :  Bonjour, mon oncle.
(ay-vee-taN d'aitr aN-brah-say) :  boN-zhoor mo-noNkl.
*(avoiding to be embraced) :  Good day, (my)  uncle.*

M. Roberts :   Comment allez-vous?
ko-maN-tah-lay-voo?
*How are you?*

M. Lesage :   Très bien, merci.  Et vous?
trai byiN mair-see.  ay voo?
*Very well, thanks.  And you?*

M. Roberts :   Pas mal non plus.
pah mall noN plêe.
*Not bad either.*

M. Lesage :   Vous avez bonne mine, Roberts.  Alors, venez chez nous prendre
voo-zah-vay bon meen ro-bairts.  ah-lor ve-nay shay noo preNdr
*You are looking well, Roberts.  Now then, come to us to have*

le petit déjeuner.  Ah, voilà ma fille avec notre voiture.
le p'tee day-zhâỹ-nay.  Ah vwah-lah mah feey ah-vaik notr vwah-têer.
*breakfast.  Oh, there is my daughter with our car.*

Vous connaissez ma fille?
Voo ko-nai-say mah feey?
*You know my daughter?*

M. Roberts :   Mais oui, je connais Mademoiselle Lucie.  Excusez-moi,
mai wee zhe ko-nai mahd-mwah-zail lêe-see.  aix-kêe-zay mwah
*But yes, I know Miss Lucie.  Excuse me.*

je vais chercher mon porteur.  (Il trouve le porteur
zhe vai shair-shay moN por-tâỹr.  eel troov le por-tâỹr
*I am going to look for my porter.  (He finds the porter*

aux bagages.)  Ah, vous voilà!  Portez les bagages
oh bah-gahzh.  ah voo vwah-lah!  por-tay lay bah-gahzh
*at the luggage office.)  Ah, there you are!  Take the luggage*

à une voiture, s'il vous plaît.  Venez avec moi.
ah êen vwah-têer see-voo-plai.  ve-nay ahvek mwah.
*to a car, please.  Come with me.*

Le porteur :   Je viens, monsieur.
zhe vyiN m'ss-yâỹ.
*I am coming, sir.*

**M. Lesage (au porteur) :  Mettez les malles là-dessus, s'il vous plaît.**
(oh por-tâŷr) : mai-tay lay mall lah d'sêê see-voo-plai.
*(To the porter) :  Put the trunks on there, please.*

**Mme Roberts :  Est-ce que les malles sont en sûreté là?**
aisk' lay mall soN-taN sêêr-tay lah?
*Are the trunks safe (literally :  in safety) there?*

**M. Lesage :         Certainement, ma chérie.    M. Roberts : Cela fait combien?**
sair-tain-maN mah shay-ree.          s'lah fai koN-byiN?
*Certainly, my dear.*                        *That makes how much?*

**Le porteur :        Neuf francs, monsieur.   Trois francs par colis.**
nâŷf fraN m'ss-yâŷ. trwah fraN pahr ko-lee.
*Nine francs, sir.   Three francs per piece of luggage.*

**M. Lesage :         Montez, s'il vous plaît, et partons.**
moN-tay see-voo-plai ay pahr-toN.
*Get in, please, and let's start.*

### SALUTATIONS

| | |
|---|---|
| **Comment allez-vous ?** . . . How are you? | Alternative forms of the |
| (Literally: How are you going?) | colloquial language are : |
| **Je vais bien** . . . I am well | **Comment ça va?** . . . How are things? |
| **Vous allez bien** . . . You are well | (Literally: How goes it?) |
| **Il (elle) va bien** . . . He (she) is well | **Ça va bien.** . . . I am all right. |
| **Nous allons bien** . . . We are well | (Literally: It goes well.) |
| **Ils (elles) vont bien** . . . They are well | **Ça va bien?** . . . You are all right? |
| | You are getting on well? |

### ROUND THE TOWN

**Un Conseil pour les Gens Avisés**

Si vous voulez vraiment connaître Paris par vous-même, vous ne pouvez mieux faire que de vous mettre entre les mains d'un chauffeur parisien, en lui disant de vous prendre chaque jour à votre gîte. Dites-lui : " Chauffeur, on voudrait connaître les restaurants où l'on mange bien, et tous les bons coins du vieux Paris." La plupart des chauffeurs sont de bons types, et à cause de leur occupation ils connaissent la ville à fond.  Il leur est facile de choisir leur restaurant dans n'importe quel quartier et s'ils montrent une préférence pour un certain établissement, celui-ci est presque toujours un restaurant où l'on mange bien et à bon marché.  Naturellement, si votre chauffeur a des velléités de vous jouer "le truc des étrangers," arrêtez les frais—et choisissez-en un autre.

**A Tip for the Wise**

If you wish really to get to know Paris well on your own, you cannot do better than to put yourself in the hands of a Paris chauffeur, and arrange that he fetches you every day where you're staying.  Say to him : " Chauffeur, we'd like to know the restaurants where one eats well, and all the interesting corners of old Paris."  The majority of the chauffeurs are "good scouts," and on account of their occupation they know the city thoroughly.  It is easy for them to choose their restaurant in no matter what district, and if they show a preference for a certain establishment, this is nearly always a restaurant where one eats well and cheaply.  Naturally, if your driver shows a disposition to play the "stranger act" on you, cut your losses—and choose another driver.

L'ÉGLISE DE LA MADELEINE ET LA RUE ROYALE

Inspiré du Parthénon, cet édifice est un des plus beaux realisés dans le style néo-classique.
Il fut commencé sous Louis XVI en 1764, pour servir d'église paroissiale. La Révolution
en fit un temple païen à la "Déesse Raison". Aujourd'hui cet edifice prédestiné a été
rendu à sa designation originelle: une église paroissiale de Paris.

| **Paroissial-e** (adj.) | **église** (f.) | **païen-ne** (adj.) | **déesse** (f.) | **raison** (f.) |
|---|---|---|---|---|
| Parish | church | pagan | goddess | reason |

The following list is from the buffet of a French railway station. Owing to fluctuations of the franc, the prices are omitted.

| TARIF | tah-reef | TARIFF |
|---|---|---|
| * | * | * |
| BIÈRES | byair | *beer* |
| Bock.............. | bock ................. | *small glass (of beer)* |
| Demi ............. | d'mee ............... | *large glass (of beer)* |
| Pilsen ............ | pill-senn ............ | *Pilsen* |
| Pale Ale, Bouteille.... | pail-ail, boo-taiy ........ | *pale ale, bottle* |
| et Demi-Bouteille .. | d'mee boo-taiy.......... | *and half-bottle* |
| Stout, Quart ........ | kahr ................. | *stout, mug (quarter of a litre)* |
| | | |
| CAFÉ—INFUSIONS | kah-fay iN-fẽẽz-yoN | *coffee, infusions* |
| Café nature ........ | kah-fay nah-tẽẽr ........ | *coffee, black* |
| Café filtre .......... | kah-fay feeltr .......... | *coffee, percolated* |
| Café glacé .......... | kah-fay glah-say........ | *coffee, iced* |
| Café au lait......... | kah-fay oh lai .......... | *coffee with milk* |
| Lait froid ......... | lai frwa ............... | *milk, cold* |
| Lait chaud ......... | lai shoh............... | *milk, hot* |
| Chocolat ........... | shoh-koh-lah .......... | *chocolate* |
| Chocolat glacé ...... | shoh-koh-lah glah-say.... | *chocolate, iced* |
| Thé .............. | tay................... | *tea* |
| Infusions .......... | iN-fẽẽz-yoN ........... | *infusions* |
| | | |
| DIVERS | dee-vair | *miscellaneous* |
| Citron pressé ....... | seet-roN prai-say........ | *lemon squash* |
| Citronnade glacée .... | seet-ro-nahd glah-say.... | *lemonade, iced* |
| Orange pressée ...... | oh-raNzh prai-say ...... | *orange squash* |
| Orangeade glacée .... | oh-raN-zhahd glah-say .. | *orangeade, iced* |
| Glaces .............. | glahs ............... | *ices* |
| Champagne, la coupe | shaN-pany la koop .... | *champagne, the glass* |
| Bordeaux Blanc, le verre | bor-doh blaN le vair .... | *white Bordeaux wine, the glass* |
| Bordeaux Rouge, le verre | bor-doh roozh le vair.... | *red Bordeaux wine, the glass* |
| Vin chaud, le verre .. | viN-shoh le vair ........ | *mulled wine, the glass* |
| | | |
| CASSE-CROÛTE | kahs-kroot | *snacks* |
| Sandwich Jambon .... | sahnd-veech zhaN-boN .. | *ham sandwich* |
| Sandwich Veau ...... | sahnd-veech voh ........ | *veal sandwich* |
| Sandwich Rosbif...... | sahnd-veech roz-beef .... | *beef sandwich* |
| Brioches ........... | bree-osh ............. | *(rolls) kind of* |
| Gâteaux ........... | gah-toh ............. | *cakes* |
| Tartes ............. | tahrt ................. | *pastries* |
| | | |
| APÉRITIFS | | |
| Vermouth Chambéry .. | vair-moot shaN-bay-ree.. | *French (dry) Vermouth* |
| Turin Martini ........ | tẽẽ-riN mahr-tee-nee .... | *Italian Vermouth* |

| | | |
|---|---|---|
| Turin Cinzano* ....., | têê-riN siN-zah-noh...... | *Vermouth* |
| Dubonnet* .......... | dêê-bo-nay ............ | *cordial wine* |
| Raphaël* .......... | rah-fah-ail ............ | *do.* |
| Amer Picon* ........ | ah-mair pee-koN........ | *bitters* |
| Amer Campari* ...... | ah-mair kaN-pah-ree .... | *do.* |
| Anis divers .......... | ah-nee dee-vair ........ | *aniseed* |
| Pernod Fils* ........ | pair-noh fees .......... | (*resembles*) *absinthe** |
| VINS DE LIQUEUR | viN de lee-kâŷr | *dessert wine* |
| Porto .............. | por-toh ................ | *port* |
| Madère ............ | mah-dair .............. | *Madeira* |
| Malaga ............ | mah-lah-gah .......... | *Malaga* |
| Xérès ............. | kay-rais................ | *sherry* |
| Frontignan .......... | froN-teen-yaN.......... | *Frontignan* |
| LIQUEURS & SIROPS | lee-kâŷr ay see-rop | *liqueurs and syrups* |
| Menthe Verte ........ | maNt vairt ............ | *spearmint* |
| Cassis-Curaçao ...... | kah-sees kêê-rah-soh .... | *blackcurrant and Curaçao* |
| Guignolet-Menthe .... | geen-yoh-lay maNt...... | *cherry brandy and mint* |
| Sirop nature ........ | see-rop nah-têêr ........ | *plain syrup* |
| Sirop alcoolisé........ | see-rop ahl-ko-lee-zay.... | *alcoholic syrup* |
| Crème de Cassis...... | kraim de kah-sees ...... | *blackcurrant* |
| Cerises à l'eau de vie.. | s'reez ah loh d'vee ...... | *brandied cherries* |
| ALCOOLS, LIQUEURS | ahl-kol lee-kâŷr | *strong liqueurs* |
| Marc de Bourgogne .. | mahr d'boor-gony ...... | *white brandy* |
| Rhum Vieux ........ | rom vyâŷ .............. | *old rum* |
| Kirsch .............. | keersh ................ | *Kirsch* |
| Mirabelle............ | mee-rah-bail............ | *mirabelle-plum* |
| Framboise .......... | fraN-bwahz ............ | *raspberry* |
| Calvados ............ | kahl-vah-doss .......... | *cider-brandy* |
| Fine Champagne...... | feen shaN-pany ........ | *liqueur brandy* (*from the* |
| Cherry Brandy ...... | shai-ree brahn-dee | *Champagne de Saintonge* |
| Bénédictine .......... | bay-nay-deek-teen | *adjoining the Bordeaux dis-* |
| Kummel ............ | kêê-mail | *trict*) *flavoured with caraway* |
| | | *seed, anise, etc.* |
| EAUX MINERALES | oh mee-nay-rahl | *mineral waters* |
| Saint-Galmier* ...... | siN gahlm-yay | * *Proprietary brands* |
| Vittel, Vichy*........ | vee-tail vee-shee | *Note: Absinthe is nowadays* |
| Evian* .............. | ayv-yaN | *forbidden in France.* |
| Perrier-Carola* ...... | pair-yay kah-roh-lah | *Pernod is a substitute.* |
| Soda................ | soh-dah | |

This list of refreshments in railway buffets is fairly representative of what you will usually find in the average French café. The café is the Frenchman's club, where he reads, writes and meets his friends. There you will find most of the day's newspapers, and it is quite usual to ask the waiter for writing materials (**de quoi écrire**).

A STREET IN PARIS

Cover over the text from the start, and see how many of the objects in the drawing you can name in French from your existing vocabulary. Consult the key only when

| **une rue barrée** | **le magasin** | **la devanture** | **le cinéma** | **un agent de police**[1] |
|---|---|---|---|---|
| street closed for traffic | shop | shop-window | cinema | policeman |

| **une affiche** | **bicyclette de livreur** | **un étudiant** | **un arrêt obligatoire** | **une midinette** |
|---|---|---|---|---|
| poster | carrier-bicycle | student | compulsory (bus) stop | milliner's girl |

[1]The word **gendarmes,** often erroneously used for Paris policemen, really applies only to a

## UNE RUE DE PARIS

necessary. Repeat until you are satisfied that you know the French for everything which is shown in the picture, whether living or inanimate.

| | | | | |
|---|---|---|---|---|
| **un arrêt facultatif** request (bus) stop | **un homme-sandwich** sandwich man | **le trottoir** pavement | **le bord du trottoir** kerb | **la chaussée** roadway |
| **un autobus** bus | **une auto** car | **le mendiant** beggar | **une église** church | **le refuge** refuge (island) | **une horloge** clock |

semi-military body of constabulary who are to be found only in the country parts of France.

### ENTERING PARIS

| | |
|---|---|
| Charles : | **Quelle est cette rue-ci, mon oncle?** <br> kai-lay sait rễễ-see mo-noNkl? <br> *What street is this, (my) uncle?* |
| M. Lesage : | **C'est la rue La Fayette, une grande voie de communication.** <br> say la rễễ lah-fah-yait ễễn graNd vwah de kom-mễễ-nee-kah-syoN. <br> *It's rue La Fayette, a main artery (of communication).* |
| Charles : | **Vous habitez loin d'ici?** <br> voo-zah-bee-tay lwiN dee-see? <br> *You live far from here?* |
| M. Lesage : | **Encore un quart d'heure, mon petit.** <br> aN-kor uN kahr dấỹr moN p'tee. <br> *Another quarter of an hour, my little (friend).* |
| Mlle Lucie : <br> (à Madeleine) | **Quel âge avez-vous, ma chérie?** <br> kai-lahzh ah-vay voo mah shay-ree? <br> *How old are you, my dear?* |
| Madeleine : | **J'ai douze ans, ma cousine.** <br> zhay doo-zaN mah koo-zeen. <br> *I am twelve, (my) cousin.* |
| Mlle L. : | **Vous parlez bien le français.   Trouvez-vous le français difficile?** <br> voo pahr-lay byiN le fraN-sai. troo-vay voo le fraN-sai dee-fee-seel? <br> *You speak well French.   Do you find French difficult?* |
| Madeleine : | **Pas trop, ma cousine.** <br> pah troh mah koo-zeen. <br> *Not too much, (my) cousin.* |

#### THREE IRREGULAR VERBS

Three irregular verbs occur in the above conversations:
**venir**=to come; **connaître**=to know (a person or place);
**savoir**=to know (something).

| *I come, am coming, etc.* | *I know (a person or thing), etc.* | *I know (about), etc.* |
|---|---|---|
| **je viens** <br> vyiN | **je connais** <br> ko-nai | **je sais** <br> sai |
| **il**   ⎱**vient** <br> **elle** ⎰**vyiN** | **il**   ⎱**connaît** <br> **elle** ⎰**ko-nai** | **il**   ⎱**sait** <br> **elle** ⎰**sai** |
| **nous venons** <br> v'noN | **nous connaissons** <br> ko-nai-soN | **nous savons** <br> sah-voN |
| **vous venez** <br> v'nay | **vous connaissez** <br> ko-nai-say | **vous savez** <br> sah-vay |
| **ils**   ⎱**viennent** <br> **elles** ⎰**vyain** | **ils**   ⎱**connaissent** <br> **elles** ⎰**ko-nais** | **ils**   ⎱**savent** <br> **elles** ⎰**sahv** |

**Les deux enfants viennent de l'hôtel et vont à l'école**

**Charles :**      **Qu'ils sont petits, les autobus de Paris!**
keel soN p'tee lay-zoh-toh-bẽes de pah-ree!
*How they are small the buses of Paris!*

**Et voilà un agent de police!**
ay vwah-lah uNah-zhaN d'po-lees!
*And there is a policeman!*

**M. Lesage :**      **C'est l'agent de la circulation, mon ami.**
say lah-zhaN d'lah seer-kẽe-lahs-yoN mo-nah-mee.
*It's the traffic policeman, my friend.*

**Madeleine :**      **Quelles belles maisons et quels beaux magasins!**
kail bail mai-zoN ay kail boh mah-gah-ziN!
*What beautiful houses and what fine shops!*

**Mlle L. :**      **C'est le centre de Paris et le quartier le plus riche.**
say le saNtr de pah-ree ay le kahr-tyay le plẽe reesh.
*It's the centre of Paris and the district the most rich.*

**Madeleine :**      **Ah, quelle belle devanture! Regardez, maman! N'allez pas**
ah kail bail d'vantẽer! re-gahr-day mah-maN! nah-lay pah
*Oh, what a beautiful shopwindow! Look, mother! Don't go*

**si vite, mon oncle, s'il vous plaît.**
see veet mo-noNkl see-voo-plai.
*so fast, (my) uncle, please.*

**M. Lesage :**   **Eh bien, si vous voulez.**     **Charles :**   **Quel est ce bâtiment-là?**
ay byiN see voo voo-lay.              kai-lay se bah-tee-maN lah?
*All right, if you want.*             *What is that building there?*

La dame vient du magasin et va au café

Les petits garçons viennent de la maison et
vont au cinéma

L'OPÉRA DE PARIS UNE NUIT DE FÊTE NATIONALE

Une foule immense se bouscule pour ne pas manquer un spectacle gratuit.  L'Opéra, pris au cours de la soirée populaire d'un jour férié, fut fondé sous Louis XIV, en 1669, sous le nom d'"Académie Nationale de Musique" qui figure d'ailleurs encore aujourd'hui

| **bousculer** | **gratuit-e** (adj.) | **jour férié** | **fonder** |
|---|---|---|---|
| to bustle, jostle | free, gratuitous | (public) holiday | to found |

## THE PARIS OPERA HOUSE ON A NATIONAL FESTIVAL NIGHT

au frontispice du monument. Le bâtiment actuel, un des plus beaux d'Europe, fut commencé sous Napoléon III et achevé en 1875. Deux constructions précédentes avaient été détruites par des incendies, pendant et après la Revolution Française de 1789.

| **bâtiment** (m.) | **précédent-e** (adj.) | **détruire** | **incendie** (m.) |
| building | former | to destroy | fire, conflagration |

| | |
|---|---|
| Mlle L. : | **C'est l'Opéra, mon petit cousin.**<br>say loh-pay-rah moN p'tee koo-ziN.<br>*It's the Opera, my little cousin.* |
| Charles : | **Merci bien, ma grande cousine.**<br>mair-see byiN mah graNd koo-zeen.<br>*Thank you very much, my big cousin.* |
| Mlle L. :<br>(à Madeleine) | **Il est rigolo, votre petit frère, n'est-ce pas?**<br>ee-lai ree-goh-loh votr p'tee frair nais pah?<br>*He is funny, your little brother, isn't he?* |
| Madeleine : | **C'est un grand fripon, vous savez.**<br>say tuN graN free-poN voo sah-vay.<br>*He is a great rascal, you know.* |
| Mme R. : | **Quelle est cette maison-là en face?**<br>kai-lay sait mai-zoN lah aN fahs?<br>*What is that building there opposite (in face)?* |
| Mlle L. : | **C'est un immeuble de rapport. Il doit avoir quinze étages.**<br>sai-tãy-nee-mãybl d'rah-port. eel dwat av-wahr kiNz ay-tazh.<br>*It's a block of flats. It must have fifteen storeys.* |
| Mme R. : | **Quel immense bâtiment!**<br>kai-lee-maNs bah-tee-maN!<br>*What an enormous building!* |
| Charles : | **C'est un gratte-ciel, vous savez.**<br>sai-tuN gratt syail voo sah-vay.<br>*It's a sky-scraper, you know.* |
| M. Lesage : | **À gauche est la Madeleine. C'est une belle église,**<br>ah gohsh ay la mahd-lain. say-tẽen bai-lay-gleez,<br>*To (the) left is the Madeleine. It's a beautiful church,*<br>**n'est-ce pas? À droite est la rue Royale.**<br>nais-pah? ah drwaht ay lah rẽe rwah-yahl.<br>*isn't it? To the right is the rue Royale.* |
| Mlle L. : | **Prenons la rue Royale, mon père.**<br>pr'noN lah rẽe rwah-yal moN pair.<br>*Let's take the rue Royale, (my) father.* |
| M. Lesage : | **Bon, si vous voulez.**<br>boN see voo voo-lay.<br>*Good, if you want to.* |
| M. Roberts : | **Quel est le nom de cette belle rue?**<br>kai-lay le noN de sait bail rẽe?<br>*What is the name of that beautiful street?* |
| M. Lesage : | **La rue St. Honoré, mon vieux.**<br>la rẽe siN-toh-noh-ray moN vyãy.<br>*The rue St. Honoré, my old (man).* |

**M. Lesage :**    **Devant nous, c'est la Place de la Concorde.**
d'vaN noo say lah plahs d'lah koN-kord.
*Before us, that's the Place de la Concòrde.*

**Madeleine :**    **Quel beau monument!**
kail boh mo-nẽẽ-maN!
*What a beautiful monument!*

**Mlle L. :**    **Approchons pour voir les statues.**
ah-proh-shoN poor vwahr lay stah-tẽẽ.
*Let us go near to see the statues.*

**Mme R. :**    **Ah, qu'il est beau, mon Paris!**
ah kee-lay boh moN pah-ree!
*Oh, how it is beautiful, my Paris!*

### CONTRACTIONS

le chapeau de
la dame

When **de** or **à** immediately precede **le** or **les**, contracted forms are used:

**du** (dẽẽ) instead of de le
**des** (day)  ,,   ,, de les
**au** (oh)    ,,   ,, à le
**aux** (oh)   ,,   ,, à les

*Note.* (1) that no contractions are used for **de la** and **de l'**.

(2) You cannot say "the lady's hat" in French. You must turn it into "the hat of the lady"; "my father's house" is "the house of my father"=**la maison de mon père**; "this boy's parents" =**les parents de ce garçon**, etc.

le parapluie du monsieur
(**du**= de le)

les enfants de l'oncle

les bagages des enfants
(**des**=de les)

**L'élève donne le livre au professeur**
**(au=à le)**

**Il donne des fleurs à la dame**

## CONCERNING ACCENTS

*Note.*—(1) There are no contractions of à la and à l'. (2) Whereas in English the "to" is omitted in sentences like "He gives the boy the book," it must be translated in French, either by à or by **au** (for à le) or by **aux** (for à les).

Strictly speaking, accents in French should appear over capital letters, thus :

$$\grave{A} \quad \acute{E} \quad \hat{U}, \text{ etc.}$$

In practice, however, they are sometimes omitted over capitals. It will be noted that accents are placed over capital letters throughout this book.

|  | Masculine | Feminine | Plural |
|---|---|---|---|
| Of (or from) the: | **DU** (de l') | **DE LA** (de l') | **DES** |
| To (or at) the: | **AU** (à l') | **À LA** (à l') | **AUX** |

The forms in brackets are used before nouns beginning with a vowel or silent h (**le nom de l'hôtel**=the name of the hotel; à l'église=to the church).

Never forget to put accents over ordinary letters, because to write **a** instead of **à** or **e** instead of **é**, is just as bad a spelling mistake as to write **chapot** instead of **chapeau.**

**Le professeur donne une pomme**
**à l'élève**

**Il parle aux élèves**
**(aux=à les)**

**SENTENCE BUILDING**

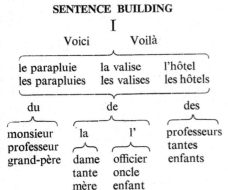

**I**

| Voici | | Voilà |
|---|---|---|
| le parapluie | la valise | l'hôtel |
| les parapluies | les valises | les hôtels |

| du | de | | des |
|---|---|---|---|
| monsieur | la | l' | professeurs |
| professeur | | | tantes |
| grand-père | dame | officier | enfants |
| | tante | oncle | |
| | mère | enfant | |

**II**

| je parle | il | nous | vous | ils |
|---|---|---|---|---|
| | elle | parlons | parlez | elles |
| | parle | | | parlent |

| au | à | | aux |
|---|---|---|---|
| machiniste | la | l' | professeurs |
| professeur | | | petites |
| contrôleur | grand'mère | oncle | filles |
| | petite fille | élève | enfants |
| | dame | enfant | |

## EXERCISES

**I**

Turn back to the pictures on pages 74, 75 and answer the following questions: 1. Qui vient de l'hôtel? 2. Qui va au cinéma? 3. D'où viennent les deux enfants? 4. Où vont-ils? 5. Qui vient du magasin? 6. Où va la dame? 7. D'où viennent les petits garçons? 8. Où vont-ils? 9. D'où vient la famille Roberts? 10. Où va-t-elle?

**II**

Answer the following questions in French, using pronouns instead of the nouns :
1. Est-ce que M. Roberts descend du train?
2. „ „ „ M. Lesage „ „ „
3. „ „ „ Madeleine „ „ „
4. „ „ „ Mlle Lesage ‚‚ „ „
5. Est-ce qu'on descend l'auto du train?

6. Est-ce que la famille Roberts descend du train?
7. „ „ „ M. et Mme R. descendent du train?
8. „ „ „ Mme R. et Madeleine „ „ „
9. Est-ce qu'on descend les valises et les malles?

**III**

**Translate into English**

1. La sixième leçon n'est pas trop difficile. 2. Le petit garçon n'aime pas être embrassé. 3. Ils vont très bien. 4. Elle ne va pas bien. 5. Il ne connaît pas vos enfants. 6. Mon frère ne vient pas avec vous. 7. Quel est le nom de ce monument? 8. Cette devanture n'est pas belle. 9. Je ne sais pas quelle heure il est. 10. Savez-vous quelle heure il est? 11. Nous venons de l'église. 12. Ils ne connaissent pas cette rue.

**IV**

**Translate into French**

1. How are you? 2. I am very well, thank you. 3. How is your little daughter? 4. How are your parents? 5. They are ill. 6. Where are they now? 7. I don't know your little sister. 8. Do you know my uncle? 9. He is going to the cinema. 10. We are coming from the station. 11. We are going to the station. 12. I am going to the café. 13. I am coming from the hotel. 14. Where are you coming from? 15. I am coming from (the) school. 16. Where are you going? 17. I am going to the cinema. 18. They are going to the station. 19. What a beautiful hat you have got! 20. What an intelligent son they have! 21. What beautiful houses are in front of us! 22. What is the name of that beautiful street? 23. My father's house is not far from here. 24. Please give these books to your teacher. 25. These are the teachers' overcoats.

(*Key to I, II, III and IV on page* 101.)

*ARE YOU LISTENING-IN EVERY DAY TO BROAD-CASTING IN FRENCH?*

LA PLACE DE LA CONCORDE (AUTREFOIS PLACE LOUIS XV)
De jour, dans une ambiance somptueuse, même les réverbères ont pris un air aristo-cratique.  De nuit, l'éclairage diffusé fait ressortir en féerie le jeu des fontaines.

| **Réverbère** (m.) | **éclairage** (m.) **diffusé** | **faire ressortir** | **jeu** (m.) |
|---|---|---|---|
| Street-lamp | floodlighting | throw up, outline | playing (of fountains) |

# SEPTIÈME LEÇON—*SEVENTH LESSON*

Most of the words connected with the hotel lounge, which Mr. Roberts is now entering, are new to you. Practise, as in other cases, with and without the text.

| | | | |
|---|---|---|---|
| **le bureau de réception** | **le gérant** | **la case** | **le tableau aux clefs** |
| bee-roh de ray-saips-yoN | zhay-raN | kahz | tahb-loh oh klay |
| *office* | *booking clerk (manager)* | *pigeon hole* | *board with keys* |
| **le casier du courrier** | **le nouvel arrivant** | **le portier** | **le domestique (valet)** |
| kahz-yay dee koor-yay | noo-vai-lah-ree-vaN | port-yay | do-mais-teek (vah-lay) |
| *letter rack* | *new guest* | *hall porter* | *boots* |
| **le liftier**    **un ascenseur** | **le hall** | **le fauteuil** | **le bar**    **le tabouret** |
| lift-yay    ahs-saN-sayr | ahl | foh-tayy | bahr    tah-boo-ray |
| *lift-boy*    *lift* | *entrance hall* | *easy chair* | *bar*    *stool* |

*How many of these objects can you now name from the picture without the text?*

### MR. ROBERTS CHOOSES HIS HOTEL

**M. Roberts :**    **Pouvez-vous me recommander un hôtel, pas trop cher?**
poo-vay voo me re-ko-maN-day ay-noh-tail pah troh shair?
*Can you recommend me an hotel, not too dear?*

**M. Lesage :**    **Le Bienvenu: c'est un excellent hôtel, près d'ici.**
le byiN-v'nee: sai-tay-nai-xe-laN-toh-tail prai dee-see.
*The Bienvenu: it's an excellent hotel, near here.*

**M. Roberts :**    **Allons-y prendre des chambres et laisser nos bagages.**
ah-loN-zee praNdr day shaNbr ay lai-say noh bah-gahzh.
*Let us go there (to) take rooms and leave our luggage.*

**M. Roberts (au gérant de l'hôtel) : Avez-vous des chambres libres?**
(oh zhay-raN de loh-tail): ah-vay voo day shaNbr leebr?
*(to the manager of the hotel): Have you any rooms vacant?*

**Le gérant :**  **Il y a trois chambres au deuxième étage.**
eel-yah trwah shaNbr oh dāyz-yai may-tahzh.
*There are three rooms on the second floor.*

**Une autre chambre au premier sera libre ce soir.**
ēē-nohtr shaNbr oh prem-yay s'rah leebr se swahr.
*Another room on the first (floor) will be free to-night.*

**M. Roberts :**  **Est-ce que vous avez deux chambres à deux lits?**
aisk' voo-zah-vay dāy shaNbr ah dāy lee?
*Have you got two rooms with double beds?*

**Le gérant :**  **Seulement au deuxième étage, monsieur.**
sāyl-maN oh dāyz-yaim-ay-tahzh, m'ss-yāy.
*Only on the second floor, sir.*

**M. Roberts :**  **Et le prix?  Combien est-ce?**
ay le pree?  koN-byiN ais-se?
*And the price?  How much is it?*

**Le gérant :**  **Cela dépend de la chambre.  Depuis trente francs par jour.**
s'lah day-paN de lah shaNbr.  d'pwee traNt fraN pahr zhoor.
*That depends on the room.  From 30 francs per day.*

**M. Roberts :**  **Combien par semaine?  Je compte rester quelques mois.**
koN-byiN pahr s'main?  zhe koNt rais-tay kailk mwah.
*How much per week?  I expect to stay (for) several months.*

**Le gérant :**  **Ça c'est différent, monsieur.  Nous avons un**
sah say dee-fay-raN m'ss-yāy.  noo-zah-voN uN
*That's different, sir.  We have a*

**tarif spécial pour longs séjours.  C'est cent vingt-cinq francs**
tah-reef spay-syal poor loN say-zhoor.  say saN viNt siNk fraN
*special tariff for long residence.  It's 125 francs*

**pour une chambre par semaine, alors ce sera deux cent cinquante**
poor ēēn shaNbr pahr s'main ah-lor se s'rah dāy saN siN-kaNt
*for one room per week, so it will be 250*

**pour les deux.**
poor lay dāy.
*for the two.*

**M. Roberts :**  **Est-ce que le petit déjeuner est compris?**
aisk' le p'tee day-zhāynay ay coN-pree?
*Is breakfast included?*

**Le gérant :**  **Mais non, monsieur, c'est à part; sept francs par jour.  Vous**
mai noN m'ss-yāy sai-tah pahr sait fraN pahr zhoor.  voo
*Oh, no, sir, it is extra;  seven francs per day.  You*

**pouvez avoir pension complète comprenant chambre,**
poo-vay zah-vwahr paN-syoN koN-plait koN-pre-naN shaNbr
*can have full board comprising room,*

**petit déjeuner, déjeuner et dîner depuis**
p'tee day-zhãÿnay day-zhãÿnay ay dee-nay d'pŵee
*breakfast, lunch and dinner from*

**soixante francs par jour.**
swah-saNt fraN pahr zhoor.
60 *francs per day.*

M. Roberts : **Puis-je voir les chambres?**
pŵee-zh vwahr lay shaNbı?
*Can I see the rooms?*

Le gérant : **Avec plaisir, monsieur. Veuillez monter dans l'ascenseur. Cette**
ah-vaik plai-zeer m'ss-yãÿ-vãÿ-yay moN-tay daN lah-saN-sãÿr. sait
*With pleasure, sir. Will you please step into the lift. This*

**chambre est très agréable. Elle donne sur le jardin.**
shaNbr ai trai-zah-gray-ahbl. ail don sẽer le zharh-diN.
*room is very pleasant. It gives (looks) on to the garden.*

Mr. Roberts chooses a pleasant bedroom which gives a fine view over Paris, looking in the direction of the world-famous Eiffel Tower.

| Un édredon | le chauffage central | la table de toilette | une esquisse |
| Eiderdown | central heating | dressing-table | sketch |

**M. Roberts :** **Où donne cette porte-là?**
oo don sait port lah?
*Where does that door lead?*

**Le gérant :** **Dans une autre chambre qui est aussi à deux lits. Elle sera**
daN zḕn ohtr shaNbr kee ay-toh-see ah dāy lee.   ail s'rah
*To another room which is also with two beds.   It will be*

**libre ce soir. Vous pouvez la voir si vous voulez.**
leebr se swahr. voo poo-vay lah vwahr see voo voo-lay.
*free this evening.   You can see it if you like.*

**M. Roberts :** **S'il vous plaît. Cette chambre n'est pas claire.**
see voo plai. sait shaNbr nay pah klair.
*Please.   This room is not bright.*

**Le gérant :** **La fenêtre donne sur une cour.   Vous**
lah f'naitr don sḕr ḕn koor.   voo
*The window gives on to a courtyard.   You*

**pouvez en avoir une autre sur le**
poo-vay-zaN-av-wahr ḕn ohtr sḕr le
*can have another at the*

**devant de la maison.   Veuillez entrer**
d'vaN de la mai-zoN. vāy-yay-zaN-tray
*front of the house.   Will you please come*

**dans cette chambre, monsieur.**
daN sait shaNbr, m'ss-yāy.
*into this room, sir.*

**M. Roberts :** **J'aime mieux cette chambre-ci.   Bon, je prends**
zhaim myāy sait shaNbr-see.   boN zhe praN
*I like better this room (here).   Good, I take*

**ces deux chambres.   Voilà un billet de cinq cents francs pour**
say dāy shaNbr.   vwah-lah uN bee-yay de siN saN fraN poor
*these two rooms.   There is a note of five hundred francs for*

**quinze jours.   Quel jour est-ce?**
kiNz zhoor.   kail zhoor ais-se?
*15 days (i.e., a fortnight).   What day is it?*

**Le gérant :** **Aujourd'hui, c'est mardi trois juin.**
oh-zhoor dw̑ee sai mahr-dee trwah zhw̑iN.
*To-day, it is Tuesday, the third (of) June.*

**M. Roberts :** **Alors, c'est payé jusqu'au dix-huit.**
ah-lor say pai-yay zhḕs-koh deezw̑eet.
*Then it is paid up to the eighteenth.*

**Le gérant :**    **C'est ça, monsieur.**   **Le valet va**
say sah m'ss-yẫy.   le vah-lay vah
*That's right, sir.*   *The boots will*

**monter vos bagages.**
moN-tay voh bah-gahzh.
*take up your luggage.*

**M. Roberts :**   **Quels sont les numéros de nos chambres?**
kail soN lay nẽẽmay-roh de noh shaNbr?
*What are the numbers of our rooms?*

**Le gérant :**   **Les numéros onze et dix-neuf, monsieur.**
lay nẽẽmayroh oNz ay deez-nẫyf m'ss-yẫy.
*(The) numbers eleven and nineteen, sir.*

### THERE IS, THERE ARE

| | |
|---|---|
| **Il y a une chambre au premier étage** ......... | There is one room on the first floor |
| **Il y a deux chambres au deuxième** ........... | There are two rooms on the second |
| **Y a-t-il une chambre au premier?** ............. | Is there a room on the first? |
| **Y a-t-il des chambres au deuxième?** ........... | Are there any rooms on the second? |

Note that **il y a** stands for both "there is" and "there are".

#### I WILL and I CAN

**je veux** vẫy=I will    **je peux** pẫy=I can

**il**
**elle** } **veut** vẫy     **il**
**elle** } **peut** pẫy

**nous voulons** voo-loN   **nous pouvons** poo-voN

**vous voulez** voo-lay    **vous pouvez** poo-vay

**ils**
**elles** } **veulent** vẫyl    **ils**
**elles** } **peuvent** pẫyv

**Il veut parler français**
He wants to speak French

**Il va parler français**
He is going to speak French

**Il ne peut pas le faire**
He cannot do it

**veuillez parler français**
Will you please speak French

*Note.*—(1) **Je veux** expresses wish or desire; **je vais** the immediate future (I am going to . . .).

(2) The "to" of "I want to" or "I am going to" is left out in French, as it is in both English and French after "I can".

(3) **Veuillez** (vẫy-yay) corresponds to English "will you please" or "would you be so kind as to . . ." or "do you mind .. "

### ROUND THE TOWN

#### Paris

Le centre géographique et historique de Paris est l'Île de la Cité, qui se trouve au milieu de la Seine. Là s'élève la cathédrale de Notre-Dame.

Sur la rive droite (au nord) de la Seine sont les quartiers commerçants et la plupart des théâtres. La rive gauche (au sud) comprend le Quartier Latin, l'Université de Paris et les grandes écoles, et plusieurs établissements militaires.

#### Paris

The geographical and historical centre of Paris is the City Island, which is in the middle of the Seine. There stands Notre-Dame Cathedral.

On the right bank (to the north) of the Seine are the commercial districts and most of the theatres. The left bank (to the south), includes the Latin Quarter, the University of Paris and the great schools (of learning) and several military establishments.

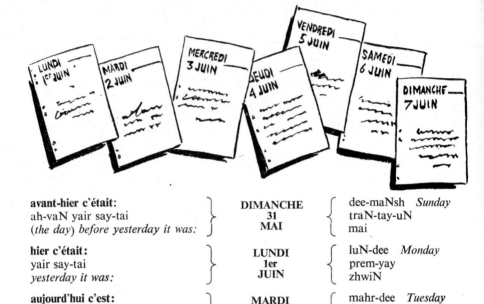

| | | |
|---|---|---|
| **avant-hier c'était:** } <br> ah-vaN yair say-tai <br> *(the day) before yesterday it was:* | DIMANCHE <br> 31 <br> MAI | { dee-maNsh *Sunday* <br> traN-tay-uN <br> mai |
| **hier c'était:** } <br> yair say-tai <br> *yesterday it was:* | LUNDI <br> 1er <br> JUIN | { luN-dee *Monday* <br> prem-yay <br> zhwiN |
| **aujourd'hui c'est:** } <br> oh-zhoord-ŵee sai <br> *to-day it is:* | MARDI <br> 2 <br> JUIN | { mahr-dee *Tuesday* <br> dâŷ |
| **demain ce sera:** } <br> d'miN se s'rah <br> *to-morrow it will be:* | MERCREDI <br> 3 <br> JUIN | { mairk-re-dee *Wednesday* <br> trwah |
| **après-demain ce sera:** } <br> ah-prai d'miN se s'rah <br> *after to-morrow it will be:* | JEUDI <br> 4 <br> JUIN | { zhâŷ-dee *Thursday* <br> kahtr |
| **dans trois jours ce sera:** } <br> daN trwah zhoor se s'rah <br> *in three days it will be:* | VENDREDI <br> 5 <br> JUIN | { vaNdr-dee *Friday* <br> siNk |
| **dans quatre jours ce sera:** } <br> daN kahtr zhoor se s'rah <br> *in four days it will be:* | SAMEDI <br> 6 <br> JUIN | { sahm'dee *Saturday* <br> sees |

**Il y a vingt-quatre heures dans un jour.    Sept jours forment une semaine.**
eel-yah viNt kaht-râŷr daN-zuN zhoor.    sait zhoor form-tẽen s'main.
*There are 24 hours in one day.    Seven days make a week.*

**Trente ou trente et un jours sont un mois; les douze mois forment une année.**
traNt oo traN-tay uN zhoor soN tuN mwah    lay dooz mwah form-tẽe-nah-nay.
*30 or 31 days are a month; the 12 months make one year.*

**Dans quel mois sommes-nous?    Nous sommes en juin.    Quel jour est-ce aujourd'hui?**
daN kail mwah som noo? noo som aN zhŵiN.    kail zhoor ais oh-zhoordŵee?
*In which month are we?    We are in June.    What day is it to-day?*

## UN CALENDRIER : A CALENDAR

|          | janvier          | février          | mars               | avril            |
|----------|------------------|------------------|--------------------|------------------|
| dimanche | .. 7 14 21 28    | .. 4 11 18 25    | .. 3 10 17 24 31   | .. 7 14 21 28    |
| lundi    | 1 8 15 22 29     | .. 5 12 19 26    | .. 4 11 18 25 ..   | 1 8 15 22 29     |
| mardi    | 2 9 16 23 30     | .. 6 13 20 27    | .. 5 12 19 26 ..   | 2 9 16 23 30     |
| mercredi | 3 10 17 24 31    | .. 7 14 21 28    | .. 6 13 20 27 ..   | 3 10 17 24 ..    |
| jeudi    | 4 11 18 25 ..    | 1 8 15 22 29     | .. 7 14 21 28 ..   | 4 11 18 25 ..    |
| vendredi | 5 12 19 26 ..    | 2 9 16 23 ..     | 1 8 15 22 29 ..    | 5 12 19 26 ..    |
| samedi   | 6 13 20 27 ..    | 3 10 17 24 ..    | 2 9 16 23 30 ..    | 6 13 20 27 ..    |

|          | mai              | juin             | juillet          | août             |
|----------|------------------|------------------|------------------|------------------|
| dimanche | .. 5 12 19 26    | . 2 9 16 23 30   | .. 7 14 21 28    | .. 4 11 18 25    |
| lundi    | .. 6 13 20 27    | . 3 10 17 24 ..  | 1 8 15 22 29     | .. 5 12 19 26    |
| mardi    | .. 7 14 21 28    | . 4 11 18 25 ..  | 2 9 16 23 30     | .. 6 13 20 27    |
| mercredi | 1 8 15 22 29     | . 5 12 19 26 ..  | 3 10 17 24 31    | .. 7 14 21 28    |
| jeudi    | 2 9 16 23 30     | . 6 13 20 27 ..  | 4 11 18 25 ..    | 1 8 15 22 29     |
| vendredi | 3 10 17 24 31    | . 7 14 21 28 ..  | 5 12 19 26 ..    | 2 9 16 23 30     |
| samedi   | 4 11 18 25 ..    | 1 8 15 22 29 ..  | 6 13 20 27 ..    | 3 10 17 24 31    |

|          | septembre        | octobre          | novembre         | décembre         |
|----------|------------------|------------------|------------------|------------------|
| dimanche | 1 8 15 22 29     | .. 6 13 20 27    | .. 3 10 17 24    | 1 8 15 22 29     |
| lundi    | 2 9 16 23 30     | .. 7 14 21 28    | .. 4 11 18 25    | 2 9 16 23 30     |
| mardi    | 3 10 17 24 ..    | 1 8 15 22 29     | .. 5 12 19 26    | 3 10 17 24 31    |
| mercredi | 4 11 18 25 ..    | 2 9 16 23 30     | .. 6 13 20 27    | 4 11 18 25 ..    |
| jeudi    | 5 12 19 26 ..    | 3 10 17 24 31    | .. 7 14 21 28    | 5 12 19 26 ..    |
| vendredi | 6 13 20 27 ..    | 4 11 18 25 ..    | 1 8 15 22 29     | 6 13 20 27 ..    |
| samedi   | 7 14 21 28 ..    | 5 12 19 26 ..    | 2 9 16 23 30     | 7 14 21 28 ..    |

**C'est aujourd'hui mardi trois juin.  Ce mois-ci est le mois**
say toh-zhoordẅee mahr-di trwah zhẅiN.  se mwah-see ay le mwah
*To-day is Tuesday the third (of) June.   This month is the month*

**de juin; le mois dernier était le mois de mai.  Le mois prochain**
de zhẅiN le mwah dair-nyay ayt-ai le mwah de mai.  le mwah proh-shiN
*of June; last month was the month of May.   Next month*

**sera le mois de juillet.  L'année a trois cent soixante-cinq jours.**
s'rah l'mwah de zhĕẽyay.  lah-nay ah trwah saN swah-saNt siNk zhoor.
*will be the month of July.   The year has 365 days.*

**Tous les quatre ans, février a vingt-neuf jours, et l'année est appelée**
too lay kat-raN fayv-ryay ah viNt-nãyf zhoor ay lah-nay ay-tah-p'lay
*All the four years (=every fourth year) February has 29 days, and the year is called*

**bissextile.  L'année bissextile a trois cent soixante-six jours.**
bee-saix-teel.  lah-nay bee-saix-teel ah trwah saN swah-saNt see zhoor.
*leap-year.  (The) leap year has 366 days.*

**L'année a quatre saisons: le printemps, l'été, l'automne et l'hiver.**
lah-nay ah kahtr sai-zoN le priN-taN lay-tay loh-ton ay lee-vair.
*The year has four seasons: spring, summer, autumn and winter.*

Nous ne sommes plus au printemps.    Nous sommes maintenant en été.    Novembre
noo ne som plḝ -zoh priN-taN.    noo som miNt-naN ah-nay-tay.    noh-vaNbr
*We are no longer in spring.*    *We are now in summer.*    *November*

est en automne et Noël est en hiver.
ay tah-noh-ton ay noh-ail ay-tah-nee-vair.
*is in autumn and Xmas is in winter.*

*Note.*—(1) There are two words for "a year", **un an** and **une année.** They are used more or less indiscriminately, but for giving the age of a person **an** is used: **Il a trois ans**=He is three years old (lit., has three years).

(2) The days, months and seasons are masculine and do not take a capital letter.

(3) "In spring"=**au printemps**; but "in summer"=**en été**, in autumn=**en automne**, in winter=**en hiver.**

### NUMBERS 21—60
(*Numbers 1—20 have been given on page* 12)
21. **vingt et un**   viN-tay uN
22. **vingt-deux**   viNt-dáy
23. **vingt-trois**   viNt-trwah
24. **vingt-quatre**   viNt-kahtr
25. **vingt-cinq**   viNt-siNk
26. **vingt-six**   viNt-sees
27. **vingt-sept**   viNt-sait
28. **vingt-huit**   viNt-ŵeet
29. **vingt-neuf**   viNt-náyf
30. **trente**   traNt
31. **trente et un**   traN-tay uN
32. **trente-deux**   traNt-dáy
33. **trente-trois**   traNt-trwah
40. **quarante**   kah-raNt
41. **quarante et un**   kah-raN-tay uN
42. **quarante-deux**   kah-raNt-dáy
50. **cinquante**   siN-kaNt
51. **cinquante et un**   siN-kaN-tay uN
52. **cinquante-deux**   siNkaNt-dáy
60. **soixante**   swah-saNt

### ORDINAL NUMBERS

1st { **le premier**   prem-yay
     { **la première**   prem-yair

2nd { **le** { **second**   s'goN
            { **deuxième**   dáyz-yaim
     { **la** { **seconde**   s'gond
            { **deuxième**   dáyz-yaim

3rd { **le** } **troisième**   trwahz-yaim
     { **la** }

4th { **le** } **quatrième**   kah-tryaim
     { **la** }

5th { **le** } **cinquième**   siN-kyaim
     { **la** }

6th { **le** } **sixième**   seez-yaim
     { **la** }

7th { **le** } **septième**   sait-yaim
     { **la** }

8th { **le** } **huitième**   ŵeet-yaim
     { **la** }

9th   **neuvième**   náyv-yaim
10th  **dixième**   deez-yaim
11th  **onzième**   onz-yaim
12th  **douzième**   dooz-yaim
13th  **treizième**   traiz-yaim
14th  **quatorzième**   katorz-yaim
15th  **quinzième**   kiNz-yaim
16th  **seizième**   saiz-yaim
17th  **dix-septième**   dees-sait-yaim
18th  **dix-huitième**   deezŵeet-yaim
19th  **dix-neuvième**   deez-náyv-yaim
20th  **vingtième**   viNt-yaim
21st  **vingt et unième**   viN-tay-ḝn-yaim
22nd  **vingt-deuxième**   viN-dáyz-yaim
30th  **trentième**   traN-tyaim
31st  **trente et unième**   traN-tay-ḝnyaim
32nd  **trente-deuxième**   traNt-dáyzyaim
40th  **quarantième**   kah-raNt-yaim
50th  **cinquantième**   siN-kaNt-yaim
60th  **soixantième**   swah-saNt-yaim

Note that the Ordinal Numbers (which denote order, place or rank) are formed by adding **-ième** to the corresponding cardinal number.

### EXCEPTIONS
(*a*) **Premier**, **première** and **second, seconde,** but the latter is used only when there is no third or more in question, otherwise **deuxième** is used for the 2nd, etc.

(*b*) **Cinquième.** The letter **u** is added.

(*c*) **Neuvième.** The **f** of **neuf** becomes **v.**

(*d*) The final **e** of **quatre, onze, douze,** etc., is omitted before the **-ième.**

*Note.*—(1) In dates the cardinal numbers are used instead of the ordinal (except **PREMIER,** first):

**le premier avril**=the first of April
**le deux avril**=the second of April
**le trois avril**=the third of April

The same applies to the number following the name of a king or pope :

**Napoléon premier**=Napoleon the First
but : **Louis quinze**=Louis the Fifteenth.

(2) "on the third of July" is **le trois juillet.** Both "on" and "of" are omitted when expressing the date.

(3) **les premières fraises**=the first strawberries.

Ordinal adjectives, like any other adjectives, agree in gender and number with the noun.

**SUMMARY**

| | | |
|---|---|---|
| avant-hier ⎫ hier ⎬ c'était | dimanche | premier | janvier février |
| aujourd'hui, c'est | lundi | deux | mars |
| | mardi | trois | avril mai |
| demain après-demain dans une semaine dans quinze jours ⎬ ce sera dans un mois dans trois mois dans une année | mercredi | quatre | juin juillet |
| | jeudi | cinq | août septembre |
| | vendredi | six | octobre novembre |
| | samedi | sept, etc. | décembre |

## EXERCISES

**I.  Give the following dates in French**

2nd of June ;  5th of March ;  12th of January ;  1st of February ;  21st of March; 15th of April ;  18th of May ;  4th of July ; 31st of August ;  Tuesday, the 3rd of December ;  Sunday, the 22nd of May.

**II.  Answer the following questions in French**

1. Quel hôtel monsieur Lesage recommande-t-il?  2.  Combien (koN-byiN= how many) de chambres sont libres?  3. À quel étage est la chambre qui sera libre ce soir?  4. Est-ce que le prix de trente francs comprend le petit déjeuner?  5. Est-ce que l'hôtel est cher?  6. Est-ce que Monsieur Roberts veut avoir des chambres avec pension complète?  7. Est-ce qu'il y a un ascenseur?  8. Où donne la fenêtre de la chambre numéro 11?  9. Est-ce qu'il peut avoir une chambre sur le devant de la maison?  10. Quels sont les numéros de ses chambres?  11. Quel mois sommes-nous?  12. Quel jour est-ce aujourd'hui?  13. Combien de semaines y a-t-il dans une année?  14. Quand (kaN=when) commence l'année?  15. Quel est le premier mois de l'année?  16. Quel est le troisième?  17. Quel est le deuxième jour de la semaine?  18. Quel est le sixième?  19. Était-ce hier mardi?  20. Sera-ce le huit lundi?  21. Quel jour sera-ce demain?  22. Dans quelle saison sommes-nous maintenant?  23. Sommes-nous au printemps?  24. Quelle heure est-il maintenant?  25. Est-ce la fin (fiN= the end) de la septième leçon?

(*Key to I, II and III on pages* 101 *and* 102.)

## III

### Translate into French

1. Can you recommend this book? 2. Do you wish to see the monument? 3. Is it far from here? 4. Only five minutes from here. 5. Let us go there. 6. What a nice room! 7. How much is it per week? 8. That is too dear. 9. That's not dear. 10. Would you mind speaking English? 11. Will you please come in. 12. Can't you see the lift? 13. Is there a room on the third floor? 14. Are there any strawberries in spring? 18. You cannot come in now.

### La Concierge

Un personnage d'une importance capitale dans la vie de Paris et d'autres villes françaises, c'est la concierge, et si vous désirez que votre séjour en France soit agréable, prenez garde de ne pas froisser ses susceptibilités. Sa loge se trouve au rez-de-chaussée de tous les immeubles de rapport et de beaucoup d'hôtels. Le système anglais des clefs de maison n'existe guère en France. C'est donc elle qui vous ouvre la porte quand vous rentrez la nuit, et c'est elle qui contrôle toutes vos allées et venues. Surtout, n'oubliez jamais ses "étrennes" au Jour de l'An!

### The Concierge

A person of capital importance in the life of Paris and of other French cities, is the concierge, and if you wish your stay in France to be enjoyable, take care not to hurt her feelings. Her lodge is to be found on the ground floor of all apartment houses and of many hotels. The English latchkey system scarcely exists in France, so it is she who opens the door to you when you return at night, and she who keeps track of all your goings and comings. Above all, never forget her New Year's "box".

### UNE CONCIERGE PARISIENNE

Sa mine renfrognée présage un accueil tumultueux pour les locataires d'habitudes tapageuses.

| Renfrogné-e (adj.) | présager | accueil (m.) | locataire (m.f.) |
|---|---|---|---|
| Buttoned-up | foretell | welcome | tenant |

Key to picture, p. 65: Une malle, une valise, un porteur, une courroie, un wagon, un compartiment, une glace, un quai, un homme, une femme, un garçon, une jeune fille, un veston, un chapeau, une pipe.

# HUITIÈME LEÇON—*EIGHTH LESSON*

### À LA TERRASSE DU CAFÉ DE LA PAIX

En se payant ici un apéritif un après-midi d'été, on voit flâner tout un monde cosmopolite.

| | | |
|---|---|---|
| **Se payer (quelque chose)** | **flâner** | **cosmopolite** (adj.) |
| To treat oneself (to something) | to stroll, saunter | cosmopolitan |

**M. Roberts :**  **Entrons dans ce café pour le petit déjeuner.**
aN-troN daN se kah-fay poor le p'tee day-zhāynay.
*Let us go into this café for (the) breakfast.*

**M. Lesage :**  **Restons à la terrasse; il fait trop chaud à l'intérieur.**
rais-toN ah lah tai-rahs eel fai troh shoh ah liN-tayr-yāyr.
*Let us stay on the terrace; it is (lit., it makes) too hot inside.*

**Voilà une table qui est assez grande pour nous tous.**
vwah-lah ễn tahbl kee ay-tah-say graNd poor noo toos.
*There is a table which is enough large for us all.*

**M. Roberts :**  **Qu'est-ce que vous préférez, du thé ou du café?**
kaisk' voo prảy-fai-ray dễ tay oo dễ kah-fay?
*What do you prefer, (some) tea or (some) coffee?*

**M. Lesage :**  **Du café pour moi, s'il vous plaît.**
dễ kah-fay poor mwah see-voo-plai.
*Coffee for me, please.*

**Madeleine :**    Je préfère du chocolat.     **Charles :**    Moi aussi.
zhe pray-fair dẽe shoh-koh-lah.       mwah oh-see.
*I prefer chocolate.*            *So do I (lit., me too).*

**M. Roberts :**    Que voulez-vous boire?     **Mme R. :**   Du lait (froid) chaud.
**(to Mme R.)**   ke voo-lay voo bwahr?        dẽe lai (frwah) shoh.
*What do you want to drink?*     *Milk (cold) hot.*

**M. Roberts :**    Garçon—trois cafés, deux chocolats et un lait chaud.
gahr-soN trwah kah-fay dãy shoh-koh-lah ay uN lai shoh.
*Waiter—three coffees, two chocolates and one hot milk.*

Aussi des petits pains, des croissants, et des brioches.
oh-see day p'tee piN day krwah-saN ay day bree-osh.
*Also some rolls, some horseshoes[1] and some buns.*

**Charles :**    Je préfère un déjeuner anglais avec du
zhe pray-fair uN day-zhãy-nay aN-glai ah-vaik dẽe
*I prefer an English breakfast with*

pain grillé et des œufs sur le plat avec du jambon.
piN gree-yay ay day-zãy sẽer l'plah ah-vaik dẽe zhaN-boN.
*bread toasted and eggs fried with ham.*

**Mlle L. :**    Et du porridge et de la marmelade d'orange, mon petit gourmand.
ay dẽe po-reedzh ay de lah mahr-me-lahd do-raNzh moN p'tee
goor-maN.
*And porridge and marmalade, my little glutton.*

**Charles :**    Naturellement, ma chère cousine.
nah-tẽe-rail'maN ma shair koo-zeen.
*Naturally, my dear cousin.*

**Mlle L. :**    Vous pouvez avoir un œuf à la coque, mon cher.    Mais en
voo poo-vay-zah-vwahr ãynãyf ah lah kok moN shair.    mai aN
*You can have a boiled egg, my dear.    But in*

France on ne mange pas d'œufs sur le plat pour le petit déjeuner.
fraNs oN ne maNzh pah dãy sẽer le plah poor le p'tee day-zhãynay.
*France one does not eat fried eggs for (the) breakfast.*

**Le garçon :**    Aimez-vous le cacao au lait ou à l'eau?
ai-may voo le kah-kah-oh oh lai oo ah loh?
*Do you like the cocoa with milk or with water?*

**M. Lesage :**    Voici le café.    Prenez-vous du lait?    Prenez-vous du
vwah-see le kah-fay.   pre-nay voo dẽe lai?   prenay voo dẽe
*Here is the coffee.    Do you take milk?   Do you take*

sucre?   Combien?     **Madeleine :**   Un peu de lait seulement, mais
sẽekr? koN-byiN?           uN pãy d'lai sãyl-maN mai
*sugar?   How many?*        *A little (of) milk only, but*

---

[1] Crescent-shaped rolls.

Could you now order yourself a light meal in this typical Paris café? Try first without the text, and afterwards with and without the text alternately.

| **le garçon**<br>waiter | **un siège**<br>seat | **un verre d'eau**<br>glass of water | **une tasse**<br>cup | **le fauteuil**<br>armchair |
| --- | --- | --- | --- | --- |
| **la serveuse**<br>waitress | **un croissant**<br>crescent roll | **le beurre**<br>butter | **un pot de café**<br>a pot of coffee | **le pain**<br>bread |
| **un petit pain**<br>roll | **le sucrier**<br>sugar basin | **un verre de citronnade**<br>glass of lemonade | | **la cuillère**<br>spoon |
| | **une soucoupe**<br>saucer | **une glace**<br>ice-cream | **le plateau**<br>tray | |

beaucoup de sucre.   Je prends trois morceaux de sucre.
boh-koo de sēēkr.   zhe praN trwah mor-soh d'sēēkr.
*lots of sugar.   I take three lumps of sugar.*

Mme R. :      **Je ne prends qu'un morceau de sucre.**
zhe ne praN kuN mor-soh de sēēkr.
*I only take one lump of sugar.*

Mlle L. :     **Je ne prends pas de sucre, mais beaucoup de lait.**
zhe ne praN pah de sēēkr mai boh-koo de lai.
*I don't take sugar, but lots of milk.*

## SOME, ANY

(1) **Voilà du café** = There is (some) coffee.

(2) **Avec de la crème** = With (some) cream.

(3) **Avez-vous du sucre?** = Have you (any) sugar?

(4) **Avez-vous des oranges?** = Have you (any) oranges?

(5) **Y a-t-il de l'eau dans ce verre?** = Is there (any) water in this glass?

Whereas in English the bracketed words may be omitted, they are essential in French. The noun is rarely used alone in French. In all those cases where in English you would use the noun without any article you have to use the so-called partitive article in French, i.e., **du** before masculine nouns, **de la** before feminines, **des** before plurals, and **de l'** before nouns beginning with a vowel or a mute **h.**

The Partitive Article is replaced by **de:—**
(*a*) After a verb used in the negative:
**J'ai du sucre** = I have sugar, *but* **Je n'ai pas de sucre** = I have no sugar.

**Il veut de la crème** = he wants cream, *but* **Il ne veut pas de crème** = he does not want cream.

**Nous avons des pommes** = We have apples, but **nous n'avons pas de pommes** = we have no apples.

(*b*) When an adjective precedes the noun:
**J'ai du pain** = I have got bread. **J'ai de bons gâteaux** = I have some good cakes.

**Nous voulons de la confiture** = We want jam. **Avez-vous de bonnes confitures?** = Have you any good jam?

**Ils ont des pommes** = They have apples.
**Ils ont de petites pommes** = They have small apples.

## HOW MUCH?

**Combien de tartines avez-vous eues?** = How many slices of bread have you had?
**Combien d'argent a-t-il?** = How much money has he got?
**J'ai mangé beaucoup de petits pains** = I have eaten many rolls
**Il a beaucoup d'argent** = He has much money
**Elle a mangé peu de pain** = She has not eaten much bread (lit., little of bread)
**Une bouteille de vin** = A bottle of wine
**Une douzaine d'œufs** = A dozen (of) eggs
**Une livre de beurre** = A pound of butter
**Une boîte d'allumettes** = A box of matches

Note that expressions of quantity are followed by **de.**
If you say **du café** you leave it to the waiter how much he shall bring you.
If you want to be more precise, you should say: **un verre de café** or **une tasse de café.**

*Note* (1) That **le livre** means "the book" and **la livre** "the pound".
(2) In French "the" is used in respect of the cost of things, where we should say "a". This applies to all kinds of measurements, e.g., **trois francs le mètre** = three francs a metre.
(3) The past participle, when used with the auxiliary verb **avoir,** is invariable unless it is preceded by a direct object, when it agrees in gender and number with the direct object.

Now, without the help of the text, can you name in French all the objects on the table, and order a meal such as the Roberts are enjoying?

**La table est mise pour le petit déjeuner.  Sur la table il y a**
lah tahbl ai meez poor le p'tee day-zhay-nay.  sĕer lah tahbl eel-yah
*The table is laid for breakfast.  On the table there are*

**des tasses, des soucoupes, des cuillères, des assiettes, du pain, des**
day tahs day soo-koop day kwee-yair day-zahs-yait dĕe piN day
*cups, saucers, spoons, plates, bread,*

**petits pains, des croissants, du beurre, de la marmelade d'orange, un pot de lait,**
p'tee piN day krwah-saN dĕe bayr de lah mahrm'lahd dor-aNzh uN po-de lai
*rolls, crescents, butter, marmalade, a milk jug,*

**un sucrier, un grand couteau pour le pain et de petits couteaux pour**
uN sĕekryay uN graN koo-toh poor le piN ay de p'tee koo-toh poor
*a sugar basin, a large knife for the bread and small knives to*

| | |
|---|---|
| **beurrer le pain.**  **M. Lesage :** | **Encore une tasse de café, Roberts?** |
| bay-ray le piN. | aN-kor ĕen tahs de kah-fay ro-bairts? |
| *butter the bread.* | *Another cup of coffee, Roberts?* |

**M. Roberts :**  **Non merci, je n'ai pas fini la mienne.**
noN mair-see zhe nai pah fee-nee lah myain.
*No, thank you, I have not finished mine.*

| | |
|---|---|
| **M. Lesage :**  **Encore un peu de cacao, ma chère?** | **Madeleine : Volontiers.** |
| aN-kor uN pay de kah-kah-oh mah shair? | vo-loNt-yai. |
| *A little more cocoa, my dear?* | *Yes, please (lit., willingly).* |

**Je vous remercie, cela suffit.**
zhe voo re-mair-see s'lah sēē-fee.
*Thank you, that is enough.*

**Mlle L. :**  **Voulez-vous que je vous beurre une tartine, mon cousin?**
voo-lay voo ke zhe voo bāyr ēēn tahr-teen moN koo-ziN?
*Do you want that I butter you a slice of bread, my cousin?*

**Charles :**  **Merci, j'ai eu suffisamment.**
mair-see zhay ēē sēē-fee-zah-maN.
*No, thank you, I have had enough.*

**Mlle L. :**  **Encore un peu de cette marmelade?**
aN-kor uN pāy de sait mahr-me-lahd?
*A little more of that marmalade?*

**Madeleine :**  **Rien qu'un tout petit peu sur cette tartine de pain bis, s'il vous plaît.**
ryiN kuN too p'tee pāy sēēr sait tahr-teen de piN bee, see voo plai.
*Only a tiny little bit on that slice of brown bread, please.*

**Mme R. :**  **Le beurre est excellent.**  **Est-ce qu'il coûte cher à Paris?**
le bāyr-ai-taixai-laNt.  aisk'eel koot shai-rah pah-ree?
*The butter is excellent.*  *Does it cost dear in Paris?*

**Mlle L. :**  **Nous le payons douze francs la livre.**  **Mme R.**  **Ce n'est pas cher.**
noo le pay-yoN dooz fraN lah leevr.  se nay pah shair.
*We pay 12 francs a pound.*  *That is not dear.*

**M. Lesage :**  **Comment trouvez-vous le café?**
ko-maN troo-vay voo le kah-fay?
*How do you like (lit., find) the coffee?*

**M. Roberts :**  **Je trouve le café excellent.**  **Mme Roberts: Il est délicieux.**
zhe troov le kah-fay aix-sai-laN.  ee lay-day-lees-yāy.
*I find the coffee excellent.*  *It is delicious.*

---

**Un verre de vin blanc, s'il vous plaît.**
uN vair de viN blaN see voo plai.
*A glass of white wine, please.*

un verre de vin      un verre à vin
uN vair de viN      uN vair ah viN
*glass of wine (full)*      *A wine-glass (empty)*

**des verres de bière**
day vair de byair
*glasses of beer*

**des verres à bière**
day vair ah byair
*beer glasses*

**une coupe de champagne**
ẽen koop de shaN-pany
*glass ( full) of champagne*

**une coupe à champagne**
ẽen koop ah shaN-pany
*a champagne glass*

**des bouteilles de vin**
day boo-taiy de viN
*bottles of wine*

**des bouteilles à vin**
day boo-taiy ah viN
*wine bottles*

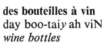

**une tasse à thé**
ẽen tahs ah tay
*a tea-cup*

**une tasse de thé**
ẽen tahs de tay
*a cup of tea*

### TO EAT, TO DRINK, TO TAKE

**manger** = *to eat*
**je** ⎫
**il**  ⎬ **mange** maNzh
**elle** ⎭
**nous mangeons** maN-zhoN
**vous mangez** maN-zhay
**ils** ⎫
**elles** ⎬ **mangent** maNzh

**prendre** = to take
**je prends** praN
**il** ⎫
**elle** ⎬ **prend** praN
**nous prenons** pr'noN
**vous prenez** pr'nay
**ils** ⎫
**elles** ⎬ **prennent** prainn

**boire** = *to drink*
**je bois** bwah
**il** ⎫
**elle** ⎬ **boit** bwah
**nous buvons** bēē-voN
**vous buvez** bēē-vay
**ils** ⎫
**elles** ⎬ **boivent** bwahv

*Note.*—Since g in front of **o** is pronounced as in "go", an e is inserted between the g and the o in the word **mangeons**, to indicate that the g is to be sounded as zh (i.e., like the s in measure).

### SUMMARY

| Prenez-vous ⎫ | | ⎧ pain |
| Avez-vous | du | vin |
| | | café |
| | | thé |
| Donnez-moi | de la | bière |
| | | limonade |
| Voulez-vous ⎬ | de l' | crème |
| | | eau |
| j'ai | | orangeade |
| | des | petits pains |
| je prends | | verres |
| | | bouteilles |
| | un verre ⎫ | ⎧ vin |
| | une tasse | café |
| | beaucoup ⎬ de ⎨ thé |
| je veux ⎭ | peu | cacao |
| | assez ⎭ | ⎩ lait |

## EXERCISES

### I

Put in **du, de la, des, au,** etc.

1. Je donne—pain—mon cousin. 2. Avez-vous—pommes? 3. Elle donne—lait —enfants. 4. Il prend—bière. 5. Il y a— livres sur la table. 6. Apportez-moi un verre—eau, s'il vous plaît. 7. Il donne— pommes—petit garçon. 8. Elle a—oranges dans sa valise. 9. Ils viennent—gare et vont—hôtel. 10. Ne donnez pas—vin— mon oncle.

### II

**Answer the following questions in French**

1. Avez-vous beaucoup d'amis? 2. Qu'est-ce que vous préférez pour votre petit déjeuner, du thé ou du café? 3. Aimez-vous la bière? 4. Prenez-vous du sucre pour le thé? 5. Combien de morceaux prenez-vous? 6. Qui apporte le café? 7. Que mange-t-on pour le petit déjeuner (*a*) en France, (*b*) en Angleterre? 8. Que mangez-vous? 9. Est-ce que nos amis vont à l'intérieur du café? 10. Où restent-ils? 11. Prenez-vous du lait avec le café? 12. Qu'a-t-on mis sur la table pour le petit déjeuner? 13. Est-ce que Madeleine prend une autre tasse de cacao? 14. Mangez-vous beaucoup de pain? 15. Quel est le prix d'une livre de beurre?

### III

**Translate into French**

1. On Mondays and Thursdays I have breakfast in a café. 2. We drink coffee at 11 o'clock. 3. What do you want to eat? 4. Will you please give me a spoon? 5. Do you like coffee with lots of milk? 6. I take only one lump of sugar. 7. Have you got any apples? 8. We have no oranges to-day. 9. There are cups on the table. 10. There are no glasses on the chair. 11. Do you want another glass of wine? 12. Yes,

please (say: willingly). 13. Thanks, I have had enough. 14. There is not enough butter. 15. How much bread is there?

*(Key to I, II and III on page 102.)*

# KEY TO THE EXERCISES

## Lesson Five

### I

1. Are you fond of books? 2. I am very fond of books. 3. My book is very interesting. 4. I don't like my father's books; they are not interesting. 5. Look at that pretty little girl; isn't she beautiful? 6. Are you going to France? 7. No, sir, I am going to England. 8. My children are going there also. 9. My father is not going to the country. 10. They are going to the seaside.

### II

1. Quelle. 2. Quelles. 3. Quel. 4. Quelles. 5. Quel. 6. Quelle. 7. Quel. 8. Quelle. 9. Quels. 10. Quelle.

### III

1. Quelle heure est-il, s'il vous plaît? 2. Il est quatre heures. 3. Il est deux heures et demie. 4. Il est cinq heures six. 5. Il est onze heures et quart. 6. Il est neuf heures vingt-cinq. 7. Il est huit heures moins le quart. 8. Il est sept heures moins vingt. 9. Il est minuit moins cinq. 10. Quel âge a votre sœur? 11. Elle n'a que douze ans. 12. Où allez-vous? Je vais à Paris. 13. Nous allons au bord de la mer. 14. Est-ce que vous allez à la campagne? 15. Votre femme y est-elle aussi? 16. Est-ce que vos enfants vont en Italie? 17. Votre fils a-t-il encore faim? 18. Merci, madame; il n'a plus faim. 19. Je ne parle jamais à mon frère. 20. Quel beau pont! 21. Quelle belle maison ils ont! 22. Quelles jolies jeunes filles elles sont! 23. Regardons le pont. 24. Préparons nos bagages. 25. Donnez-moi la moitié de votre pomme, s'il vous plaît. 26. Ne parlez pas si vite.

## Lesson Six

### I

1. Les deux enfants. 2. Les deux petits garçons y vont. 3. Ils viennent de l'hôtel. 4. Ils vont à l'école. 5. La dame. 6. Au café. 7. De la maison. 8. Au cinéma. 9. De l'Angleterre. 10. Elle va en France.

### II

1. Oui, il... 2. Non, il ne... pas... 3. Oui, elle... 4. Non, elle ne... pas... 5. Non, on ne la descend pas. 6. Oui, elle... 7. Oui, ils... 8. Oui, elles... 9. Oui, on les descend.

### III

1. The sixth lesson is not too difficult. 2. The little boy does not like to be kissed. 3. They are very well. 4. She is not well. 5. He does not know your children. 6. My brother is not coming with you. 7. What is the name of this monument? 8. This shop-window is not beautiful. 9. I don't know what time it is. 10. Do you know what time it is? 11. We come from (the) church. 12. They don't know that street.

### IV

1. Comment allez-vous? 2. Je vais (*or* Ça va) très bien, merci. 3. Comment va votre petite fille? 4. Comment vont vos parents? 5. Ils sont malades. 6. Où sont-ils maintenant? 7. Je ne connais pas votre petite sœur. 8. Connaissez-vous mon oncle? 9. Il va au cinéma. 10. Nous venons de la gare. 11. Nous allons à la gare. 12. Je vais au café. 13. Je viens de l'hôtel. 14. D'où venez-vous? 15. Je viens de l'école. 16. Où allez-vous? 17. Je vais au cinéma. 18. Ils vont à la gare. 19. Quel beau chapeau vous avez! 20. Quel fils intelligent ils ont! 21. Quelles belles maisons ce sont devant nous! 22. Quel est le nom de cette belle rue? 23. La maison de mon père n'est pas loin d'ici. 24. Donnez ces livres à votre professeur, s'il vous plaît. 25. Ce sont les pardessus des professeurs.

## Lesson Seven

### I

Le deux juin; le cinq mars; le douze janvier; le premier février; le vingt et un mars; le quinze avril; le dix-huit mai; le quatre juillet ; le trente et un août; mardi trois décembre; dimanche vingt-deux mai.

## II

1. Il recommande l'hôtel Bienvenu. 2. Il y a trois chambres qui sont libres. 3. Elle est au premier. 4. Il ne comprend pas le petit déjeuner. 5. Il n'est pas trop cher. 6. Non, il ne veut pas de chambres avec pension complète. 7. Il y a un ascenseur. 8. Elle donne sur le jardin. 9. Oui, il peut... 10. Les numéros onze et dix-neuf. 11. Nous sommes en... 12. C'est aujourd'hui... 13. Il y a cinquante-deux semaines dans une année. 14. Elle commence le premier janvier. 15. Janvier est... 16. Mars. 17. Lundi. 18. Vendredi. 19. Oui, c'était (non, ce n'était pas). 20. Oui, ce sera... Non, ce ne sera pas... 21. Demain, ce sera... 22. Nous sommes maintenant en été. 23. Nous ne sommes pas au printemps. 24. Il est... heures. 25. Ce n'est pas encore la fin de la leçon.

## III

1. Pouvez-vous recommander ce livre? 2. Voulez-vous voir le monument? 3. Est-ce loin d'ici? 4. Seulement à cinq minutes d'ici. 5. Allons-y. 6. Quelle jolie chambre! 7. Combien est-ce par semaine? 8. C'est trop cher. 9. Ce n'est pas cher. 10. Veuillez parler anglais. 11. Veuillez entrer. 12. Ne pouvez-vous pas voir l'ascenseur? 13. Y a-t-il une chambre au troisième étage? 14. Y a-t-il des fraises au printemps? 15. Vous ne pouvez pas entrer maintenant.

## Lesson Eight

### I

1. du, à. 2. des. 3. du, aux. 4. de la. 5. des. 6. d'. 7. des, au. 8. des. 9. de la, à l'. 10. de, à.

### II

1. J'ai beaucoup d'amis (je n'ai pas beaucoup d'amis). 2. Je préfère du... 3. J'aime la bière (je n'aime pas la bière). 4. Je prends du sucre (je ne prends pas de sucre). 5. Je prends deux morceaux. 6. Le garçon. 7. (a) En France on mange du pain, des petits pains et des croissants; (b) En Angleterre on mange du pain grillé, des œufs sur le plat, etc. (see page 94). 8. Je mange du pain bis avec du beurre et de la marmelade. 9. Non, monsieur, ils ne vont pas à l'intérieur. 10. Ils restent à la terrasse. 11. Je prends du lait (je ne prends pas de lait). 12. Il y a des tasses, du pain, etc. (see page 97). 13. Oui, elle prend une autre tasse. 14. Je mange (ne mange pas) beaucoup de pain. 15. Douze francs.

### III

1. Le lundi et le jeudi je prends le petit déjeuner au café. 2. Nous buvons du café à onze heures. 3. Que voulez-vous manger? 4. Veuillez me donner une cuillère. 5. Aimez-vous le café avec beaucoup de lait? 6. Je ne prends qu'un morceau de sucre. 7. Avez-vous des pommes? 8. Nous n'avons pas d'oranges aujourd'hui. 9. Il y a des tasses sur la table. 10. Il n'y a pas de verres sur la chaise. 11. Voulez-vous encore un verre de vin? 12. Volontiers, je vous remercie. 13. Merci, j'ai eu assez. 14. Il n'y a pas assez de beurre. 15. Combien de pain y a-t-il?

## ROUND THE TOWN

### L'argot Parisien

L'argot est moins en usage entre les gens bien élevés en France, qu'en Angleterre, et l'étudiant doit se garder d'utiliser des expressions qu'il recueille pendant ses excursions. Il vaut mieux se souvenir seulement des expressions qui ont cours entre les Français de votre connaissance personnelle.

### Paris Slang

Slang is less current in polite circles in France, than in England, and the learner should be careful about using phrases he may pick up during his wanderings. It is better to remember only those expressions which are current among French people of your own acquaintance.

# NEUVIÈME LEÇON—*NINTH LESSON*

| **Le soleil se lève** | **Le soleil à midi** | **Le soleil se couche** |
|---|---|---|
| le so-lai*y* se laiv | le so-lai*y* ah mee-dee | le so-lai*y* se koosh |
| *The sun rises* | *The sun at noon* | *The sun sets* |

### THE WEATHER—LE TEMPS

**Le matin;**    **le lever du soleil.**    **Le soleil est à l'est; il se lève.**
le mah-tiN    le le-vay d**ēē** so-lai*y*    le so-lai*y* ay-tah laist eel se laiv.
*The morning; the rise of the sun.*    *The sun is in the east; it is rising.*

**Midi;**    **le soleil est au sud.**    **Le soir;**    **le coucher du soleil.**
mee-dee    le so-lai*y* ay-toh s**ēē**d    le swahr    le koo-shay d**ēē** so-lai*y*.
*Noon;*    *the sun is in the south.*    *The evening; the sunset.*

**Le soleil est à l'ouest;**   **il se couche.**   **La nuit;**   **le soleil n'est pas visible;**
le so-lai*y* ay-tah lwest   eel se koosh   lah n**w**ee   le so-lai*y* nay pah vee-zeebl
*The sun is in the west;*   *it is setting.*   *The night;*   *the sun is not visible;*

**il fait noir.**    **Le jour;**    **il fait clair.**    **Le soleil est dans le ciel.**
eel fai nwahr.    le zhoor    eel fai klair.    le so-lai*y* ay daN le syail.
*it is dark.*    *The day;*    *it is light.*    *The sun is in the sky.*

**Pendant le jour il fait clair et nous pouvons voir sans allumer le**
paN-daN le zhoor eel fai klair ay noo poo-voN vwahr saN-zah-l**ēē**-may le
*During the day it is light and we can see without lighting the*

**gaz ou l'électricité.**    **Pendant la nuit le soleil n'est pas visible,**
gahz oo lay-laik-tree-see-tay.    paN-daN lah n**w**ee le so-lai*y* nay pah vee-zeebl
*gas or the electricity.*    *During the night the sun is not visible,*

**mais nous pouvons voir la lune et les étoiles.**    **Il fait noir et**
mai noo poo-voN vwahr la l**ēē**n ay lay-zay twahl.    eel fai nwahr ay
*but we can see the moon and the stars.*    *It is dark and*

**nous allumons le gaz ou l'électricité.**    **Le soleil se lève le matin;**
noo-zah-l**ēē**moN le gahz oo lay-laik-tree-see-tay.    le so-lai*y* se laiv le mah-tiN
*we light the gas or the electric light.*    *The sun rises in the morning;*

**il se couche le soir. En été le soleil se lève de bonne heure. Il fait jour**
eel se koosh le swahr.  ah-nay-tay le so-laiy se laiv de bo-nãyr.  eel fait zhoor
*it sets in the evening.  In summer the sun rises early.  It is light*

**à trois heures du matin et les jours sont longs. En hiver le**
ah trwah-zãyr dẽe mah-tiN ay lay zhoor soN loN.  ah-nee-vair le
*at three o'clock in the morning and the days are long.  In winter the*

**soleil se lève tard, à sept heures ou encore plus tard. Il fait déjà nuit**
so-laiy se laiv tahr ah sai-tãyr oo aN-kor plẽe tahr.  eel fai day-zhah nw̃ee
*sun rises late at seven o'clock or still later (lit. more late).  It is already night*

**à cinq heures du soir, et les jours sont courts. Quand le ciel est bleu, il fait du**
ah siN-kãyr dẽe swahr ay lay zhoor soN koor.  kaN le syail ay blãy eel fait dẽe
*at five o'clock in the evening, and the days are short.  When the sky is blue, it makes*

**soleil—il fait beau temps. Quand le ciel est gris, il est couvert de nuages—**
so-laiy   eel fai boh taN.  kaN le syail ay gree ee-lay koo-vair de nẽeahzh
*sunshine—it makes fine weather.  When the sky is grey, it is covered with clouds—*

**il fait mauvais temps. À Londres il pleut souvent. À Paris il pleut**
eel fai moh-vai taN.  ah loNdr eel plãy soo-vaN.  ah pah-ree eel plãy
*it makes bad weather.  In London it rains often.  In Paris it rains*

**quelquefois. À Nice il pleut rarement; il fait généralement beau. Il neige**
kailk-fwah.  ah nees eel plãy rahr'maN eel fai zhay-nay-rahl'maN boh.  eel naizh
*sometimes.  In Nice it rains rarely; it is generally fine.  It snows*

**quelquefois à Paris en hiver; en été il ne neige jamais. Au**
kailk-fwah ah pah-ree ah-nee-vair   ah-nay-tay eel ne naizh zhah-mai.  oh
*sometimes in Paris in winter; in summer it snows never.  At the*

**pôle nord il fait toujours froid; il ne fait jamais chaud.**
pol nor eel fai too-zhoor frwah  eel ne fai zhah-mai shoh.
*North Pole it is always cold; it is never warm.*

**la nouvelle lune**          **la lune à son décours**       **la pleine lune**
lah noo-vail lẽen            lah lẽen ah soN day-koor        lah plain lẽen
*new moon*                   *waning moon*                   *full moon*

| il fait jour | il fait nuit | le soleil | la lune | une étoile | une étoile filante |
|---|---|---|---|---|---|
| eel fai zhoor | eel fait nw̃ee | so-lai*y* | l@n | ay-twahl | ay-twahl fee-laNt |
| *it is daytime* | *it is night* | *sun* | *moon* | *star* | *shooting star* |

| la pluie (il pleut) | la neige (il neige) | il fait froid | il fait chaud | la tempête |
|---|---|---|---|---|
| plw̃ee (eel plãy) | naizh (eel naizh) | eel fai frwah | eel fai shoh | taN-pait |
| *the rain (it is raining)* | *the snow (it snows)* | *it is cold* | *it is hot* | *storm* |

| il fait du vent | il fait du brouillard | le nuage | un orage | un éclair | la grêle |
|---|---|---|---|---|---|
| eel fai d@ vaN | broo-yahr | n@-ahzh | oh-rahzh | ay-klair | grail |
| *it is windy* | *it is foggy* | *cloud* | *thunderstorm* | *lightning* | *hail* |

## COMPARISON OF CENTIGRADE AND ENGLISH (FAHRENHEIT) THERMOMETERS

**Le Thermomètre**
(Centigrade)

$$-20 \quad -10 \quad -5 \quad 0 \quad +5 \quad 10 \quad 15 \quad 20 \quad 25 \quad 30 \quad 35 \quad 40 \quad 45 \quad 50 \quad 100$$

point de congélation
pwiN de koN-zhay-lahs-yoN

point d'ébullition
pwiN day-b@lees-yoN

*The Thermometer*
(*Fahrenheit*)

$$-4 \quad +14 \quad 23 \quad 32 \quad 41 \quad 50 \quad 59 \quad 68 \quad 77 \quad 86 \quad 95 \quad 104 \quad 113 \quad 122 \quad 212$$

*freezing point*

*boiling point*

To convert Fahrenheit degrees to Centigrade subtract 32 and multiply by 5/9ths; for example, 50 degrees F. = (50−32) × 5/9 = 10 degrees C.

To convert Centigrade degrees to Fahrenheit multiply by 9/5ths and add 32; for example, 5 degrees Centigrade = (5 × 9/5 + 32) = 41 degrees F.

### THE CARDINAL POINTS—LES POINTS CARDINAUX

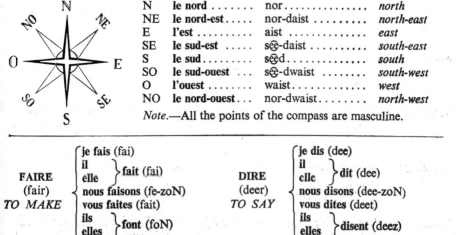

| N | le nord ....... | nor .............. | *north* |
|---|---|---|---|
| NE | le nord-est ..... | nor-daist ......... | *north-east* |
| E | l'est .......... | aist .............. | *east* |
| SE | le sud-est ..... | s@-daist .......... | *south-east* |
| S | le sud ......... | s@d .............. | *south* |
| SO | le sud-ouest ... | s@-dwaist ........ | *south-west* |
| O | l'ouest ........ | waist ............. | *west* |
| NO | le nord-ouest ... | nor-dwaist ........ | *north-west* |

*Note.*—All the points of the compass are masculine.

**FAIRE**
(fair)
*TO MAKE*

- je fais (fai)
- il
- elle } fait (fai)
- nous faisons (fe-zoN)
- vous faites (fait)
- ils
- elles } font (foN)

**DIRE**
(deer)
*TO SAY*

- je dis (dee)
- il
- elle } dit (dee)
- nous disons (dee-zoN)
- vous dites (deet)
- ils
- elles } disent (deez)

*Note.*—There are three verbs only which have the ending -tes (only the t is pronounced) instead of -ez : **vous êtes, vous faites** and **vous dites.**

### Mlle LESAGE MAKES A DRESS

In making this frock for her mother, Lucie Lesage is using a sewing machine, scissors, and a dressmaker's dummy. Do you know what the corresponding terms are in French? If not you will find them on page 401.

**Mlle L. :**    **Je dois partir maintenant. Je vais travailler.**
zhe dwah pahr-teer miNt-naN.   zhe vai trah-vah-yay.
*I must leave now.   I am going to work.*

**Madeleine : Qu'allez-vous faire?**    **Mlle L. : Une robe pour ma mère.**
kah-lay voo fair?    ẽn rob poor mah mair.
*What are you going to make?*    *A dress for my mother.*

**Madeleine : Une robe de laine?**    **Mlle L. : Non, une robe de soie pour l'été.**
ẽn rob de lain?    noN ẽn rob de swah poor lay-tay.
*A dress of wool (woollen dress)?*    *No, a silk dress for the summer.*

**Madeleine : De quelle couleur?**    **Mlle L. : Bleu clair.**
de kail koo-lãyr?    blãy klair.
*(of) What colour?*    *Light blue.*

**Madeleine : Cela sera bien joli.**    **Mme R. : Mon Dieu,[1] qu'il fait chaud ici!**
s'lah s'rah byiN zho-lee.    moN dyãy keel fai shoh ee-see!
*That will be very nice.*    *Heavens, how hot it is here!*

---

[1] Lit. "My God," but corresponding to "Heavens!" or "Good Gracious!"

**M. Lesage :** Oui, il fait chaud aujourd'hui. C'est le jour le plus chaud de
ŵee eel fai shoh oh-zhoord ŵee. sai le zhoor le plẽ shoh de
*Yes, it is hot to-day. It is the hottest day of*

l'année. Trente degrès à l'ombre et trente-cinq au soleil.
lah-nay. traNt de-gray ah loNbr ay traNt siNk oh so-laiy.
*the year. Thirty degrees in the shade and thirty-five in the sun.*

**Charles :** Combien cela fait-il au thermomètre anglais?
koN-byiN slah fay-teel oh tair-moh-maitr aN-glai?
*How much is that on the English thermometer?*

**M. Roberts :** À peu près quatre-vingt six à l'ombre et exactement
ah pẽ pray kahtr viN siNk ah loNbr ay ai-xakt-maN
*About 86 in the shade and exactly*

quatre-vingt quinze au soleil. **Mlle L. :** Il fait lourd. Je crois
kahtr viN kiNz oh so-laiy. eel fai loor. zhe krwah
*95 in the sun.* *It is close. I think*

qu'il y aura de l'orage. **Madeleine :** Croyez-vous, ma chère?
keel ee oh-rah de loh-rahzh. krwah-yay voo mah shair?
*that there will be a storm.* *Do you think so, my dear?*

**Mme R. :** Que dit votre cousine?
ke dee votr koo-zeen?
*What does your cousin say?*

**Madeleine :** Elle croit qu'il va faire de l'orage.
ail krwah keel vah fair de loh-rahzh.
*She thinks that there will be a storm.*

**M. Lesage :** Dites, Roberts, l'hiver est-il froid en Angleterre?
deet ro-bairts lee-vair ai-teel frwah ah-naN-gle-tair?
*Tell me, Roberts, is the winter cold in England?*

**M. Robert :** Il n'est pas très rigoureux. Il tombe peu de neige,
eel nai pah trai ree-goo-rẽ. eel toNb pẽ de naizh
*It is not very severe. It falls little snow,*

excepté dans le nord où il y en a beaucoup.
ai-xep-tay daN le nor oo eel-yah-nah boh-koo.
*except in the north where there is of it a lot.*

**M. Lesage :** Est-ce qu'il neige en hiver à Londres?
ais-keel naizh ah-nee-vair ah loNdr?
*Does it snow in winter in London?*

**M. Robert :** Il neige quelquefois à Londres en hiver.
eel naizh kailk'fwah ah loNdr ah-nee-vair.
*It snows sometimes in London in winter.*

PARIS: UN JOUR DE SOLEIL

La brume matinale a fait place à la chaleur accablante d'un après-midi d'été.

| **Brume** (f.) | **matinal-e** (adj.) | **faire place** | **chaleur** (f.) | **accablant-e** (adj.) |
|---|---|---|---|---|
| Haze, mist | morning | to give place | heat | overpowering |

## PARIS: UN JOUR DE PLUIE

L'aspect luisant et désert de cette ruelle, laisse deviner qu'à Paris aussi il pleut de temps en temps.

| aspect (m.) | luisant-e (adj.) | désert-e (adj.) | ruelle | laisser deviner |
|---|---|---|---|---|
| appearance | glistening | deserted | by-street | to suggest |

### NOT A NICE DAY

In this picture some of the weather conditions which you have already learned are illustrated. The others are listed on page 114. Consult that list, then turn back and see if you can describe in French what is happening on this particularly nasty day.

**Mlle L. :**     **Charles, quelle saison aimez vous le mieux?**
Shahrl kail sai-soN ai-may voo le myāȳ?
*Charles, which season do you like (the) best?*

**Charles :**     **J'aime bien l'hiver quand on joue au football.**
zhaim byiN lee-vair kaN-toN zhoo oh foot-bahl.
*I like very much the winter when one plays football.*

**Mlle L. :**     **J'aime mieux l'été, parce qu'il y a de belles fleurs.**
zhaim myāȳ lay-tay pahrs keel-yah de bail flāȳr.
*I like best the summer, because there are beautiful flowers.*

**Madeleine :**   **Moi aussi.    Regardez cette femme qui vend des fleurs.    Elle a de**
mwah oh-see.    re-gahr-day sait fam kee vaN dāȳ flāȳr.    ai-lah-de
*So do I.    Look (at) that woman who sells flowers.    She has*

**jolis bouquets.       Mme R. : Quelles belles fleurs! Qu'est-ce qu'il y a?**
zho-lee boo-kai.           kail bail flāȳr!    kaisk-eel-yah?
*nice bunches.            What beautiful flowers!    What is there?*

**La bouquetière : Il y a des roses, des œillets, des violettes, des pensées, des**
la boo-ktyair: eel-yah day rohz day-zāȳyay day vyoh-lait day paN-say day
*The flower girl : There are roses, carnations, violets, pansies,*

## AT THE FLORIST'S

After studying the list of flowers given below, cover it over and name in French as many of the flowers shown in the picture as you can recognise.

| | | | | |
|---|---|---|---|---|
| **l'azalée (f.)** az-ah-lay *azalea* | **le laurier-rose** loh-ryay-rohz *oleander* | **le coquelicot anglais** kohk-lee-ko aN-glai *Shirley poppy* | **le pavot** pah-voh *poppy* | **le pois de senteur** pwah de saN-tayr *sweet pea* |
| **la clématite** klay-mah-teet *clematis* | **la primevère** preem-vair *primrose* | **la jonquille** zhoN-keey *jonquil*    **la glycine** glee-seen *wistaria* | **le nénuphar** nay-nee-fahr *water-lily* | **le perce-neige** pairs naizh *snowdrop* |
| **la pensée** paN-say *pansy* | **l'asphodèle (m.)** ahs-foh-dail *daffodil* | **l'œillet (m.)** ay-yay *carnation*    **l'iris (f.)** ee-rees *iris* | **le glaïeul** glah-yayl *gladiolus*   **le lis** lees *lily* | **la rose** rohz *rose* |
| **le dahlia** dahl-yah *dahlia*   **la tulipe** tee-leep *tulip*   **le lilas** lee-lah *lilac* | | **la violette** vyoh-lait *violet*   **le souci** soo-see *marigold* | **le chrysanthème** kree-zaN-taim *chrysanthemum* | **le bluet** blee-ay *cornflower* |
| **la marguerite** mahr-ge-reet *daisy* | **le jasmin** zhahs-miN *jasmine* | **le muguet** mee-gay *lily of the valley*   **le narcisse** nahr-sees *narcissus* | **l'orchidée (f.)** or-kee-day *orchid* | **la giroflée** zhee-rof-lay *wallflower* |
| **le fleuriste** flay-reest *florist* | **le bouquet** boo-kay *bunch of flowers* | **le pot de fleurs** poh de flayr *pot of flowers* | **le panier** pah-nyay *basket* | **la couronne** koo-ron *wreath* |

*Note.*—Flowers play a somewhat greater role in French life than in ours, and are presented on many occasions. A guest dining out, for instance, will very likely bring a bouquet for his hostess.

soucis, des lis et des tulipes.   **Mme R. :** **Prenons un bouquet**
soo-see day lees ay day t$\widehat{ee}$-leep.        pre-noN uN boo-kay
*marigolds, lilies, and tulips.*       *Let us take a bunch*

**d'œillets pour votre tante.**   **Combien coûtent-ils?**
d$\widehat{a}$yyay poor votr taNt.   coN-byiN koot-teel?
*of carnations for your aunt.*   *How much cost they?*

**La bouquetière:** **Ils sont à trois francs la pièce, madame.**
eel soN-tah trwah fraN lah pyais mah-dahm.
*They are three francs each, madam.*

**Mme R. :**      **Veuillez me faire un bouquet d'une douzaine.**
v$\widehat{a}$y-yay me fair uN boo-kay d$\widehat{ee}$n doo-zain.
*Will you please make me a bunch of a dozen.*

**Mlle L. :**      **Mademoiselle, pouvez-vous me faire une boutonnière de**
mahd-mwah-zail poo-vay voo me fair $\widehat{ee}$n boo-ton-yair de
*Miss, can you make me a buttonhole of*

**quelques violettes?**   **La bouquetière :** **À votre service, mesdames.**
kailk vyo-lait?             ah votr sair-vees may-dahm.
*some violets?*                  *At your service, my ladies.*

## THE NUMBERS FROM 60  (*see also pages* 12 *and* 90)

| | | | | | |
|---|---|---|---|---|---|
| 60 | **soixante** swah-saNt | | 89 | **quatre-vingt-neuf** kahtr' viN n$\widehat{a}$yf |
| 61 | **soixante et un** swah-saN-tay uN | | 90 | **quatre-vingt-dix** kahtr' viN dees |
| 62 | **soixante-deux** swah-saNt d$\widehat{a}$y | | 91 | **quatre-vingt-onze** kahtr' viN oNz |
| 63 | **soixante-trois** swah-saNt trwah | | 92 | **quatre-vingt-douze** kahtr' viN dooz |
| 70 | **soixante-dix** swah-saNt dees | | 93 | **quatre-vingt-treize** kahtr' viN traiz |
| 71 | **soixante et onze** swah-saN-tay oNz | | 94 | **quatre-vingt-quatorze** |
| 72 | **soixante-douze** swah-saNt dooz | | | kahtr' viN kah-torz |
| 73 | **soixante-treize** swah-saNt traiz | | 99 | **quatre-vingt-dix-neuf** |
| 74 | **soixante-quatorze** swah-saNt kah-torz | | | kahtr' viN deez-n$\widehat{a}$yf |
| 75 | **soixante-quinze** swah-saNt kiNz | | 100 | **cent** saN |
| 76 | **soixante-seize** swah-saNt saiz | | 101 | **cent un** saN uN |
| 77 | **soixante-dix-sept** swah-saNt dees-sait | | 102 | **cent deux** saN d$\widehat{a}$y |
| 78 | **soixante-dix-huit** swah-saN deez-$\widehat{w}$eet | | 103 | **cent trois** saN trwah |
| 79 | **soixante-dix-neuf** | | 200 | **deux cents** d$\widehat{a}$y saN |
| | swah-saNt dees-n$\widehat{a}$yf | | 201 | **deux cent un** d$\widehat{a}$y saN uN |
| 80 | **quatre-vingts** kahtr' viN | | 202 | **deux cent deux** d$\widehat{a}$y saN d$\widehat{a}$y |
| 81 | **quatre-vingt-un** kahtr' viN-uN | | 300 | **trois cents** trwah saN |
| 82 | **quatre-vingt-deux** kahtr' viN d$\widehat{a}$y | | 834 | **huit cent trente-quatre** |
| 83 | **quatre-vingt-trois** kahtr' viN trwah | | | $\widehat{w}$ee saN traNt kahtr |
| 84 | **quatre-vingt-quatre** kahtr' viN kahtr | | 996 | **neuf cent quatre-vingt-seize** |
| 85 | **quatre-vingt-cinq** kahtr' viN siNk | | | n$\widehat{a}$yf saN kahtr viN saiz |
| 86 | **quatre-vingt-six** kahtr' viN sees | | 1,000 | **mille** meel |
| 87 | **quatre-vingt-sept** kahtr' viN sait | | 1,001 | **mille un** meel uN |
| 88 | **quatre-vingt-huit** kahtr' viN $\widehat{w}$eet | | 2,000 | **deux mille** d$\widehat{a}$y meel |

## AU "BAR DE LA BEAUTÉ"

Quelle **idée** surprenante, débiter la beauté comme on le ferait d'une boisson! À ce "bar", c'est le souci du velouté de leur peau, et non pas **celui** d'un vermouth-cassis à déguster, qui attire les femmes du monde au comptoir.

| **Surprenant-e** (adj.) | **débiter** | **souci** (m.) | **velouté** (m.) | **attirer** |
|---|---|---|---|---|
| Surprising, astonishing | to sell (retail) | care | softness | to attract |

10,000    **dix mille**    dee meel
100,000    **cent mille**    saN meel
1,000,000    **un million**    uN meel-yoN
In the year 1066=**en mil soixante-six**
               aN meel swah-saNt sees
*Note.*—(1) There are no special words
for 70, 80 and 90 (except in Belgian and
other dialects, where **septante, octante** and
**nonante** are used).    70 is sixty ten, 71 is
sixty eleven, etc.    80 is four twenties, 90 is
80+10, 91 is 80+11, etc.    (2) **et** is used
only in 21, 31, 41, 51, 61 and 71.    (3) In
dates **mille** is often written **mil.**    (4) **en**
stands for "in the year".

## SUMMARY

| | **What is the weather like?** | | **Quel temps fait-il?** |
|---|---|---|---|
| it is | hot<br>cold<br>fine weather<br>bad weather<br>nasty weather<br>sunny<br>close<br>cool<br>foggy<br>windy<br>stormy<br>light<br>dark | il fait | chaud<br>froid<br>beau (temps)<br>mauvais (temps)<br>un sale temps<br>du soleil<br>lourd<br>frais<br>du brouillard<br>du vent<br>un vent furieux<br>jour<br>noir |
| it | rains, is raining<br>snows, is snowing<br>hails, is hailing<br>freezes, is freezing<br>thaws, is thawing<br>thunders, is thundering | il | pleut<br>neige<br>grêle<br>gèle<br>dégèle<br>tonne |

there is a thunderstorm (lightning)        il y a de l'orage (des éclairs)

## EXERCISES

### I   Answer in French

1. Où est le soleil? 2. Le soleil est-il visible pendant la nuit? 3. Quand allumons-nous l'électricité, le jour ou la nuit? 4. Quand le soleil se lève-t-il? 5. Quand le soleil se couche-t-il? 6. À quelle heure le soleil se lève-t-il en été? 7. Les jours sont-ils longs en hiver? 8. Les nuits sont-elles courtes en été? 9. Fait-il jour à trois heures du matin en hiver? 10. Que faisons-nous pour voir pendant la nuit? 11. Le soleil se couche-t-il de bonne heure en été? 12. Pouvez-vous voir s'il ne fait pas clair? 13. Fait-il encore jour à six heures du soir en hiver? 14. De quelle couleur sont les nuages? 15. Pleut-il beaucoup à Londres? 16. Neige-t-il en été? 17. Les dames ouvrent-elles leurs parapluies quand il fait du soleil? 18. Fait-il du soleil quand le ciel est gris? 19. Fait-il beau temps aujourd'hui? 20. Fait-il chaud au pôle nord? 21. Neige-t-il quelquefois en juillet? 22. Avez-vous froid? 23. Aimez-vous les fleurs? 24. Quelle saison aimez-vous le mieux? 25. Est-ce qu'il y a des violettes en février?

### II   Translate into French

1. What is the time, please? 2. It is eleven o'clock in the morning. 3. Is the sun visible now? 4. Is it dark? 5. Will you please light the gas. 6. I am always cold in winter. 7. What is your brother doing? 8. He is making bunches of pansies. 9. Does it rain? 10. It snows sometimes in winter.

### III   Write in French

4 ; 6 ; 11 ; 56 ; 78 ; 87 ; 91 ; 95 ; 99 ; 106 ; 234 ; 354 ; 456 ; 692 ; 1,087 ; 2,156 ; 8,967 ; 13,405.

(*Key to I, II and III on pages* 150 *and* 151.)

# DIXIÈME LEÇON—*TENTH LESSON*

### LETTERS FOR THE LESAGE'S

See how many of the objects listed on pp. 116-117 you can find in this picture of the postman calling at the Lesage villa. Then make your own list of them in French.

**La famille Lesage habite une jolie petite villa dans un des**
lah fah-mee*y* le-sahzh ah-beet ễn zho-lee p'teet vee-lah daN-zuN day
*The Lesage family lives in a nice little villa in one of the*

**faubourgs de Paris.   Quoique petite, la maison est bien bâtie et**
foh-boor de pah-ree.   kwahk' p'teet lah mai-zoN ay byiN bah-tee ay
*suburbs of Paris.   Although small, the house is well built and*

**contient tout ce qu'il faut pour le confort de la famille.   C'est une maison**
koN-tyiN too se keel foh poor le koN-for de lah fah-mee*y*.   sai-tễn mai-zoN
*contains all that it needs for the comfort of the family.   It is a house*

**de douze pièces.   Au rez-de-chaussée il y a la salle-à-manger, la cuisine et un**
de dooz pyais.   oh raid-shoh-say eel-yah lah sahl-ah maN-shay lah kŵee-zeen ay uN
*of twelve rooms.   On the ground floor there is the dining-room, the kitchen and a*

**petit salon.   Au premier étage il y a le salon et le bureau du**
p'tee sah-loN.   oh prem-yay-ray-tahzh eel yah le sah-loN ay le bễroh dễ
*small sitting-room.   On the first floor there is the drawing-room and the study of the*

**maître de la maison.   Au deuxième étage il y a deux chambres à coucher, la**
maitr de lah mai-zoN.   oh dễyz-yaim-ay-tahzh eel yah dễy shaNbr-ah koo-shay lah
*master of the house.   On the second floor there are two bedrooms, the*

## A VILLA : UNE VILLA

### English

1. Chimney; 2. Lightning-conductor; 3. Attic; 4. Maid's room; 5. Loft; 6. Skylight; 7. Aerial; 8. Roof; 9. Shutter; 10. Frieze; 11. Play-pen; 12. Nursery; 13. Bedroom; 14. 2nd floor; 15. 1st floor; 16. Diffused lighting; 17. Bathroom; 18. Grand-father clock; 19. Drawing-room; 20. Rocking chair; 21. Bookcase; 22. Awning; 23. Balcony; 24. Ground floor; 25. Stove chimney; 26. Door curtain; 27. Dining-room; 28. Kitchen stove; 29. Basement; 30. Sawn wood; 31. Sawing-horse; 32. Central-heating stove; 33. Stock of coal, coke or anthracite; 34. Cistern; 35. Wine-barrels; 36. Wine-rack; 37. Staircase; 38. Ladder; 39. Porch; 40. Door-bell; 41. Steps to House; 42. Lawn; 43. Deck-chair; 44. Garden-railings; 45. Garden-gate; 46. Roller; 47. Lawn-mower.

### French

1. Cheminée (*f.*); 2. Paratonnerre (*m.*); 3. Mansarde (*f.*); 4. Chambre de domestique; 5. Grenier (*m.*); 6. Lucarne (*f.*); 7. Antenne (*f.*); 8. Toit (*m.*); toiture (*f.*); 9. Volet (*m.*); persiennes (*f. pl.*); 10. Bordure (*f.*) (de papier peint); 11. Baby-parc (*m.*); 12. Chambre des enfants; 13. Chambre à coucher; 14. Deuxième étage (*m.*); 15. Premier étage; 16. Éclairage (*m.*) diffusé; 17. Salle (*f.*) de bain(s); 18. Horloge (*f.*) comtoise; 19. Salon (*m.*); salle (*f.*) de réception; 20. Fauteuil (*m.*) à bascule; 21. Bibliothèque (*m.*); 22. Store (*m.*); 23. Balcon (*m.*); 24. Rez-de-chaussée (*m. inv.*); 25. Tuyau (*m.*) de poêle; 26. Portière (*f.*); 27. Salle à manger; 28. Fourneau (*m.*) de cuisine; 29. Sous-sol (*m.*); 30. Du bois scié; 31. Chevalet (*m.*) de sciage; 32. Poêle (*m.*) du chauffage central; 33. Approvisionnement de charbon, de coke ou d'anthracite; 34. Citerne (*f.*); réservoir (*m.*) à eau; 35. Fûts (*m. pl.*) de vin; 36. Porte boutcilles; 37. Escalier (*m.*); 38. Échelle (*f.*); 39. Porche (*m.*); portique (*m.*); 40. Timbre (*m.*); 41. Perron (*m.*); 42. Pelouse (*f.*); 43. Transatlantique (*m.*); 44. Grille, palissade (*f.*); 45. Grille d'entrée; 46. Cylindre (*m.*) compresseur; 47. Tondeuse (*f.*).

chambre des enfants (aujourd'hui divisée en deux chambres pour Georges et
shaN-br day-zaN-faN (oh-zhoor-dw͡ee dee-vee-zay aN da͡y shaNbr poor zhorzh ay
*bedroom of the children (nowadays divided into two rooms for Georges and*

Lucie) et la salle de bain.    Au-dessus du deuxième étage il y a
le͡esee) ay lah sahl de biN.    oh de-se͡e de͡e da͡yz-yaim-ay-tahzh eel-yah
*Lucie) and the bathroom.    Above the second floor there is*

une mansarde, qui est la chambre à coucher de la bonne.    Au-dessous
e͡en maN-sahrd kee ay lah shaNbr ah koo-shay de lah bon.    oh de-soo
*an attic which is the bedroom of the maid.    Under*

du rez-de-chaussée est la cave.    Devant la maison il y a un
de͡e ray de shoh-say ay lah kahv.    de-vaN lah mai-zoN eel-yah uN
*the ground floor is the cellar.    In front of the house there is a*

jardin, qui est bien entretenu.    La pelouse est ornée de
zhahr-diN kee ay byain-aNtr-t'ne͡e.    lah pe-looz ai-tor-nay de
*garden, which is well kept.    The lawn is adorned with*

parterres de fleurs.    Derrière la maison il y a un plus grand
pahr-tair de fla͡yr.    dair-yair lah mai-zoN eel-yah uN ple͡e graN
*flower-beds.    Behind the house there is a larger*

jardin, qui fournit la famille Lesage en fruits et en légumes.
zhahr-diN kee foor-nee lah fah-meey le-sahzh aN frwee ay aN lay-ge͡em.
*garden, which supplies the Lesage family with fruit and vegetables.*

Au grenier se trouvent les bagages, une vieille chaise cassée, un vieux
oh gren-yay se troov lay bah-gahzh e͡en vyaiy shaiz kah-say uN vya͡y
*In the loft are to be found the luggage, an old broken chair, an old*

paravent, un cheval à bascule, et une échelle.    La mansarde est la
pah-rah-vaN uN sh'vahl ah bahs-ke͡el ay e͡enay-shail.    lah man-sahr-dai lah
*screen, a rocking horse, and a ladder.    The attic is the*

chambre de la bonne.    Dans la salle de bain il y a une grande baignoire
shaNbr de lah bon.    daN la sahl de biN eel-yah e͡en graNd bainy-wahr
*room of the maid.    In the bathroom there is a big porcelain*

en porcelaine.    On monte et descend l'escalier.    On reçoit les
aN porslain.    oN moNt ay dai-saN lais-kahl-yay.    oN r'swah lay
*bath.    One goes up and down the stairs.    One receives*

visiteurs dans le salon.    Le maître de la maison lit des livres,
vee-zee-ta͡yr daN le sah-loN.    le maitr de lah mai-zoN lee day leevr
*visitors in the drawing-room.    The master of the house reads his books,*

écrit ses lettres et fume des cigares dans son cabinet de travail.
ay-kree say laitr ay fe͡em day see-gahr daN soN kah-bee-nay de trah-vahy.
*writes his letters and smokes his cigars in his study.*

## IN THE HALL AT THE LESAGE'S

Your vocabulary is now increasing. Try to name in French ten objects in this picture, without looking at the text below. Check later from the list.

**le plafonnier**
plah-fo-nyay
*ceiling lamp*

**l'abat-jour** (*m.*)
abah-zhoor
*lamp-shade*

**le tiroir**
teer-wahr
*drawer*

**un escalier**
ais-kahl-yay
*stairs*

**la rampe**
raNp
*banister*

**la portière**
port-yair
*door-curtain*

**le vestibule**
ves-tee-bũl
*hall*

**le portemanteau**
port-maN-toh
*hall-stand*

**la glace**
glahs
*mirror*

**le porte-parapluies**
port pah-rah-plw͡ee
*umbrella stand*

**le parapluie**
pah-rah-plw͡ee
*umbrella*

**la canne**
kahn
*walking stick*

**le vase à fleurs avec un bouquet**
vahz-ah flãyr ah-vaik-uN boo-kai
*flower vase with cut flowers*

**le porte-brosses**
port-bros
*brush-holder*

**la petite table**
p'teet tahbl
*small table*

**le tapis-brosse**
tah-pee-bros
*mat*

**le plancher**
plaN-shay
*floor*

**le mur**
mẽ͡r
*wall*

**le plafond**
plah-foN
*ceiling*

**le compteur électrique**
coN-tãyr ay-laik-treek
*meter*

**le téléphone**
tay-lay-fohn
*telephone*

**la lampe**
laNp
*lamp*

**il ôte son pardessus**
il oht soN pahr-de-sẽ͡
*he takes off his overcoat*

**elle met son chapeau**
ail mai soN shah-poh
*she is putting on her hat*

**Dans le vestibule on ôte son pardessus.   On prend ses repas dans la**
daN le vais-tee-bęęl on oht soN par-de-sęę.   oN praN say re-pah daN lah
*In the vestibule one takes off one's overcoat.   One takes one's meals in the*

**salle à manger.   Dans la cuisine il y a un fourneau de cuisine, un**
sah-lah-maN-zhay.   daN lah kŵee-zeen eel yah uN foor-noh de kŵee-zeen uN
*dining-room.   In the kitchen there is a kitchen stove, a*

**buffet et une table.   Il y a aussi de la vaisselle, des casseroles et toutes sortes**
bęę-fay ay ęęn tahbl.   eel yah oh-see de lah vai-sail day kahs-rohl ay toot sort
*dresser and a table.   There is also crockery, saucepans and all sorts*

**de choses pour faire la cuisine.   Mme Lesage est une excellente**
de shohz poor fair lah kŵee-zeen.   Mah-dahm le-sahzh ai-tęę-nai-xai-laNt
*of things to do the cooking.   Mrs. Lesage is an excellent*

**cuisinière.   Dans la cave il y a du charbon, du bois, du vin,**
kŵee-zeen-yair.   daN lah kahv eel-yah dęę shahr-boN dęę bwah dęę viN
*cook.   In the cellar there is coal, wood, wine,*

**des tonneaux et un sac.   Entrons dans la maison et examinons**
day to-noh ay uN sahk.   aN troN daN lah mai-zoN ay ai-xah-mee-noN
*barrels and a sack.   Let us go into the house and look over the*

**l'intérieur.   Nous entrons dans le vestibule.   À gauche nous**
liN-tayr-yāŷr.   noo-zaN-troN daN le vais-tee-bęęl.   ah gohsh noo
*interior.   We go into the hall.   On the left we*

**voyons le porte-manteau avec les chapeaux et les manteaux.   A côté**
vwah-yoN le port-maN-toh ah-vaik lay shahpoh ay lay maN-toh.   ah koh-tay
*see the coat-rack with the hats and coats.   By the side*

**du porte-habits est une grande glace.   De l'autre côté il y a une**
dęę port-ah-bee ay-tęęn graNd glahs.   de lohtr koh-tay eel-yah ęęn
*of the hall-stand is a large mirror.   On the other side is a*

**petite table avec l'appareil téléphonique.   Un fauteuil est près**
p'teet tahbl ah-vaik lah-pah-raiy tay-lay-foh-neek.   uN foh-tāŷy ay pray
*small table with the telephone apparatus.   An armchair is near*

**de la table.   Au milieu du vestibule sur le plancher est un**
de lah tahbl.   oh meel-yāŷ dęę vais-tee-bęęl sęęr le plaN-shay ai-tuN
*the table.   In the middle of the hall on the floor is a*

**tapis-brosse.   Au fond nous voyons une porte qui donne dans la**
tah-pee bros.   oh foN noo vwa-yoN ęęn port kee don daN la
*mat.   In the rear we see a door which leads into the*

**salle à manger.   Cette porte est à demi ouverte.   À droite est une autre**
sah-lah maN-zhay.   sait port ait ah de-mee oo-vairt.   ah drwaht-ay-tęę-nohtr
*dining-room.   This door is half open.   To the right is another*

**porte, qui donne dans un petit salon.  Elle est fermée.  Au fond**
port kee don daN-zuN p'tee sah-loN.  elle ay fair-may.  oh foN
*door which leads into a small sitting-room.  It is shut.  In the rear*

**à droite nous voyons l'escalier qui mène au premier étage.**
ah drwaht noo vwah-yoN lais-kahl-yay kee mai-noh pr'myay-ray-tahzh.
*to the right we see a staircase which leads to the first floor.*

**Dans le vestibule il y a deux personnes.  Un visiteur**
daN le vais-tee-bēēl eel-yah dāȳ pair-son.  uN vee-zee-tāȳr
*In the hall there are two persons.  A visitor*

**qui ôte son pardessus et une jeune dame qui met son chapeau.**
kee oht soN par-de-sēē ay ēēn zhāȳn dahm kee mai soN shah-poh.
*who is taking off his overcoat and a young lady who is putting on her hat.*

**C'est une Anglaise qui donne des leçons d'anglais à Georges Lesage**
sai-tēē-naN-glaiz kee don day l'soN daN-glai ah zhorzh le-sahzh
*It's an Englishwoman who gives lessons in English to Georges Lesage*

**deux fois par semaine.**
dāȳ fwah pahr s'main.
*twice a week.*

### LES JARDINS ET PALAIS DU LUXEMBOURG
Pour les jeunes amateurs de yachts en miniature, les bassins du Luxembourg parmi les pelouses fleuries des jardins constituent un paradis à deux pas de chez eux.

| **Amateur-trice** (m.f.) | **yacht** (m.) **en miniature** | **bassin** (m.) | **paradis** (m.) **terrestre** |
|---|---|---|---|
| Lover, amateur | model yacht | pond | earthly paradise |

## "OLD" AND "NEW"

| | |
|---|---|
| le vieux monsieur (vyay͡) | the old gentleman |
| la vieille dame (vyaiy) | the old lady |
| le vieil oncle (vyaiy) | the old uncle |
| le nouveau fauteuil (noo-voh) | the new armchair |
| la nouvelle saison (noo-vail) | the new season |
| le nouvel an (noo-vail) | the new year |

These two adjectives, besides having an irregular feminine, have a special form when used before masculine singular nouns beginning with a vowel or h mute. This special liaison form is similar to the feminine form of these two adjectives.

There are a few other adjectives which also have a special masculine singular liaison form : beau (*fem.* belle) = beautiful becomes bel before a masculine noun beginning with a vowel or h mute; un bel hôtel = a beautiful hotel.

Ce (*fem.* cette) meaning "this" or "that" becomes cet before a masculine noun beginning with a vowel or h mute; cet enfant = this (or that) child ; cet hôtel = this (or that) hotel.

## TO PLAY, TO TAKE OFF, TO GO DOWN, TO GO UP, TO SLEEP, TO PUT (ON)

jouer = *to play*, ôter = *to take off*, monter = *to go up*, are regular verbs and their forms can be ascertained by examining the construction of other regular verbs (*see page 50*).

| descendre = *to go down* | mettre = *to put* | dormir = *to sleep* |
|---|---|---|
| je descends (dais-saN) | je mets (may) | je dors (dor) |
| il elle }descend (dais-saN) | il elle }met (may) | il elle }dort (dor) |
| nous descendons (dais-saN-doN) | nous mettons (mai-toN) | nous dormons (dor-moN) |
| vous descendez (dais-saN-day) | vous mettez (mai-tay) | vous dormez (dor-may) |
| ils elles }descendent (dais-saNd) | ils elles }mettent (mait) | ils elles }dorment (dorm) |

Note.—mettre means both *to put* and *to put on* (*clothes*) : Mettez les fleurs dans ce vase = *Put the flowers into that vase*; Mettez vos gants = *Put on your gloves*.

## EXERCISES

### I Answer in French

1. Où est la villa de la famille Lesage? 2. Combien de pièces a-t-elle? 3. Où est la salle à manger? 4. Quelles pièces sont au premier étage? 5. Où est la salle de bain? 6. Qu'est-ce qu'il y a au-dessus du deuxième étage? 7. Qu'y a-t-il au-dessous du rez-de-chaussée? 8. Qu'est-ce qui est devant la maison? 9. Où y a-t-il des légumes et des fruits? 10. Où dorment les enfants? 11. Où le maître de la maison écrit-il ses lettres? 12. Où met-on le charbon? 13. Où est le téléphone? 14. Quelle porte est ouverte? 15. Qui est dans le vestibule? 16. Que fait le monsieur? 17. Que fait la vieille dame? 18. Qui est-elle? 19. Prenez-vous des leçons de français? 20. Où est l'escalier?

### II Add the correct ending

1. Je ne parl- pas. 2. Ne dorm- vous pas? 3. Il ôt- son chapeau. 4. Nous ne descend- pas. 5. Ils dorm-. 6. Que dit- vous? 7. Elles ne vienn- pas. 8. Ne fait- pas cela. 9. Je dor-. 10. Elle arriv-.

### III Translate into French

1. Where do you live? 2. Is it far from here? 3. How many rooms has your house? 4. Is there a bathroom in his house? 5. On what floor is the nursery? 6. It is on the second floor. 7. Your trunks are in the loft. 8. You have beautiful flower-beds in your garden, haven't you ? 9. Have you got vegetables in your garden? 10. You only have a few flowers. 11. Is this child asleep? 12. Let us go down into the cellar. 13. The kitchen is near the dining room. 14. The dining room is to the left. 15. The telephone is to the right by the side of the hall-stand.

(*Key to* I, II *and* III *on page* 151).

# ONZIÈME LEÇON—*ELEVENTH LESSON*

### IN THE LESAGE SITTING ROOM

It all *looks* quite straightforward, but our artist has again introduced several deliberate errors as compared with the text below. How many can you find after reading the French text only? For answer see bottom of page 138.

**Nous voici dans le salon de la famille Lesage.   À gauche nous**
noo vwah-see daN le sah-loN de lah fah-meey le-sahzh.   ah gohsh noo
*We are here in the sitting room of the Lesage family.   On the left we*

**voyons le foyer et au-dessus de la cheminée une grande glace.   Sur**
vwah-yoN le fwah-yay ay oh d'sṻ de la sh'mee-nay ṻn graNd glahs.   sṻr
*see the fireplace and over the mantelpiece a large mirror.   On*

**la cheminée est une pendule.   Elle est en marbre.   Devant**
la sh'mee-nay ay-tṻn paN-dṻl.   ai-lay-taN mahrbr.   de-vaN
*the mantelpiece is a clock.   It is (made) of marble.   In front of*

**le foyer est un fauteuil.   Le grand-père est assis ; il fume,**
le fwah-yay ai-tuN foh tṻy.   le graN paɪr ee ay tah-see eel fṻm.
*the fireplace is an easy chair.   Grandfather is sitting ; he is smoking.*

**À côté de la cheminée est un secrétaire.   Mme Lesage est assise devant.**
ah koh-tay de lah sh'mee-nay ay-tuN se kray-tair.   mah-dahm L. ai-tah-seez de vaN.
*By the side of the fire-place is a bureau.   Mrs. Lesage is sitting in front of it.*

**Elle écrit une lettre à sa sœur qui est en Amérique.   Au fond**
ai-lay-kree-t&#234;&#234;n laitr ah sah s&#226;&#375;r kee ay-tah-nah-may-reek.   oh foN
*She is writing a letter to her sister who is in America.   In the rear*

**du salon est une porte-fenêtre.   C'est la porte du balcon.   À droite nous**
d&#234;&#234; sah-loN ay -t&#234;&#234;n port-f'naitr.   say lah port d&#234;&#234; bahl-koN.   ah drwaht noo
*of the sitting-room is a window-door.   It is the balcony door.   On the right we*

**voyons la bibliothèque.   M. Lesage est debout devant la**
vwah-yoN lah beeb-lyoh-taik.   m'ssy&#226;&#375; l'sahzh ay de-boo de-vaN lah
*see the bookcase.   M. Lesage is standing in front of the*

**bibliothèque, lisant un livre.   À côté de la bibliothèque dans**
beeb-lyoh-taik leezaN-tuN leevr.   ah koh-tay de lah beeb-lyoh-taik daN
*bookcase, reading a book.   By the side of the bookcase in*

**un coin est une niche.   Il y a un canapé.   Georges est assis dessus.**
zuN kwiN ay-t&#234;&#234;n neesh.   eel-yah uN kah-nah-pay.   zhorzh ay-tahsee des-s&#234;&#234;.
*a corner is a recess.   There is a sofa.   George is sitting there.*

**De l'autre côté de la bibliothèque est une table à ouvrage,**
de lohtr koh-tay de lah beeb-lyoh-taik ay-t&#234;&#234;n tahb-lah oov-rahzh
*On the other side of the bookcase is a work table,*

**devant laquelle la grand'mère est assise ; elle reprise.   Au milieu de la**
de-vaN lah-kail lah graN mair ay tah-sees ail reprees.   oh meel-y&#226;&#375; de
*in front of which the grand-mother is sitting ; she is darning.   In the middle of*

**chambre est une table ronde, sur laquelle sont un album de photos,**
lah shaNbr ay-t&#234;&#234;n tahbl roNd s&#234;&#234;r lah-kail soN uN ahl-bom de foh-toh
*the room is a round table on which are an album of photos,*

**un vase de fleurs et un portrait.   Devant cette table est un piano.**
uN vahz de fl&#226;&#375;r ay uN por-trai.   de-vaN sait tahbl ay-tuN pyah-noh.
*a vase of flowers and a portrait.   In front of that table is a piano.*

**Mlle Lucie est assise sur un tabouret; elle joue du piano.   Dans le coin**
Mlle L&#234;&#234;-see ay-tah-seez s&#234;&#234;r uN tah-boorayt ail zhoo d&#234;&#234; pyah-noh.   daN le kwiN
*Miss Lucie is sitting on a stool ; she is playing the piano.   In the corner*

**à gauche de la porte est un guéridon sur lequel il y a un appareil**
ah gohsh de lah port ai-tuN gay-ree-doN s&#234;&#234;r le-kail eel-yah uN ah-pah-raiy
*to the left of the door is a small table on which there is a wireless*

**de T.S.F.   La famille écoute souvent, surtout de la musique de Londres.**
de tay ais aif.   lah fah-meey ay-koot soo-vaN s&#234;&#234;r-too de lah m&#234;&#234;-zeek de loNdr.
*set.   The family listens in often, especially to music from London.*

**Sur le plancher du salon est un tapis et au plafond au dessus du**
s&#234;&#234;r le plaN-shay d&#234;&#234; sah-loN ay-tuN tah-pee ay oh plah-foN oh dai-s&#234;&#234; d&#234;&#234;
*On the floor of the sitting-room is a carpet and on the ceiling over the*

piano il y a un lustre.   Le chien est couché devant le foyer.   Il
pyah-noh eel-yah uN lḙ̃str.   le shyiN ai koo-shay de-vaN le fwah-yay.   eel
*piano there is a chandelier.   The dog is lying in front of the fireplace.   He is*

dort.   Sur les murs du salon il y a plusieurs tableaux.
dor.   sḙ̃r lay mḙ̃r dḙ̃ sah-loN eel-yah plḙ̃z-yãyr tahb-loh.
*asleep.   On the walls of the sitting room there are several pictures.*

### OBJECTS IN THE SITTING ROOM

| le guéridon | un appareil de T.S.F.[1] | la cheminée | la pendule |
|---|---|---|---|
| gay-ree-doN | ah-pah-raiy de tay ais aif | she-mee-nay | paN-dḙ̃l |
| *small round table* | *wireless set* | *fire-place* | *clock* |

| le fauteuil | le secrétaire | la porte-fenêtre | la fenêtre | le rideau |
|---|---|---|---|---|
| foh-tãyy | se-kray-tair | port f'naitr | f'naitr | ree-doh |
| *easy chair* | *bureau* | *window-door (French window)* | *window* | *curtain* |

| le store | la niche | la bibliothèque | la table à ouvrage | une table ronde |
|---|---|---|---|---|
| stohr | neesh | beeb-lyoh-taik | tahbl ah oov-rahzh | tahbl roNd |
| *window-blind* | *recess* | *book-case* | *work-table* | *round table* |

| un album à photos | le vase de fleurs | le piano | le tabouret | un album de musique |
|---|---|---|---|---|
| ahlbom ah foh-toh | vahz de flãyr | pyah-noh | tah-boo-raiy | ahl-bom de mḙ̃zeek |
| *photo-album* | *vase with flowers* | *piano* | *stool* | *book of music* |

| le tapis | le tableau | le canapé | le coussin | le lustre |
|---|---|---|---|---|
| tah-pee | tahb-loh | kah-nah-pay | koo-siN | lḙ̃str |
| *carpet* | *picture* | *sofa* | *cushion* | *chandelier* |

[1] **Télégraphie sans fil** = telegraphy without wire

SEPT PONTS DE PARIS
Une vue panoramique du Paris fluvial, prise des toitures de l'Hôtel de Ville.   **En arrière-plan**, cette Tour Eiffel célèbre, symbole de Paris, s'estompe à l'horizon.

| **Fluvial-e** (adj.) | **toiture** (f.) | **en arrière-plan** | **s'estomper** |
|---|---|---|---|
| Riverside | roof | in the background | to loom up |

Cover over the English lines below and see if with the help of the picture you can translate the French sentences.  Later you can check the number of errors made.

### REST AND MOVEMENT

| | | | | |
|---|---|---|---|---|
| 1. | il est assis | ay-tah-see | | *he is sitting* |
| 2. | elle est assise | ay-tah-seez | | *she is sitting* |
| 3. | il est debout | ay de-boo | | *he is standing* |
| 4. | elle est debout | ay de-boo | | *she is standing* |
| 5. | le chien est couché | shyiN ay koo-shay | | *the dog is lying* |
| 6. | la petite fille est couchée | p'teet feey ay koo-shay | | *the little girl is lying* |
| 7. | il entre | aNtr | | *he is coming in* |
| 8. | elle sort | sor | | *she is going out* |
| 9. | il est à genoux | ay-tah zh'noo | | *he is on his knees* |
| 10. | elle marche | mahrsh | | *she is walking* |
| 11. | il court | koor | | *he is running* |

### CLOCKS AND WATCHES

**Une pendule est plus grande qu'une montre.   Un bracelet-montre est plus petit**
ēēn paN-dēēl ay plēē graNd kēēn moNtr. uN brahs-lai moNtr ay plēē p'tee
*A clock is bigger than a watch.   A wrist-watch is smaller*

**qu'une montre que nous portons dans la poche.   Une montre est en or,**
kēēn moNtr ke noo portoN daN lah posh. ēēn moNtr ayt-ah-nor
*than a watch which we carry in the pocket.   A watch is (made) of gold,*

**en argent, en nickel ou en acier.   Une pendule est en bois, en marbre**
ah-nahr-zhaN aN nee-kail oo ah-nahs-yay. ēēn paN-dēēl ay-taN bwah aN mahrbr
*of silver, of nickel or of steel.   A clock is (made) of wood, marble*

| une montre | un bracelet-montre | une pendule | un réveil |
| moNtr | brahs-lait moNtr | paN-dẽẽl | uN ray-vaiy |

**ou en bronze. Un réveil n'est pas aussi grand qu'une pendule, que nous**
oo aN broNz.  uN ray-vaiy nai pah-zo-see graN kẽẽn paN-dẽẽl ke noo
*or of bronze.  An alarm clock is not as big as a clock which we*

**mettons sur la cheminée ou contre le mur.  Ma montre va très bien.  Elle**
mai-toN sẽẽr lah she-mee-nay oo koNtr le mẽẽr. mah moNtr vah trai byiN. ail
*put on the mantelpiece or against the wall.  My watch goes very well.  It*

**n'avance ni ne retarde.  Dans notre salon il y a une pendule qui ne marche**
nah-vaNs nee ne re-tahrd.  daN notr sah-loN eel-yah ẽẽn paN-dẽẽl kee ne
*is neither fast nor slow.  In our sitting-room there is a clock which does*

**pas.  Elle est arrêtée, parce qu'elle n'est pas remontée.**
mahrsh pah.  ai-lay-tah-rai-tay pahrs kail nay pah re-moN-tay.
*not go.  It has stopped, because it is not wound up.*

**Voici la clef pour la remonter.**
vwah-see lah klay poor lah re-moN-tay.
*Here is the key to wind it up.*

| trois heures précises | trois heures moins dix | trois heures cinq |
| trwah-zãyr pray-sees | trwah-zãyr mwiN deez | trwah-zãyr siNk |

| l'heure exacte | la montre retarde | la montre avance |
| lãyr aixahkt | lah moNtr re-tahrd | lah moNtr ah-vaNs |
| *the right time* | *the watch is slow* | *the watch is fast* |

## INSIDE A FRENCH KITCHEN
*(See page 12 for notes*

### English

1. Saucepan; 2. Frying-pan; 3. Grid-iron; 4. Stove-pipe; 5. Plates; 6. Plate-rack; 7. Cutlery : spoons, forks, knives ; 8. Carving-knife; 9. Tin-opener; 10. Gas-stove; 11. Kitchen range; 12. Ingredients (rice, sugar, cloves, pepper, salt, raisins, olive oil, yeast, etc.); 13. Kitchen-sink; 14. Refrigerator; 15. Gas-oven; 16. Kettle; 17. Serving-hatch; 18. Tray; 19. Flour-bin; 20. Bread-bin; 21. Coffee-mill; 22. Coffee-pot; 23. Kitchen-table; 24. Gas-tap; 25. Corkscrew; 26. Steamer; 27. Double-saucepan; 28. Chef, male cook; 29. Stock-pot; 30. Dresser; 31. Rolling-pin; 32. Female cook; apron; 33. Fish-slice; 34. Dish-cloth; 35. Overalls ; (chef's cap); 36. Tap-water.

### French

1. Casserole (*f.*); 2. Poêle (*f.*) à frire; 3. Gril(*m.*); 4. Tuyau(*m.*) de poêle; 5. Assiettes (*f.pl.*); 6. Porte-assiettes; 7. Couvert (*m.*):

| Further Useful Expressions | mijoter | œufs (m.pl.) sur le plat | moudre le café |
|---|---|---|---|
| | to simmer | fried eggs | to grind coffee |

## DANS UNE CUISINE FRANÇAISE
*on how to use this picture).*

cuillères (*f. pl.*), fourchettes (*f. pl.*) couteaux (*m. pl.*); 8. Couteau à découper; 9. Ouvre-boîtes (*m. inv.*); 10, Fourneau (*m.*) à gaz; 11. Fourneau de cuisine; 12. Ingrédients : riz (*m.*); sucre (*m.*); clous (*m. pl.*) de girofle; poivre (*m.*); sel (*m.*); raisins (*m. pl.*) secs; huile (*f.*) d'olive; levure (*f.*) etc. 13. évier (*m.*) de cuisine; 14. Appareil (*m.*) frigorifique (*fam.* "*frigo*"); 15 Four (*m.*) à gaz; 16. Bouilloire (*f.*); 17. Passe-plats (*m. inv.*); 18. Plateau (*m.*); 19.

Farinière (*f.*); 20. Huche (*f.*) au pain; 21. Moulin (*m.*) à café; 22. Cafetière (*f.*); 23. Table (*f.*) de cuisine; 24. Robinet (*m.*) à gaz; 25. Tirebouchon (*m.*); 26. Marmite (*f.*) à vapeur; 27. Bain-marie (*m.*) (*pl.* bains-marie); 28. Chef de cuisine (cuisinier); 29. Pot-au-feu (*m.*); 30. Armoire (*f.*); 31. Rouleau (*m.*); 32. Cuisinière (*f.*); tablier (*m.*); 33. Truelle (*f.*) à poisson; 34. Torchon (*m.*); 35. Blouse (*f.*); (bonnet, *m.*); 36 Eau (*f.*) de la ville.

| **faire la vaiselle** | **rôtir; cuire au four** | **bouillir** | **griller** | **assaisonner** |
|---|---|---|---|---|
| to wash up | to roast | to boil | to grill | to season |

**TO SEE, TO LISTEN, TO READ, TO WRITE, TO ENTER, TO GO OUT**

**écouter**=*to listen* and **entrer**=*to enter* are regular verbs.

| **voir**=*to see* | **lire**=*to read* | **écrire**=*to write* | **sortir**=*to go out* |
|---|---|---|---|
| je **vois**  vwah | **lis**  lee | j'**écris**  ay-kree | **sors**  sor |
| il }  **voit**  vwah | **lit**  lee | **écrit**  ay-kree | **sort**  sor |
| elle | | | |
| nous **voyons**  vwahyoN | **lisons**  lee-zoN | **écrivons**  ay-kree-voN | **sortons**  sor-toN |
| vous **voyez**  vwah-yay | **lisez**  lee-zay | **écrivez**  ay-kree-vay | **sortez**  sor-tay |
| ils }  **voient**  vwah | **lisent**  leez | **écrivent**  ay-kreev | **sortent**  sort |
| elles | | | |

**COMPARISONS**

**Ce chien est grand**

**Ce chien est plus grand**

**Ce chien est le plus grand**

Ce chien est petit

**Ce chien est plus petit**

Ce chien est le plus petit

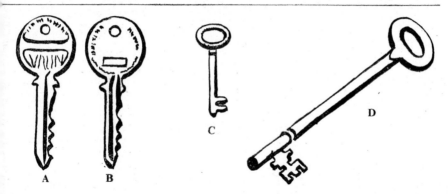

A          B          C          D

1. La clef (klay) A est aussi grande que la clef B.

2. La clef C n'est pas si grande que les clefs A et B.
La clef C est moins (mwiN) grande que les clefs A et B.

3. La clef D est plus grande que les clefs A et B.
La clef D est la plus grande de ces clefs.

4. La clef C est la moins grande (la plus petite) de ces clefs.

Note.—(1) Whereas in English there are two ways of expressing the Comparative degree of Adjectives, i.e., either by adding "-er" or by the use of "more", in French only the latter method is used; **Il est plus grand que vous**=He is taller than you.

(2) With a negative **aussi** becomes **si** :
**Il est aussi grand que vous**=He is as tall as you.

Il n'est pas si grand que vous=He is not so tall as you.

**EITHER . . . OR ; NEITHER . . . NOR**

1. **Ou vous entrez ou vous sortez**=You either come in or go out.

2. **Il ne mange ni ne boit**=He neither eats nor drinks.

3. **Nous allons ou au bord de la mer ou à la campagne**=We go either to the sea-side or to the country.

4. **Ils ne sont ni à la maison ni au jardin**= They are neither in the house nor in the garden.

5. **Il n'est ni trop intelligent ni trop stupide** =He is neither too intelligent nor too stupid.

Note (1) Either . . . or . . .=**ou . . . ou . . .**

(2) Neither . . . nor . . . is **ne . . . ni, ne . . .** in connection with verbs (Example 2) and **ne . . . ni . . . ni . . .** in connection with nouns or adjectives (Examples 4 and 5).

## EXERCISES

**I  Answer these Questions in French**

1. Quelles personnes sont dans le salon? 2. Que fait M. Lesage? 3. Que fait Mme Lesage? 4. Qui joue du piano? 5. Combien de personnes y a-t-il dans le salon? 6. Que font le grand-père et la grand'mère? 7. Qu'y a-t-il sur la cheminée? 8. Où est le canapé? 9. Georges est-il debout? 10. Qui n'est pas assis? 11. Qu'est-ce qui est au milieu de la chambre? 12. Y a-t-il un secré-taire dans ce salon? 13. Où est-il? 14. Avez-vous une montre? 15. Quelle heure est-il? 16. Votre montre est-elle remontée? 17. Votre pendule avance-t-elle? 18. La table est-elle plus grande que la chaise? 19. La fenêtre est-elle aussi large que le mur? 20. Écrivez-vous beaucoup de lettres? 21. Lisez-vous beaucoup?

**II  Translate into French**

1. Do you see my grandfather? **2.** He is sitting in the garden. 3. Is she standing

or sitting? 4. Do you play the piano? 5. I don't play, but I often listen, especially to music from Wagner. 6. Is your watch made of gold? 7. No, it is made of silver. 8. My alarm clock is smaller than your clock, which is on the mantelpiece. 9. My watch has stopped. 10. Please listen, don't read. 11. What are you writing? 12. A letter to my mother, who is in France.

### III

Translate the questions, and say or write down several answers to the questions which can be derived from the following substitution tables. (*Key to* I, II & III *on pages* 151 *and* 152).

| 1) Est-ce-que | vous êtes | plus | jeune | que | votre frère? |
|---|---|---|---|---|---|
| | je suis | moins | âgé | | mon oncle? |
| | mon frère est | | grand | | notre cousin? |
| | etc. | | petit | | sa tante? |
| | | | fort | | etc. |
| | | | mince | | |
| | | | etc. | | |

| 2) Est-ce qu'il fait | plus | chaud | au printemps | qu' | en hiver? |
|---|---|---|---|---|---|
| | moins | froid | en été | | en automne? |
| | | | en automne | | en été? |
| | | | en hiver | | au printemps? |

| 3) Est-ce que les jours les | plus | beaux | sont | au printemps? |
|---|---|---|---|---|
| | moins | mauvais | | en été? |
| | | longs | | en automne? |
| | | courts | | en hiver? |

### DANS LA BEAUCE

Cette plaine dorée de la Beauce—ce grenier de la France—encore bordée des beaux épis de blé qui l'ont rendue célèbre, est située entre la Seine et la Loire.

| **Doré** | **le grenier** | **épi** (m.) | **le blé** |
|---|---|---|---|
| golden | granary | ear (of corn) | corn |

# DOUZIÈME LEÇON—*TWELFTH LESSON*

## CHARLES SAYS GOODNIGHT

How many objects in the room can you name in French? For key see page 125.

**Charles :  Je suis très fatigué.**            **Je vais me coucher.**
  zhe swee trai fah-tee-gay.          zhe vai me koo-shay.
  *I am very tired.*                   *I am going to bed.*

**Charles était très fatigué, parce qu'il n'avait pas dormi de toute la nuit.**
shahrl ay-tai trai fah-tee-gay, pahrs keel nah-vai pah dor-mee de toot la nŵee.
*Charles was very tired because he had not slept the whole night.*

**La famille Lesage insiste pour que Charles reste chez eux pour la nuit.  Georges**
lah fah-meey le-sahzh iN-seest poor ke shahrl raist shay-zaŷ poor lah nŵee.  zhorzh
*The Lesage family insists that Charles stays with them for the night.  George*

**partage sa chambre avec lui,**
pahr-tahzh sah shaNbr ah-vaik lŵee.
*shares his room with him.*

**Mme Roberts, avant d'aller à son hôtel, a dit à Charles de ne pas**
Mme Robairts ah-vaN dah-lay ah so-noh-tail ah dee ah shahrl de ne pah
*Mrs. Roberts, before going (lit., to go) to her hotel, has told (lit., said to) Charles not*

**oublier de se laver.**
zoo-blee-ay de se lah-vay.
*to forget to wash himself.*

### PARIS : PORT DE MER (I)

Amarrés dans un bras pittoresque de la Seine, à l'ombre de beaux arbres, ces chalands attendent qu'on les forme en convoi. Pour les mariniers, ce recoin si calme constitue "*leur*" Paris, où, là, ils sont contents.

| **Amarré** (adj.) | **bras** (m.) | **chaland** (m.) | **marinier** (m.) | **recoin** (m.) |
|---|---|---|---|---|
| Anchored, made fast | arm | barge | bargee | nook, recess |

## PARIS : PORT DE MER (II)

Ces péniches, poursuivant lentement leur chemin en aval, relient la métropole à la mer, par Rouen et Le Havre. Les péniches sont tantôt formées en convoi que hale un remorqueur, et tantôt mues de leurs propres moyens.

| **Péniche** (f.) **à moteur** | **en aval** | **remorqueur** (m.) | **mues de leurs propres moyens** |
|---|---|---|---|
| Motor barge | downstream | tug | moved by their own power |

**Mme Lesage :**  **Bonne nuit, Charles, dormez bien.**
bon nŵee shahrl dor-may byiN.
*Good night, Charles, sleep well.*

**Georges :**  **N'oubliez pas de vous laver.   Vous l'avez promis à votre**
nooblyay pah de voo lah-vay.   voo lah-vay pro-mee ah votr
*Don't forget to wash yourself.   You (it) have promised to your*
**mère, vous savez.   Charles : Sans blague !**
mair voo sah-vay.            saN blahg !
*mother, you know.           You don't say so ! (lit., without kidding)*

**M. Lesage :**  **Est-ce que vous voulez être réveillé demain matin de bonne heure?**
aisk' voo voo-lay-zaitr ray-vai-yay d'miN mah-tiN de bo-nâyr?
*Do you want to be called in the morning early?*[1]

**Charles :**  **Je veux me lever à sept heures.   J'ai beaucoup à faire.**
zhe vâŷ me le-vay ah sai-tâŷr.   zhay boh-koo pah fair.
*I want to get up at seven o'clock.   I have a lot to do.*

**M. Lesage :**  **Vraiment?     Mme L. : Qu'est-ce que vous avez à faire, Charles?**
vrai-maN?        kaisk' voo-zah-vay ah fair shahrl?
*Really?         What have you got to do, Charles?*

**Charles :**  **Voir Paris ; les monuments, les musées, les parcs,**
vwahr pah-ree lay mo-nêêmaN lay mêêzay lay pahrk
*See Paris; the monuments, the museums, the parks,*
**enfin tout ce qui est intéressant.**
aN-fiN toos' kee ai-tiN-tay-rai-saN.
*in short everything that is interesting.*

**M. Lesage :**  **`À la bonne heure.**     **Charles : Alors bonne nuit tout le monde.**
ah lah bo-nâŷr.                 ah-lor bon nŵee too le mond.
*That's right.*[2]               *Good night then everybody (lit.,*
                                  *all the world).*

**Charles se lave le cou.**
shahrl se lahv le coo
*Charles is washing his neck.*

---

[1] Lit. " in good time ".     [2] **à la bonne heure** is a frequently used expression, meaning " that's good ", " that's right ", " all right ".

## TO WASH, TO GET UP, TO LIE DOWN

**laver** = *to wash*

**se laver** = *to wash oneself*

**je me lave**   lahv = *I wash myself*

**il se lave**   lahv = *he washes himself*

**elle se lave**   lahv = *she washes herself*

**nous nous lavons**   lah-voN = *we wash ourselves*

**vous vous lavez**   lah-vay = *you wash yourself* (-ves)

**ils (elles) se lavent**   lahv = *they wash themselves*

**lavez-vous** = *wash yourself!*

**lavons-nous** = *let us wash ourselves!*

**laver** by itself means either to wash somebody else or to do some washing. Whereas in English " I wash " is used also in the meaning of " I wash myself ", the latter form in French is **je me lave** ; "you wash (yourself) ", etc., as above.

A verb like " to wash oneself " is called a reflexive verb, i.e., one in which the action is done by yourself and to yourself. Many verbs are reflexive in French which are not in English.

**se lever** = *to get up*

**je me**
**il se**   **lève** laiv   *I am getting up ; I get up*
**elle se**

**nous nous levons**   l'voN

**vous vous levez**   l'vay

**ils**
**elles**   **se lèvent**   laiv

**levez-vous** = *get up!*

**levons-nous** = *let us get up!*

**se coucher** = *to lie down, to go to bed*

**je me**
**il se**   **couche** koosh   *I am lying down, I lie down*
**elle se**

**nous nous couchons**   koo-shoN

**vous vous couchez**   koo-shay

**ils**
**elles**   **se couchent**   koosh

**couchez-vous** = *lie down!*

**couchons-nous** = *let us lie down!*

**je ne me lève pas** = *I don't get up; I am not getting up*

**vous levez-vous ?** = *are you getting up? do you get up?*

**je ne me couche pas** = *I don't lie down; I am not lying down*

**vous couchez-vous?** = *are you lying down? do you lie down?*

## I HAD, I WAS, I SPOKE, I PUT, I WASHED

*I had, I was having*
**j'avais**   ah-vai

**il**
**elle**   **avait**   ah-vai

**nous avions**   ahv-yoN
**vous aviez**   ahv-yai

**ils**
**elles**   **avaient**   ah-vai

*I was, I was being*
**j'étais**   ay-tai

**il**
**elle**   **était**   ay-tai

**nous étions**   ayt-yoN
**vous étiez**   ayt-yay

**ils**
**elles**   **étaient**   ay-tai

*I spoke, I was speaking*
**je parlais**   pahr-lai

**il**
**elle**   **parlait**   pahr-lai

**nous parlions**   pahrl-yoN
**vous parliez**   pahrl-yay

**ils**
**elles**   **parlaient**   pahr-lai

*I put, I was putting*
**je mettais**   mai-tai

**il**
**elle**   **mettait**   mai-tai

**nous mettions**   mait-yoN
**vous mettiez**   mait-yay

**ils**
**elles**   **mettaient**   mai-tai

*I washed, I was washing* (*myself*)
**je me lavais**   lah-vai

**il**
**elle**   **se lavait**   lah-vai

**nous nous lavions**   lahv-yoN
**vous vous laviez**   lahv-yay

**ils**
**elles**   **se lavaient**   lah-vai

## PERFECT AND IMPERFECT

The perfect in French denotes not only what has happened (as the English perfect does), but also what happened. In everyday language it is the tense most frequently used to denote a past event. But when states and conditions in the past are described the Imperfect is used, which is also the tense used to denote habitual or repeated action.

Study the following examples very carefully :

**Perfect.** (1) What has happened.

**J'ai fini ma leçon.**
> *I have finished my lesson.*

**Où avez-vous mis votre chapeau?**
> *Where have you put your hat?*

**A-t-il écrit?** *Has he written?*

(2) What happened

**Je l'ai vu il y a trois mois.**
> *I saw him three months ago.*

**À quelle heure avez-vous dîné hier?**
> *At what time did you have dinner yesterday?*

**Qu'est-ce qu'il a dit?** *What did he say?*

**Imperfect.** (1) What was (description)

**Il faisait froid.** *It was cold.*

**C'était une femme âgée.**
> *It was an old woman.*

**Le soleil brillait, les oiseaux chantaient.**
> *The sun was shining, the birds were singing.*

(2) What used to happen (habitual or repeated action)

**Il se couchait tard.**
> *He used to go to bed late.*

**Nous nous levions toujours à six heures.**
> *We used to get up always at six o'clock.*

(3) What was going on when something else happened. .

**Il écrivait pendant que je lisais.**
> *He was writing while I was reading.*

## ARTICLES IN A BEDROOM

| | | | | | |
|---|---|---|---|---|---|
| **le rideau** | **le store** | **le divan** | **le lit** | **la couverture** | **l'édredon** (m.) |
| ree-doh | stohr | dee-vaN | lee | koo-vair-tẽer | ay-dre-doN |
| *curtain* | *window blind* | *couch* | *bed* | *blanket* | *quilt* |

| | | | |
|---|---|---|---|
| **le mate!as** | **le drap de lit** | **l'oreiller** (m.) | **le traversin** |
| mah-te-lah | drah de lee | oh-rai-yay | trah-vair-siN |
| *mattress* | *sheet* | *pillow* | *bolster* |

| | | | |
|---|---|---|---|
| **la descente de lit** | **la pantoufle** | **la table de nuit** | **la lampe de chevet** |
| dais-saNt de lee | paN-toofl | tahbl de n(w)ee | laNp de sh'vay |
| *(bedside) rug* | *slipper* | *bedside table* | *bedside lamp* |

| | | | | |
|---|---|---|---|---|
| **la prise de courant** | **le réveil** | **une armoire** | **la glace** | **le vaporisateur** |
| preez de koo-raN | ray-vail | ahr-mwahr | glahs | vah-poh-ree-zah-t(ay)r |
| *plug* | *alarm-clock* | *wardrobe* | *mirror* | *scent spray* |

| | | | | |
|---|---|---|---|---|
| **le poudrier** | **la houpette** | **la brosse** | **le peigne** | **le tiroir** |
| pood-ryay | oo-pait | bros | pain*y* | tee-rwahr |
| *powder-box* | *powder-puff* | *brush* | *comb* | *drawer* |

In the portion of the Lesage sitting-room shown on page 123 there is not "a large mirror" over the mantelpiece, but a painting (**peinture**, f.). M. Lesage is not seated at the bureau which is beside the fireplace. The bookcase, as shown in the picture, is really to the left of the fireplace, not on the right as stated, and M. Lesage is not standing in front of it "reading a book". The round table mentioned certainly has an album of photos upon it, but neither vase of flowers nor portrait; and further, since we are only shown a corner of the sitting-room, it cannot be "in the middle of the room", but should correctly be described as "near grandfather Lesage's armchair". The radio is not "on the left of the window-door", but is on the opposite side of the room.

## LUCIE LESAGE'S BEDROOM

The list on page 138 has given you the French names of almost all the objects in the room. Cover over the text and see how many of them you know.

**Ce tableau nous montre la chambre à coucher de Mlle Lesage.**
se tahb-loh noo moNtr lah shaNb-rah koo-shay de mahd-mwah-zail le-sahzh.
*This picture shows us the bedroom of Miss Lesage.*

**Elle a un grand lit confortable, qui est en bois.   À droite on peut**
ai-lah uN graN lee koN-for-tahbl kee ai-taN bwah.   ah drwah-toN pay
*She has a large comfortable bed, which is of wood.   On the right one can*

**voir la table de toilette avec une grande glace, devant laquelle**
vwahr lah tahbl de twah-lait ah-vaik ẽn graNd glahs de-vaN lah-kail
*see the dressing table with a large mirror, in front of which*

**elle passe beaucoup de temps chaque jour.   La table de toilette a**
ail pahs boh-koo de taN shahk zhoor.   lah tahbl de twah-lait ah
*she passes a lot of time every day.   The dressing table has*

**des tiroirs dans lesquels Mademoiselle met ses bijoux et ses**
day tee-rwahr daN lay-kail mahd-mwah-zail mai say bee-zhoo ay say-
*some drawers into which Mademoiselle puts her jewels and her*

**objets de toilette: ses brosses, ses peignes, ses boîtes à poudres, ses bâtons de rouge**
zob-zhay de twah-lait say bros say painy say bwaht-zah poodr say bahtoN de roozh
*articles of toilet: her brushes, her combs, her powder boxes, her lipsticks*

## PARIS QUI DANSE

Tandis qu'en haut un monde cosmopolite se divertit en regardant danser le cancan, en bas, dans un bal-musette du quartier de la Bastille, on danse avec entrain une valse-chaloupée aux sons d'un orchestre composé de violon et d'accordéon.

| Se divertir | bal-musette (m.) | entrain (m.) | valse-chaloupée (f.) |
|---|---|---|---|
| To amuse oneself | "shilling hop" | liveliness | apache-dance |

**et ses parfums.  De l'autre côté on voit une armoire**
ah say pahr-fuN.  de lohtr koh-tay oN vwah ēēnahr-mwahr
*and her perfumes.  At the other side one sees a cupboard*

**comprenant deux parties: la garde-robe, qui contient ses robes et une armoire**
koN-pre-naN dāy pahr-tee lah gahrd-rob kee koN-tyiN say rob ay ēēnahr-mwahr
*consisting of two parts:  the wardrobe, which contains her frocks and a linen*

**à linge avec beaucoup de rayons.  Près du lit il y a une**
ah liNzh ah-vaik boh-koo de ray-oN.  prai dēē lee eel-yah ēēn
*cupboard with many shelves.  Near the bed is a*

**petite table de chevet sur  laquelle se trouvent[1] un livre, une bonbonnière**
p'teet tahbl de sh'vai sēēr lah-kail se troov uN leevr ēēn boN-bon-yair
*small bedside table on which there are a book, a box of sweets*

**et un réveil.  Mlle Lesage aime lire dans son lit en mangeant**
ay uN ray-vaiy.  mahd-mwah-zail le-sahzh aim leer daN soN lee aN maN-zhaN
*and an alarm-clock.  Miss Lesage likes to read in her bed eating*

**des bonbons ou du chocolat.  Elle dit, que c'est plus agréable et moins**
day boN-boN oo dēē shoh-koh-lah.  ail dee ke sai plēē-zah-gray ahbl ay mwiN
*sweets or chocolate.  She says that it is more agreeable and less*

**dangereux que de fumer dans son lit, comme c'est l'habitude de**
daN-zhye-rāy ke de fēē-may daN soN lee kom sai lah-bee-tēēd de
*dangerous than to smoke in one's bed as it is the habit of*

**beaucoup de jeunes personnes de nos jours.**
boh-koo de zhāyn pair-son de noh zhoor.
*lots of young people nowadays (lit. of our days).*

**Elle lit dans son lit en mangeant des bonbons et du chocolat.**
ail lee daN soN lee aN maN-zhaN day boN-boN ay dēē shoh-koh-lah.
*She reads in her bed eating sweets and chocolate.*

---

[1] Lit. find themselves.

## EXERCISES

### I  Answer in French

1. Vous couchez-vous de bonne heure? 2. À quelle heure vous levez-vous? 3. Est-ce que Charles se couche à sept heures du soir? 4. Veut-il se lever à neuf heures du matin? 5. Qu'est qu'il veut faire? 6. Est-ce qu'il était très fatigué? 7. Vous lavez-vous dans la salle à manger? 8. Qu'est-ce que vous dites avant de vous coucher? 9. Lisez-vous dans votre lit? 10. Aimez-vous manger du chocolat?

### II  Translate into French

1. We get up at six o'clock. 2. Don't you go to bed early? 3. They don't wash in the bedroom. 4. You are going to bed at eight o'clock. 5. Are there any chairs in the bedroom? 6. Don't forget to wake me up. 7. He forgot. 8. They went to their hotel. 9. What did he have to do? 10. Everybody was asleep. 11. It was hot. 12. He did not want to wash before breakfast. 13. She was putting her jewels into the third drawer of her toilet table. 14. He liked to read in (his) bed. 15. You are getting up, aren't you?

### III  Put the following into the Imperfect Tense

1. Je suis malade. 2. Il ne reste pas à l'hôtel. 3. Elle a beaucoup d'argent. 4. Ils sont fatigués. 5. Nous avons faim. 6. Ils n'ont pas de chaises. 7. Est-ce que vous vous couchez? 8. Le train arrive. 9. Il fait beau. 10. Pourquoi mettez-vous les fleurs sur l'armoire? (*Key to* I, II *and* III *on page* 152).

### DANS LA CHARENTE

Armées de serpettes, ces braves paysannes de la Charente sont penchées sur les ceps de vigne pour les tailler.   La vendange de l'année prochaine s'annonce abondante.

| **Serpette** (f.) | **cep** (m.) | **tailler** | **vendange** (f.) |
|---|---|---|---|
| pruning-bill | vine-stock | to prune | vine-harvest |

# TREIZIÈME LEÇON

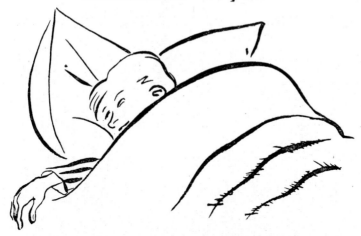

**Laissez-moi dormir.   Je ne veux pas encore me lever.**
lai-say mwah dor-meer.   zhe ne vay pah-zaN-kor me le-vay.
*Let me sleep.   I don't want yet to get up.*

## CHARLES GETS UP

Charles :   **Entendez-vous, Georges?**      Georges :   **Quoi?**
aN-taN-day voo zhorzh?                     kwah?
*Do you hear, George?*                      *What?*

Charles :   **On frappe à la porte.**        Georges :   **C'est mon père.**
oN frahp ah lah port.                       sai moN pair.
*Someone is knocking at the door.*          *It is my father.*

Charles :   **Pourquoi frappe-t-il?**         Georges :   **Pour me réveiller.**
poor-kwah frahp-teel?                        poor me ray-vai-yay.
*Why does he knock?*                         *To wake me.*

Charles :   **Quelle heure est-il?**          Georges :   **Il est sept heures.**
kai-layr ay-teel?                            ee-lay sai-tayr.
*What is the time?*                          *It is seven o'clock.*

Charles :   **Est-ce qu'il fait beau ce matin?**    Georges :   **Oui, il fait très beau.**
ais-keel fai boh se mah-tiN?                        wee eel fai trai boh.
*Is the weather fine this morning?*                  *Yes, it is very fine.*

**Le soleil brille.**      Charles :  **Avez-vous bien dormi, Georges?**
le so-laiy breey.          ah-vay voo byiN dor-mee zhorzh?
*The sun is shining.*       *Did you sleep well, George?*

Georges :   **Oui, merci, j'ai bien dormi.   Ne voulez-vous pas**
wee mair-see zhay byiN dor-mee.   ne voo-lay voo pah
*Yes, thank you, I have slept well.   Don't you want*

vous lever?
voo le-vay?
*to get up?*

**Charles :**   **Pas encore.  Je**
pah-zaN-kor. zhe
*Not yet.   I*

**ne suis pas pressé.**
ne sw͡ee pah prai-say.
*am not in a hurry.*

**Je suis en vacances.**
zhe sw͡ee-zaN vah-kaNs.
*I am on holiday.*

**Je n'ai pas besoin de me lever.**
zhe nai pah b'zwiN de me le-vay.
*I have no need to get up.*

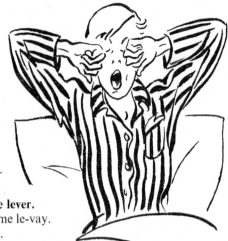

**Georges :**   **Mais hier vous avez dit que vous vouliez être réveillé**
mai yair voo-zah-vay dee ke voo voo-lyay-zaitr ray-vai-yay
*But yesterday you have said that you wanted to be called*

**de bonne heure.**      **Charles :  J'ai changé d'avis.   Il est si**
de bo-nãyr.                      zhay shaN-zhay dah-vee. ee-lai see
*early.*                           *I have changed my mind.   It is so*

**bon de rester au lit.**   **Georges :  Vous avez dit hier que**
boN de rais-tay oh lee.              voo-zah-vay dee yair ke
*good to stay in bed.*             · *You have said yesterday that*

**vous aviez beaucoup à faire.**   **Charles :  J'ai bien le temps.**
voo-zah-vyay boh-koo ah fair.              zhay byiN le taN
*you had lots of things to do.*           · *I have plenty of time.*

**Georges**      **(se levant) : Vous êtes heureux.   Je me lève, autrement je serai**
se le-vaN    voo-zait-zãy-rãy. zhe me laiv ohtr'maN zhe s'rai
*(getting up) :   You are lucky. I am getting up, otherwise I shall be*

**en retard.   Je serai habillé avant vous.**
aN re-tahr.   zhe s'ray ah-bee-yay ah-vaN voo.
*late.   I shall be dressed before you.*

**Charles :**   **C'est très probable.**      **Georges :   C'est curieux.**
say trai proh-bahbl              say kẽer-yãy
*That is very likely.*             *That's funny.*

**Charles :**   **Qu'avez-vous?**      **Georges :   Je ne peux pas**
kah-vay voo?              zhe ne pãy pah
*What is the matter with you?*      *I can't*

| | |
|---|---|
| trouver ma chemise.<br>troo-vay mah sh'meez.<br>*find my shirt.* | **Charles :** **La voilà sur le lit.**<br>lah vwah-lah sᾱᾱr le lee.<br>*There it is on the bed.* |

**Georges :** **Merci bien. Pouvez-vous voir mon caleçon?**
mair-see byiN. poo-vay voo vwahr moN kahl-soN?
*Can you see my pants?*

| | |
|---|---|
| **Charles :** **Cherchez-le bien.**<br>shair-shay le byiN.<br>*Look for them well.* | **Georges :** **Le voici sous la table.**<br>le vwah-see soo lah tahbl.<br>*There they are under the table.* |
| **Où sont mes chaussettes?**<br>oo soN may shoh-sait ?<br>*Where are my socks ?* | **Charles :** **Les voilà sur la**<br>lay vwah-lah sᾱᾱr lah<br>*There they are on the* |
| **commode.**<br>ko-mohd.<br>*chest of drawers.* | **Georges :** **Vous êtes un vrai détective.**<br>voo-zait uN vrai day-taik-teev.<br>*You are a real detective.* |

**Charles :** **Peut-être le serai-je un jour.**
pᾱy taitr le s'rai zhe uN zhoor
*Perhaps I shall be one, one day.*

## ARTICLES IN THE BATHROOM

| | | | |
|---|---|---|---|
| **le bain**<br>biN<br>*bath* | **la baignoire**<br>bain-ywahr<br>*bath-tub* | **le savon de toilette**<br>sah-voN de twah-lait<br>*bath soap* | **le porte-savon**<br>port sah-voN<br>*soap-dish* |

| | | | |
|---|---|---|---|
| | **le gant de toilette**<br>gaN de twah-lait<br>*face-flannel* | | |

**une éponge** — ay-poNzh — *sponge*    **le peignoir de bain** — pain-ywahr de biN — *bath-wrap*    **la douche** — doosh — *shower*    **le chauffe-bain** — shohf biN — *geyser*

**la descente de bain** — dais-saNt de biN — *bath-mat*    **le lavabo** — lah-vah-boh — *wash-basin*    **le verre à eau** — vai-rah oh — *tumbler*    **la brosse à dents** — bros-ah daN — *tooth-brush*

**la pâte dentifrice** — paht daN-tee-frees — *tooth-paste*    **le flacon d'eau dentifrice** — flah-koN doh daN-tee-frees — *mouth-wash*    **le rasoir de sûreté** — rahzwahr de sᾱᾱr-tay — *safety-razor*

**le savon à barbe** — sah-voN ah bahrb — *shaving soap*    **le blaireau** — blai-roh — *shaving-brush*    **la serviette de bain** — sair-vyait de biN — *bath-towel*    **le porte-serviette** — port sair-vyait — *towel-rail*

**le savon** — sah-voN — *soap*    **la bascule** — bahs-kᾱᾱl — *weighing machine*    **le bain de siège** — biN de syaizh — *hip-bath*    **le W.C.** — doobl vay say — *W.C.*

**la chaîne** — shain — *chain*    **le couvercle** — koo-vairkl — *lid*    **le papier hygiénique** — pahp-yay eezh-yay-neek — *toilet-paper*    **le portemanteau** — port-maN-toh — *clothes-rack*

### CHARLES IN THE BATHROOM

Try making a list in French of the objects you see before consulting the list on page145. Then turn back and fill the gaps in your list without making use of the text.

**Georges :**     **Alors aidez-moi à trouver mon rasoir.**
ah-lor ai-day mwah ah troo-vay moN rahzwahr.
*Then help me to find my razor.*

**Charles :**     **Le voilà sous votre nez.**
le vwah-lah soo votr nay.
*There it is in front of your eyes (lit., under your nose).*

**Georges :**     **Mais ça, c'est extraordinaire.**
mai sah say-taix-trah-or-dee-nair.
*But that's extraordinary (that is).*

**Charles :**     **Peut-être le savon y est-il aussi.**
pay-taitr le sah-voN ee ay-teel oh-see.
*Perhaps the soap is also there.*

**Georges :**     **Vraiment, vous avez raison. Maintenant j'ai mon pantalon,**
vrai-maN voo-zah-vay rai-zoN. miNt-naN zhay moN paN-tah-lon
*Really, you are (lit., have) right. Now I have my trousers,*

        **mon gilet, mon col, ma cravate, mes bottines, mon**
moN zhee-lay moN kol mah krah-vaht may bo-teen moN
*my waistcoat, my collar, my tie, my boots, my*

**veston, et les choses pour me raser.  Je vais me raser,**
vais-toN ay lay shohz poor me rah-zay.   zhe vai me rah-zay
*jacket, and the things for shaving.   I am going to shave,*

**me laver, et m'habiller dans la salle de bain.  J'espère que**
me lah-vay ay mah-bee-yay daN lah sahl de biN.   zhais-pair ke
*to wash, and to dress in the bathroom.   I hope that*

**vous serez habillé, quand je reviendrai.**
voo se-ray zah-bee-yay kaN zhe re-vyiN-dray.
*you will be dressed, when I come back.*

Charles :  **Il n'y a pas de danger.**
eel nyah pah de daN-zhay.
*There is no danger of that.*

Georges :  **Levez-vous, paresseux; je serai prêt avant vous.**
le-vay voo pah-rai-sŷ; zhe s'rai prai-ah-vaN voo.
*Get up, lazybones; I shall be ready before you.*

Charles :  **Cela m'est égal.**
s'lah mai-tay-gahl.
*I don't care (lit., That to me is equal).*

**Georges sort.   Charles reste encore quelques minutes**
zhorzh sor.   shahrl rais-taN-kor kailk mee-nêêt
*George leaves.   Charles remains still a few minutes*

**dans son lit.  Puis, après un**
daN soN lee.  pŵee ah-prai-zuN
*in his bed.  Then, after an*

**immense effort, il se lève.  Il**
nee-maNs ai-for eel se laiv.   eel
*immense effort, he gets up.   He*

**ôte la veste de son pyjama**
oht lah vaist de soN pee-zhah-mah
*takes off the coat of his pyjamas*

**et met ses pantoufles.  Il se lave**
ay mai say paN-toofl.   eel se lahv
*and puts on his slippers.   He washes*

**les mains, la figure, le cou et les oreilles, après quoi il se sèche**
lay miN lah fee-gêêr le koo ay lay-zoh-raiy ah-prai kwah eel se saish
*his hands, his face, his neck and his ears, after which he dries himself*

**avec une serviette.  Il se nettoie les dents avec sa brosse à dents et**
ah-vai-kêên sair-vyait.   eel se nai-twah lay daN ah-vaik sah bros ah daN ay
*with a towel.   He cleans his teeth with his toothbrush and*

**un peu de dentifrice.   Cela fait, il s'habille.   Il met ses chaussettes, puis**
ʋN pay̆ de daN-tee-frees.   s'lah fai eel sah-beey.   eel mai say shoh-sait pwee
*a little tooth-paste.   This done, he dresses.   He puts on his socks, then*

**sa chemise, son caleçon, son pantalon et ses bretelles.   Pour mettre sa**
sah sh'meez soN kahl-soN soN paN-tah-loN ay say bre-tail.   poor maitr sah
*his shirt, his pants, his trousers and his braces.   To put on his*

**cravate il va devant la glace; il se brosse aussi les**
krah-vaht eel vah de-vaN lah glahs eel se bros oh-see lay
*tie he goes before the mirror; he also brushes his*

**cheveux et se peigne.   Après cela il met son gilet, son veston**
sh'vay̆ ay se painy.   ah-prai s'lah eel mai soN zhee-lai soN vais-toN
*hair and combs it.   After that he puts on his waistcoat, his jacket*

**et ses souliers.   Il ne se dépêche pas, il prend son temps.   À**
ay say sool-yay.   eel ne se day-paish pah eel praN soN taN.   ah
*and his shoes.   He does not hurry, he takes his time.   At*

**neuf heures moins vingt il descend et entre dans la salle à manger, où**
nay̆vay̆r mwiN viN eel dais-saN ay aNtr daN lah sah-lah maN-zhay oo
*twenty to nine he goes down and enters (in) the dining-room, where*

**la famille a presque fini le petit déjeuner.   Il dit "bonjour,"**
lah fah-meey ah praisk' fee-nee le p'tee day-zhay̆nay.   eel dee boN-zhoor
*the family has almost finished (the) breakfast.   He says "good morning,"*

**et s'excuse d'être en retard, en disant: "Je vous demande pardon".**
ay saix-kẽez daitr aN re-tahr aN dee-saN zhe voo de-maNd pahr-doN.
*and apologises for being late, by saying: "I am sorry".*

**Mme Lesage répond: "Il n'y a pas de quoi".**
mah-dahm le-sahzh ray-poN   eel nyah pah de kwah.
*Mme. Lesage replies : " Don't mention it."*

### HOW TO APOLOGISE

**Je vous demande pardon,** which literally means "I beg your pardon", also stands for "I am sorry", "Excuse me", "I apologise". The usual reply to these is **Il n'y a pas de quoi,** which literally means "There is not of what". "To apologise" is also s'excuser, another reflexive verb.

### TO KNOCK ; TO RING ; TO LISTEN

**Frapper**=to knock, **sonner**=to ring, and **écouter**=to listen to, are regular verbs. **On frappe** means "there is a knock", "someone is knocking"; similarly **on sonne**="the bell is ringing", "someone is ringing".

### VERBS ENDING IN -RE

**Entendre**=to hear
**Present Tense**

j'entends   aN-taN

il ⎱
elle ⎰ entend   aN-taN

nous entendons   aN-taN-doN
vous entendez   aN-taN-day

ils ⎱
elles ⎰ entendent   aN-taNd

## Imperfect

j'entendais aN-taN-dai

il ⎫
elle ⎬ entendait aN-taN-dai

nous entendions aN-taN-dyoN
vous entendiez aN-taN-dyay

ils ⎫
elles ⎬ entendaient aN-taN-dai

## Perfect

j'ai entendu aN-taN-dǖ

il ⎫
elle ⎬ a entendu

nous avons entendu

ils ⎫
elles ⎬ ont entendu

### Répondre=to reply
#### Present Tense

je réponds ray-poN

il ⎫
elle ⎬ répond ray-poN

nous répondons ray-poN-doN
vous répondez ray-poN-day

ils ⎫
elles ⎬ répondent ray-poNd

## Imperfect

je répondais ray-poN-dai

il ⎫
elle ⎬ répondait ray-poN-dai

nous répondions ray-poN-dyoN
vous répondiez ray-poN-dyay

ils ⎫
elles ⎬ répondaient ray-poN-dai

## Perfect

j'ai répondu ray-poN-dǖ

il ⎫
elle ⎬ a répondu

nous avons répondu

ils ⎫
elles ⎬ ont répondu

Verbs in -re usually have the same forms as given above for entendre and répondre. Such a regular verb in -re is for instance descendre; irregular verbs in -re we havê come across so far are mettre=to put, faire=to make, and dire=to say. The Present Tense of these verbs has already been given in previous pages. Their Imperfects can be derived, as those of every verb whatsoever, from the form of the Present Tense used in connection with nous. If you leave out the ending -ons of mettons, faisons and disons you get mett-, dis- and fais-. To these stems the Imperfect endings -ais, ait, -ions, -iez, -aient are added. And this rule holds good for every French verb, except être=to be, which, however, is not a proper verb, but a so-called auxiliary verb.

The Perfect of faire, dire, lire, prendre, écrire and mettre is irregular : j'ai fait=I have made, j'ai dit=I have said, j'ai mis= I have put (on), j'ai lu=I have read, j'ai pris=I have taken, j'ai écrit=I have written.

### SOME MORE REFLEXIVE VERBS

se dépêcher=to hurry; s'habiller=to get dressed; se brosser=to brush (oneself); se peigner=to comb (oneself); se baigner= to have a bath, to bathe; se raser=to shave (oneself) are reflexive verbs, the forms of which are identical with those given in the previous lesson (page 137).

### IDIOMATIC EXPRESSIONS

The following have occurred in this lesson:

être pressé=to be in a hurry (lit., to be hurried).

avoir besoin=to need, to require (lit., to have need).

avoir raison=to be right (lit., to have reason).

changer d'avis=to change one's mind (lit., to change of opinion).

j'ai le temps=I have time.

être en retard=to be late (lit., to be in delay).

le voici (voilà)=here (there) it is (if the object referred to is masculine); here (there) he is.

la voici (voilà)=here (there) it is (if the object referred to is feminine); here (there) she is.

les voici (voilà)=here (there) they are.

### PARTS OF THE BODY

| | | |
|---|---|---|
| la tête | tait | *head* |
| un cheveu | sh'vay͡ | *hair* |
| un œil | ay͡y | *eye* |
| le nez | nay | *nose* |
| la bouche | boosh | *mouth* |
| la dent | daN | *tooth* |
| le cou | koo | *neck* |
| une oreille | oh-raiy | *ear* |
| le bras | brah | *arm* |
| la main | miN | *hand* |
| la jambe | zhaNb | *leg* |
| le pied | pyay | *foot* |

Note.—The plural of **un œil** (ay͡y) is **les yeux** (yay͡); **le cheveu** (sh'vay͡)=*hair* like any other noun ending in **-eu** or **-eau** has the plural ending in **-x** instead of **-s.**

### DEFINITE ARTICLE WITH PARTS OF THE BODY

**il se lave les mains**=
> *he washes his hands.*

**elle se brosse les cheveux**=
> *she brushes her hair.*

**ils se sèchent les mains**=
> *they dry their hands.*

**je me nettoie les dents**=
> *I clean my teeth.*

**elle a les yeux bleus**=
> *she has blue eyes.*

**il a les cheveux courts**=
> *he has short hair.*

When there is no doubt as to the possessor, the definite article is used in French instead of the possessive adjective before parts of the body.

## EXERCISES

### I   Answer in French

1. Où est-ce que Georges avait mis sa chemise? 2. Pourquoi Charles ne voulait-il pas se lever? 3. Avait-il besoin de se lever de bonne heure? 4. Pourquoi pas (=why not)? 5. Qui frappe à la porte de la chambre? 6. Est-ce que Charles se lève à sept heures? 7. Où Georges se lave-t-il? 8. Qu'est-ce qu'on fait avant de s'habiller? 9. Est-ce que vous vous mettez devant une glace pour vous peigner? 10. Qu'est-ce que Charles dit, quand il entre dans la salle à manger? 11. Est-ce que vous vous excusez, quand vous êtes en retard? 12. Qu'est-ce que Mme Lesage répond?

### II   Translate into English

1. Pour le déjeuner il y a du café au lait avec du pain et du beurre. 2. Je mets mes chaussettes sur une chaise. 3. Je me lave les mains avec de l'eau chaude et du savon. 4. Il n'y avait pas de savon. 5. Sur la tête il y a les cheveux. 6. Les dents sont dans la bouche. 7. Nous avons deux jambes et deux bras. 8. Les dames ont les cheveux longs. 9. Votre frère, a-t-il les cheveux courts? 10. Nous marchons avec les pieds. 11. Avec les yeux nous voyons. 12. Avec les oreilles nous entendons.

### III   Translate into French

1. Who was knocking? 2. Don't you have to get up? 3. Why did you change your mind? 4. They have plenty of time. 5. I cannot find my collar—here it is. 6. Where are my shoes?—There they are. 7. Won't you brush your hair? 8. Why is she late? 9. She has not heard the alarm-clock. 10. I am sorry for being late, but I was very tired. (*Key to I, II and III on page* 152.)

## KEY TO THE EXERCISES

### Lesson Nine—I

1. Il est dans le ciel. 2. Il n'est pas visible pendant la nuit. 3. La nuit. 4. Il se lève le matin. 5. Il se couche le soir. 6. À trois heures ou quatre heures. 7. Non, ils sont courts. 8. Oui, elles sont courtes. 9. Non, il fait noir. 10. Nous allumons le gaz ou

l'électricité. 11. Non, il se couche tard. 12. Je ne peux pas voir. 13. Il ne fait plus jour. 14. Ils sont gris. 15. Quelquefois il pleut beaucoup. 16. Non, il ne neige pas en été. 17. Non, ils n'ouvrent pas leurs parapluies. 18. Non, il ne fait pas de soleil. 19. Oui, il fait beau (Non, il ne fait pas beau). 20. Non, il fait froid. 21. Non, il ne neige pas en juillet. 22. J'ai froid (je n'ai pas froid). 23. J'aime les fleurs. 24. L'été. 25. Non, il n'y a pas de violettes en février.

## II

1. Quelle heure est-il, s'il vous plaît? 2. Il est onze heures du matin. 3. Le soleil est-il visible maintenant? 4. Fait-il noir? 5. Veuillez allumer le gaz. 6. J'ai toujours froid en hiver. 7. Que fait votre frère? 8. Il fait des bouquets de pensées. 9. Pleut-il (or est-ce qu'il pleut)? 10. Il neige quelquefois en hiver.

## III

Compare your answers with pages 12, 90 and 112.

## Lesson Ten

### I

1. Elle est dans un faubourg. 2. Douze. 3. Au rez-de-chaussée. 4. Le salon et le bureau. 5. Au deuxième étage. 6. La mansarde et le grenier. 7. La cave. 8. Un petit jardin. 9. Dans le grand jardin qui est derrière la maison. 10. Au deuxième étage. 11. Dans le cabinet de travail. 12. Dans la cave. 13. Au vestibule. 14. La porte de la maison. 15. Un visiteur et une vieille dame sont dans le vestibule. 16. Il ôte son pardessus. 17. Elle met son chapeau. 18. Une Anglaise, qui donne des leçons. 19. Je prends des leçons de français. 20. Dans le vestibule au fond et à droite.

### II

1. -e. 2. -ez. 3. -e. 4. -ons. 5. -ent. 6. -es. 7. -ent. 8. -es. 9. -s. 10. -e.

## III

1. Où habitez-vous? 2. Est-ce loin d'ici? 3. Combien de pièces a votre maison? 4. Y a-t-il une salle de bain dans sa maison? 5. À quel étage est la chambre des enfants? 6. Elle est au deuxième étage. 7. Vos malles sont au grenier. 8. Vous avez de beaux parterres de fleurs dans votre jardin, n'est-ce pas? 9. Avez-vous des légumes dans votre jardin? 10. Nous n'avons que quelques fleurs. 11. Est-ce que cet enfant dort? 12. Descendons dans la cave! 13. La cuisine est près de la salle à manger. 14. La salle a manger est à gauche. 15. Le téléphone est à droite à côté du porte-manteau.

## Lesson Eleven

### I

1. Le grand-père, la grand'mère, M. et Mme Lesage, etc., sont dans le salon. 2. Il lit. 3. Elle écrit une lettre. 4. Mlle Lesage. 5. Il y a six personnes. 6. Il fume et elle reprise. 7. Une pendule. 8. Dans la niche. 9. Non, il n'est pas debout. 10. M. Lesage. 11. Une table ronde. 12. Oui. 13. Il est à gauche. 14. J'ai une montre (Je n'ai pas de montre). 15. Il est . . . heures. 16. Oui, elle est remontée (Non, elle n'est pas remontée). 17. Elle (n') avance (pas.). 18. Oui. 19. Elle n'est pas si large. 20. J'écris (Je n'écris pas) beaucoup de lettres. 21. Je (ne) lis (pas) beaucoup.

## II

1. Voyez-vous mon grand-père? 2. Il est assis dans le jardin. 3. Est-elle debout ou assise? 4. Jouez-vous du piano? 5. Je ne joue pas, mais j'écoute souvent, surtout de la musique de Wagner. 6. Est-ce que votre montre est en or? 7. Non, elle est en argent. 8. Mon réveil est plus petit que votre pendule, qui est sur la cheminée. 9. Ma montre est arrêtée. 10. Écoutez s'il vous plaît, ne lisez pas. 11. Qu'est-ce que vous écrivez? 12. Une lettre à ma mère qui est en France.

### III

1. Are you younger (older) than your brother (my uncle), etc.? 2. Is it warmer (less warm; colder) in spring than in winter, etc.? 3. Are the most (least) beautiful (bad, long, short) days in spring, etc.?

## Lesson Twelve

### I

1. Je (ne) me couche (pas) de bonne heure. 2. Je me lève à . . . heures. 3. Non, il ne se couche pas à sept heures. 4. Non, il veut se lever à sept heures. 5. Il veut voir Paris. 6. Oui, il était très fatigué. 7. Non, je ne me lave pas dans la salle à manger. 8. Je dis "bonne nuit". 9. Je (ne) lis (pas) dans mon lit. 10. J'aime (Je n'aime pas) manger du chocolat.

### II

1. Nous nous levons à six heures. 2. Ne vous couchez-vous pas de bonne heure? 3. Ils (elles) ne se lavent pas dans la chambre à coucher. 4. Vous allez vous coucher à huit heures. 5. Y a-t-il des chaises dans la chambre à coucher. 6. N'oubliez pas de me réveiller. 7. Il oubliait. 8. Ils allaient à leur hôtel. 9. Qu'est-ce qu'il avait à faire? 10. Tout le monde dormait. 11. Il faisait chaud. 12. Il ne voulait pas se laver avant le petit déjeuner. 13. Elle mettait ses bijoux dans le troisième tiroir de sa table de toilette. 14. Il aimait à lire dans son lit. 15. Vous vous levez, n'est-ce pas?

### III

1. J'étais malade. 2. Il ne restait pas à l'hôtel. 3. Elle avait beaucoup d'argent. 4. Ils étaient fatigués. 5. Nous avions faim.

6. Ils n'avaient pas de chaises. 7. Est-ce que vous vous couchiez? 8. Le train arrivait. 9. Il faisait beau. 10. Pourquoi mettiez-vous les fleurs sur l'armoire?

## Lesson Thirteen

### I

1. Sur son lit. 2. Parce qu'il était paresseux. 3. Non, il n'avait pas besoin de se lever de bonne heure. 4. Parce qu'il était en vacances. 5. Le père de Georges. 6. Non, il ne se lève pas. 7. Il se lave dans la salle de bain. 8. On se lave. 9. Oui, me mets devant une glace. 10. Il dit "Bonjour". 11. Oui, je m'excuse. 12. Elle répond : "Il n'y a pas de quoi".

### II

1. For breakfast there is coffee with milk and bread and butter. 2. I put my socks on a chair. 3. I wash my hands with hot water and soap. 4. There was no soap. 5. On the head is the hair. 6. The teeth are in the mouth. 7. We have two legs and two arms. 8. Ladies have long hair. 9. Has your brother short hair? 10. We walk with our feet. 11. With the eyes we see. 12. With the ears we hear.

### III

1. Qui frappait? 2. N'avez-vous pas besoin de vous lever? 3. Pourquoi avez-vous changé d'avis? 4. Ils ont bien le temps. 5. Je ne peux pas trouver mon col— le voici. 6. Où sont mes souliers?—Les voici. 7. Ne voulez-vous pas brosser vos cheveux? 8. Pourquoi est-elle en retard? 9. Elle n'a pas entendu le réveil. 10. Je vous demande pardon d'être en retard, mais j'étais très fatigué(e).

### TAKE THE COURSE WITH YOU TO FRANCE !

When next business or pleasure takes you to France, you will be well advised to take the Course with you. It is so designed as to be useful not only to those who wish to learn French at home, but also to those who may wish to take a long motor tour or make an extended stay in France. It may be at the garage when you wish to explain the repairs needed to some part of your car, or at the butcher's when you want to describe some cut of meat, or in the train or on the racecourse, that you will find the Course invaluable.

# QUATORZIÈME LEÇON

Could you approach the **grille** (wire partition), pass your sterling through the **guichet** (paying-slot) and change money as Mr. Roberts is doing? If not, study the text below, then cover it over and repeat until you are satisfied that you know what you would have to say in French, in order to carry out a similar transaction.

### ACHATS DIVERS—VARIOUS PURCHASES

**Monsieur Roberts n'a pas d'argent français et pour faire ses achats**
m'ss-yãy robairts nah pah dahr-zhaN fraN-sai ay poor fair say-zah-shah
*Mr. Roberts has no French money and to do his shopping*

**il en aura besoin.   C'est pourquoi il entre dans un bureau de change.**
ee-lah-noh-rah bez-wiN.   say poor-kwah ee-laNtr daN-zuN bẽe-roh de shaNzh.
*he of it will have need.   That is why he enters (in) an exchange office.*

**M. Roberts :**   **Monsieur, voulez-vous changer des billets de banque anglais ?**
             m'ss-yãy voo-lay voo shaN-zhay day bee-yay de baNk aN-glai?
             *Will you change English banknotes?*

**Changeur :**   **Certainement.   Combien monsieur veut-il changer ?**
             sair-tain-maN.   koN-byiN m'ss-yãy vãy teel shaN-zhay
             *Certainly.   How much does the gentleman wish to change?*

**M. Roberts :**   **Je changerai une livre seulement, s'il vous plaît, monsieur.**
             zhe shaNzh-ray ẽen leevr sãyl-maN see-voo plai m'ss-yãy.
             *I will change one pound only, please.*

**Changeur :**      Comment voulez-vous prendre l'argent[1], en billets ou en monnaie?
ko-maN voo-lay voo prandr lahr-zhaN aN bee-yay oo aN mo-nai?
*How do you wish to take the money, in notes or in silver?*

**M. Roberts :**      Un billet de cent francs et de la monnaie[1] pour le reste, s.v.p.
uN bee-yai de saN fraN ay de lah mo-nai poor le raist s.v.p.
*One note of* 100 *francs and the rest in small change, please.*

**Changeur :**      Voici, monsieur, cent francs, cinquante, soixante,
vwah-see m'ss-yãy saN fraN, siN-kaNt swah-saNt
*Here you are, sir, hundred francs, fifty, sixty,*

            **70, 71, 72, 73, 74, 75 francs et 50 centimes, cela fait**
(see page 112) fraN ay siN-kaNt saN-teem, s'lah fai
70, 71, 72, 73, 74, 75 *francs and* 50 *centimes, that makes*

            **175 francs 50.**             **M. Roberts (après avoir**
saN-swah-saNt kiNz fraN siN-kaNt.         ah-prai-zahvwahr
175 *francs* 50.                           *(after having*

            **compté l'argent) : Merci, c'est juste.    Bonjour, monsieur.**
koN-tay lahr-zhaN.   mair-see, say zhèest.   boN-zhoor m'ss-yãy.
*counted the money) : Thanks, that is right.   Good morning, sir.*

**Ses poches remplies d'argent, M. Roberts entre dans un bistrot**
say posh raN-plee dahr-zhaN M. ro-bairts aNtr daN-zuN beest-roh
*His pockets full of money, Mr. Roberts goes into a public-house*

**pour acheter des cigarettes.    Il a appris que c'est dans des**
poor ahsh-tay day see-gah-rait.   ee-lah ah-pree ke say daN day
*to buy some cigarettes.   He has learnt that it is in*

**bistrots qu'on trouve les bureaux de tabac.     Le tabac, les**
beest-roh koN troov lay bèe-roh de tah-bah.   le tah-bah lay
*public-houses that one finds the tobacco shops.   The tobacco, the*

**cigarettes, les cigares, les allumettes et les cartes à jouer**
see-gah-rait lay see-gahr lay zah-lèe-mait ay lay kahrt ah zhoo-ay
*cigarettes, the cigars, the matches and the playing cards*

**sont des monopoles de l'État, c'est à dire que l'État seul a**
soN day moh-noh-pol de lay-tah, say-tah deer ke lay-tah sãyl ah
*are monopolies of the State, that is to say the State alone has*

**le droit de les fabriquer et de les vendre.    Dans un bureau de tabac**
le drwah de lay fah-bree-kay ay de lay vaNdr.   daN-zuN bèe-roh de tah-bah
*the right to manufacture them and to sell them.   In a tobacco shop*

---

[1] **l'argent** means both "money" and "silver"; **la monnaie** is "small change" only.

**on vend aussi des timbres-poste, des cartes-postales et**
oN vaN-toh-see day tiNbr pohst day kahrt pohs-tahl ay
*one sells also postage-stamps, postcards and*

**des cartes-lettres; en outre on y vend des pipes, des blagues, des fume-**
day kahrt laitr ah-nootr o-nee vaN day peep day blahg day fẽẽm
*letter-cards; in addition one sells there pipes, pouches, cigar-*

**cigares, des fume-cigarettes et toutes sortes de choses à l'usage**
sẽe-gahr day fẽẽm see-gah-rait ay toot sort de shohz ah lẽẽ-zahzh
*holders, cigarette-holders, and all kinds of things for the use*

**des fumeurs. M. Roberts s'adresse à la patronne qui vient de**
day fẽẽ-mãyr. M. ro-bairts sah-drais ah lah pah-tron kee vyiN de
*of smokers. Mr. Roberts addresses himself to the proprietress*

**vendre[1] quelques timbres-poste à un autre client.**
vaNdr kailk tiNbr post ah ãy-nohtr klee-aN.
*who has just been selling some stamps to another customer.*

**M. Roberts :  Bonjour, madame, voulez-vous me donner un paquet de**
boN-zhoor mah-dahm voo-lay voo me do-nay uN pah-kay de
*Good morning, madam, will you give me a packet of*

---

[1]Lit.  Comes from selling.

    This officer of the French Colonial cavalry dazzles the ladies, but he need not
dazzle you.  Our artist has here shown several objects which you know.  Consult the list
on page 156 only when your vocabulary breaks down, then turn back.  Continue until you
are satisfied that you could cover all your requirements in any French tobacconist's.

**cigarettes, s'il vous plaît?**    **La patronne:** **Avec plaisir, monsieur,**
see-gah-rait see voo plai?                     ah-vaik plai-zeer m'ss-yâŷ
*cigarettes, please?*                           *With pleasure, sir,*

**quelles cigarettes désirez-vous?**    **M. Roberts :** **Donnez-moi . . .**
kail see-gah-rait day-zee ray voo?                do-nay mwah
*what cigarettes do you want?*                   *Give me . . .*

**je ne connais pas les marques françaises.**
zhe ne ko-nay pah lay mahrk fraN-saiz.
*I don't know the French brands.*

**Patronne :**    **Désirez-vous des douces ou des fortes?**
day-zee-ray voo day doos oo day fort?
*Do you want mild or strong ones?*

**M. Roberts :**    **Vous n'avez pas de cigarettes anglaises, par hasard?**
voo nah-vay pah de see-gah-rait-zaN-glaiz pahr-ah-zahr?
*You haven't any English cigarettes, by (any) chance?*

**Patronne :**    **Mais si,**[1] **monsieur, nous avons toutes les marques connues.**
mai see m'ss-yâŷ noo-zah-voN toot lay mahrk ko-nê̂.
*But yes, sir, we have all the (well) known brands.*

**Mr. Roberts :**    **Je préfère les marques anglaises, parce que je ne**
zhe pray-fair lay mahrk-zan-glaiz pahrs ke zhe ne
*I prefer the English brands, because I don't*

---

### AT THE TOBACCONIST'S

| **le cigare** | **la cigarette** | **la pipe** | **le cigarillo** | **le fume-cigare** |
|---|---|---|---|---|
| see-gahr | see-gah-rait | peep | see-gah-rilloh | fê̂m see-gahr |
| *cigar* | *cigarette* | *pipe* | *small cigar* | *cigar-holder* |

| **le fume-cigarette** | **la boîte de cigares** | **le paquet de cigarettes** |
|---|---|---|
| fê̂m see-gah-rait | bwaht de see-gahr | pah-kai de see-gah-rait |
| *cigarette-holder* | *box of cigars* | *packet of cigarettes* |

| **un étui à cigares** | **un étui à cigarettes** | **une blague** | **le coupe-cigare** |
|---|---|---|---|
| ay-twee ah see-gahr | ay-twee ah see-gah-rait | blahg | koop see-gahr |
| *cigar-case* | *cigarette-case* | *tobacco-pouch* | *cigar-cutter* |

| **une boîte d'allumettes** | **une allumette** | **le cendrier** | **la bougie** | **la tabatière** |
|---|---|---|---|---|
| bwaht dah-lê̂mait | ah-lê̂mait | saN-dryay | boo-zhee | tah-bah-tyair |
| *box of matches* | *match* | *ash-tray* | *candle* | *snuff-box* |

| **le paquet de tabac** | **la pochette d'allumettes** | **le briquet** | **le cure-pipe** |
|---|---|---|---|
| pah-kai de tah-bah | po-shait dah-lê̂mait | bree-kai | kê̂r peep |
| *packet of tobacco* | *book matches* | *lighter* | *pipe-cleaner* |

---

[1] **si** is used instead of **oui** in reply to a negative question.

connais pas les autres.    Alors donnez-moi un paquet de
ko-nai pah lay-zohtr    ah-lor do-nay mwah uN pah-kay de
*know the others.*    *Then give me a packet of*

vingt Player's.    La patronne : Et Celtique ou Gitane aussi?
viN play-air.            ay sail-teek oo zhee-tahn oh-see?
*twenty Player's.*        *And Celtic or Gitane also?*

**M. Roberts :**    Gitane, c'est ça.    Donnez-m'en un paquet, s'il vous plaît.
           zhee-tahn say sah.    do-nay maN uN pah-kai see-voo-plai.
           *Gitane, that's it.*    *Give me (of it) a packet, please.*

Et qu'est-ce que ça coûte?    La patronne : Trois francs le paquet
ay kaisk' sah koot?            trwah fraN le pah-kay
*And how much is that?*        *Three francs the packet*

de dix, et huit francs les Player's.
de deez ay ŵee fraN lay play-air
*of ten, and eight francs the Player's.*

**M. Roberts :**    Oh, j'ai presque oublié.    Donnez-moi encore une
           oh zhay praisk' oo-blee-yay.    do-nay mwah aN-kor ễn
           *Oh, I have almost forgotten.*    *Give me also a*

boîte de cigares de la Havane, c'est pour un parent,
bwaht de see-gahr de lah ahvan say poor uN pah-raN
*box of Havana cigars, it is for a relation (of mine),*

et une boîte d'allumettes.    La patronne : Ce sera tout?
ay ễn bwaht dah-lễ-mait.            se s'rah too?
*and a box of matches.*        *That will be all?*

**M. Roberts :**    Oui, madame, c'est tout pour aujourd'hui.
           wee mah-dahm sai too poor oh-zhoord-ŵee.
           *Yes, madam, that is all for to-day.*

### CHEZ LE PAPETIER—AT THE STATIONER'S

**M. Roberts a besoin d'écrire beaucoup de lettres et n'a pas**
M. ro-bairts a be-zwiN day-kreer boh-koo de laitr ay nah pah
*Mr. Roberts has (need) to write lots of letters and has not (got)*

**ce qu'il faut.    C'est pourquoi il entre chez un papetier**
s'keel foh.    sai poor-kwah ee-laNtr shay-zuN pah-pe-tyay
*the necessary things.[1]    That is why he enters (at) a stationer's*

**pour y faire les achats nécessaires.**
poor-ee fair lay-zah-shah nay-sai-sair.
*to make the necessary purchases.*

---

[1] Lit. that which it needs.

**Le vendeur :**    **Qu'y a-t-il pour votre service, monsieur?**
le vaN-dâȳr    kyah-teel poor votr sair-vees m'ss-yâȳ?
*The salesman :* *What is there for your service, sir?*

**M. Roberts :**    **Je voudrais du papier à lettres.**
zhe vood-rai dêē pahp-yay ah laitr.
*I want some note-paper.*

**Vendeur :**    **De quelle couleur le désirez-vous, monsieur?**
de kail koo-lâȳr le day-zee-ray voo m'ss-yâȳ?
*(Of ) what colour do you want it, sir?*

**M. Roberts :**    **Montrez-moi du blanc, mais de très belle qualité, s'il vous plaît.**
moN-tray mwah dêē blaN mai de trai bail kah-lee-tay see voo plai
*Show me some white, but of very good quality, please.*

**Vendeur :**    **Désirez-vous aussi des enveloppes?**
day-zee-ray voo oh-see day-zaN-ve-lop?
*Do you also want envelopes?*

**M. Roberts :**    **C'est ça ; et puis donnez-moi de l'encre.**
say sah ay pŵee do-nay mwah de laNkr.
*That's so ; and then give me some ink.*

     This little girl seems to know how to ask for what she wants at the stationer's—can you? Our artist has helped with many objects. Try making your own list in French before you consult the list which is given on the opposite page.

## ARTICLES IN THE STATIONER'S

| | | | | |
|---|---|---|---|---|
| **du papier à lettres** | **une enveloppe** | **un cahier** | **un carnet** | **un crayon** |
| pahp-yay ah laitr | aN-ve-lop | kah-yay | kahr-nay | krai-yoN |
| *note-paper* | *envelope* | *exercise-book* | *note-book* | *pencil* |

| | | | | | |
|---|---|---|---|---|---|
| **de la mine de plomb** | **un porte-plume** | **une plume** | **un stylo** | **de l'encre (f.)** | **un encrier** |
| meen de ploN | port plĕem | plĕem | stee-loh | aNkr | aN-kryay |
| *pencil refill* | *pen-holder* | *nib* | *fountain-pen* | *ink* | *inkstand* |

| | | | | |
|---|---|---|---|---|
| **une gomme** | **un canif** | **une carte** | **un pèse-lettres** | **une carte postale illustrée** |
| gom | kah-neef | kahrt | paiz laitr | kahrt pos-tahl ee-lĕes-tray |
| *india-rubber* | *pen-knife* | *map* | *letter-scale* | *picture postcard* |

| | | | | |
|---|---|---|---|---|
| **une carte de visite** | **une règle** | **une étiquette** | **de la cire à cacheter** | **un calendrier** |
| kahrt de vee-zeet | raigl | ay-tee-kait | see-rah kahsh-tay | kah-laN-dryay |
| *visiting card* | *ruler* | *label* | *sealing wax* | *calendar* |

---

**Vendeur :**    **De l'encre ordinaire ou à stylo?**    **M. Roberts :** **De l'encre à stylo,**
de laNkr or-dee-nair oo ah stee-loh?      de laNkr ah steelo
*Ordinary ink or for fountain pen?*      *Fountain-pen ink,*

**noire, s'il vous plaît.**    **Avez-vous des cartes postales illustrées?**
nwahr see voo plai.    avay-voo day kahrt postahl ee-lĕe-stray?
*black, please.*    *Have you any picture postcards?*

**Vendeur :**    **J'en ai même un grand assortiment.**    **Je vais vous en**
zhah-nay maim uN graN-tah-sor-tee-maN.   zhe vai voo-zaN
*I (of them) have (even) a large selection.*    *I'll you (of them)*

**montrer.**    **(Il apporte une grande boîte, la met sur le**
mon-tray.    ee-lah-por-tĕen graNd bwaht lah mais sĕer le
*show.*    *(He brings a large box, puts it on the*

**comptoir et l'ouvre.)**    **Les voici, monsieur.**    **Il y a des vues**
koN-twahr ay loovr.    lay vwah-see m'ss-yãy.    ill-yah day vĕe
*counter and opens it.)*    *Here they are, sir.*    *There are views*

**de la ville, des portraits des vedettes de l'écran, des**
de lah veel day por-trai day ve-dait de lay-kraN day
*of the town, portraits of the stars of the screen,*

**reproductions des grandes peintures qui se trouvent[1]**
re-pro-dĕeks-yoN day graNd piNtĕer kee se troov
*reproductions of the great paintings which are to be found*

**au Louvre[2].**    **M. Roberts :** **Combien celles-ci?**
oh loovr.      koN-byiN sail see?
*in the Louvre.*      *How much are these?*

---

[1] Lit. Find themselves.    [2] Famous museum.

**Vendeur :**

**50 centimes la pièce, Monsieur, mais j'en ai encore**
siN-kaNt saN-teem lah pyais m'ss-yāy mai zhah-nay aN-kor
*50 centimes each, sir, but I also have*

**à 3 francs le paquet.**
a trwah fraN le pah-kai.
*(at) 3 francs a packet.*

**M. Roberts : Veuillez m'en faire voir,**
vāy-yay maN fair vwahr
*Will you show me some,*

**s'il vous plaît.**
see voo plai.
*please.*

**Vendeur : Avec grand plaisir, monsieur.**
ah-vaik graN plai-zeer m'ss-yāy.
*With great pleasure, sir.*

**En voici.**
aN vwah-see.
*Here are some.*

**M. Roberts : Je prends ce paquet-ci.**
zhe praN se pah-kai see.
*I'll take this packet.*

**Maintenant j'ai tout ce qu'il me faut.  Voilà un**
miNt-naN zhay toos-keel me foh.  vwah-lah uN
*Now I have all that I need.  There is a*

### AU MUSÉE DU LOUVRE

Une foule enthousiaste entoure la statue de la Vénus de Milo, qui possède la réputation de ressembler, comme aucune autre, à l'idéal de la beauté féminine.

| **Foule** (f.) | **enthousiaste** (adj.) | **entourer** | **posséder** | **ressembler** |
|---|---|---|---|---|
| Crowd | enthusiastic | to surround | to possess | to resemble |

billet de cent francs.
bee-yai de saN fraN
*100 francs note.*

**Vendeur : Monsieur n'a pas de petite**
m'ss-yⓐy nah pah de p'teet
*The gentleman has no small*

monnaie?
mo-nai?
*change?*

**M. Roberts : Je regrette.**
zhe re-grait.
*I regret (it).*

## TO BUY AND TO SELL

**acheter**—*to buy*
**j'achète**   ah-shait
**il (elle) achète**   ah-shait
**nous achetons**   ahsh-toN
**vous achetez**   ahsh-tay
**ils (elles) achètent**   ah-shait
*Imperfect :* **j'achetais,** etc.
*Perfect :* **j'ai acheté,** etc.

**vendre**—*to sell*
**je vends**   vaN
**il (elle) vend**   vaN
**nous vendons**   vaN-doN
**vous vendez**   vaN-day
**ils (elles) vendent**   vaNd
*Imperfect :* **je vendais,** etc.
*Perfect :* **j'ai vendu,** etc.

Note that **acheter,** which has e mute in the last syllable but one, takes a grave accent when the next syllable has e mute.

## DEAR AND CHEAP

*Dear*—**cher** (m.), **chère** (f.), are both pronounced **shair.**
*Cheap*—**bon marché** (boN mahr-shay) literally means *good market.*
*Cheaper* — **meilleur** (mai-yⓐr) **marché,** lit., *better market.*
*Cheapest*—**le meilleur** (mai-yⓐr) **marché,** lit., *the best market.*

Note from the above the irregular Comparative and Superlative of **bon, bonne.**

## GOOD, BETTER, BEST

| *Good:* | *Better:* | *Best:* |
|---|---|---|
| **bon** | **meilleur** | **le meilleur** |
| **bonne** | **meilleure** | **la meilleure** |

## THE DEFINITE ARTICLE IN PRICE QUOTATIONS

**Les cartes postales coûtent 10 francs la douzaine**—*These postcards cost 10 francs a dozen.*
**Trois francs le paquet.**—*Three francs a packet.*
**Le beurre coûte 12 francs la livre.**—*(The) butter costs 12 francs a pound.*
**J'ai payé sept francs le mètre.**—*I paid seven francs a metre.*

When giving price quotations, measurements, weights, etc., the definite article **(le, la)** is used in French instead of the indefinite article or "per" as used in English.

## AGO

**Il y a trois mois**—*three months ago.*
**Il y a quelques jours**—*a few days ago.*
**Il y a quinze jours**—*a fortnight ago.*

## WISHES AND REQUESTS

**Je voudrais** (voo-drai)—*I should like.*
**Voudriez-vous** (voo-dryai voo)—*would you like?*
**Veuillez** (vⓐy-yay)—*would you please, will you be so kind as to?*
**je désire** (day-zeer)—*I wish, I want to.*
**je veux** (vⓐy)—*I want, I wish to.*
**voulez-vous** (voo-lay-voo)—*do you want, do you wish to?*

## THE FUTURE

*I shall be*
**je serai**   s'ray
**il (elle) sera**   s'ra
**nous serons**   s'roN
**vous serez**   s'ray
**ils (elles) seront**   s'roN

*I shall speak*
**je parlerai**   pahrl'rai
**il (elle) parlera**   pahrl'rah
**nous parlerons**   pahr-le-roN
**vous parlerez**   pahr-le-ray
**ils (elles) parleront**   pahr-le-roN

## LA BOURSE DE PARIS

En haut, nous voyons une foule rassemblée sur les marches de la Bourse, occupée à lire la cote affichée par les courtiers. En bas, ce qui semble une scène de film arrangée par un régisseur de génie est une véritable photographie prise un jour de hausse.

The upper photograph shows a crowd on the steps of the Stock Exchange, busily reading the quotations on the stockbrokers' lists. Below, what looks like a scene from a film arranged by a clever director, is an actual photograph taken on a day of boom prices.

*I shall have*

**j'aurai** oh-ray
**il (elle) aura** oh-rah
**nous aurons** oh-roN
**vous aurez** oh-ray
**ils (elles) auront** oh-roN

*I shall reply*

**je répondrai** ray-poN-drai
**il (elle) répondra** ray-pon-drah
**nous répondrons** ray-poN-droN
**vous répondrez** ray-poN-dray
**ils (elles) répondront** ray-poN-droN

The Future is formed by putting the endings of the present tense of **avoir** on to the Infinitive : **Je parler-ai** is *I have to speak*, i.e., *I shall speak*, etc.

Note that verbs ending in **re** drop the e before the addition of **ai**, etc., e.g., **je répondrai**—*I shall speak*, **je descendrai**—*I shall go down*, **j'entendrai**—*I shall hear*, etc.

## EXERCISES

### I

Use (*a*) the Present tense, (*b*) the Imperfect, (*c*) the Perfect, (*d*) the Future of the following verbs after the Pronoun **il** :

1. donner. 2. prendre. 3. mettre. 4. acheter. 5. dire.

### II Translate into English

1. Ce livre-ci est un bon livre, mais ce livre-là est meilleur : c'est le meilleur de tous mes livres. 2. Le printemps est la meilleure saison. 3. Georges est le garçon le plus heureux de la ville. 4. Je me laverai dans la salle de bain. 5. Il sera très fatigué. 6. Seront-ils en retard pour le petit déjeuner? 7. Nous passerons les vacances au bord de la mer. 8. Quand serez-vous en vacances? 9. Elle ne changera pas son argent. 10. Pourquoi ne comptez-vous pas la monnaie? 11. Est-ce qu'ils vendront leur maison? 12. Je voudrais me coucher de bonne heure.

### III Translate into French

1. My cigars are better than your cigarettes. 2. The best tobacco is very dear. 3. French cigarettes are cheaper. 4. They are 25 centimes each. 5. How much is a packet of 10? 6. He will have to write many letters. 7. Will you change your English bank-notes? 8. I shall not forget to buy a box of matches and some ink. 9. Is there a stationer's near here? 10. We shall go into a public-house, where one can buy some stamps. 11. I would like some picture postcards. 12. Would you like to go with me? (*Key on page* 209.)

### AVEZ VOUS ACHETÉ UN DICTIONNAIRE?

Un dictionnaire peut être très utile pour augmenter votre vocabulaire et vous aider à apprendre à mesure que vous avancez. Vous pouvez y chercher les mots que vous rencontrez dans vos lectures ou que vous entendez à la radio et que vous ne connaissez pas. N'importe quel dictionnaire de poche usuel suffira pour le moment. Plus tard, si vous désirez faire une étude plus avancée du français, le "Study Guide" à la fin de ce volume vous donnera d'utiles conseils sur ce point. Cependant, assurez-vous que vous connaissez les noms français des objets de tous les jours avant d'essayer d'apprendre des mots difficiles ou rares.

### HAVE YOU BOUGHT A DICTIONARY?

A dictionary can be very useful in adding to your vocabulary, and in assisting you to learn as you go along. In it you can look up any word which you read or hear on the radio, and do not know. Any ordinary pocket dictionary will serve for the moment. Later, should you desire to study more advanced French, the "Study Guide" at the end of this volume gives you valuable advice in this respect. Make certain, however, that you know the French for all everyday things before you attempt to learn any difficult or unusual words.

**AUX HALLES CENTRALES**

Après minuit, sous de puissantes lampes électriques, les négociants en produit alimentaires viennent s'approvisionner dans ce fameux marché.

| **Puissant-e** (adj.) | **négociant-e** (m.f.) | **produits** (m.pl.) **alimentaires** | **s'approvisionne** |
|---|---|---|---|
| Powerful | (wholesale) merchant | foodstuffs | to lay in stock |

# QUINZIÈME LEÇON

## M. LESAGE AS HOST

Try to describe in French the above picture, in which Mr. and Mrs. Roberts are seen lunching as M. Lesage's guests.  For key, see page 401.

### DÉJEUNER AU RESTAURANT

**M. et Mme Roberts et M. Lesage sont assis autour d'une table dans un**
M. ay Mme ro-bairts ay M. le-sahzh soN-tah-see oh-toor dễn tahbl daN-zuN
*Mr. and Mrs. Roberts and Mr. Lesage are sitting around a table in a*

**restaurant.  C'est l'heure du déjeuner.**
rais-toh-raN.  sai lãyr dễ day-zhãy-nay.
*restaurant.  It is lunch-time.*

**M. Lesage :  Garçon, donnez-**
gahr-soN do-nay
*Waiter, give*

**moi la carte, s'il vous plaît.**
mwah lah kahrt see-voo plai.
*me the menu, please.*

**Garçon :  La voici, monsieur.**
lah vwah-see m'ss-yãy.
*Here it is, sir,*

**M. Lesage :  Merci.  Qu'est-ce que vous prenez comme hors d'œuvre?**
mair-see.  kaisk' voo pre-nay kom or-dãyvr?
*Thanks.   What are you taking as hors d'œuvre?*

**Moi, je**
mwah zhe
*As for me, I*

**prendrai du filet de hareng.**
praN-dray dễ fee-lay de ah-raN.
*will take filleted herring.*

**M. Roberts :  La même chose pour moi.**
lah maim shohz poor mwah.
*The same (thing) for me.*

**Mme Roberts :** **Je préfère la salade de tomates.**
zhe pray-fair lah sah-lahd de toh-maht.
*I prefer (the) tomato-salad.*

**M. Lesage :**   **Bien.   Garçon, apportez-nous deux filets de hareng**
byiN.   gahr-soN ah-por-tay noo dȳ fee-lay de ah-raN
*Good.    Waiter, bring us two portions of filleted herring*

**et une salade de tomates et n'oubliez pas le pain.**
ay ȇn sah-lad de toh-maht ay noo-blyay pah le piN.
*and one tomato-salad and don't forget the bread.*

**Garçon :**   **Le pain est sur la table, monsieur.**
le piN ay sȇr lah tahbl m'ssyȳ.
*The bread is on the table, sir.*

**M. Lesage :**   **Excusez-moi, je ne l'avais pas vu.**
aix-kȇ-zay mwah zhe ne lah-vai pah vȇ.
*Excuse me, I had not seen it.*

**Garçon :**   **Qu'est-ce que vous choisissez comme viande, messieurs, dames?**
kaisk' voo shwah-zee-say kom vyaNd mais'yȳ dahm?
*What do you choose as meat, gentlemen, ladies?*

**M. Lesage :**   **Apportez-moi une escalope.   Comme légumes**
ah-por-tay mwah ȇn-ais-kah-lop.   kom lay-gȇm
*Bring me a collop.[1]    As vegetables*

**je prendrai des pommes de terre et de la salade verte.**
zhe praN-dray day pom de tair ay de lah sah-lahd vairt.
*I'll take potatoes and green salad.*

**Garçon :**   **C'est entendu.**                **Mme Roberts :** **Pour moi**
sai-taN-taN-dȇ.                                                    poor mwah
*Very good, sir (lit., this is understood).*                      *For me*

**une tranche de bœuf avec des champignons, s'il vous plaît.**
ȇn traNsh de bȳf ah-vaik day shaN-peen-yoN see voo plai.
*(a portion of) roast beef with mushrooms, please.*

**M. Roberts :**   **Pouvez-vous recommander votre lapin rôti?**
poo-vay voo re-ko-maN-day votr lah-piN ro-tee?
*Can you recommend your roast rabbit?*

**Garçon :**   **Je vous le recommande beaucoup, nous le servons**
zhe voo le re-ko-maNd boh-koo noo le sair-voN
*I (to you) recommend it very much, we serve it*

---

[1] The French word **escalope** is more often used for this thin slice of meat.

## PARIS QUI MANGE

En haut, on déguste dans un fameux restaurant des mets de choix et de vins de marque. En bas, des employés de la Halle aux Vins savourent un bon "gueuleton".

| **Déguster** | **mets** (m.) | **vins de marque** | **savourer** | **gueuleton** (m.) |
|---|---|---|---|---|
| To taste | viand; (prepared) food | vintage wines | to relish | "blow-out" (slang) |

# CARTE DU JOUR—MENU

## HORS D'ŒUVRE[1]

| | | | |
|---|---|---|---|
| **Filet de hareng** | **Anchois** | **Maquereaux au vin blanc** | **Beurre** |
| fee-lai de a-raN | aN-shwah | mak-roh oh viN blaN | bãyr |
| *Filleted herring* | *Anchovies* | *Mackerel in white wine* | *Butter* |
| | | | |
| **Huîtres** | **Pâté de lapin** | **Hors d'œuvre variés** | **Saucissons** |
| w̃eetr | pa-tay de lah-piN | or dãyvr vah-ryay | so-see-soN |
| *Oysters* | *Rabbit pie* | *Assorted hors d'œuvre* | *Sausage* |

## SOUPES

| | |
|---|---|
| **Soupe à l'oignon** | **Consommé Julienne** |
| soop a lon-yoN | koN-so-may zhẽẽl-yain |
| *Onion soup* | *Clear vegetable soup* |

## ENTRÉES

| | | |
|---|---|---|
| **Salade de bœuf** | **Veau sauté petit pois** | **Homard mayonnaise** |
| sah-lahd de bãyf | voh soh-tay p'tee pwah | o-mahr mah-yo-naiz |
| *Beef salad* | *Stewed veal with peas* | *Lobster with mayonnaise* |
| | | |
| **Omelette paysanne** | **Œufs brouillés aux pointes d'asperge** | |
| om-lait pai-eezahn | ãy broo-yay oh pwiNt dahs-pairzh | |
| *Omelette with chopped vegetables* | *Scrambled eggs with asparagus tips* | |

## LÉGUMES—VEGETABLES

| | | |
|---|---|---|
| **Pommes nouvelles au beurre** | **Haricots verts à l'huile** | **Asperges** |
| pom noo-vail oh bãyr | ah-ree-koh vair ah lw̃eel | ah-spairzh |
| *New potatoes in butter* | *French beans in oil* | *Asparagus* |
| | | |
| **Petits pois au lard** | **Chou-fleur au gratin** | **Céleri braisé** |
| p'tee pwah oh lahr | shoo-flãyr oh grah-tiN | sayl'ree brai-zay |
| *Peas in bacon fat* | *Cauliflower au gratin* | *Braised celery* |

## RÔTIS—JOINTS

| | | |
|---|---|---|
| **Noix de veau rôtie** | **Faisan rôti** | **Côte de porc sauce piquante** |
| nwah de voh roh-tee | fai-saN roh-tee | koht de por sohs pee-kaNt |
| *Roast knuckle of veal* | *Roast pheasant* | *Rib of pork, piquant sauce* |
| | | |
| **Aloyau, pommes nouvelles** | **Côtelette de mouton aux pommes soufflées** | |
| ah-lwah-yoh pom noo-vail | koht-lait de moo-toN oh pom soof-lay | |
| *Sirloin of beef, new potatoes* | *Mutton chop, puffed potatoes* | |

## FROMAGES—CHEESE

| | | | | |
|---|---|---|---|---|
| **Crème d'Isigny** | **Camembert** | **Roquefort** | **Gruyère** | **Brie** |
| kraim dee-zeen-yee | kah-maN-bair | rock-for | grẽẽ-yair | bree |
| *Crème d'Isigny* | *Camembert* | *Roquefort* | *Gruyère* | *Brie* |
| (*Cream cheese*) | | (*Kind of strong cheese*) | | |

## DESSERTS

| | | | | | |
|---|---|---|---|---|---|
| **Compote de pêches** | **Glaces** | **Confitures** | **Fraises** | **Gâteaux** | **Cerises** |
| koN-poht de paish | glahs | koN-fee-tẽẽr | fraiz | gah-toh | se-reez |
| *Stewed peaches* | *Ices* | *Jams* | *Strawberries* | *Cakes* | *Cherries* |

---

[1]Usually, but incorrectly, spelt in English **hors d'œuvres**. The French words **hors d'œuvre** (without final **s**) mean "outside the (finished) work," in other words, a side-dish.

Here our artist has done half the work for you, since you can scarcely miss which are lobsters, oysters, salmon, mussels, etc. But there are still others for which you must consult the list below. Use this list as in other lessons, until you feel satisfied that you could order anything you wanted at the fishmonger's.

### LE POISSON—FISH

| **le hareng** | **le maquereau** | **la carpe** | **l'anguille** (f.) | **l'anchois** (m.) | **la sardine** |
|---|---|---|---|---|---|
| ah-raN | mahk-roh | kahrp | aN-geey | an-shwah | sahr-deen |
| *herring* | *mackerel* | *carp* | *eel* | *anchovy* | *sardine* |

| **la truite** | **l'éperlan** | **le saumon** | **la perche** | **la raie** | **la barbue** |
|---|---|---|---|---|---|
| trw̃eet | ay-pair-laN | soh-moN | pairsh | rai | bahr-bẽe |
| *trout* | *smelt* | *salmon* | *perch* | *skate* | *brill* |

| **le thon** | **l'aigrefin** (m.) | **la morue** | **la sole** | **le homard** | **la langouste** | **l'huître** (f.) |
|---|---|---|---|---|---|---|
| toN | aygr-fiN | mo-rẽe | sohl | o-mahr | laN-goost | w̃eetr |
| *tunny* | *haddock* | *cod* | *sole* | *lobster* | *sea crayfish* | *oyster* |

| **la crevette** | **l'escargot** (m.) | **la moule** | **la tortue** | **le carrelet** | **les crustacés** |
|---|---|---|---|---|---|
| kre-vait | ais-kahr-goh | mool | tor-tẽe | kah-r'lay | krẽe-stah-say |
| *shrimp* | *snail* | *mussel* | *turtle* | *plaice* | *shell fish* |

| **le poisson d'eau douce** | **le poisson de marée** | **mariné** | **étuvé** | **frit** |
|---|---|---|---|---|
| pwah-soN doh doos | pwah-soN de mah ray | mah-ree-nay | ay-tẽe-vay | free |
| *river fish* | *salt-water fish* | *pickled, soused* | *stewed* | *fried* |

| **au four** | **à la brochette** | **grillé** | **au bleu** | **en coquille** | **aux câpres** |
|---|---|---|---|---|---|
| oh foor | ah la broh-shait | gree-yay | oh blãy | aN ko-keey | oh kahpr |
| *baked* | *broiled* | *grilled* | *cooked in wine* | *served in shell* | *with caper sauce* |

| **bonne femme** | **Colbert** | **maître d'hôtel** | **friture** (f.) |
|---|---|---|---|
| bon fahm | kol bair | maitr doh tail | free-tẽer |
| *with bitter sauce* | *with white sauce* | *done in butter* | *dish of small fried fish* |

**au vin blanc, c'est délicieux, monsieur.**
oh viN blaN sai day-lees-ya͡y m'ss-ya͡y.
*with white wine, it is delicious, sir.*

**M. Roberts :** **Bon, j'ai confiance en vous.**    **Garçon :** **Qu'est-ce que vous**
boN zhay koN-fyaNs aN voo.      kaisk' voo
*Good, I have confidence in you.*      *What do you*

**prenez comme légumes, monsieur?**
pre-nay kom lay-ge͡͡em m'ss-ya͡y?
*take as vegetables, sir?*

**M. Roberts :** **Des petits pois, s'il vous plaît.**    **Garçon :** **Comme vin je**
day p'tee pwah see voo plai.      kom viN zhe
*Peas, if you please.*      *As (a) wine I*

**vous recommande surtout notre Bordeaux rouge.**
voo re-ko-maNd se͡͡er-too notr bor-doh roozh.
*recommend you especially our red Bordeaux.*

**Il est exquis.**      **M. Lesage :** **Non, apportez-nous plutôt**
ee-lai-taix-kee.      noN ah-por-tay noo ple͡͡e-toh
*It is exquisite.*      *No, bring us rather*

**une demi-bouteille de Montrachet avec les**
e͡͡n d'mee-boo-taiy de moN-rah-shay ah-vaik lay
*a half-bottle of Montrachet with the*

**hors-d'oeuvre et une bonne bouteille de Bourgogne rouge**
or-da͡yvr ay e͡͡n bon boo-taiy de boor-gony roozh
*hors-d'oeuvres and a good bottle of red Burgundy*

**avec le rôti.**      **Garçon :** **Bien, monsieur, et qu'est-ce**
ah-vaik le roh-tee.      byiN m'ss-ya͡y ay kaisk'
*with the (roast) meat.*      *All right, sir, and what*

**que vous prenez comme dessert?**    **M. Lesage :** **Du fromage et des**
voo pre-nay kom dai-sair?      de͡͡e fro-mahzh ay day
*will you take as dessert?*      *Cheese and*

**fruits pour moi.**      **Mme Roberts :** **La même chose pour nous.**
fru͡ee pour mwah.      lah maim shohz poor noo.
*fruit for me.*      *The same (thing) for us.*

**Garçon :** **Je vais vous servir tout de suite, messieurs, dames.**
zhe vai voo sair-veer tood's͡weet mais-ya͡y dahm.
*I am going to serve you at once, gentlemen, ladies.*

**Mme Roberts :** **C'est un coquet petit restaurant.**
sai-tuN ko-kai p'tee rais-toh-raN.
*It is a charming little restaurant.*

**M. Lesage :**  Un de mes amis me l'a recommandé; il semble qu'on
uN de may-zah-mee me lah re-ko-maN-day eel seNbl
*One of my friends has recommended it to me; it seems that one*

y mange bien et pas cher.
ko-nee maNzh byiN ay pah shair.
*(here) eats well and not expensively.*

### LÉGUMES (m.pl.)—VEGETABLES

| les petits pois | les haricots | haricots verts | la tomate | le concombre | l'asperge (f.) |
|---|---|---|---|---|---|
| p'tee pwah | ah-ree-koh | ah-ree-koh vair | toh-maht | koN-koNbr | ahs-pairzh |
| *green peas* | *beans* | *French beans* | *tomato* | *cucumber* | *asparagus* |

| le radis | la carotte | le raifort | le poireau | l'oignon | le céleri | l'épinard |
|---|---|---|---|---|---|---|
| rah-dee | kah-rot | rai-for | pwah-roh | on-yoN | say-le-ree | ay-pee-nahr |
| *radish* | *carrot* | *horse-radish* | *leek* | *onion* | *celery* | *spinach* |

| le chou | le chou de Bruxelles | le chou-fleur | la laitue | la pomme de terre | la betterave |
|---|---|---|---|---|---|
| shoo | shoo de brē̂-sail | shoo-flāyr | lai-tē̂ | pom de tair | bait'rahv |
| *cabbage* | *Brussels sprouts* | *cauliflower* | *lettuce* | *potato* | *beetroot* |

| le cresson | le navet | la courge | la chicorée | l'artichaut (m.) | la citrouille, le potiron |
|---|---|---|---|---|---|
| krai-soN | nah-vai | koorzh | shee-koh-ray | ahr-tee-shoh | see-trooy · poh-tee-roN |
| *watercress* | *turnip* | *marrow* | *endive* | *artichoke* | *pumpkin* |

Certain popular vegetables are here clearly shown—but supposing you wanted a lettuce, cress, beetroot and radishes for a salad?   Consult the list above, then cover it over and practise making in French your own lists of the things  shown on these greengrocer's stalls.

**M. Roberts :**  Est-ce que l'avenue des Champs-Élysées est loin d'ici?
aisk' lah-venēē day shaN-zay-lee-zay ai lwiN dee see?
*Is the avenue des Champs Elysees far from here?*

**M. Lesage :**  Non, nous sommes tout près des Champs-Élysées.   Avez-vous
noN noo som too prai day shaN-zay-lee-zay. ah-vay voo
*No, we are quite near the Champs Elysees.   Have you*

l'intention d'y aller après le repas?
liN-taNs-yoN dee ah-lay ah-prai le re-pah?
*the intention to go there after the meal?*

**Mme Roberts :** Je voudrais tant prendre une tasse de café à
zhe voo-drai taN praNdr ēēn tahs de kah-fay ah
*I should like so much to have a cup of coffee at*

la Hungaria après le déjeuner.   On
lah uN-garyah ah-prai le day-zhāȳnay.   oN
*the Hungaria after (the) lunch.   One*

m'a dit qu'il y a là un bon orchestre hongrois avec
mah dee kee-lyah lah uN bo-nor-kaistr oN-grwah ah-vaik
*has told me that there is a good Hungarian band with*

des chanteurs tziganes.        **M. Lesage :** J'ai une course à
day shaN-tāȳr tsee-gahn.               zhay ēēn koors ah
*gipsy singers.*                        *I have an errand to*

faire, mais je veux bien vous accompagner jusqu'à la
fair mai zhe vāȳ byiN voo-zah-koN-pahn-yay zhēēs-kah lah
*do, but I should like very much to accompany you to the*

Hungaria.   Si vous pouvez m'attendre, je vous y
uN-garyah.   see voo poo-vay mah-taNdr zhe voo-zee
*Hungaria.   If you can wait for me, I shall*

rejoindrai vers quatre heures et demie.
re-zhwiN-dray vair kaht-rāȳr ay d'mee.
*rejoin you there towards half-past four.*

**Mme Roberts :** Bien sûr, nous vous attendrons.   Nous n'avons
byiN sēēr noo voo-zah-taN-droN.   noo nah-voN
*Certainly, we shall wait for you.   We have*

rien à faire de tout l'après-midi.   Voilà le
ryāȳ-nah fair too lahp-rai mee-dee.   vwah-lah le
*nothing to do the whole afternoon.   Here comes the*

garçon qui arrive.        **Garçon :** Veuillez m'excuser,
gahr-soN kee ah-reev.            vāȳyay maix-kēē-zay
*waiter.*                         *Will you excuse me,*

## LE JOUEUR D'ACCORDÉON

Par cette belle après-midi d'automne les passants sont rares, mais c'est peut-être l'art pour l'art qui retient ce musicien à son poste sur le quai.

| **Accordéon** (m.) | **passant-e** (m.f.) | **l'art pour l'art** | **quai** (m.) |
|---|---|---|---|
| Melodeon, concertina | passer-by | art for art's sake | quay |

**madame, il n'y a plus de tomates.**   **Mon collègue vient**
mah-dahm ill nyah plēē de toh-maht.   moN ko-laig vyiN
*madam, there are no more tomatoes.*   *My colleague has*

**de servir[1] les dernières.**    **Mme Roberts : C'est dommage.**
de sair-veer lay dairn-yair.       say do-mahzh.
*just served the last.*        *That's a pity.*

**Alors apportez-moi des sardines.**   **Il y en a**
ah-lor ah-por-tay mwah day sahr-deen.   eel yaN nah
*Then bring me some sardines.*   *There are some*

**encore, j'espère?**   **Garçon : Sans aucun doute, madame.  Je**
aN-kor zhais-pair?      saN-zoh-kuNdoot mah-dahm. zhe
*left, I hope?*       *Without any doubt, madam.  I*

**vous les servirai tout de suite.**   **M. Lesage : Ne nous faites**
voo lay sair-vee-ray tood' sŵeet.     ne noo fait
*shall serve them to you at once.*   *Don't let us*

**pas trop attendre, je vous prie.**
pah troh ah-taNdr zhe voo pree
*wait too much, I beg you.*

**Garçon :**     **Il y a tant de monde aujourd'hui, mais je ferai mon**
eel-yah taN de moNd oh-zhoor-dŵee mai zhe fe-ray moN
*There are so many people today, but I shall do all*

**possible, monsieur. (Il s'éloigne.)**   **M. Lesage: Pas de tomates!**
po-seebl m'ss-yâŷ.  eel say-lwany.      pah de toh-maht!
*I can, sir.  (He goes off.)*      *No tomatoes!*

**C'est drôle, tout de même.**   **Enfin, c'est vrai, il y a beaucoup de**
say drohl too de maim.  aN-fiN say vrai eel-yah boh-koo de
*It is strange, all the same.*   *After all, it's true it is very*

**monde[2], soyons indulgents.**   **Garçon : Voilà les filets de**
moNd swah-yoN-ziN-dēēl-zhaN.     vwahl-ah lay fee-lai de
*crowded, let's be tolerant.*     *Here are the fillets of*

**hareng et les sardines.**   **Je vous apporte en même temps**
ah-raN ay lay sahr-deen.  zhe voo-zah-port aN maim taN
*herring and the sardines.*   *I bring you at the same time*

**votre Montrachet.**   **La viande et les légumes vont suivre dans**
votr moN-trah-shay.  lah vyaNd ay lay lay-gēēm voN sŵeevr daN
*your Montrachet.*   *The meat and the vegetables will follow in*

---

[1] Lit. comes from serving.   [2] Lit. there are lots of people.

un instant.    **M. Lesage : Bien. (Il lève son verre.)**  À **votre**
zuN-niN-staN.       byiN.  ill laiv soN vair.  ah votr
*a moment.*       *Good.*  *(He raises his glass.)*  *Your*

**santé. (Tout le monde boit.)  Je voulais vous faire**
saN-tay.  too le moNd bwah.  zhe voo-lai voo fair
*health. (They all drink.)  I wanted to let you*

**goûter de ce Montrachet, l'un de nos vins blancs bien**
goo-tay de ce moN-trah-shay luN de noh viN blaN byiN
*taste this Montrachet, one of our white wines far*

**trop peu connu à l'étranger.**
troh pa͡y kon-ne͡e ah lay-traN-zhay.
*too little known abroad.*

**M. Roberts :**  **Il est délicieux.  Je vous en suis vraiment**
eel ay day-lees-ya͡y.  zhe voo-zaN-sw͡ee vrai-maN
*It is delicious.  I am really grateful to you*

**reconnaissant.**    **M. Lesage (un peu plus tard) : La cuisine**
rek-on-nai-saN.            lah k͡wee-zeen
*for (introducing me to) it.*        *The cooking*

DANS UN VIGNOBLE DE BEAUNE

Les grappes de raisins tombent dans les paniers.  Les vignerons auront tôt fait d'achever
la vendange.  Votre verre de Bourgogne est assuré!

| **Vignoble** (m.) | **grappe** (f.) | **vigneron** (m.) | **avoir tôt fait de** | **vendange** (f.) |
|---|---|---|---|---|
| Vineyard | bunch | vine-grower | not to be long in (doing) | wine-harvest |

n'est pas mauvaise, pas mauvaise du tout, n'est-ce pas?
nay pah moh-vaiz pah moh-vaiz dée too nais' pah?
*is not bad, not bad at all, isn't it so?*

**M. Roberts :**   Quant à moi, je suis très content.
kaN-tah mwah zhe swee trai koN-taN.
*As for me, I am very pleased.*

**Garçon :**   Voilà le fromage et le dessert.
vwah-lah le fro-mazh ay le dai-sair.
*Here is the cheese and the dessert.*

**M. Lesage :**   Je vous remercie.   Vous nous servez vraiment vite.
zhe voo re-mair-see. voo noo sair-vay vrai-maN veet.
*I thank you.   You serve us really quickly.*

Maintenant apportez l'addition, s'il vous plaît.
miNt-naN ah-por-tay lah-dees-yoN see voo plai.
*Now, bring the bill, please.*

**Garçon :**   Bien, monsieur.    **M. Lesage** (s'adressant à un vendeur de
byiN,m'ss-yáy             sah-drai-saN ah uN vaN-dáyr de
*Good, sir.*               (*addressing himself to a*

journaux qui passe) :   Donnez-moi Paris-
zhoor-noh kee pahs do-nay mwah pah-ree
*newspaper seller who passes*) *Give me Paris-*

Midi!    **M. Roberts :** Il y a du nouveau?
mee-dee!          eel-yah dée noo-voh?
*Midi!*            *Is there any news?*

**M. Lesage :**   Rien d'extraordinaire.
ryiN daix-trah-or-dee-nair.
*Nothing extraordinary.*

Tiens!   On a arrêté le
tyiN! o-nah ah-rai-tay le
*I say!   One has* (*they have*) *arrested the*

meurtrier de la rue
máyr-tray de lah rée
*murderer of the rue*

de Clichy.
de klee-shee.
*de Clichy.*

**Mme Roberts :** Vous lisez les histoires de meurtres?
voo lee-zay lay-zees-twahr de máyrtr?
*You read* (*the*) *stories of murders?*

**M. Lesage :**    **C'est un cas extraordinaire, vous n'en avez pas**
sai-tuN kah aix-trah-or-dee-nair voo naN-nah-vay pah
*It is an extraordinary case, you haven't heard*

**entendu parler?    Mais tout Paris en parle.    C'était**
zaN-taN-dẽ pahr-lay?    mai too pah-ree aN pahrl. say-tai
*speak of it?    But all Paris is speaking of it.    It was*

**il y a deux ou trois jours...**         **Garçon : Voilà l'addition,**
eel-yah dãy-zoo trwah zhoor              vwah-lah lah-dees-yoN
*two or three days ago...*                *Here is the bill,*

**messieurs.**       **M. Lesage : Je vais régler ça.    Voilà,**
mais-yãy.           zhe vai raig-lay sah vwah-lah
*gentlemen.*         *I am going to settle this.    Here you are,*

**gardez le reste!**         **Garçon : Merci, monsieur.**
gahr-day le rest!
*keep the rest!*

## DANS UNE RÔTISSERIE PARISIENNE

Devant soi, en plein restaurant, on voit tourner à la broche le poulet qu'on a choisi pour déjeuner.    C'est avec difficulté qu'on réprime son impatience.

| En plein restaurant | tourner à la broche | rôtisserie (f.) | réprimer |
|---|---|---|---|
| Right in the restaurant | to turn on the spit | grill-room | to repress |

## LA VIANDE—MEAT
## LE GIBIER—GAME
## LA VOLAILLE—POULTRY

| le bœuf | le veau | le porc | le mouton | l'agneau (m.) | le lapin | le lièvre | la bécasse |
|---------|---------|---------|-----------|---------------|----------|-----------|------------|
| bayf | voh | por | moo-toN | ahn-yoh | lah-piN | lyaivr | bay-kahs |
| *ox* | *calf* | *pig* | *mutton* | *lamb* | *rabbit* | *hare* | *woodcock* |

| la caille | la perdrix | le faisan | le coq de bruyère | le pluvier |
|-----------|------------|-----------|-------------------|------------|
| kahy | pair-dree | fai-zaN | kok de brēeyair | plēevyay |
| *quail* | *partridge* | *pheasant* | *grouse* | *plover* |

| le poulet | le canard | l'oie | la dinde | le dindon | la pintade | le chevreuil |
|-----------|-----------|-------|----------|-----------|------------|--------------|
| poo-lai | kah-nahr | wah | diNd | diN-doN | piN-tahd | shev-ray-y |
| *chicken* | *duck* | *goose* | *turkey* | *turkey* | *guinea-fowl* | *roe-buck* |

du boeuf—*beef*
du veau—*veal*
du porc—*pork*
de la viande de bœuf—*beef*
de la viande de veau—*veal*
de la viande de porc—*pork*
du rôti de bœuf—*roast beef*
du rôti de veau—*roast veal*
du rôti de porc—*roast pork*
l'aile f.—*wing (of poultry)*
le bifteck  (beef-taik)—*beefsteak*
au pot  (oh poh)—*boiled*
en ragoût—*stewed*
en daube—*braised*
bouilli  (boo-yee)—*boiled*
grillade  (gree-yahd)—*grilled*
sur le gril—*grilled*
à la casserole—*stewed in stewpan*
au four—*baked*
hachis—*minced*
rognon  (ron-yoN)—*kidney*
le foie—*liver*
la langue  (laNg-)—*tongue*
le pied  (pyay)—*foot*
la cervelle—*brain*
le collet  (co-lai)—*neck*
la côte—*rib*
la côtelette—*chop, cutlet*
le dos  (doh)—*saddle*
la tête—*head*

la poitrine  (pwaht-reen)—*breast*
le gigot—*leg of mutton*
la cuisse—*leg of game or poultry*
le cuissot—*leg of venison*
le ris  (ree)—*sweetbread*
farci—*stuffed*
le jambon  (zhaN-boN)—*ham*
la saucisse  (soh-sees)—*sausage*
le saucisson—*large sausage eaten cold*
le lard  (lahr)—*bacon*
andouille  (an-dooy)—*sausage of tripe*
blanquette—*stew in thick white sauce*
bouchée  (boo-shay)—*pie or patty*
le boudin—*black pudding*
bourguignon—*with carrots and onions*
châteaubriant—*fillet of steak with fried potatoes*
cocotte—*cooked with bacon in casserole*
cœur de filet—*tender loin steak*
escalope (f.)—*thin slice of meat*
financière—*with mushrooms and truffles in Madeira wine*
jardinière—*with mixed vegetables*
maître d'hôtel—*done in butter*
velouté de—*creamed or pulped*
pot-au-feu—*boiled beef and broth*
civet de—*jugged*
fricandeau—*stew of larded meat*
vol-au-vent—*raised pie filled with goose liver, kidneys, mushrooms, &c.*

### FOR STUDENTS TO REMEMBER !

Le commencement est la moitié de tout.
Well begun is half done.

L'oisiveté est la mère de tous les vices.
Idleness is the root of all evil.

**Mme Roberts : Alors nous pouvons partir.**
ah-lor noo poo-voN pahr-teer.
*Now we can go.*

**M. Lesage :    Je vous raconterai l'histoire du meurtre en route.**
zhe voo rah-koN-tray lees-twahr dẽe mãỹrtr aN root.
*I will tell you the story of the murder on the way.*

**C'est vraiment sensationnel.   Quelle chance qu'on ait**
sai vrai-maN saN-sah-syoh-nail.  kail shaNs ko-nai
*It is really sensational.   What luck that one has*

**pu arrêter le meurtrier si vite.   Elle travaille**
pẽe ah-ray-tay le mãỹr-tryay see veet.  ail trah-vah*y*
*been able to arrest the murderer so quickly.   It works*

**bien, la police, il faut l'avouer.   Mais je veux**
byiN lah po-lees eel foh lah-voo-ay.  mai zhe vãỹ
*well, the police, one has to admit it.   But I want*

**commencer par le commencement.   Alors c'était. . . .**
ko-maN-say pahr le ko-maNs-maN.  ah-lor say-tai
*to start with the beginning.   Well, there was . . .*

**(Ils quittent le restaurant.   Dans la rue M. Lesage continue**
eel keet le rais-toh-raN.  daN lah rẽe m'ss-yãỹ le-sahzh koN-tee-nẽe
*(They leave the restaurant.   In the street Mr. Lesage continues*

**à raconter l'histoire étrange du meurtre de la rue de Clichy.)**
ah rah-koN-tay lees-twahr ay-traNzh dẽe mãỹrtr de lah rẽe de klee-shee.
*to tell the strange story of the murder in the rue de Clichy.)*

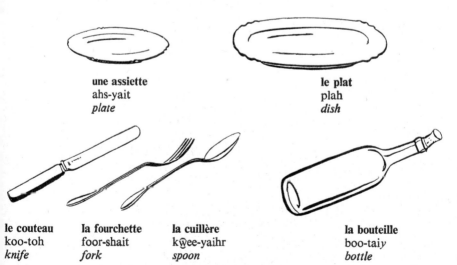

**une assiette**          **le plat**
ahs-yait                 plah
*plate*                  *dish*

**le couteau**   **la fourchette**   **la cuillère**      **la bouteille**
koo-toh         foor-shait          k$\widehat{w}$ee-yaihr      boo-tai*y*
*knife*         *fork*              *spoon*             *bottle*

**MANGER** = TO EAT ; **BOIRE** = TO DRINK

### Present Tense

(See Lesson 8, page 100)

#### Imperfect

je mangeais   maN-zhai

il ⎫
elle ⎰ mangeait   maN-zhai

nous mangions   maN-zhyoN
vous mangiez   maN-zhyay

ils ⎫
elles ⎰ mangeaient   maN-zhai

je buvais   bē͞e-vai

il ⎫
elle ⎰ buvait   (bē͞e-vai

nous buvions   bē͞ev-yon
vous buviez   bē͞ev-yay

ils ⎫
elles ⎰ buvaient   bē͞e-vai

#### Future

je mangerai   maNzh'ray, etc.
je boirai   bwah-ray, etc.

#### Perfect

j'ai mangé   maN-zhay
j'ai bu   bē͞e, etc.

Nous mangeons (maN-zhoN) la soupe avec une cuillère.   Nous mangeons la viande avec une fourchette.   Nous coupons la viande avec un couteau.

Nous buvons le vin dans un verre.   Nous buvons le thé dans une tasse.   On apporte la viande sur un plat, mais nous la mangeons dans une assiette.

*Note.*—The **g** in **manger** is soft (pronounced like the s in " pleasure ").   **g** is always soft before **e** and **i,** otherwise it is hard (as in "go").

Now, in order to indicate that the **g** remains soft when used in connection with **nous** an **e** is inserted before the ending **ons**. The same is done right through the Imperfect.   Notice that this extra **e** is not pronounced.

#### HIM, HER, THEM

**Connaissez-vous M. Lesage?   Je le connais.**
*Do you know Mr. Lesage?   I know him.*

**Je ne le connais pas.**
*I don't know him.*

**Prenez-vous ce billet?   Je le prends.**
*Do you take this ticket?   I take it.*

**Je ne le prends pas.**
*I don't take it.*

**Connaissez-vous Mme. Lesage?   Je la connais.**
*Do you know Mrs. Lesage?   I know her.*

**Je ne la connais pas.**
*I don't know her.*

**Prenez-vous cette boîte?   Je la prends.**
*Do you take that box?   I take it.*

**Je ne les prends pas.**
*I don't take them.*

**Connaissez-vous les Lesages?   Je les connais.**
*Do you know the Lesages?   I know them.*

**Je ne les connais pas.**
*I don't know them.*

**Prenez-vous ces billets (boîtes)?**
*Do you take these tickets (boxes)?*

**Je les prends.**
*I take them.*

**Je ne les prends pas.**
*I don't take them.*

**Voici le garçon.   Appelez-le.**
*Here is the waiter.   Call him.*

**Voici le billet.   Prenez-le.**
*Here is the ticket.   Take it.*

**Ne le prenez-pas.**
*Don't take it.*

**Voici la serveuse.   Appelez-la.**
*Here is the waitress.   Call her.*

**Ne l'appelez pas.   Voici la boîte.**
*Don't call her.   Here is the box.*

**Prenez-la.   Ne la prenez pas.**
*Take it.   Don't take it.*

**Voici les billets (boîtes).**
*Here are the tickets (boxes).*

**Prenez-les.   Ne les prenez pas.**
*Take them.   Don't take them.*

When we are constantly referring to a certain person we do not consider it necessary to repeat his (or her) name over and over again: we refer to him as "he", to her as "she", to a thing as "it", to several persons or things as "they".   Words like "he", "she", "it", "they", "them", etc., which are used instead of nouns are called Pronouns.   "I", "he", "she", and "they", are used as subjects of sentences;

"he", "him", "her", and "them", are used objects. "It", "you", can be used her as subjects or objects, e.g. "it is autiful" ("it" is the subject of (the ntence); "can you see it? (here "it" is the ject, "you" the subject); "I like you" I" is the subject, "you" the object).

Careful study of the above examples will ow you that in French : 1. Le is used th for "him" and for "it" (when the ject is masculine). 2. La is used both r "her" and for "it" (when the object is minine). 3. Les is used for "them".

With regard to the order of words in the ntence note that :

1. Pronouns, when objects, are placed fore the verb instead of after it as in nglish.

2. When the verb expresses a command, ., when it is in the Imperative Affirmative, e Pronoun Object is placed after the verb d joined on to it by a hyphen.

3. If the Imperative is negative (i.e., gins with Don't) pronoun objects are aced before the verb.

renez-le but ne le prenez pas.
oyons-les but ne les voyons pas.
coutez-nous but ne nous écoutez pas.

Note from the last example that there is difference in French between "we" and us", both forms rendered by nous.

### ME

st-ce qu'il vous connaît? Does he know you?
me connaît. He knows me.
ne me connaît pas. He does not know me.
coutez-moi. Listen to me.
ttendez-moi. Wait for me.
e m'attendez pas. Don't wait for me.

*Note.*—1. When me is to be placed after e verb in the Imperative it becomes moi nwah). 2. me, le, la, become m', l', l', fore a vowel or mute h.

### IT

Voici le vin. Il est bon.
Here is the wine. It is good.
Je le prends. I take it.
Voici la bière. Elle est bonne.
Here is the beer. It is good.
Je la prends. I take it.

In these four lines we have the four equivalents for English "it".

1. In the first line the "it" in "it is good" must be translated by il, because "it" is the subject and replaces a masculine noun.

2. In the second line "it" must be translated by le, because it is the object, replacing a masculine noun.

3. In the third line "it" is the subject, replacing a feminine noun.

4. In the fourth line "it" is the object, replacing a feminine noun.

IL ("he" or "it") replaces any masculine noun, if the subject.

ELLE ("she" or "it") replaces any feminine noun, if the subject.

LE ("him" or "it") replaces any masculine noun, if the object.

LA ("her" or "it") replaces any feminine noun, if the object.

### SUMMARY
(*Sentence building*)

### EXERCISES

#### I Replace the words in bold type by Pronouns

1. **Charles** n'écoute pas le **professeur**.
2. **Les enfants** regardent **les belles fleurs**.

3. Nous allons voir **nos parents.** 4. Elle met **la main** sur sa bouche. 5. Il ne mange pas **les légumes.** 6. Aimez-vous **la bière?** 7. Il ne trouve pas **ses livres.** 8. Elle attend **son oncle.** 9. **Les enfants** ne ferment pas **la porte.** 10. **Le professeur** prend-t-il **la boîte?**

## II Translate into French

1. Are you taking (the) salad? Yes, I am taking it. 2. Is she taking herring? She is not taking it. 3. Does the teacher open the window? No, he does not open it. 4. They eat meat, vegetables and fruit. 5. I don't eat fish. 6. I like to eat strawberries. 7. Do you like to eat cherries? 8. Do you put sugar in your (the) coffee? 9. I put three lumps in my coffee. 10. The waiter has not brought us the wine. 11. The cheese is very good; I recommend it.

12. I cannot accompany them. 13. W₂ for me. 14. Don't wait for me. 15. W₂ for her. 16. Don't wait for her.

## III Answer in French

1. Y a-t-il quelque chose sur la table ( votre salle à manger? 2. Mangez-vo₁ beaucoup de pain? 3. Buvez-vous du vi₁ 4. Mangez-vous des fruits? 5. Mettez-vo₁ du lait dans le café? 6. Buvez-vous c café noir? 7. Avec quoi mangez-vous soupe? 8. Avec quoi coupons-nous viande? 9. Aimez-vous manger c fromage? 10. Aimez-vous boire de ] bière? 11. Aimez-vous lire les histoir₁ de meurtre? 12. M. Lesage, qu'est-ce qu' prend comme dessert? 13. M. et Mɯ Roberts, où vont-ils après le déjeuner? 1₄ Qui les accompagne? 15. Quand M. Lesag les rejoindra-t-il? (*Key on pp. 209 and 210*

### SOUS LES PONTS DE PARIS

Même le voisinage menaçant de la Sûreté qu'on entrevoit à travers le crépuscule n suffit plus à émouvoir ces pauvres loques humaines.

| **Voisinage (m.)** | **Sûreté** | **crépuscule (m.)** | **loques (f.) humaine** |
|---|---|---|---|
| Neighbourhood | Paris Scotland Yard | twilight | human wreckage |

# SEIZIÈME LEÇON

From the text below and the list on the next page, you can learn how to buy all you want at the fruiterer's. Try afterwards to make specimen lists in French on your own.

### AT THE FRUITERER'S, THE BUTCHER'S AND THE BAKER'S

**Mme Lesage a invité ses parents pour un grand dîner de famille**
Mme Le-sahzh ah iN-vee-tay say pah-raN poo-ruN graN dee-nay de fah-mee*y*
*Mrs. Lesage has invited her relations to a great family dinner*

**et est en train de faire les achats nécessaires chez quelques**
ay ai-taN triN de fair lay-zah-shah nay-sai-sair shay kailk
*and is about to make the necessary purchases at some*

**marchands de son quartier. Elle entre d'abord dans une**
mahr-shaN de soN kahr-tyay. ail aNtr dah-bor daN-zē̃n
*shopkeepers of her district. She enters first into a*

**boutique de fruits et de primeurs.**
boo-teek de frwee ay de pree-mayr.
*shop of fruit and early vegetables.*

**Le fruitier : Bonjour, madame ; vous désirez, madame?**
bon-zhoor mah-dahm voo day-zee-ray mah-dahm?
*Good morning, madam; what would you like, madam?*

**Mme L. :**   **Donnez-moi une douzaine de bananes, s'il vous plaît,**
do-nay mwah ẽn doo-zain de bah-nahn see voo plai
*Give me a dozen bananas, please,*

**mais de la meilleure qualité.   Ensuite vous pouvez me donner**
mai de lah mai-yâyr kah-lee-tay.   aN-sŵeet voo poo-vay me do-nä
*but of the best quality.   Then you can give me*

**une livre de cerises anglaises.   Je ne**
ẽn leevr de se-reez aN-glaiz.   zhe ne
*a pound of English cherries.   I don't*

**les aime pas personnellement, seulement j'ai des**
lay-zaim pah pair-so-nail-maN sâyl-maN zhay day-
*like them personally, only I have*

**invités anglais à dîner.**
ziN-veetai-zaN-glai ah dee-nay.
*English guests for dinner.*

**Fruitier :**   **Goûtez-les, madame, elles sont excellentes.**
goo-tay lay mah-dahm, ail soN-tai-xai-laNt.
*Taste them, madam, they are excellent.*

**Mme L. :**   **Non, merci, pour moi je préfère les cerises sucrées.**
noN mair-see poor mwah zhe pray-fair lay se-reez sẽek-ray.
*No, thank you, as for me, I prefer the sweet cherries.*

**Fruitier :**   **C'est tout ce que vous désirez, madame?**
sai toos' ke voo day-zee-ray mah-dahm?
*That is all that you want, madam?*

**Regardez les belles pêches.   Ne voulez-vous pas**
re-gahr-day lay bail paish.   ne voo-lay voo pah
*Have a look at the beautiful peaches.   Wouldn't you like*

---

### FRUIT

| la banane | l'abricot | la pêche | la prune | la figue | la datte | le melon |
|---|---|---|---|---|---|---|
| bah-nahn | ahb-ree-koh | paish | prẽn | feeg | dahtt | me-loN |
| *banana* | *apricot* | *peach* | *plum* | *fig* | *date* | *melon* |

| l'orange (f.) | le citron | la mandarine | la groseille | la groseille à maquereau |
|---|---|---|---|---|
| oh-raNzh | see-troN | maN-dah-reen | gro-zaiy | gro-zaiy ah mah-kroh |
| *orange* | *lemon* | *tangerine* | *red currant* | *gooseberry* |

| le cassis | l'amande (f.) | la noix | la noisette | la noix d'Amérique |
|---|---|---|---|---|
| kah-sees | ah-maNd | nwah | nwah- zait | nwah dah-may-reek |
| *black currant* | *almond* | *walnut* | *hazel-nut* | *brazil-nut* |

| la châtaigne | le coing | la framboise | le raisin | la pomme | la poire |
|---|---|---|---|---|---|
| shah-tainy | kwiN | fraN-bwahz | rai-ziN | pom | pwahr |
| *chestnut* | *quince* | *raspberry* | *grape* | *apple* | *pear* |

en prendre une livre?          Mme Lesage : Donnez-moi plutôt un
zaN praNdr ễn leevr?                    do-nay mwah plễ-toh
*to have a pound of them?*              *Give me rather a*

kilo d'abricots.               Fruitier : Voilà, madame.
uN kee-loh dahb-ree-koh.
*kilo of apricots.*

Mme Lesage : Combien vous dois-je?
koN-byiN voo dwah zhe?
*How much do I owe you?*

Fruitier :      Ça vous fait 17 francs 50, madame.
sah voo fai dees-sait fraN siN-kaNt mah-dahm.
*That makes 17 francs 50, madam.*

Mme Lesage :   Voilà vingt francs, donnez-moi une livre de reines-Claude
vwah-lah viN fraN do-nay mwah ễn leevr de rain klohd
*Here is twenty francs, give me a pound of greengages*

pour faire un compte juste.     Fruitier : Avec plaisir, madame,
poor fair uN koNt zhễst.
*to make up the difference.*

voilà.   Je vous remercie.   Au revoir, madame.

Mme Lesage quitte la boutique et se rend chez le boucher.   Elle regarde
Mme Le-sazh keet la boo-teek ay se raN shay le boo-shay.   ail re-gahrd
*Mrs. Lesage leaves the shop and goes to the butcher's.   She looks at*

l'étalage et examine les prix.   Puis elle entre dans la boucherie
ay-tah-lahzh ay eg-za-meen lay pree.   pŵee ail aNtr daN lah boo-sh'-ree
*the shop-window and considers the prices.   Then she enters into the butcher's*

et s'adresse à un garçon boucher.
ay sah-drais ah uN gahr-soN boo-shay
*and addresses an assistant.*

Mme L. :        Bonjour, monsieur!   Je ne suis pas contente de vous.
boN-zhoor m'ss-yẫy zhe ne sŵee pah koN-taNt de voo.
*Good morning.   I am not satisfied with you.*

Les biftecks que vous m'avez vendus l'autre jour étaient
lay beef-taik ke voo mah-vay vaN-dễ lohtr zhooı ay-tai
*The beefsteaks which you sold me the other day were*

tellement durs qu'il était impossible de les manger.
tail-maN dễr kee-lay-tai-tiN-po-seebl de lay maN-zhay.
*so tough that it was impossible to eat them.*

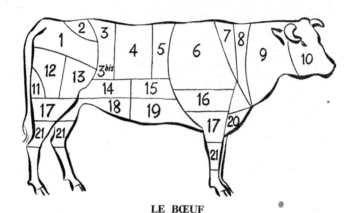

LE BŒUF

1. **la culotte**   kc̈c̈-lot
2. **le romsteck**   rom-staik
3. **l'aloyau** (m.)   ah-lwah-yoh
3 *bis*. **le filet**   fee-lay
4. **le faux filet**   foh-fee-lay
5. **côtes** (f. pl.)   koht
6. **les entrecôtes**   aNtr-koht
7. **la surlonge**   sc̈c̈r-loNzh
8. **le talon de collier**   tah-loN de kol-yay
9. **le collier**   kol-yay
10. **la tête**   tait
11. **le quasi**   kah- zee

12. **le gîte à la noix**   zhee-tah lah nwah
13. **la tranche grasse**   traNsh grahs
14. **la bavette d'aloyau**   bah-vait dah-lwah-yoh
15. **les plates côtes** (f.)   plaht koht
16. **la boîte à moelle**   bwaht ah mwail
17. **le gîte**   zheet
18. **le flanchet**   flaN-shai
19.⎫ **la poitrine**   pwaht-reen
20.⎭
21. **la crosse**   kros

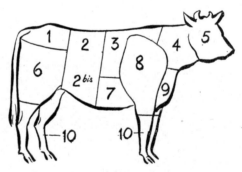

LE VEAU

1. **le quasi**   kah-zee
2. **le filet**   fee-lai
2 *bis*. **la panse**   paNs
3. **le carré**   kah-ray
4. **le collet**   ko-lai
5. **la tête**   tait

6. **le cuisseau**   kŵee-soh
7. **le tendron**   taN-droN
8. **l'épaule** (f.)   ay-pol
9. **la poitrine**   pwaht-reen
10. **le jarret**   zhah-rai

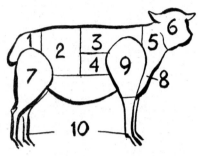

### LE MOUTON

. **la selle**   sail
. **le filet**   fee-lai
. **le carré**   kah-ray
. **le haut de côtelettes**   oh de koht-lait
. **le collet**   ko-lai

6. **la tête**   tait
7. **le gigot**   zhee-goh
8. **la poitrine**   pwaht-reen
9. **l'épaule (f.)**   ay-pol
10. **les pieds (m. pl.)**   pyay

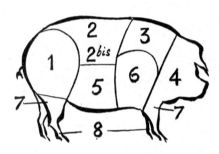

### LE PORC

1. **le jambon**   zhaN-boN
2. **le lard gras**   lahr grah
2 *bis*. **le filet**   fee-lai
3. **les côtes (f. pl.)**   koht
4. **la tête**   tait

5. **le ventre (la poitrine)**   vaNtr (pwaht-reen)
6. **l'épaule (f.)**   ay-pol
7. **le jambonneau**   zhaN-bo-noh
8. **les pieds (m. pl.)**   pyay

### ENGLISH EXPLANATION OF DIAGRAMS

*(In certain cases there are no equivalent cuts)*

**Beef :** 1. Buttock. 2. Rump-steak. 3. Sirloin. 3a. Fillet (undercut). 4. Fore-rib. . Ribs. 6. Roasting ribs. 7. No equivalent. 8. Clod. 9. Neck. 10. Head. 11. Chump-end. 12. Silverside. 13. Round (top-rump). 14. Top of sirloin. 15. Top ribs. 16. Stewing steak. 17. Leg of beef. 8. Flank. 19/20. Brisket. 21. Knuckle.

**Veal :** 1. Chump-end. 2. Fillet. 2a. Belly. 3. Loin. 4. Neck. 5. Head. 6. Leg fillet. 7. Gristle. 8. Shoulder. 9. Breast. 10. Knuckle.

**Mutton :** 1. Saddle. 2. Fillet. 3. Loin. 4. Best ribs. 5. Neck. 6. Head. 7. Leg. 8. Breast. 9. Shoulder. 10. Feet.

**Pork :** 1. Leg of pork. 2. Fat bacon. 2a. Loin. 3. Ribs. 4. "Pig's Cheek". 5. Belly. 6 and 7 correspond to "Hand and spring" and "Half-leg". 8. Feet.

**Le boucher :**   Je m'excuse, madame, je ne comprends pas . . .
zhe maix-kēēz mah-dahm zhe ne koN-praN pah
*I apologize, madam, I don't understand . . .*

**Mme Lesage :** N'en parlons plus, mais servez-moi bien cette
naN pahr-loN plēē mai sair-vay mwah byiN sait
*Don't let us speak about it any more, but serve me well this*

fois; j'ai des invités et je ne veux pas qu'ils se
fwah zhay day-ziN-vee-tay ay zhe ne vāӯ pah keel se
*time; I have guests and I don't want them to*

cassent les dents en mangeant vos biftecks.
kahs lay daN aN maN-zhaN voh beef-taik.
*break their teeth by eating your beefsteaks.*

**Boucher :**   Comptez sur moi, madame!   Que désirez-vous aujourd'hui?
koN-tay sēēr mwah mah-dam! ke day-zee-ray voo oh-zhoord-ŵee
*Count on me, madam!   What do you want to-day?*

**Mme L. :**   Donnez-moi un beau morceau de noix de veau—disons un
do-nay mwah uN boh mor-soh de nwah de voh dee-zoN uN
*Give me a good piece of knuckle of veal—let us say one*

kilo; et deux petites tranches de foie.
kee-loh ay dāӯ p'teet traNsh de fwah.
*kilo; and two small slices of liver.*

**Boucher :**   Du foie de veau, madame, ou de bœuf?
dēē fwah de voh mah-dahm oo de bāӯf?
*Calves' liver, madam, or ox's?*

**Mme L. :**   Du veau.   C'est pour mes petits-enfants, je leur achète
dēē voh. sai poor may p'tee-zaN-faN zhe lāӯr-ah-shait
*Calves'.   It's for my grandchildren, I buy them*

toujours le meilleur.
too-zhoor le mai-yāӯr.
*always the best.*

Après avoir fait ses achats, Mme Lesage paye sa note à la
ah-prai-zah-vwahr fai say-zah-shah Mme Lesage pay sah not ah lah
*After having made her purchases, Mme Lesage pays her bill at the*

caisse et se rend chez le boulanger.
kais ay se raN shay le boo-laN-zhay.
*cash-desk and betakes herself to the baker.*

**Le boulanger :** Bonjour, Madame Lesage, comment allez-vous?
boN-zhoor, mah-dahm le-sahzh, ko-man-tah-lay voo?
*Good morning, Madam Lesage, how are you?*

Without looking at the text, you should now be able to make a list in French of everything you can recognise in this butcher's and poulterer's. If you cannot do so, study the last Lessons again.

**Mme Lesage :** **Ça va, je vous remercie, et vous, ça va toujours**
sah vah zhe voo re-mair-see ay voo sah vah too-zhoor
*Very well, thank you, and you are keeping*

**bien?[1]** **Quelle chaleur!** **Donnez-moi une livre de pain de**
byiN? kail shah-lãyr! do-nay mwah ẽen leevr de piN de
*well?* *What heat!* *Give me one pound of household*

**ménage et un kilo de pain bis . . . oh, comme j'ai chaud!**
may-nahzh ay uN kee-loh de piN bee . . . oh kom zhay shoh!
*bread and one kilo of brown bread . . . oh, how hot I am!*

**Le boulanger :** **Voilà, Madame Lesage.** **Mme L. : Donnez-moi encore une**
do-nay mwah aN-kor ẽen
*Give me also a*

**douzaine de croissants et deux morceaux de gâteau comme**
doo-zain de krwah-saN ay dãy mor-soh de gah toh kom
*dozen horse-shoes and two pieces of cake as the*

**l'autre jour.** **Le boulanger : Ah, je vois, c'est pour les petits-**
lohtr zhoor. ah zhe vwah sai poor lay p'tee
*other day.* *Ah, I see, this is for the grand-*

---
[1] Lit. "It goes, I thank you, and you, it goes always well?"

L'AVENUE DES CHAMPS-ÉLYSÉES

Paris est redevable de cette noble avenue au génie du Baron Haussman (1809-91).
Devenu préfet de la Seine, il entreprit la reconstruction de la ville entière.   L'Arc de

**Être redevable de q'ch à q'qn**   **génie** (m.)  **devenir**   **entreprendre**
To be indebted to s'one for s'thing  genius   to become   to undertake

## ET L'ARC DE TRIOMPHE

Triomphe fut érigé pour célébrer les victoires de Napoléon 1er. Consacrée autrefois aux
hôtels particuliers, l'Avenue est aujourd'hui devenue quartier commerçant.

| **Ériger** | **consacrer à q'ch** | **hôtel** (m.) **particulier** | **quartier** (m.) **commerçant** |
|---|---|---|---|
| To erect | dedicated to s'thing | private house | business quarter |

**enfants. Je vous ai vue dans la rue avec les gosses.**
zaN-faN. zhe voo-zai vẽẽ daN lah rẽẽ ah-vaik lay gos.
*children. I saw you in the street with the youngsters.*

**Ils sont gentils, très gentils.**     **Mme L. : Je crois bien**[1]
eel soN zhaN-tee trai zhaN-tee.            zhe krwah byiN
*They are nice, very nice.*              *I think (indeed)*

**qu'ils sont gentils, mes petits-enfants. Quelle heure est-il?**
keel soN zhaN-tee may p'tee-zaN-faN.   kai-lãŷr ai-teel?
*that they are nice, my grandchildren.  What time is it?*

**Onze heures? Il faut que je me sauve.**[2] **. . au revoir.**
oN-zãŷr? eel foh ke zhe me sohv   oh re-vwahr.
*Eleven o'clock?  I must hurry . . . good-bye.*

### THE USE OF "EN"

1. **Avez-vous du pain? Oui, j'en ai.** Have you any bread? Yes, I have some.
**Avez-vous de la viande? J'en ai.** Have you any meat? I have some.
**Avez-vous des sardines? J'en ai.** Have you any sardines? I have some.
**Je n'en ai pas.** I haven't got any.
The French for "some" or "any" used instead of the noun is **en,** which is placed directly before the verb.

2. **Avez-vous des cigarettes? Oui, monsieur, j'en ai.** Yes, I have.
**Combien de cigarettes avez-vous? J'en ai trois.** I have three.
**Avez-vous de l'argent? Oui, j'en ai.** Yes, I have.
**Je n'en ai pas.** I haven't.
**J'en ai beaucoup.** I have much.

Note that **en** must be used to replace the French partitive article, even in cases where the English may be omitted.

3. Meaning "of it," "of them", "with it", "with them", "for it", "for them", etc.
**J'en ai assez.** I have enough of it.
**N'en parlons plus.** Don't let us speak about it any more.
**Il a volé l'argent; j'en suis sûr.** He has stolen the money; I am sure of it.

**J'ai vu la maison et j'en suis charmé.** I have seen the house and I am delighted with it.
**Combien a-t-il d'enfants? Il en a quatre.** How many children has he? He has four (of them).
**J'ai payé la note; en voici le reçu.** I paid the bill; here is the receipt for it.
**Est-ce qu'il y a des cigares?** Are there any cigars?
**Il y en a plusieurs.** There are several (of them).

4. **en** may also be a preposition:
**en été** In summer
**en hiver** In winter
**en automne** In autumn
**en France** In France
**en Angleterre** In England
**en Allemagne** In Germany

### POSITION OF ADJECTIVES

**Le grand garçon est intelligent.** The big boy is intelligent.
**Le grand garçon intelligent est le fils de mon ami.** The big intelligent boy is the son of my friend.
**C'est une jolie petite fille.** She is a pretty little girl.
**Ces jeunes filles françaises.** These French girls.
**Elle est assise sur la vieille chaise.** She is sitting on the old chair.

---

[1] **Je crois bien** here means something like "I should jolly well think."
[2] Lit. "save myself."

**Quel mauvais temps!**
What bad weather!

**Ils mangent de bons raisins.**
They eat good grapes.

**Elle regarde de jolis tableaux.**
She is looking at pretty pictures.

**Ils ont de gros melons.**
They have big melons.

**Il aime de vieux vin rouge.**
He likes old red wine.

Most adjectives in French usually follow the noun. But a number of short and frequently used adjectives precede it. Among the latter are : **grand, petit, bon, mauvais, jeune, vieux, beau, joli, cher, gros.**

Note that when the noun is preceded by an adjective, **de** only is used instead of **du, de la, de l'**, or **des:**

**du gâteau**  cake
**de bon gâteau**  good cake
**de la viande**  meat
**de bonne viande**  good meat
**des enfants**  children
**de petits enfants**  little children
**de l'argent**  money
**de mauvais argent**  bad money
**des chiens**  dogs
**de jolis chiens**  pretty dogs
but: **des chiens intelligents,**
**de l'argent anglais,** etc.

## SENTENCE BUILDING

| Question | | Answer |
|---|---|---|
| | du pain? | |
| | du poisson? | |
| Avez-vous | du vin rouge? | J'en ai.  I have some. |
| | de la viande? | |
| | de l'argent? | |
| Voulez-vous | des légumes? | Merci, j'en ai déjà.  Thank you, I |
| | des fruits? | have got some already. |
| | des oranges? | |
| | beaucoup de pain? | |
| | de jolis crayons? | Je n'en ai pas.  I haven't got any. |
| | de l'argent français? | |
| | de l'encre noire? | |
| Voulez-vous } me donner | de bonnes oranges? | Je regrette infiniment, mais je n'en ai |
| Pouvez-vous } | un peu de fromage? | pas.  I greatly regret, but I have |
| | de beaux tableaux? | not got any. |
| | de bon vin blanc? | |
| | de vieux vin rouge? | |

## *EXERCISES*

### I  Answer in French

1. Est-ce que vous avez beaucoup d'argent? 2. Mangez-vous des fruits? 3. Avez-vous beaucoup de livres français? 4. Où achetez-vous des légumes? 5. Où est-ce qu'on achète de la viande? 6. Qui vend des fruits? 7. Avez-vous assez de pain? 8. Est-ce que Mme Lesage achète des poires? 9. Qu'est-ce qu'elle achète? 10. Est-ce qu'elle était contente de son boucher? 11. Pourquoi pas? 12. Combien prend-elle de gâteaux? 13. Est-ce que M. Robert est chez le boulanger? 14. Où a-t-il acheté ses cigarettes? 15. Qu'est-ce qu'il a fait dans le bureau de change?

### II  Replace with pronouns the words in bold type

1. **La grand'mère** achète du pain. 2. On mange **de la viande**. 3. Elle a **des crayons** dans sa valise. 4. **Mon père** boit le vin blanc. 5. **Mon père** boit **du vin blanc**. 6. **Ma sœur** a acheté la viande. 7. **Sa cousine** achète de la viande. 8. **Le garçon** apporte

les légumes. 9. **Mes parents** mangent beaucoup de **légumes.** 10. Ils regardent **les livres.** 11. Elle n'a pas de **livres français.** 12. Il veut de **l'encre rouge.**

### III Translate into French

1. I have some bread, but I have no butter. 2. Have you got any? 3. I have a little. 4. I haven't any. 5. There are no cherries at the fruiterer's. 6. Are there none? 7. Don't you drink red wine? 8. Do you never drink any? 9. I want some good oranges. 10. Have you got any? 11. I have apples, but I haven't any pears. 12. Does your father drink white wine? 13. Your aunt asks if there is any meat. 14. The maid says that there is not any. 15. She is going to buy cheese, vegetables and meat. (*Key on page* 210).

PARIS : LA CONCIERGERIE

Cette ancienne prison, dont la construction remonte au XVe siècle, fut la dernière demeure de Marie Antoinette avant sa mort sur l'échafaud. Aujourd'hui elle fait partie du Palais de Justice.

| **Remonter à** | **demeure** (f.) | **échafaud** (m.) | **Palais** (m.) **de Justice** |
|---|---|---|---|
| To date back to | dwelling | scaffold | Law Courts |

# DIX-SEPTIÈME LEÇON

## LE DÎNER CHEZ LES LESAGES

**L'appartement de grand-père et grand'mère Lesage.   Dans la**
la-pahrte-maN de graN-pair ay graN-mair le-sahzh.   daN lah
*The flat of grandfather and grandmother Lesage.   In the*

**salle à manger la table est mise pour six personnes.   Grand-père**
sah-lah maN-zhay lah tahbl ai meez poor see pair-son.   graN-pair
*dining room.   The table is laid for six persons.   Grandfather*

**(regardant sa montre): Je ne comprends pas.   Il est sept heures passées,**
re-gahr-daN sah moNtr zhe ne koN-praN pah. ee-lay sai-tāȳr pah-say
*(looking at his watch): I don't understand.   It is past seven o'clock,*

**et ils n'arrivent toujours pas.**
ay eel nah-reev too-zhoor pah.
*and they still don't arrive.*

**Grand'mère :**   **Il ne faut pas oublier qu'ils ne sont pas**
eel ne foh pah-zoo-blee-yay keel ne soN pah
*One must not forget that they are not*

**parisiens.**       **Grand-père : Tout de même, j'ai une**
pah-reez-yiN.       too de maim zhay ēēn
*Parisians.*        *Nevertheless, I have a*

**faim de loup.**                    **(On sonne.)**
fiN de loo.                         oN son.
*wolf's hunger ("I'm as hungry as a hunter"). (The bell is ringing.)*

**Grand-père :**   **Les voilà, enfin. (M. et Mme Roberts entrent.)**
lay vwah-lah aN-fiN.
*There they are, at last.*

**Mme Roberts :  Bon soir tout le monde!   Veuillez nous excuser,**
bon-swahr too le moNd!   vāȳ-yay noo-zaix-kēē-zay
*Good evening, everybody!   Will you excuse us,*

**mais ce n'est vraiment pas notre faute si nous sommes**
mai se nai vrai-maN pah notr foht see noo som-zaN
*but it is really not our fault if we are*

**en retard.**       **M. Roberts :  C'est vrai.  Le métro était**
re-tahr.            sai vrai. le mayt-roh ay-tai
*late.*             *It is true.   The tube was*

**bloqué pendant un bon quart d'heure.   Je ne sais pas pour**
blo-kay paN-daN uN boN kahr dāȳr.   zhe ne sai pah poor
*blocked during a good quarter of an hour.   I don't know for*

## DINNER AT GRANDMOTHER LESAGE'S

Here you have a typically French interior on an evening when a cosy repast is being prepared for a few intimate friends.

Before consulting the list on the next page, it should now be easy for you to name twenty objects on the table or in the room, in French. For key see page 198.

**quelle raison. J'espère qu'il n'y a pas eu**
kail rai-zoN. zhais-pair keel nyah pah·ee
*what reason. I hope that there has not been*

**d'accident. Donc, excusez notre retard.**
dah-xee-daN. doNk aix-kee-zay notr re-tahr.
*an accident. Therefore excuse our being late.*

La bonne:    **Le dîner est servi, madame.**      Grand-père : **Vous êtes tous**
le dee-nay ai sair-vee mah-dahm.          voo-zait toos
*Dinner is served, madam.*            *You are all*

**excusés. Mais maintenant vite à table. Vous prenez**
aix-kee-zay. mai miNt-naN vee-tah tahbl. voo pre-nay
*excused. But now quick to (the) table. You take an*

**l'apéritif?**      M. Roberts : **Non, merci, nous n'aimons pas ça.**
lah-pay-ree-teef?          noN mair-see noo nai-moN pah sah.
*appetiser?*           *No, thanks, we don't like that.*

Grand-père :    **Tant pis pour vous. Mais vous ne déclinerez pas notre**
taN pee poor voo. mai voo ne day-kleen'ray pah notr
*So much the worse for you. But you will not refuse our*

---

## LA SALLE À MANGER — THE DINING-ROOM

| | | | |
|---|---|---|---|
| **La table mise pour le dîner** tahbl meez poor le dee-nay *table laid for dinner* | **le buffet** bee-fai *sideboard* | **la nappe** nahp *table-cloth* | **la desserte** dais-sairt *side-table* |
| **la lampe à suspension** laNp ah sees-paN-syoN *hanging lamp* | **la soupière** soo-pyair *soup-tureen* | **la gravure** la gravure *picture* | **une assiette plate** ah-syait plaht *flat plate* |
| **une assiette creuse** ah-syait krayz *deep plate* | **le couteau** koo-toh *knife* | **la fourchette** foor-shait *fork* | **la cuillère à potage** kwee-yair ah po-tahzh *soup spoon* |
| **la serviette** sair-vyait *serviette, dinner-napkin* | **le moutardier** moo-tahr-dyay *mustard-pot* | **la saucière** soohs-yair *sauce-dish*   **la salière** sahl-yair *salt-cellar* | **la cloche à fromage** klosh ah fro-mahzh *cheese dish* |
| **la bouteille de vin** boo-taiy de viN *bottle of wine* | **la cuillère à dessert** kwee-yair ah dai-sair *dessert-spoon* | **la carafe** kah-rahf *decanter* | **le couvert à poisson** koo-vair ah pwah-soN *fish knife and fork* |
| **la corbeille à pain** kor-baiy ah piN *bread basket* | **le légumier** lay-geem-yay *vegetable-dish* | **une assiette à dessert** ahs-yait ah dai-sair *dessert-plate* | **le plat à rôti** plah ah roh-tee *meat dish* |
| **l'huilier** weel-yay *oil cruet* | **le verre à vin** vair ah viN *wine glass* | **la ménagère** may-nah-zhair *cruet-stand* | **le vinaigrier** vee-naig-ree-ay *vinegar cruet* |

**bon vin de France, j'espère.**     M. Roberts : **Tout au**
boN viN de fraNs zhais-pair.            too-toh
*good wine of France, I hope.*          *Quite on the*

**contraire.   Votre vin, je le préfère à tout autre.**
koN-trair.   votr viN zhe le pray-fair ah too-tohtr.
*contrary.   Your wine I prefer to any other.*

Grand'mère :   **Voulez-vous du potage, mon gendre?**
             voo-lay voo-dē̄ po-tahzh moN zhaNdr?
             *Do you want some soup, my son-in-law?*

M. Roberts :   **J'en prendrai un tout petit peu.**
            zhaN praN-dray uN too p'tee pā̄y.
            *I'll (of it) have only very little.*

Georges :   **Voulez-vous me passer le pain, s'il vous plaît?   Merci.**
          voo-lay voo me pah-say le piN seel voo plai?   mair-see.
          *Will you pass me the bread, please?   Thank you.*

Grand-père :   **Avez-vous déjà visité la ville?**
            ah-vay voo day-zhah vee-zee-tay lah veel?
            *Have you already visited the town?*

M. Roberts :   **Nous avons visité des musées, surtout le Louvre.   Hier**
          noo-zah-voN vee-zee-tay day mē̄-zay sē̄r-too le loovr.   yair
          *We have visited some museums, especially the Louvre.   Last*

**soir nous étions au théâtre du Châtelet.   C'était**
swahr noo zayt-*y*oN-zoh tay-ahtr dē̄ shaht-lai.   say-tai
*night we were in the Châtelet theatre.   It was*

**vraiment très amusant.   Vous avez de bons**
vrai-maN trai-zah-mē̄-zaN.   voo-zah-vay de boN-
*really very amusing.   You have good*

**acteurs à Paris.**     Mme Roberts : **Demain soir nous**
zahk-tā̄yr ah pah-rèe.            de-miN swahr noo-
*actors in Paris.*               *To-morrow night we*

**irons à l'Opéra.   Paul nous a invités.**
zee-roN-zah loh-pay-rah.   pol noo-zah iN-vee-tay.
*shall go to the Opera.   Paul has invited us.*

Grand'mère :   **Et les enfants, vont-ils bien?   N'oubliez pas de**
            ay lay-zaN-faN voN-teel byiN?   noo-blyay pah de
            *And the children, are they all right?   Don't forget*

---

Twenty objects (p. 196) are: la table, la chaise, la fenêtre, la lampe, la portière, la tasse, la soucoupe, le pain, le fromage, l'assiette, le vin, le verre à vin, le couteau, la fourchette, la cuillère, du sel, de la moutarde, de l'huile, la gravure, la corbeille à fleurs.

**les amener avec vous demain pour le déjeuner.**
leh-zah-me-nay ah-vaik voo d'miN poor le day-zhā̄y-nay.
*to bring them along with you for lunch.*

**Comment la ville leur plaît-elle?**
ko-maN lah veel lā̄yr plai-tail?
*How do they like the town?*

**M. Roberts : Oh, ils trouvent**
oh eel troov
*Oh, they find*

**Paris très intéressant.**
pah-ree trai-ziN-tay-rai-saN.
*Paris very interesting.*

**Georges : Avez-vous déjà**
ah-vay-voo day-zhah
*Have you already*

**été à Versailles?**
ay-tay ah vair-sah*y*?
*been to Versailles?*

**M. Roberts : Non, pas encore. Mais je**
noN pah-zaN-kor. mai zhe
*No, not yet. But I*

**ne partirai pas sans l'avoir vu. Est-ce loin d'ici?**
ne pahr-tee-ray pah saN la-vwahr vē̄. ai-se lwiN dee-see?
*won't leave without having seen it. Is it far from here?*

**Georges : Pas du tout! Vous n'avez qu'à prendre le métro**
pah dē̄ too! voo nah-vay kah praNdr le may-troh
*Not at all! You only have to take the underground*

**jusqu'au pont de Sèvres. Là vous prendrez l'autobus.**
zhē̄s-koh poN de saivr. lah voo praN-dray loh-toh-bē̄s.
*up to Sèvres bridge. There you'll have to take the bus.*

**C'est très simple. Vous y serez dans une heure**
say trai siNpl. voo-zee s'ray daN-zē̄-nā̄yr
*It's very simple. You will be there in one hour*

**environ. D'ailleurs je peux vous accompagner, si vous le**
aN-vee-roN. dah-yā̄yr zhe pā̄y voo-zah-koN-pahn-yay see voo
*approximately. Besides I can accompany you, if you*

**voulez. Qu'en dites-vous?**
voo-lay. kaN deet voo?
*want to. What do you say to that?*

**Mme Roberts : Nous acceptons avec le plus grand plaisir.**
noo-zahk-saip-toN ah-vaik le plē̄ graN plai-zeer.
*We accept with the greatest pleasure.*

**Vous nous accompagnerez aussi, chère cousine?**
voo-noo-zah-koN-pahn-ye-ray oh-see shair koo-zeen?
*You will also accompany us, dear cousin?*

**Mlle Lesage : Très volontiers. Quand voulez-vous faire l'excursion?**
trai vo-loN-tyay. kaN voo-lay voo fair laix-kē̄r-syoN?
*Very gladly. When do you want to make the excursion?*

## VERSAILLES: LA VILLE ROYALE

En haut, le Palais, aujourd'hui un musée, où Louis XIV, le Roi Soleil, tenait jadis sa cour, qui servait de modèle à toute l'Europe. En bas, les jardins où, les jours des "Grandes Eaux", les citoyens viennent admirer les fontaines.

**"Le Roi Soleil"**,
"King Sun", flatterers' title for Louis XIV

**"Les Grandes Eaux"**
Special fountain displays at Versailles

**Je suis libre presque tous les jours.**
zhe sw̃ee leebr praisk too lay zhoor.
*I am free almost every day.*

M. Roberts : **Disons après-demain, pour ne pas remettre trop**
dee-zoN ahp-rai d'miN poor ne .pah re-maitr troh
*Let us say the day after to-morrow, in order not to put it off too*

**longtemps.    Mlle Lesage : C'est entendu pour après-demain.**
loN-taN                    sai-taN-taN-dễ poor ah-prai d'miN.
*long.*                    *That's arranged for the day after*
                                             *to-morrow.*

Grand'mère : **Eh bien, je crois que nous pouvons passer à la viande.**
eh byiN zhe krwah ke noo poo-voN pah-say ah lah vyaNd.
*Well, I think that we can pass on to the meat.*

**(Elle sonne la bonne.)        La bonne: Madame a sonné?**
ail son lah bon.                        mah-dahm ah so-nay?
*(She rings for the servant.)            Did you ring, Madam?*

Grand'mère : **Vous pouvez changer les assiettes et servir la viande.**
voo-poo-vay shaN-zhay lay-zahs-yait ay sair-veer lah vyaNd.
*You can change the plates and serve the meat.*

**(On sert la viande et ils mangent tous avec beaucoup**
oN sair lah vyaNd ay eel maNzh toos ah-vaik boh-koo
*(The meat is served and they all eat with much*

**d'appétit.)    Grand-père : Voulez-vous du vin rouge ou**
dah-pay-tee.                    voo-lay voo dễ viN roozh oo
*appetite.)*                    *Will you have red wine or*

**du blanc?    M. Roberts : Du rouge, s'il vous plaît.    Ah, quelle**
dễ blaN?                    dễ roozh seel voo plai.    ah kail
*white?*                    *Some red, please.    Ah, how*

**merveille!    On dirait du Bordeaux de marque.**
mair-vaiy!    oN dee-rai dễ bor-doh de mark.
*exquisite!    One would say choice (or vintage) claret.*

Grand-père : **C'est bien cela.    Il sort de ma propre cave.    On dirait**
sai byiN s'lah.    eel sor de mah propr kahv.    oN dee-rai
*That's what it is.    It comes from my own cellar.    One would*

**du soleil en bouteille.    Un peu plus tard vous allez**
dễ so-laiy aN boo-taiy.    uN pãy plễ tahr voo-zah-lay
*think sunshine in a bottle.    A little later you are going to*

**déguster un autre vin rouge.**
day-gễs-tay ãy-nohtr viN roozh.
*taste another red wine.*

**Grand'mère :** **Encore un peu de ce rôti?**
aN-kor uN pay de se ro-tee?
*Some more of this joint?*

**M. Roberts :** **Rien qu'un petit morceau, s'il vous plaît.** **Ça c'est**
ryiN kuN p'tee mor-soh seel voo plai.　sah say
*Only a tiny piece, please.　That is*

**beaucoup trop. Mme Roberts: Merci, j'en ai eu suffisamment.**
boh-koo troh.　·　　　　　mair-see zhah-nai ée sée-fee-zah-maN
*far too much.　　　　　　Thank you, I have had plenty.*

**Grand'mère :** **Voilà le gâteau et les fruits.** **Après vous aurez**
vwah-lah le gah-toh ay lay frwee.　ahp-rai voo-zoh-ray
*Here is the cake and the fruit.　Afterwards you'll have*

**de bon café.** **J'espère que vous êtes tous contents.**
de boN kah-fay.　zhes-pair ke voo-zait toos koN-taN.
*some good coffee.　I hope you are all pleased.*

**M. Roberts :** **C'était excellent.** **C'est vraiment très agréable**
say-tai tai-xai-laN.　sai vrai-maN trai-zah-gray-ahbl
*It was excellent.　It really is very nice (to be)*

**chez vous.** **Mlle Lesage : Comme il est bon ce gâteau!**
shay voo.　　　　　　　ko-mee-lai boN se gah-toh!
*with you.　　　　　　　How good this cake is!*

**Grand'mère :** **Je l'ai fait moi-même.** **C'en était du travail.** **Il y a de**
zhe lay fai mwah maim.　sah-nay-tai dée trah-vay.　eel-yah de
*I made it myself.　It was some work.　There are some*

**bonnes choses là-dedans.** **Mme Lesage : On le note tout de suite**
bon shohz lah-de-daN.　　　　　oN le not tood swheet.
*good things inside.　　　　　　You realize it at once.*

**Grand-père :** **Vous fumez le cigare?**
voo fée-may le see-gahr?
*You smoke a cigar?*

**M. Roberts :** **Merci, je préfère une cigarette.**
mair-see zhe pray-fair één see-gah-rait.
*No thank you, I prefer a cigarette.*

**Grand'mère :** **Georges, pourquoi ne mangez-vous pas votre dessert?**
zhorzh poor-kwah ne maN-zhay voo pah votr dai-sair?
*George, why don't you eat your dessert?*

**Georges :** **Oh, vous savez, je n'aime pas les choses sucrées.**
oh voo sah-vay zhe naim pah lay shohz sée-kray.
*Oh, you know, I don't like sweet things.*

**Grand'mère :**  Mais il y a des fruits.  Puis-je vous peler une orange?
mai eel-yah day frŵee.  pŵee zhe voo pe-lay ĕ͠e-noh-raNzh?
*But there is fruit.   May I peel an orange for you?*

**Grand-père :**  Où donc est mon briquet?   (Il cherche dans ses poches.)
oo doNk ay moN bree-kay?   eel shairsh daN say posh.
*Where on earth is my lighter?   (He looks in his pockets.)*

**M. Roberts :**  J'ai des allumettes sur moi.   Voilà.   (Il lui
zhay day-zah-lĕ͠e-mait sĕ͠er mwah.  vwah-lah.  (eel lwee
*I have matches with me.   There you are.   (He*

offre du feu.)        **Grand-père :** Merci.   Vous jouez aux cartes?
ofr dĕ͠e fa͠y.)                      mair-see.  voo zhoo-ay zoh kahrt?
*offers him a light.)*              *Thanks.   Do you play cards?*

**M. Roberts :**  Assez rarement.   Mais si je me rappelle bien, vous
ah-say rahr-maN.  mai see zhe me rah-pail byiN voo
*Very rarely.       But if I remember right, you*

jouiez aux échecs.   **Grand-père :** C'est exact.   Alors
zhoo-yay oh-zay-shaik.             sai-taix-ahkt.  ah-lor.
*used to play chess.               That's right.   So let*

faisons une partie!          **M. Roberts :** Avec plaisir.
fai-zoNz-ĕ͠en pahr-tee!                       ah-vaik plai-zeer.
*us have a game!*                             *With pleasure.*

D'ailleurs, un ami va me téléphoner.
dah-ya͠yr a͠yn-nah-mee vah me tay-lay-foh-nay.
*By the way, a friend (of mine) is going to ring me up.*

Je me suis permis de donner votre numéro de
zhe me sŵee pair-mee de do-nay votr nĕ͠e-may-roh de
*I took the liberty of giving your telephone*

téléphone.   J'espère que cela ne vous gênera pas.
tay-lay-fohn.  zhais-pair ke s'lah ne voo zhain'rah pah.
*number.   I hope that this will not inconvenience you.*

**Grand'mère :**  Mais non, pas du tout.   Allez faire votre partie
mai noN pah dĕ͠e too.  ah-lay fair votr pahr-tee
*But no, not at all.   Go and have your game*

d'échecs.   Je vous appellerai quand votre ami vous
day-shaik.  zhe voo-zah-pail'ray kaN vot-rah-mee voo
*of chess.   I'll call you when your friend will*

demandera.   **Grand'mère :** Je me sens un peu fatiguée,
de-maNd-rah.                zhe me saNz-uN pa͠y fah-tee-gay
*ask for you.*              *I feel a bit tired,*

**et je vais m'étendre pour une demi-heure.    Amusez-**
ay zhe vai may-taN-dr poor êen d'mee-âyr.    ah-mêe-zay
*and I am going to lie down for half an hour.    Have a good*

**vous bien.    À tout à l'heure!**
voo byiN.    ah too-tah-lâyr!
*time.    Until later!*

**Les autres :    A tout à l'heure!    Reposez-vous bien!**
lay-zohtr :    ah too-tah-lâyr!    re-poh-zay voo byiN!
*The others :    Until later!    Have a good rest!*

**Mlle Lesage :    Avez-vous envie de faire une petite promenade?**
ah-vay voo-zaN-vee de fair êen p'teet pro-m'-nahd?
*Would you like to go for a little walk?*

**Georges :    Pour moi, j'accepte.    Et vous ma chère tante?**
Poor mwah zhahk-saipt.    ay voo mah shair taNt?
*As for me, I accept.    And you, my dear aunt?*

**Mme Roberts : Je veux bien, si vous n'allez pas trop loin.**
zhe vây byiN see voo nah-lay pah troh lwiN.
*I should love to, if you don't go too far.*

**Georges :    Oh, non, nous n'allons faire qu'un petit tour.**
oh noN, noo nah-loN fair kuN p'tee toor.
*Oh no, we are only going for a little stroll.*

**(riant) C'est bon pour la digestion, vous savez.**
ryaN    sai boN poor lah dee-zhaist-yoN voo sah-vay.
*(laughing) That is good for the digestion, you know.*

**Mme Roberts : Dans ce cas, je vous accompagne.    Je vais seulement**
daN se kah zhe voo-zah-koN-pahny.    zhe vai sâyl-maN
*In that case, I'll come with you.    I am only going*

**chercher mon chapeau et mon sac.**
shair-shay moN shah-poh ay moN sahk.
*to get my hat and my handbag.*

**Georges :    Prenez votre temps.    Nous vous attendons. (Quelques minutes**
pre-nay votr taN.    noo voo-zah-taN-doN.    kailk mee-nêet-
*Take your time.    We'll wait for you.    (A few minutes*

**après, Mme Roberts revient, et ils s'en vont.)**
zah-prai mah-dahm ro-bairts revyiN ay eel saN voN.
*later Mrs. Roberts comes back, and they go away.)*

## S'EN ALLER—TO GO (AWAY)

### Present Affirmative

je m'en vais  I am going
il (elle) s'en va  he (she) is going
nous nous en allons  we are going
vous vous en allez  you are going
ils (elles) s'en vont  they are going

### Present Negative

je ne m'en vais pas, etc.

### Present Interrogative

s'en va-t-il?  is he going?
vous en allez-vous?  are you going?

### Imperative Affirmative

allons-nous-en!  let us go!
allez-vous-en!  go away!

### Imperative Negative

ne nous en allons pas!  don't let us go!
ne vous en allez pas!  don't go!

## COMPRENDRE—TO UNDERSTAND

### Present

je comprends
il (elle) comprend
nous comprenons
vous comprenez
ils (elles) comprennent

### Imperfect

je comprenais, etc.

### Future

je comprendrai, etc.

### Perfect

j'ai compris, etc.

### VERBS ENDING IN -IR

partir = to leave;  dormir = to sleep;
servir = to serve;  sentir = to feel, to smell;
sortir = to go out;  venir = to come.

### Present

| | |
|---|---|
| je pars | je dors |
| il (elle) part | il (elle) dort |
| nous partons | nous dormons |
| vous partez | vous dormez |
| ils (elles) partent | ils (elles) dorment |

| | |
|---|---|
| je sers | je sens |
| il (elle) sert | il (elle) sent |
| nous servons | nous sentons |
| vous servez | vous sentez |
| ils (elles) servent | ils (elles) sentent |

| | |
|---|---|
| je sors | je viens |
| il (elle) sort | il (elle) vient |
| nous sortons | nous venons |
| vous sortez | vous venez |
| ils (elles) sortent | ils (elles) viennent |

### Imperfect

| | | |
|---|---|---|
| je partais | je dormais | je servais |
| je sentais | je sortais | je venais |

### Future

| | | |
|---|---|---|
| je partirai | je dormirai | je servirai |
| je sentirai | je sortirai | je viendrai |

### Perfect

| | | |
|---|---|---|
| je suis parti | j'ai dormi | j'ai servi |
| j'ai senti | je suis sorti | je suis venu |

## THE PAST PARTICIPLE

je dîne  I am having  j'ai dîné  I have had
  dinner; I dine    dinner; I dined

il dort  he is  il a dormi  he has
  asleep; he sleeps  been sleeping; he slept

elle vend des bas  elle les a vendus
  she sells (is selling)  she has sold them;
  stockings    she sold them

Forms of the verb like "dined", "slept", "sold", "arrived", "left", etc., are called Past Participles. In English the usual ending of the Past Participle is -ed (the same as for the Imperfect). In French the usual ending of the Past Participle is -é; it is the ending of all verbs of which the Infinitive ends in -er.

| Infinitive | Past Participle |
|---|---|
| dîner = to dine | dîné = dined |
| aller = to go | allé = gone |
| donner = to give | donné = given |
| dormir = to sleep | dormi = slept |
| vendre = to sell | vendu = sold |
| prendre = to take | pris = taken |

The endings of the past participle are:

-é with all verbs in -er.
-i with most verbs in -ir.
-u with most verbs in -re.

| (I am going out) | (I have gone out) |
| je sors | je suis sorti(e) |
| (the train is leaving) | (the train has left) |
| le train part | le train est parti |
| (they arrive) | (they have arrived) |
| ils arrivent | ils sont arrivé(e)s |

The Perfect Tense of the vast majority of French verbs is formed (as in English) by the Present Tense of avoir (j'ai, il a, etc.) and the Past Participle.

A few verbs (they are mostly verbs denoting motion from one place to another) form their Perfect with être (je suis, il est, etc.).

Instead of saying, for example: "he has gone", the French say il est parti ("is gone").

The following verbs form their Perfect with être:

aller = to go; venir = to come; entrer = to enter; sortir = to go out; arriver = to arrive; partir = to leave; monter = to go (come) up; descendre = to go (come) down; tomber = to fall; rester = to stay.

1. **Mon oncle est venu.**
   My uncle has come.

   **Il est arrivé à six heures.**
   He arrived at six o'clock.

2. **Ma tante est venue.**
   My aunt has come.

   **Elle est arrivée à onze heures.**
   She arrived at eleven o'clock.

3. **Mes cousins sont venus.**
   My cousins have come.

   **Ils sont arrivés à une heure.**
   They arrived at one o'clock.

4. **Mes cousines sont venues.**
   My cousins (women) have come.

   **Elles sont arrivées à midi et demie.**
   They arrived at half past twelve.

Note from the above: 1. The Perfect Tense in French denotes not only what has just been happening, but also what happened in the past.

2. The Past Participle used in connection with être agrees with the subject. (In sentence 2, the subject is feminine, therefore -e is added to venu and arrivé; in sentence 3, the subject is plural masculine, therefore -s is added; in 4, the subject is plural feminine, so -es is added.)

## SENTENCE BUILDING

| | |
| --- | --- |
| j'ai | I have, etc. |
| vous avez | |
| nous avons | |
| il (elle) a | |
| ils (elles) ont | |
| je n'ai pas | I haven't, etc. |
| vous n'avez pas | |
| nous n'avons pas | |
| il n'a pas | |
| elle n'a pas | |
| ils n'ont pas | |
| elles n'ont pas | |

| (n') | ai-je | Have I |
| | avez-vous | (Haven't I), etc. |
| | avons-nous | (pas) |
| | a-t-il (elle) | |
| | ont-ils (elles) | |

| | |
| --- | --- |
| mangé | eaten |
| déjeuné | lunched |
| dîné | dined |
| fermé la porte | shut the door |
| ouvert la fenêtre | opened the window |
| été en France | been in France |
| regardé les fleurs | looked at the flowers |
| parlé français | spoken French |
| dit au revoir | said good-bye |
| pris un bain | taken a bath |
| eu des lettres | had letters |
| fait les malles | packed the trunks |
| bien dormi | slept well |
| mis des gants | put on gloves |
| vu Paris | seen Paris |
| lu ce roman | read this novel |
| écrit des lettres | written letters |
| demandé pardon | apologized |

I have, etc.
je suis
vous êtes
nous sommes
il ⎫
elle ⎬ est
ils ⎫
elles ⎬ sont

I haven't, etc.
je ne suis pas
vous n'êtes pas
il n'est pas
elle n'est pas
nous ne sommes pas
ils ne sont pas
elles ne sont pas

Have I (haven't I), etc.
(ne) suis-je ⎫
(n') êtes-vous ⎪
(n') est-il ⎪
(n') est-elle ⎬ (pas)
(ne) sommes-nous ⎪
(ne) sont-ils ⎪
(ne) sont-elles ⎭

| | |
|---|---|
| allé(es) à Paris | gone to Paris |
| arrivé(es) en auto | arrived in a car |
| venu(es) hier | come yesterday |
| sorti(es) de la maison | left the house (gone out of) |
| entré(es) tard | come in late |
| parti(es) pour l'Amérique | left for America |
| monté(es) l'escalier | gone up the stairs |
| descendu(es) pour le dîner | come down for dinner |
| tombé(es) dans l'eau | fallen into the water |
| resté(es) à la maison | stayed indoors |

*Note.*—Add -e to the Past Participle if the subject of the sentence is feminine; -s if it is masculine plural; -es if feminine plural. These endings do not affect the pronunciation.

### SOME FRENCH PROVERBS

**Quand le chat n'y est pas, les souris dansent.** When the cat is away the mice play.
**Quand les fous vont au marché, les marchands se réjouissent.** When fools go buying there is joy in the market place.
**Quand on sème le vent, on récolte la tempête.** Sow the wind and reap the whirlwind.
**Qui dort, dîne.** Sleeping is as good as eating.
**Qui ne risque rien, n'a rien.** Nothing venture, nothing win.
**Qui s'excuse, s'accuse.** He who excuses accuses himself.
**Rira bien qui rira le dernier.** He who laughs last, laughs longest.
**Tel père tel fils.** Like father like son.
**Tout est bien qui finit bien.** All's well that ends well.
**Vouloir c'est pouvoir.** Where there's a will there's a way.

## EXERCISES

### I Put into the Perfect

1. Je ne comprends pas. 2. Il est malade. 3. J'ai une faim de loup. 4. Est-ce que Madame sonne? 5. Elle n'aime pas la bière. 6. Nous ne fermons pas les yeux. 7. Il prend le métro. 8. La domestique apporte la viande. 9. Personne ne veut de potage. 10. Elle fait une robe.

### II Answer in French

1. Avez vous lu beaucoup de livres? 2. A quelle heure avez-vous dîné hier? 3. Avez-vous bu du vin hier? 4. Avez-vous mangé quelque chose ce matin? 5. Avez-vous fait une promenade hier soir? 6. M. Roberts a-t-il pris du potage? 7. M. et Mme Roberts ont-ils déjà visité la ville?

### GENS DE LOISIR

Des "trimardeurs" et des gens quasi respectables font la sieste sur les bords du fleuve.

| **Loisir** (m) | **trimardeur** (m.) | **quasi** (adv.) | **sieste** (f.) | **fleuve** (m.) |
|---|---|---|---|---|
| Leisure | tramp (slang) | almost | siesta, after-lunch sleep | river |

. Ont-ils déjà été à Versailles? 9. Qui a fait
e gâteau? 10. Qui est allé faire une
promenade? 11. Êtes-vous allé au théâtre
ier soir? 12. Êtes-vous resté à la maison
dimanche dernier (dairn-yay=last)? 13.
:tes-vous sorti mardi dernier? 14. Êtes-
ous allé à Paris l'année dernière? 15. M.
t Mme Roberts sont-ils arrivés en retard?

### III  Translate into French

1. At what time do you have dinner? 2.
At what time did you have dinner yester-
ay? 3. Did you drink wine last night?
. Have you been to Paris? 5. Not yet, but
shall go in summer. 6. I have been to
Boulogne. 7. Last year we went to Nice.
. They have not arrived yet. 9. They left
or America last month. 10. We stayed in
he theatre (for) four hours. 11. I did not
o out last night. 12. My parents have
rrived. We went to the station.

*(Key on page 210).*

# KEY TO THE EXERCISES

## Lesson Fourteen

### I

1. il donne, donnait, a donné, donnera.
. il prend, prenait, a pris, prendra. 3. il
net, mettait, a mis, mettra. 4. il achète,
chetait, a acheté, achètera. 5. il dit,
isait, a dit, dira.

### II

1. This book is a good one, but that book
a better one; it is the best of all my
ooks. 2. Spring is the best season. 3.
George is the happiest boy of the town.
. I shall wash in the bathroom. 5. He will
e very tired. 6. Will they be late for
reakfast? 7. We shall spend the holidays
t the seaside. 8. When will you have your
olidays? 9. She will not change her
noney. 10. Why don't you count your
nange? 11. Will they sell their house?
2. I should like to go to bed early.

### III

1. Mes cigares sont meilleurs que vos
cigarettes. 2. Le meilleur tabac est très
cher. 3. Des cigarettes françaises sont
meilleur marché. 4. Elles sont vingt-cinq
centimes pièce. 5. Combien coûte le
paquet de dix? 6. Il aura à écrire beaucoup
de lettres. 7. Changerez-vous vos billets de
banque anglais? 8. Je n'oublierai pas
d'acheter une boîte d'allumettes et de
l'encre. 9. Y a-t-il une papeterie près d'ici?
10. Nous entrerons dans un bistrot, où l'on
peut acheter des timbres-poste. 11. Je
voudrais des cartes postales illustrées. 12.
Voudriez-vous aller avec moi?

## Lesson Fifteen

### I

1. Il ne l'écoute pas. 2. Ils les regardent.
3. Nous allons les voir. 4. Elle la met sur
la bouche. 5. Il ne les mange pas. 6.
L'aimez-vous? 7. Il ne les trouve pas.
8. Elle l'attend. 9. Ils ne la ferment pas.
10. La prend-il?

### II

1. Prenez-vous la salade? Oui, je la
prends. 2. Est-ce qu'elle prend du hareng?
Elle ne le prend pas. 3. Est-ce que le
professeur ouvre la fenêtre? Non, il ne
l'ouvre pas. 4. Ils mangent de la viande,
des légumes et des fruits. 5. Je ne mange
pas de poisson. 6. J'aime manger des
fraises. 7. Aimez-vous manger des cerises?
8. Mettez-vous du sucre dans le café? 9.
Je mets trois morceaux dans mon café.
10. Le garçon ne nous a pas apporté le vin.
11. Le fromage est très bon; je le recommande. 12. Je ne peux pas les accompagner. 13. Attendez-moi. 14. Ne
m'attendez pas. 15. Attendez-la. 16. Ne
l'attendez pas.

### III

1. Il y a quelque chose (il n'y a rien). 2.
Je mange beaucoup de pain (je ne mange
pas beaucoup de pain). 3. Je bois du vin
(je ne bois pas de vin). 4. Je mange des

fruits. 5. Je (ne) mets (pas de) du lait dans le café. 6. Je (ne) bois (pas de) du café noir. 7. Je la mange avec une cuillère. 8. Nous la coupons avec un couteau. 9 and 10. Je l'aime (Je ne l'aime pas). 11. Je (') (n') aime (pas) les lire. 12. Du fromage et des fruits. 13. Ils vont à un café. 14. M. Lesage les accompagne. 15. Il les rejoindra à quatre heures et demie.

## Lesson Sixteen

### I

1. J'en ai beaucoup (je n'en ai pas beaucoup). 2. J'en mange (je n'en mange pas). 3. Same as 1. 4. J'en achète chez le fruitier. 5. Chez le boucher. 6. Le fruitier en vend. 7. J'en ai assez. 8. Elle n'en achète pas. 9. Elle achète des cerises et des abricots. 10. Non, elle n'était pas contente de son boucher. 11. Il avait vendu de la viande dure. 12. Elle en prend deux. 13. Non, il n'est pas chez le boulanger. 14. Dans un bureau de tabac. 15. Il a changé de l'argent anglais.

### II

1. Elle en achète. 2. On en mange. 3. Elle en a. 4. Il le boit. 5. Il en boit. 6. Elle l'a achetée. 7. Elle en achète. 8. Il les apporte. 9. Ils en mangent beaucoup. 10. Ils les regardent. 11. Elle n'en a pas. 12. Il en veut.

### III

1. J'ai du pain, mais je n'ai pas de beurre. 2. En avez-vous? 3. J'en ai un peu. 4. Je n'en ai pas. 5. Il n'y a pas de cerises chez le fruitier. 6. N'y en a-t-il pas? 7. Ne buvez-vous pas de vin rouge? 8. N'en buvez-vous jamais? 9. Je veux de bonnes oranges. 10. En avez-vous? 11. J'ai des pommes, mais je n'ai pas de poires. 12. Est-ce que votre père boit du vin blanc? 13. Votre tante demande s'il y a de la viande. 14. La bonne dit qu'il n'y en a pas.

15. Elle va acheter du fromage, de légumes et de la viande.

## Lesson Seventeen

### I

1. Je n'ai pas compris. 2. Il a é malade. 3. J'ai eu une faim de loup. Est-ce que Mme a sonné? 5. Elle n'a pa aimé la bière. 6. Nous n'avons pas fern les yeux. 7. Il a pris le métro. 8. L domestique a apporté la viande. Personne n'a voulu de potage. 10. Elle fait une robe.

### II

1. J'en ai lu beaucoup (je n'en ai pas beaucoup). 2. Hier j'ai dîné à sept heure 3. Je n'en ai pas bu hier. J'en ai bu hie 4. Oui, j'ai mangé quelque chose ce mati 5. Je n'ai pas fait de promenade. J' fait une promenade hier soir. 6. Il en pris. 7. Ils l'ont déjà visité. 8. Ils n'o pas encore été à Versailles. 9. Mme Lesa l'a fait. 10. Mme Roberts, Mlle Lesage Georges sont allés faire une promenac 11. Je (ne) suis (pas) allé au théâtre hi soir. 12. Je (ne) suis (pas) resté à maison. 13. Je (ne) suis (pas) sorti mar dernier. 14. Je (ne) suis (pas) allé à Par l'année dernière. 15. Oui, ils sont arriv en retard.

### III

1. À quelle heure dînez-vous? 2. quelle heure avez-vous dîné hier? 3. Ave vous bu du vin hier soir? 4. Avez-vous é à Paris? 5. Pas encore, mais j'irai cet é 6. J'ai été à Boulogne. 7. L'année derniè nous sommes allés à Nice. 8. Ils ne so pas encore arrivés. 9. Ils sont partis po l'Amérique le mois dernier. 10. No sommes restés au théâtre quatre heure 11. Je ne suis pas sorti hier soir. 12. M parents sont arrivés. Nous sommes al à la gare.

**ANOTHER FRENCH PROVERB**

**Le menteur n'est plus écouté, quand même il dit la vérité.**
A liar is not believed, even when he speaks the truth.

# PRONUNCIATION AT SIGHT

WE have now reached a stage in this Course where we no longer consider it necessary to provide students with phonetic transcriptions. We feel sure that by now every one of our readers will be able to pronounce at sight frequent words as monsieur, madame, mademoiselle, je suis, un peu, tu, du and s'il vous plaît. The phonetic transcriptions have been given so often, that it would really amount to a waste of space to continue them.

As we explained in the beginning, our system of imitated pronunciation did not aim to do more than to offer a nearest English equivalent, not an exact reproduction of French sounds. For that reason we advised students to listen in to French being spoken by Frenchmen, and to check their own pronunciation as they listened. Many students will have done this, and the material which follows should aid them in the task of perfecting what they have learned.

While in English the same letter or combination of letters is quite often sounded differently in different words, in French every letter and every combination of letters can—with very few exceptions—be pronounced in one way only. Whereas ou is pronounced differently in soup, soul, house, enough, etc., French ou is always pronounced the same, namely as in English soup; whereas au is pronounced differently in daughter, laughter, automatic, etc., French au is always pronounced oh; whereas English "u" is differently sounded in but, sure, supply, survey, etc., French u is always pronounced "ee." It is therefore impossible to give, to a foreign student of English, rules of pronunciation that will enable him to pronounce correctly words that he has never heard before. It is the object of this section to show how every letter and every combination of letters should be pronounced in French.

## I. THE VOWELS

Vowels are generally either long or short (see page 214).          *Examples*

| | |
|---|---|
| as in "far", when long. | *page, dame, par, la, a, ma, papa.* |
| like the "a" in "rat" when short. | |
| like "ah!", always long. | *âme* (soul), *âge, tâche* (task). |
| like "ay" in "gay", but shorter. | *été, donné, thé.* |
| like "ai" in "pair". | *père, mère, je lève.* |
| as in "her", at the end of a word or syllable. | *le, me, retenir* (to retain). |
| like é when followed by a mute consonant. | *les, mes, ses.* |
| like è when followed by a sounded consonant. | *elle, lettre, terre* (earth). |
| like "ee" in "seen". | *qui, il, ici, ami.* |
| like "i", but always long. | *île* (island). |
| long as in "hole". | *rose, poser.* |
| short as in "hot". | *trop, comme, poste, robe.* |
| as in "hole", always long. | *trône* (throne) *tôt, rôti.* |
| "ee" with rounded lips. | *lu, vu, mûr* (ripe), *sûr.* |
| like *i*, but always long. | *style, y, cylindre.* |
| usually like è. | *vrai, jamais, palais.* |
| like é in *gai, j'ai* (but è in *ai-je*) and the termination of 1st person singular Future. | *je donnerai.* |
| like "e" in "her" in *faisons*, and in Imperfect of *faire.* | *je faisais,* etc. |
| like *a* if followed by *l* or *ll*. | *travailler, le travail, volaille.* |

**ay** like *è* and *i* in *pays*=country.      *crayon, payer.*

**au** ⎱ like "oh".      *auto, au, autre.*
**eau** ⎰      *beau, couteau, eau.*

**ei** like *è*, always long.      *reine* (queen), *peine.*

**eu** like "i" in " fir".

     when followed by a hard consonant ;      *neuf, beurre.*
     like *é* pronounced with rounded lips ;
     when followed by a soft consonant or by a silent      *deux, feu, heureuse.*
       consonant, or at the end of a word.
     like &ecirc;&ecirc;, when meaning "had" (past participle of      *J'ai eu peur.*
       *avoir*) or in *eut*, the Preterite of *avoir*.

**oi** like "wah".      *trois, moi, froid.*

**œu** like "i" in "fir" (in the plural of **œuf**—"egg", the *œu*      *cœur, sœur, œuf, les œufs.*
    is sounded like ay pronounced with rounded lips).

**ou** like "oo" in "tool".      *poule, fou, jour, pour.*

**oy** like "oi".      *nettoyer, royal, loyer* (lwah-yay)

**ui** like *ui* making the "u" very short, the "i" follow-      *lui, huit, nuit, puis.*
    ing immediately.


## II. CONSONANTS

(unless mentioned below, they are the same as in English)

**c** pronounced "k" before *a, o, u* or a consonant.      *cage, cacao, crédit.*
    pronounced "s" before *e, i, y.*      *ce, cigare, bicyclette.*

**cc** pronounced "k" before *a, o, u* or a consonant, "ks"      *occuper* (o-k&ecirc;&ecirc;-pay),
    before *e* or *i.*        *accepter* (ahk-saip-tay),
       *accident* (ahk-see-daN).

**ç** always like "s".      *Français, garçon.*

**ch** like English "sh".      *chien, cheval, chef.*
    "k" in some words, e.g.      *écho, Christ, chrétien* (kray-tyiN
       =Christian), *chœur* (k&acirc;&ycirc;r
       =choir), *choléra, technique,*
       *orchestre.*

**g** hard as in "go" before *a, o, u* or a consonant other      *gare, goût, guide* (geed), *grand.*
    than *n.*
    soft, like "s" in "measure", before *e, i, y.*      *gentil, gilet, gymnastique.*

**ge** like soft "g" before *a, o, u* (the "e" is mute here, it      *je mangeais, nous mangeons.*
    is merely an indication that the "g" is soft).

**gn** like "ni" in English "onion".      *oignon, Bretagne, signe.*

**gu** like hard "*g*" (the "*u*" is mute here, it only shows      *langue, guerre, guitare.*
    that the "*g*" retains its hard sound).

**h** is always silent. Most words beginning with "h"      *l'heure, l'homme, l'hôtel, le*
    are treated exactly as if they began with a vowel      *heures* (lay-z&acirc;&ycirc;r), *les homme*
    ("*h*" mute).      (lay-zom).

    in some words, however, the "h" is treated as a con-      *le hareng* (herring) ; *le hasar*
    sonant (*h aspiré*), i.e. there is neither liaison nor      (chance, risk) ; *la hâte*
    elision. Some of the most frequent ones are :      (haste) ; *haut* (oh = high)
       *la Hollande* (Holland) ; *l*
       *Hongrie* (Hungary), *le Havre*

(This difference is made because *h aspiré* was sounded in former times. In modern French both are equally silent.)

**j** like soft "g" (zh).                                    *je, jamais, journal.*
**l** as in "lamp" (never as in "all").                      *la, lampe, boule* (ball).
**ll** preceded by *i* pronounced double "l" when a word     *illégal, illustration.*
begins with " ill".
pronounced like "y" in English *yes* in the middle or        *fille, bouteille, famille.*
at the end of a word.
like single "l" in                                           *mille, million, ville, village, tran-*
                                                             *quille* and in a few others.

**q**
**qu** } like "k".                                           *coq, cinq, que, quand, question.*

**r** is pronounced more distinctly than in English.         *rose, Charles, rouge.*
**s** at the beginning of a word as in "see".                *sont, sac, sucre.*
between vowels like "z" also in the following words          *Alsace, alsacien, transaction,*
(although preceded by a consonant) :                         *transition, transatlantique.*
**ss** always like "s" in "see".                             *poisson, assassinat* (murder).
**sc** like "sk" before *a, o, u* or a consonant.            *scandale, sculpteur.*
like "s" (in "see") before *e, i,* or *y.*                   *descendre, science.*
**t** usually as in English.                                 *tenir, question, vingtième.*
like "s" (in "see") in words ending in *-tial, -tiel,*       *nation, essentiel, patience,*
*-tience, -tieux, -tie, -tion* (when not *-stion*)           *partial, ambitieux, aristo*
                                                             *cratie.*
**th** like "t".                                             *thé, théâtre.*
**w** like English "v".                                      *wagon.*
**x**—"eggz" when at the beginning followed by a vowel       *exact, exagérer, exhibition.*
or *h.*
like "z" in                                                  *deuxième, sixième, dixième.*
like "ks" in all other cases.                                *luxe, excuse, excellent.*

## III. FINAL LETTERS

*Final* e without any accent is not sounded, unless it is the only vowel of the word, as in *je, le, me,* etc.

Final consonants are usually not pronounced, except final **c,f,k,l,q** and **r**; e.g. *parc, sac, avec,* etc. (c pronounced as k).

s pronounced in *bref* (short); *sauf* (except); *soif* (thirst); *neuf,* etc.

k final only in foreign words: *Danemark; bifteck, bock,* etc.

l is pronounced in *il; fil; mil; avril; exil;* and others.

q final is pronounced as **k:** *cinq; coq* (cock).

r final is usually pronounced (*mer; cher; hiver; hier; car; par; sortir; or; noir; cour;* etc.) but it is mute in the ending of the infinitive *-er,* which is pronounced

like "é", and the ending *-ier,* which is pronounced "yay".

**ent,** the ending of the 3rd person plural is silent: *ils donnent.*

Exceptions to the rules given above:—

**b** final is pronounced in proper names and in foreign words: Jacob, club.

**c** final is mute in *tabac, estomac* (stomach), *porc, caoutchouc* (rubber).

**d** final is pronounced in *sud* (south) and in proper names like *David.*

**f** final is mute in *clef* (key), also written *clé.*

**l** final is mute in *fusil* (rifle), *gentil* (nice), *outil* (tool), *sourcil* (eyebrow). *il* is pronounced **y** in *travail* (work), *soleil* (sun), *fauteuil* (armchair) and a few others. For the pronunciation of *ille* see Section II above.

**m** final: see section **IV** (below).

**n** final: see section **IV** (below).

**r** final: the " r " is pronounced in *hier* (yesterday) and *fier* (proud); it is mute in *monsieur* and *messieurs*;

**s** final is pronounced in *omnibus*; *tennis*; *gratis*; *as*; *atlas*; *hélas*; *bis* (twice); *ours* (bear), and in certain proper names.

**t** final is pronounced in *mat, net, sept, est* (east), *ouest* (west), *déficit, tact, strict, huit*, except when followed by plural beginning with a consonant: *huit cents*; *huit livres*, etc.).

**x** final is pronounced " s " in *six* and *dix*, but silent when followed by plural beginning with a consonant (*six livres*), etc.

**z** final is sounded in *gaz* and in foreign words.

## IV. NASALS

Nasals occur whenever a vowel comes before *m* or *n* at the end of a word, or when these letters are followed by one or several consonants. They are purely vowel sounds, and there is no difference whether *n* or *m* follows. How to nasalize vowels has been explained in the Introduction to French Pronunciation in the first part of this Course.

**an, am, en, em** nasalized "ah"
*anglais, lampe, patient, temps*;

**on, om** nasalized "oh"
*on, concert, bon, nom, compliment*;

**un, um** nasalized "a͡y"
*un, commun, parfum, humble*;

**in, im, ain, aim, ein, eim, yn, ym** nasalized "ai"
*vin*; *quinze, impossible, bain, faim, plein, Reims, sympathique, syncope* (fainting fit).

**en** is pronounced like "iN" in *vient, tient, mien, bien, combien, examen, européen, égyptien, parisien* and *moyen* (= means).

*Note.*—If the **m** or **n** is followed by a vowel (or "*h*") or doubled, it loses its nasal sound: *une, bonne, immense, bonheur, brune*, etc.

## V. SIGNS AND ACCENTS

(1) l'accent **aigu** (′) to show that e is pronounced *ay*: *été, donné, thé*.

(2) l'accent **grave** (`) to show that e is pronounced *ai*: *père, mère, il lève;* to distinguish meanings, without changing pronunciation, e.g. *a* = has; *à* = to; *ou* = or, *où* = where; *la* = the; *là* = there.

(3) l'accent **circonflexe** (^) to show that e is open and long: *tête, fenêtre*; to lengthen other vowels: *âme* (soul), *île* (island), *côte* (coast).

(4) le **tréma** (··) to show that the vowel bearing it is not blended with the preceding vowel: *Noël* (Christmas), *naïf* (nah-if).

(5) la **cédille** (say-deey) to give the *ç* the sound of "s" before "a, o, u:" *ça, leçon, reçu*.

(6) l'**apostrophe** to indicate the omission of a vowel: *l'hôtel, j'ai, s'il*.

## VI. LENGTH OF VOWELS

Vowels are long:

(1) Before a single soft consonant (*vr, ch*, and *ll* when sounded "y" count as one consonant):
*page, dame, rouge, rose, livre, fille, gauche*.

(2) When having an accent circonflexe:
*tête, côte, sûr*.

Vowels are short:

(1) When followed by a hard consonant or by two consonants:
*os, force, juste, carte, lourd*.

(2) When a final syllable ends in a vowel sound:
*ma, la, si, est, vous, tu, bleu, couteau*.

(3) When é or e:
*je, me, été, fermé, donner, cheval, revenir*.

Vowels are of medium length:
In all other cases.
Nasals are long:
When followed by a consonant which is sounded:

France, oncle, tante, ronde, grande.

Nasals are of medium length:
In all other cases.

Nasals are short: Never.

## VII. LIAISON

When a word ending in a consonant stands before a word beginning with a vowel or **h** mute, the consonant is frequently pronounced and the two words joined in pronunciation. They are spoken as if the final consonant were detached from its own word and became the initial sound of the following one, e.g., *mes amis* is pronounced *may-zahmee*, etc.

It is impossible to give definite and infallible rules as to where liaison should or should not take place. It is much less frequent in conversation than in reading.

Liaison is obligatory, if the two words are closely connected in sense, namely:

(1) after *les, des, ces, aux, nous, vous, ils, elles*: *les amis, des enfants, ces hommes, des hôtels, aux États-Unis, nous avons, ils ont, elles aiment.*

(2) Between adjectives and the following nouns: *le petit enfant, un grand amour, plusieurs hôtels, quelques amis, trois hommes.*

(3) Between prepositions and the following words: *en été, dans un jardin, sous une table, pendant une heure, chez elle,* etc.

(4) Between *bien, très, plus, moins,* and a following adjective: *très actif, plus intéressant, moins intelligent.*

(5) After auxiliary verbs (but not after *tu es* or *tu as*): *il est occupé, elles ont entendu, ils sont arrivés, il avait eu, ils ont acheté,* etc.

(6) In expressions and compounds: *tout à coup* (=suddenly), *de temps en temps* (=from time to time), *vis à vis* (face to face, opposite), *de plus en plus* (=more and more), etc.

Liaison must never be used:

(1) Between a noun used as a subject and *est*: *la maison est belle.*

(2) With a mute consonant following "r": *il sort à midi, cela ne sert à rien.*

(3) after infinitives in -er: *il faut aller immédiatement, elle va retourner à Paris.*

(4) Before aspirated "h", before *huit* or *onze*: *la Hollande, les huit jours, les onze harengs.*

(5) after *et*=and: *une fourchette et un couteau.*

### NOTE:

(1) In liaison, **d** is sounded like "t", **f** like "v", **s** and **x** like "z": *un grand hôtel, neuf heures, deux enfants, trois images,* etc.

(2) A nasal sound loses its nasal quality in liaison and a pure vowel sound is heard: *mon ami* (mo-nah-mee), *ton enfant* (to-naN-faN), *un homme* (ai-nom), *en avant* (ah-nah-vaN), etc.

## PUNCTUATION MARKS

| . | *point* |
|---|---|
| , | *virgule* |
| : | *deux points* |
| ; | *point-virgule* |
| ! | *point d'exclamation* |
| ? | *point d'interrogation* |
| - | *trait d'union* |
| — | *tiret* |
| " " | *guillemets* |
| ( ) | *parenthèse* |

## THREE MORE PROVERBS

**Il ne faut pas mettre le doigt entre l'arbre et l'écorce.** Do not interfere between a man and his wife. (Literally : Do not put your finger between the tree and the bark.)

**Pierre qui roule n'amasse pas mousse.** A rolling stone gathers no moss.

**Loin des yeux, loin du cœur.** Out of sight, out of mind.

### AU VIEUX MONTMARTRE

On mange en plein air sur la fameuse Place du Tertre, au sommet de la Butte Montmartre. À l'arrière-plan, la flèche de la Basilique du Sacré-Cœur.

| **Manger en plein air** | tertre (m.) | butte (f.) | à l'arrière-plan | flèche (f.) |
|---|---|---|---|---|
| To eat in the open | hillock | knoll | in the background | spire (of church) |

# DIX-HUITIÈME LEÇON

### EN VILLE—IN TOWN

**M. et Mme Roberts désireux de connaître Paris se promènent dans les rues**
Mr. and Mrs. Roberts desirous to know Paris are walking in the streets

**en regardant les vieux quartiers et les vieilles maisons qui ont déjà vu**
looking at the old parts and the old houses which have already seen

**tant de siécles.   Ils visitent le vieux Montmartre avec ses petites rues montantes**
so many centuries.   They visit old Montmartre with its small steep streets

**et ses innombrables escaliers.   Ils visitent le "Père-Lachaise" et**
and its countless stairs.   They visit the "Père-Lachaise" and

**regardent les tombeaux des célébrités qui y reposent.   Ils ont déjà vu**
look at the tombs of the famous who rest there.   They have already seen

**tant de choses que finalement Mme Roberts dit à son mari:**
so many things that finally Mrs. Roberts says to her husband:

## LE PEINTRE MONTMARTROIS
Nullement gêné par la présence des laïques, le peintre poursuit sa tâche.

| **Nullement** (adv.) | **gêner** | **laïque** (m.f.) | **poursuivre** | **tâche** (f.) |
|---|---|---|---|---|
| Not at all, in no way | to embarrass | layman | to continue with | task |

"Ne trouves-tu pas que nous en avons assez vu aujourd'hui?"
"Don't you find that we have seen enough to-day?"

**M. Roberts :** **Plus je regarde Paris, plus je l'aime.   Je ne veux pas**
The more I look at Paris, the more I like it.   I don't want

**quitter cette ville sans en avoir vu le plus possible.**
to leave this town without having seen as much as possible.

**Mme Roberts : Pour vraiment connaître Paris il faudrait des années . . .**
In order really to know Paris one would need years . . .

**M. Roberts :** **Je sais, mais je veux tout de même voir ce que tout étranger**
I know, but I want, nevertheless, to see what every foreigner

**visite à Paris     Mme Roberts : Je te comprends parfaitement;**
visits in Paris.                              I understand you perfectly;

**néanmoins, je suis trop fatiguée aujourd'hui.   Je te ferai une**
nevertheless, I am too tired to-day.   I'll make you a

LE CIMETIÈRE DU PÈRE-LACHAISE

Le "Monument des Morts" au Père-Lachaise.   Dans ce cimetière sont ensevelis
Héloïse et Abélard, amants tragiques dont le roman a attristé le monde entier, et Oscar
Wilde, exilé volontaire après avoir été relâché de la prison de Reading.

| **Cimetière** (m.) | **ensevelir** | **attrister** | **relâcher** |
| Cemetery | to bury | to render sad | **to** release |

**proposition.   Tu verras l'Arc de Triomphe sans moi, et moi,**
suggestion.   You will see the "Triumphal Arch" without me, and

**j'attendrai dans ce petit café, où je prendrai**
I shall wait in this little cafe, where I shall have

**une glace.     M. Roberts : Bien, tu es très gentille ma chère ;**
an ice-cream                  All right, you are very kind, my dear;

**à tout à l'heure.   (S'adressant à un passant) :   Monsieur,**
bye-bye, until later. (Addressing himself to a passer-by) :   Sir,

**pouvez-vous m'indiquer le chemin pour aller à l'Arc de Triomphe?**
can you indicate to me the way (to go) to the Arc de Triomphe?

**Passant :     Je regrette, monsieur, je ne suis pas du quartier.**
I regret, sir, I am a stranger myself (lit., I am not of the district).

**Voilà un facteur qui pourra certainement**
There is a postman who will certainly be able

**vous renseigner.     M. Roberts : Merci beaucoup, monsieur.  (Il**
to direct you.                   Thank you very much, sir. (He

**s'approche du facteur.)   Pardon,**
goes up to the postman).   Excuse me,

**monsieur, pouvez-vous me dire quel**
sir, could you tell me which

**chemin je dois prendre pour aller**
way I have to take to go

**à l'Arc de Triomphe?     Facteur : Avec**
to the Arc de Triomphe?            With

**plaisir, monsieur.   Suivez cette rue**
pleasure, sir.   Follow that street

**jusqu'au bout, puis tournez à droite et continuez tout**
up to the end, then turn to the right and continue straight

**droit.   Vous arriverez à un carrefour, d'où vous verrez**
ahead.   You will arrive at a cross-roads, where you will see

**l'Arc de Triomphe au bout de la deuxième rue à gauche.**
the Arc de Triomphe at the end of the second street on the left.

**M. Roberts :   Vous êtes très aimable.   Est-ce loin?**
That is very kind of you.   Is it far?

**Facteur :**     **Pas du tout, c'est tout près, à peine dix minutes d'ici.**
Not at all, it's quite near, hardly ten minutes from here.

**M. Roberts : Merci bien, monsieur. (Il suit**
Thanks very much, sir.   (He follows

**le chemin indiqué pendant dix minutes,**
the way indicated for ten minutes,

**à peu près, sans arriver à son**
approximately, without arriving at his

**but.    Alors il s'adresse à un agent de police.)**
goal.    Then he speaks to a policeman.)

**Pardon, monsieur l'agent, est-ce bien par**
Excuse me, officer, is it (right) by

**ici que je peux arriver à l'Arc de**
this way that I can get to the Arc de

**Triomphe?**     **Agent : Pas du tout, monsieur, c'est juste dans le sens**
Triomphe?                   Not at all, sir, it's just in the opposite

**opposé.    Retournez jusqu'à la première à gauche,**
direction.    Go back as far as the first street on the left,

**prenez la grande avenue que vous trouverez devant vous,**
take the broad thoroughfare which you will find in front of you,

**et vous verrez l'Arc de Triomphe au bout de cette avenue.**
and you will see the Arc de Triomphe at the end of this avenue.

**Je t'aime**
I love you

### "THOU" IN FRENCH

The Familiar Form.—While in English the familiar form—THOU, THY, THEE—is almost extinct, it is used in French when speaking to small children and intimate friends.

### Present Tense

| Ordinary Form | Familiar Form | |
| --- | --- | --- |
| vous avez | tu as | you have |
| vous êtes | tu es | you are |
| vous parlez | tu parles | you speak |
| vous donnez | tu donnes | you give |
| vous aimez | tu aimes | you love |
| vous allez | tu vas | you go |
| vous faites | tu fais | you make |
| vous prenez | tu prends | you take |
| vous mettez | tu mets | you put |
| vous venez | tu viens | you come |

| | | |
|---|---|---|
| ous dormez | tu dors | you sleep |
| ous partez | tu pars | you leave |
| ous sortez | tu sors | you go out |
| ous attendez | tu attends | you wait |
| ous pouvez | tu peux | you can |
| ous voulez | tu veux | you want, wish, will |

Note that the forms of the verb used in connection with **tu**, as far as pronunciation is concerned, are identical with the forms used in connection with **il** or **elle**. With regard to spelling, however, note that they all, with the exception of the last two examples given, end in **-s**.

## Other Tenses

| | | |
|---|---|---|
| ous aviez | tu avais | you had |
| ouz étiez | tu étais | you were |
| ous parliez | tu parlais | you spoke |
| ous donniez | tu donnais | you gave |
| ouz aimiez | tu aimais | you loved |
| ous alliez | tu allais | you went |
| ous faisiez | tu faisais | you made |
| ous disiez | tu disais | you said |
| ous veniez | tu venais | you came |
| ous dormiez | tu dormais | you slept |
| ous partiez | tu partais | you left |
| ous attendiez | tu attendais | you waited |
| ous pouviez | tu pouvais | you could |
| ous vouliez | tu voulais | you wanted |

| | | |
|---|---|---|
| ous aurez | tu auras | you will have |
| ous serez | tu seras | you will be |
| ous parlerez | tu parleras | you will speak |
| ous donnerez | tu donneras | you will give |
| ous irez | tu iras | you will go |
| ous viendrez | tu viendras | you will come |
| ous ferez | tu feras | you will make |
| ous direz | tu diras | you will say |
| ous prendrez | tu prendras | you will take |
| ous mettrez | tu mettras | you will put |
| ous dormirez | tu dormiras | you will sleep |
| ous partirez | tu partiras | you will leave |
| ous pourrez | tu pourras | you will be able |
| ous voudrez | tu voudras | you will want |

| | | |
|---|---|---|
| vous avez eu | tu as eu | you have had |
| vous avez été | tu as été | you have been |
| vous avez parlé | tu as parlé | you have spoken |

| | | |
|---|---|---|
| vous avez donné | tu as donné | you have given |
| vous avez fait | tu as fait | you have made |
| vous avez dit | tu as dit | you have said |
| vous avez pris | tu as pris | you have taken |
| vous avez attendu | tu as attendu | you have waited |
| vous avez dormi | tu as dormi | you have slept |
| vous êtes venu(e)s | tu es venu(e) | you have come |
| vous êtes parti(e)s | tu es parti(e) | you have left |
| vous êtes sorti(e)s | tu es sorti(e) | you have gone out |

Note that all these forms, as far as pronunciation is concerned, are identical with the forms used in connection with **il** or **elle,** and that with regard to spelling they all end in **-s**, which, however, is not sounded.

---

## Imperative

| | | |
|---|---|---|
| donnez! | donne! | give! |
| parlez! | parle! | speak! |
| mangez! | mange! | eat! |
| attendez! | attends! | wait! |
| prenez! | prends! | take! |
| dormez! | dors! | sleep! |
| allez! | va! | go! |
| ayez! | aie! | have . . .! |
| soyez! | sois! | be . . .! |

Note that the Imperative is the same as the first person (i.e. the form of the present tense used in connection with **je**), with the exception of the last three examples given above.

## The Possessive Adjective

| | | |
|---|---|---|
| votre livre | ton livre | your book |
| votre chaise | ta chaise | your chair |
| votre père | ton père | your father |
| votre mère | ta mère | your mother |
| vos parents | tes parents | your parents |
| vos livres | tes livres | your books |
| vos chaises | tes chaises | your chairs |

**Ton** (toN), **ta** (tah), **tes** (tay) are the French equivalents for "thy".

**Ton** is used with masculine nouns, singular, **ta** with feminines (singular) and **tes** with plurals (masculine and feminine). Compare **mon, ma, mes** with **ton, ta, tes**:

mon chapeau . . . . . . . . . . . . . . . .my hat
ton chapeau . . . . . . . . . . . . . . . .thy hat
ma robe . . . . . . . . . . . . . . . . . . .my dress
ta robe . . . . . . . . . . . . . . . . . . .thy dress
mes chapeaux . . . . . . . . . . . . . .my hats
tes chapeaux . . . . . . . . . . . . . . .thy hats
mes robes . . . . . . . . . . . . . . . . .my dresses
tes robes . . . . . . . . . . . . . . . . . .thy dresses

### The Object Pronoun

| | | |
|---|---|---|
| je vous donne | je te donne | I give you |
| je vous aime | je t'aime | I love you |
| vous vous lavez | tu te laves | you wash yourself |
| vous habillez-vous? | t'habilles-tu? | are you getting dressed? |
| levez-vous! | lève-toi! | get up! |
| ne vous levez pas! | ne te lève pas! | don't get up! |
| vous vous en allez | tu t'en vas | you are going away |
| allez-vous en! | va-t-en! | go away! |
| ne vous en allez pas! | ne t'en va pas! | don't go away! |

The familiar form of the object pronoun (THEE) is **te** or **t'** in front of a vowel or **h** mute.

va-t-en!
go away!

ne t'en va pas!
don't go away!

Compare **te** (t') with **me** (m'):
il me donne . . . . . . . . . . . . .he gives me
il te donne . . . . . . . . . . . . .he gives thee
elle m'aime . . . . . . . . . . . . .she loves me
elle t'aime . . . . . . . . . . . . .she loves thee

### POUVOIR—TO BE ABLE

| *I can* | *Can I?* |
|---|---|
| je peux | puis-je? |
| tu peux | peux-tu? |
| il (elle) peut | peut-il (elle)? |
| nous pouvons | etc. |
| vous pouvez | |
| ils (elles) peuvent | |

| *I cannot* | *I could* |
|---|---|
| je ne peux pas | je pouvais |
| or: je ne puis | tu pouvais |
| tu ne peux pas | il pouvait |
| etc. | etc. |

| *I shall be able* | *I have been able* |
|---|---|
| je pourrai | j'ai pu |
| tu pourras | tu as pu |
| il pourra | il a pu |
| etc. | etc. |

The English "I can" is a defective verb, i.e., it has only a Present and a Past Tense; for the other tenses "to be able" has to be used. In French, however, "I can" is a full verb, capable of forming all tenses except the Imperative.

Note that the first person of the Present Interrogative is irregular, and also that there is an alternative form for the first person of the Present Negative, which is frequently used.

## EXERCISES

### I Answer in French

1. Est-ce que tu es plus grand que ton ère? 2. Est-ce que tu écris beaucoup de ttres? 3. Est-ce que tu as parlé français ier? 4. Est-ce que tu manges des pommes? Qu'est-ce que tu as mangé pour le petit éjeuner? 6. Est-ce que tu prends du ncre dans ton café? 7. M'as-tu vu hier oir? 8. Bois-tu du bon vin blanc? 9. As-tu u du vin à midi? 10. Quel livre lis-tu aintenant? 11. As-tu lu "Les Misérables" ar Victor Hugo? 12. T'es-tu levé de onne heure aujourd'hui?

### Replace vous, votre, vos by the more intimate form—tu, te, ton, ta, tes, etc.

1. Vous mettez les fruits sur la table. Ne prenez-vous pas de légumes? 3. 'écrivez-vous pas? 4. Vous êtes bien imable. 5. Avez-vous vos cartes? 6. Regardez-vous votre tableau? 7. Vous pouvez venir avec votre frère. 8. Vous vous couchez tard. 9. Il vous voit. 10. Ne vous lavez-vous pas? 11. Partez-vous avec votre fille? 12. Vous vous en allez.

### III Translate

1. Do you want to go for a walk? 2. I shall not be able to go out to-day. 3. Don't you want to see your sister? 4. Will you not be able to see her? 5. Have you seen your friends? 6. Can you tell me please which way I have to go to get to Rue Montmartre? 7. I am sorry, I cannot tell you. 8. There is a policeman who will be able to tell you. 9. I saw you last night. 10. Did you see me too? 11. I have seen your brother and your parents, but I haven't seen your sister. 12. Don't do that. 13. Don't speak so fast! 14. Don't go. 15. Wait, please.

*(Key on page 252.)*

L'AVENUE DES CHAMPS-ÉLYSÉES VUE DE L'ARC DE TRIOMPHE

En descendant l'Avenue, bordée tout le long de beaux platanes, l'on traverse Rond-Point des Champs-Élysées pour aboutir à la Place de la Concorde.

| 'atane (m.) | rond-point (m.) | aboutir |
|---|---|---|
| ane tree | circus (meeting of several roads) | to end in, at |

# DIX-NEUVIÈME LEÇON.

### LA FAMILLE ROBERTS AU VIEUX MONTMARTRE

Madame et Monsieur Roberts visitant le Vieux Montmartre ont monté la colline.  Ils remarquent quelques maisons délabrées, ils longent quelques ruelles écartées et ils grimpent d'anciens escaliers de tout genre.

| colline (f.) | délabré-e (adj.) | écarté-e (adj.) | grimper |
|---|---|---|---|
| hill | dilapidated | secluded | to climb |

**M. et Mme Roberts se promènent dans les rues de Paris et visitent plusieurs**
Mr. and Mrs. Roberts are walking in the streets of Paris and visit several

**magasins, pour y faire des achats.   Leurs enfants, Charles et Madeleine,**
shops to make some purchases there.   Their children, Charles and Madeleine,

**les accompagnent.   En ce moment ils entrent dans un magasin à prix unique.**
accompany them.   At this moment they are entering a one-price store.

**M. Roberts (s'adressant à une vendeuse) : Pardon, mademoiselle, où**
(addressing himself to a saleswoman) : Pardon, miss, where

**est le rayon des articles de toilette, s'il vous plaît?**
is the department for toilet articles, please?

**La vendeuse : Par là, monsieur, vous le trouverez au bout de ce passage.**
This way, sir, you will find it at the end of this passage.

**M. Roberts :   Merci, mademoiselle.   Vendeuse : À votre service, monsieur.**
Thank you, miss.                              At your service, sir.

Charles :           **Maman, tu ne vas pas oublier ce que tu m'as promis?**
                    Mummy, you won't forget what you have promised me?

Mme Roberts :       **Tu auras ta glace tout à l'heure.   Ne peux-tu pas**
                    You will have your ice-cream in a moment.   Can't you have a

                    **patienter un peu?   Charles: Oui, maman, mais tu m'as promis**
                    little patience?              Yes, mummy, but you have promised me

                    **encore autre chose . . .      Mme Roberts : Ah, le ping-pong?**
                    still something else . . .                  Ah, the ping-pong?

                    **Petit polisson, n'as-tu pas confiance en ta mère?   D'ailleurs,**
                    Little rascal, have you no trust in your mother?   Besides,

                    **avec qui veux-tu jouer?   Tu n'as pas de copain à Paris.**
                    with whom will you play?   You have no pal in Paris.

Charles :           **Ça ne fait rien.   Je peux jouer avec Madeleine, et puis**
                    That doesn't matter.   I can play with Madeleine, and then

                    **Georges voudra sûrement jouer au ping-pong avec moi.**
                    George would surely (like to) play ping-pong with me.

M. Roberts :        **Nous y voilà.   Vous me servez, mademoiselle?**
                    There we are.   Are you serving me, miss?

Une vendeuse :      **Certainement, monsieur, que désirez-vous?**
                    Certainly, sir, what would you like?

M. Roberts :        **Donnez-moi un morceau de ce savon!**
                    Give me a cake of this soap!

Vendeuse :          **Le voilà, monsieur!   C'est tout ce qu'il vous faut?**
                    There you are, sir!   Is that all (that) you require?

M. Roberts :        **Non, mademoiselle, donnez-moi encore ce petit paquet**
                    No, miss, give me also this small packet

                    **de lames de rasoir; elles sont bonnes, j'espère?**
                    of razor blades; they are good, I hope?

Vendeuse :          **Ah oui, monsieur, ce sont les meilleures.   C'est une marque**
                    Oh, yes, sir, these are the best.   It's a well-known

                    **très connue.   M. Roberts : Ça sera tout pour aujourd'hui. Combien**
                    brand.                    That will be all for to-day.   How much

                    **est-ce que je vous dois?   Vendeuse : Ça fait sept francs, monsieur.**
                    do I owe you?              Seven francs, sir.

## A FRENCH TOWN

With the text below covered, how many objects in the picture can you name in French? If you have to consult the text, cover it over again, and fill in any gaps in your list.

| | | | |
|---|---|---|---|
| **La mairie**<br>Town hall | **le stationnement des véhicules**<br>taxi-rank | **le marché**<br>market | **la grand'rue**<br>main street |
| **Les (sapeurs) pompiers**<br>Fire brigade | **la mouette**<br>seagull | **la place**<br>square | **l'aiguille** (f.<br>spire |
| **Le faubourg**<br>Suburb | **l'usine** (f.)<br>factory | **le clocher**<br>belfry, steeple | **la caserne**<br>barracks |

**M. Roberts :** **Les voilà. Au revoir, mademoiselle.**
Here it is. Good bye, miss.

**Mme Roberts :** **J'aimerais mieux aller dans un magasin de nouveautés.**
I would prefer to go to a draper's stores.

**Je ne crois pas que je trouve ici ce qu'il me faut.**
I don't think that I shall find here what I want.

**M. Roberts :** **Ça m'est égal, allons-y!**
It's the same to me, let's go there!

**Charles :** **Mais, maman, comme ça je n'aurai pas ce que tu m'as promis.**
But, mummy, like this I won't get what you have promised me.

**Mme Roberts :** **Charles, vraiment, tu m'énerves.**
Charles, really, you are unnerving (worrying) me.

**(Ils quittent le magasin à prix unique et entrent dans une maison de nouveautés.)**
(They leave the one-price shop and enter (in) a department stores.)

**Un vendeur :** **Bonjour, monsieur, dame! Vous désirez?**
Good day, sir, madam! You want something?

**Mme Roberts :** **Je cherche un sac-à-main; où est-ce que je peux trouver ça?**
I am looking for a handbag; where can I find that?

**Le vendeur :** **Le rayon de maroquinerie se trouve au premier étage,**
The leather goods department is on the first floor,

**madame. Si vous voulez prendre l'ascenseur . . .**
madam. If you will take the lift . . .

## IN THE STORES

### English

1. Jewellery Dept.; 2. Trimmings Dept.; 3. Grand staircase; 4. Lift; 5. Liftman; 6. Tea chest; 7. Wrapping paper; 8. Packing counter; 9. Shop assistant; 10. Package; 11. Male customer; 12. Sack; 13. Barrel; 14. Shopping basket; 15. Female customer; 16. Paper bag; 17. Spring balance; 18. Jar; 19. Tins; 20. Show-board; 21. Haberdashery Dept.; 22. Weighing machine; 23. Shopwalker; 24. Price-ticket; 25. Knitted goods Dept.; 26. Shopping-ticket; 27. Paying-slot; 28. Cashier (f.); 29. Cash-desk; 30. Clock Dept.; 31. Commissionaire; 32. Shop-front; 33. Shop-window; 34. Goods in window; 35. Tailor's dummy; 36. Revolving door; 37. Show-case for watches.

### French

1. Bijouterie (f.); 2. Passementerie (f.); 3. Grand escalier (m.); 4. Ascenseur (m.); 5. Garçon d'ascenseur, liftier (m.); 6.

| Further Useful Expressions | **Le dernier cri**<br>The latest fashion | **Le dernier chic**<br>The last word (in smartness) | **Marchander**<br>To bargain |

## DANS UN GRAND MAGASIN

Caisse (f.) à thé; 7. Papier (m.) d'emballage; 8. Comptoir (m.) d'emballage; 9. Employé-e (m.f.) de magasin; vendeur-se (m.f.); 10. Paquet, colis (m.); 11. Chaland, client (m.); 12. Sac (m.); 13. Tonneau, baril, fût (m.); barrique (f.), etc. (according to nature of contents); 14. Panier, cabas (m.); 15. Chalande, cliente (f.); 16. Sac en, de, papier; 17. Peson (m.); balance (f.) à ressort; 18. Pot, bocal (m.); jarre (f.), etc. (according to the contents); 19. Boîte (f.) à, de, conserves; 20. Planche (f.) à affiche; écriteau (m.) d'annonces; 21. Mercerie (f.); 22. Machine (f.) à peser; 23. Chef (m.) de rayon; 24. Étiquette (f.); 25. Bonneterie (f.); 26. Pancarte (f.); 27. Guichet (m.); 28. Caissière (f.); 29. Caisse (f.); 30. Horlogerie (f.); 31. Portier, commissionnaire (m.); 32. Devanture (f.); 33. Vitrine (f.); 34. Étalage (m.); 35. Figure (f.) de cire; 36. Porte (f.) revolver; 37. Vitrine (f.) porte-montres.

| | | |
|---|---|---|
| **Faire son marché** | **Les bas indémaillables** | **Un fromage bien à point** |
| To do one's shopping | Ladder-proof stockings | A cheese nicely ripe |

**Mme Roberts : Ça ne vaut pas la peine.   Nous prendrons l'escalier.**
That's not worth while.   We shall go there by the staircase.

**Je vous remercie, monsieur.**
I thank you, sir.

**(Ils montent au premier étage où ils s'adressent à**
(They go up to the first floor, where they address themselves to

**une vendeuse du rayon de maroquinerie.   Mme Roberts, après avoir**
a saleswoman of the leather goods department.   Mme Roberts, after having

**longtemps hésité s'est enfin décidée à acheter un très beau et**
hesitated for a long time, has at last decided to buy a very beautiful and

**très solide sac-à-main.   Après avoir payé, les Roberts visitent encore**
strong handbag.   After having paid, the Roberts also visit

**d'autres rayons.   Ils achètent des bas, des chaussettes, du linge, et même une**
other departments.   They buy stockings, socks, linen, and even a

**jolie robe pour Madeleine.   Mme Roberts a tenu parole en achetant quelques**
pretty frock for Madeleine.   Mrs. Roberts has kept her word by buying some

**jouets pour les enfants, et Charles, tout fier et heureux, est enfin devenu**
toys for the children, and Charles, all proud and happy, has at last become

**le propriétaire d'un ping-pong.)**
the owner of a ping-pong set.)

**M. Roberts :   Tu dois être très fatiguée?   Je te propose d'aller prendre un**
You must be very tired.   I suggest that you have a

**rafraîchissement au salon de thé.   Moi, j'irai acheter**
refreshment in the tea-room.   I shall go and buy

**des cigarettes dans un bureau de tabac, et je vous rejoindrai**
cigarettes in the tobacconist's, and I will rejoin you

**dans un quart d'heure.**
in a quarter of an hour.

### SHOPPING EXPRESSIONS

The word used for the designation of the shop usually also applies to the designation of the trade or business and often also to the goods handled.   **La mercerie** means not only the haberdasher's shop, but also his trade and his goods.   **L'épicerie** means (1) the grocer's shop, (2) groceries, (3) the grocery business.

At the grocer's is ................... **chez l'épicier,** or **dans l'épicerie.**
At the butcher's ................... **chez le boucher,** or **dans la boucherie,** etc.
At a stationer's................... **chez un libraire** or **dans une librairie,** etc.

La **boutique** is only "the small shop". The usual word for "shop" is **le magasin**; a department store is **un grand magasin**.

to go shopping **faire des courses**

a bargain **une occasion**

reduced in price **à prix réduit**

to pay cash **payer comptant**

a deposit **des arrhes**, (ahr) f.pl.

to leave a deposit of 20 francs **laisser vingt francs d'arrhes**

by instalments **par acomptes**

the invoice **la facture**

the bill **la note**

a receipt **un reçu**

to pack **emba.ler**

the size **le numéro; la pointure** (of shoes, gloves and stockings)

the colour **la couleur**

the quality **la qualité**

something in blue **quelque chose de bleu**

dark blue **bleu foncé**

light blue **bleu clair**

How much is it? **Combien est-ce?**

It is too dear **C'est trop cher**

I'il have it **Je le (la) prendrai**

I'll have them **Je les prendrai**

I'll take it (them) with me **Je (les) l'emporterai avec moi**

Please have it sent to this address **Veuillez me le livrer à cette adresse**

I have not enough money with me **Je n'ai pas assez d'argent sur moi**

I shall pay on delivery **Je paierai à la livraison**

cash on delivery **Contre remboursement**

## Idiomatic Expressions

**tout à l'heure** a moment ago; in a moment; just now

**par ici** this way

**paı là** that way

**ça ne fait rien** that does not matter

**le voilà!** there he is!

**me voici!** here I am!

**nous voilà!** there we are!

**nous y voilà** we are there

**j'aimerais mieux** I would rather, I should prefer (lit. I would like better)

**tout ce qu'il faut** all that is needed

**tout ce qu'il me faut** all that I need

**je n'en peux plus** I can't go on any longer

**je vous en prie** I beg you

### THERE

**Où est la lettre? Elle est là sur la table.** Where is the letter? It is there on the table.

**Est-il à Paris? Oui, il y est.** Is he in Paris? Yes, he is (there).

**Où est la gare? Elle est là au bout de la rue.** Where is the station? It is there at the end of the street.

**Je vais à la gare. J'y vais aussi.** I am going to the station. I am going there too.

**Ce magasin est très grand. On y trouve tout ce qu'on peut désirer.** This shop is very big. One finds there all that one can wish (for).

If the word "there" is being used to point to a certain place it is translated by **là**.

If "there" indicates a place already mentioned, it is translated by **y**.

Note that **y** is placed before the verb. When **en** and **y** are together, the order is always **y en**.

### THERE IS, THERE ARE

**voilà votre journal** there is your newspaper

**voilà vos journaux** there are your newspapers

**il y a un article intéressant dans le journal** there is an interesting article in the newspaper.

**il y a des nouvelles importantes** there is important news.

**qu'est-ce qu'il y a de nouveau?** what news is there?

**il n'y a rien** there is nothing

**il n'y a pas de nouvelles** there is no news.

**y a-t-il des lettres?** are there any letters?

## THE SHOPPING STREET

Here our artist has in many cases made it clear what types of goods these various shops are handling. With the help of the drawing make a list of the types of businesses

**La librairie; le libraire**
Bookshop and bookseller

**la crémerie; le/la crémier-ère**
dairy and dairyman/woman

**la pharmacie; le pharmacien**
chemist's and chemist

**La pâtisserie; le/la pâtissier-ère**
Pastrycook's and pastrycook

**la chapellerie; le/la chapelier-ère**
hatter's and hatter

You should also know the following, not shown on the drawing.

**La boucherie; le boucher**
Butcher's and butcher

**la mercerie; le/la mercier-ère**
haberdasher's and haberdasher

**La bijouterie; le bijoutier**
Jeweller's and jeweller

**le tailleur; la couturière**
tailor ; dressmaker

## LA RUE COMMERÇANTE

and the titles of those who run them. Fill in any blanks by reference to the key below, which gives masculine and feminine. Such businesses are frequently run by women.

| | | |
|---|---|---|
| **'épicerie; l'épicier-ère** | **le coiffeur; la coiffeuse** | **la quincaillerie; le quincaillier** |
| grocer's and grocer | male and female hairdresser | ironmonger's and ironmonger |

| | |
|---|---|
| **plomberie; le plombier** | **serrurrie; le serrurier** |
| plumber's and plumber | locksmith's and locksmith |

| | |
|---|---|
| **a charcuterie; le/la charcutier-ère** | **le magasin d'étoffes; le marchand d'étoffes** |
| cooked meats shop and pork butcher | cloth-merchant's and cloth-merchant |

| | |
|---|---|
| **a boulangerie; le/la boulanger-ère** | **le magasin (le marchand) de chaussures** |
| the bakery and baker | bootshop and proprietor |

il y en a trois   there are three
il y en a une   there is one

Use **voilà** when pointing to persons or things, and use **il y a** when not pointing. The English sentence " There is bread " can either mean a general statement that there is bread available, or that bread is actually there and being pointed out. In French, the general statement is : **Il y a du pain.** The pointing to it is expressed by : " **Voilà du pain** ".

### REFLEXIVE VERBS

Se **promener**=to go for a walk

#### Present

I am going for a walk, I go for a walk
Je me promène
tu te promènes
il se promène
elle se promène
nous nous promenons
vous vous promenez
ils se promènent
elles se promènent

#### Imperfect

I was going for a walk
Je me promenais
etc.

#### Future

I shall go for a walk
Je me promènerai
tu te promèneras
il se promènera
elle se promènera
nous nous promènerons
vous vous promènerez
ils se promèneront
elles se promèneront

#### Perfect

I went for a walk, I have been for a walk
je me suis promené(e)
tu t'es promené(e)
il s'est promené
elle s'est promenée
nous nous sommes promené(e)s
vous vous êtes promené(e)s
ils se sont promenés
elles se sont promenées

Se **décider**=to make up one's mind

#### Present

je me décide
tu te décides etc.

#### Imperfect

je me décidais
tu te décidais etc.

#### Future

je me déciderai
tu te décideras etc.

#### Perfect

je me suis décidé(e)
tu t'es décidé(e)
il s'est décidé
elle s'est décidée
nous nous sommes décidé(e)s
vous vous êtes décidé(e)s
ils se sont décidés
elles se sont décidées

Note.—The perfect of reflexive verbs is conjugated with **être**, e.g., **je me suis lavé** I have washed myself; **s'est-il habillé?** has he got dressed? **elle s'est couchée** she has lain down.

### DEVENIR=to become

All the forms of the verb **devenir** are like **venir** (see page 205).
Note that "I have become" is **je suis devenu**, "he has become" is **il est devenu** etc.

### PROMETTRE=to promise

This verb is conjugated like **mettre** (see pages 122, 137); "I have promised" is **j'ai promis**; "I will promise" is **je promettrai**.

## EXERCISES

### I. Replace the words in italic type by le, la, les, en or y

1. Le petit garçon achète *des pommes.* 2. Je mets *les jouets sur la table.* 3. Charles regarde *le sac-à-main.* 4. Elle a vendu *les robes.* 5. Nous irons voir *notre grand' mère.* 6. Il achète *le gâteau chez le boulanger.* 7. Il achète *du gâteau chez le boulanger.* 8. Elle achète *les sardines chez l'épicier.* 9. Il a acheté *ses cigarettes dans*

*un bistrot.* 10. Il a acheté *des cigarettes dans un bureau de tabac.*

## II Answer in French

1. Mme Roberts était-elle fatiguée? 2. M. et Mme Roberts, où sont-ils allés? Sont-ils restés longtemps dans le premier magasin? 4. Quel est le rayon qui intéresse Mme Roberts? 5. Qu'est-ce que Charles veut avoir? 6. De quoi parle-t-il toujours? 7. Avec qui veut-il jouer? 8. Le magasin à prix unique vend-il des automobiles? 9. À qui parle Mme Roberts dans le magasin de nouveautés? 10. Que font-ils après avoir fait leurs achats? 11. M. Roberts accompagne-t-il sa famille dans le salon de thé? 12. Où va-t-il?

## III Translate into French

1. There is a pencil. Where is it? There it is. 2. There are the books. Where are they? There they are. 3. Have you got any paper? 4. Have you got any? 5. I have some. 6. There is some in the bookcase. 7. There is some. 8. Haven't you got any envelopes? 9. There are some in the drawer. 10. There are not any. 11. There isn't any ice-cream. 12. There isn't any bread. 13. There isn't any. 14. Isn't there any? 15. Are you going there? 16. Did he go there? 17. I am not going there. 18. He did not go there. 19. They are not going there any more. 20. There is your ticket. Where is it? There on the table, and there is one at the cash-desk. (*Key on page* 252).

**Another reminder:**
**Are you listening in daily to broadcasts in French?**

## PRÈS D'EPERNAY (CHAMPAGNE): LA VENDANGE

Le champagne n'est ni un vin ancien ni le vin favori des Français mais c'est lui qui tient la première place dans le commerce extérieur. Des affaires importantes dont le chiffre s'élève à des milliards de francs s'exécutent journellement entre la France et presque tous les pays du monde.

| les affaires (f.pl.) | le chiffre | journellement | le pays | le monde |
|---|---|---|---|---|
| business | amount | daily | country | world |

# VINGTIÈME LEÇON

### A PARIS BUS

Here is a typical Paris bus, and below are a few phrases connected with it. Learn these, then read carefully the account of the Roberts' bus journey. Then close the book and make a list of the terms needed on any ordinary Paris bus journey.

| | | | |
|---|---|---|---|
| **Un arrêt d'autobus**<br>Bus-stop | **le chauffeur**<br>driver | **la plate-forme**<br>platform | **le marchepied**<br>step |
| **Les voyageurs**<br>Passengers | **la banquette**<br>seat | **le conducteur**<br>conductor | **le contrôle**<br>ticket-inspection |

### DANS L'AUTOBUS—IN THE BUS

**Château de Vincennes, terminus d'une ligne de métro, point de départ de**
Castle of Vincennes, terminus of a line of the metro, starting point of

**nombreux autobus partant pour des centres d'excursion dans la banlieue de**
numerous buses leaving for excursion centres in the outskirts of

**Paris.  M. et Mme Roberts avec leurs enfants Charles et Madeleine et**
Paris.  Mr. and Mrs. Roberts with their children Charles and Madeleine and

**leur oncle, Monsieur Paul Lesage, à l'arrêt d'un autobus.**
their uncle, Mr. Paul Lesage, at the stopping place of a bus.

**M. Lesage (au conducteur) : Pardon, monsieur, est-ce qu'on peut aller au bord**
        (to the conductor) : Excuse me, conductor, can one go to the banks

        **de la Marne par cette ligne?**
        of the Marne by this line?

**Conducteur :**   Ça dépend!   À quel endroit voulez-vous aller?
It depends!   To what place do you want to go?

**Charles :**   Là naturellement, où nous pourrons nous baigner.
There, of course, where we shall be able to bathe.

**Conducteur :**   Vous pouvez aller à Noisy-le-Grand, par exemple.
You can go to Noisy-le-Grand, for instance.

Prenez le 120, ici à côté.        M. Lesage : Merci beaucoup,
Take the 120, here close by.                      Thank you very much,

monsieur.   (Toute la famille se rend à l'arrêt du 120, mais
sir.   (The whole family goes to the stop of the bus 120, but

le conducteur ne les admet[1] pas.)
the conductor does not admit them.)

**Conducteur :**   Complet!   Prenez le prochain, qui partira dans dix minutes.
Full up!   Take the next (one), which will leave in ten minutes.

(Le conducteur sonne, l'autobus part, le suivant arrive.   Comme il y a
(The conductor rings, the bus leaves, the following arrives.   As there are

beaucoup de gens qui attendent, ils montent vite et prennent place en
many people who wait, they get in quickly and take (their) seats in the

première classe.   En deuxième il n'y a plus de place libre.   Même la plate-forme
first class.   In the second there is no seat left.   Even the platform

est pleine de monde.   Déjà le conducteur s'écrie "Complet!"   Une vieille
is full of people.   Already the conductor is calling out "Full up!"   An old

dame, qui n'a pas trouvé de place, reste debout à l'intérieur.)
lady, who has not found a seat, remains standing in the inside.)

**Conducteur :**   Vous ne pouvez pas rester dans le passage, madame; voulez-vous
You cannot stand in the gangway, madam; will you

aller sur la plate-forme, s'il vous plaît?
go on to the platform, please?

**Mme Roberts (s'adressant à son fils) :**   Lève-toi, Charles, et offre ta
(addressing herself to her son) :   Stand up, Charles, and offer your

place à cette dame.
seat to this lady.

---

[1] From **admettre**—to admit, conjugated like **mettre**.

**Charles :**   Oui, maman, je veux bien.   (Il se lève et s'adresse à la vieille
Yes, mummy, I should like to.   (He stands up and addresses the old

dame.)   Pardon, madame, puis-je vous offrir ma place?
lady.)   Excuse me, Madam, may I offer you my seat?

**La dame :**   Merci, beaucoup, mon petit ami, c'est très gentil de votre part.
Thank you very much, my little friend, it's very nice of you.

**Charles :**   Il n'y a pas de quoi,[1] madame.
Don't mention it, madam.

**M. Lesage :**   (à M. Roberts) : Il est bien élevé,[2] ton fils.
He is well mannered, your son.

**M. Roberts :**   C'est tout naturel d'offrir sa place à une vieille dame.
It is quite natural to offer one's seat to an old lady.

**Conducteur :**   Vous avez vos billets?
You have (got) your tickets?

**M. Lesage :**   Non.   Combien de billets[3] faut-il pour Noisy-le-Grand,
No.   How many tickets does one need for Noisy-le-Grand,

s'il vous plaît?   Conducteur : Cinq par personne, monsieur.
if you please?   Five each (lit., per person), sir.

**M. Lesage :**   Eh, bien, nous sommes cinq personnes, donnez-moi 25 billets,[3]
Well, then, we are five persons, give me 25 tickets,

s'il vous plaît.   Conducteur : Ne voulez-vous pas prendre deux
if you please.   Won't you take two

carnets?   Cela vous coûtera moins cher.
booklets?   That will cost you less (dear).

**M. Roberts :**   Combien de billets y a-t-il dans un carnet?
How many tickets are there in one booklet?

**Conducteur :**   Vingt, monsieur.   Si vous prenez deux carnets, vous pourrez utiliser
Twenty, sir.   If you take two booklets, you will be able to use

le reste au retour.
the rest on the return (journey).

---

[1] Lit. there isn't of what.   [2] Lit. well brought up.   [3] Bus-fares in Paris are cheaper if you
buy **un carnet**, a booklet of 20 tickets. **Un billet** is good for one section only. For a longer
journey, several tickets, according to the number of fare stages, are required.

**M. Lesage :** C'est entendu, monsieur, donnez-moi deux carnets, s'il vous plaît.
All right, conductor, give me two booklets, please.

**Conducteur :** Voilà! Ça fait 21 francs, monsieur.
There you are. That makes 21 francs, sir.

**M. Lesage (à M. Roberts) :** As-tu de la monnaie? Je n'ai qu'un
Have you any change? I have only a

billet de 100 francs.    **M. Roberts :** Je crois que oui. (Il cherche
100 francs note.                                 I think so. (He looks

dans ses poches.) Voilà 21 francs. Dites, monsieur, quand est-ce
in his pockets.) Here is 21 francs. Tell me, conductor, when shall

que nous serons à Noisy-le-Grand?
we be at Noisy-le-Grand?

**Conducteur :** Dans une demi-heure à peu près.
In half an hour, approximately.

**M. Roberts :** Est-ce qu'il y a un arrêt fixe à Noisy-le-Grand?
Is there a compulsory stop at Noisy-le-Grand?

**Conducteur :** Bien sûr, monsieur, puisque c'est le terminus.
Certainly, sir, since it is the terminus.

## EN ROUTE—ON THE ROAD

| | | | |
|---|---|---|---|
| **un autobus** / bus | **un autocar** / charabanc | **une limousine** / limousine | **une conduite intérieure** / saloon car |
| **une torpédo** / open tourer | **un cabriolet** / drop head coupé | **une auto de course** / racing car | **une bicyclette** / bicycle |
| **une motocyclette** / motorcycle | **un camion** / lorry | **le chauffeur** / driver | **un dépôt d'essence** / petrol station |
| **la route** / road | **un chemin de traverse** / side-road, short cut | **un passage à niveau** / level crossing | |
| **un poteau indicateur** / road sign | **un virage** / bend | **vidange gratuite** / "sump drained free" | |
| **gonflage gratuit** / "free air" (gonfler to pump up) | **l'huile (f.)** / lubrication-oil | **la bougie** / sparking plug | |

## THREE MORE PROVERBS

**Il faut prendre les hommes comme ils sont, et les choses comme elles viennent.**
One must take men as they are and things as they come.

**Le bon marché coûte toujours cher.**
Cheap things are always dear.

**Chien qui aboie ne mord pas.**
Barking dogs don't bite.

All the vehicles and objects shown in this drawing of a typical section of road near Paris are in the list on the preceding page.   Study this, until you can make your own list in French without having to consult the text.

### TERMES CONTRAIRES—OPPOSITE TERMS

| gras(se) | maigre | grand(e) | petit(e) | long(ue) | court(e) |
|---|---|---|---|---|---|
| fat | lean | tall | short, small | long | short |
| corpulent(e) | mince | large | étroit(e) | vide | plein(e) |
| stout | slim | wide | narrow | empty | full |
| épais(se) | mince | haut(e) | bas(se) | premier | dernier |
| thick | thin | high; tall | low | première | dernière |
| | | | | first | last |
| léger(ère) | lourd(e) | droit(e) | courbé | | |
| light | heavy | straight | curved | heureux | malheureux |
| droit(e) | incliné(e) | ouvert(e) | fermé(e) | heureuse | malheureuse |
| upright | slanting | open | closed | happy | unhappy |
| tranchant(e) | émoussé(e) | vertical(e) | horizontal(e) | clair(e) | obscur(e) |
| sharp | blunt | perpendicular | horizontal | light | dark; dim |
| chaud(e) | froid(e) | riche | pauvre | généreux(se) | avare |
| hot | cold | rich | poor | generous | miserly |
| vrai(e) | faux(sse) | gauche | droit(e) | lent(e) | rapide |
| true | false | left | right | slow | fast |

## ENDINGS OF ADJECTIVES

**Ce monsieur est furieux, parce**
This man is furious, because

**que le beau chapeau neuf de sa**
the beautiful new hat of his

**femme est trop cher.**
wife is too dear.

**Cette femme est furieuse, parce**
This woman is furious, because

**que la belle robe neuve de sa**
the beautiful new dress of her

**fille est trop chère.**
daughter is too dear.

*Note.*—(1) Adjectives ending in **-eux** form their feminine by changing **-eux** into **-euse.**

| Masculine | Feminine | |
|---|---|---|
| furieux | furieuse | furious |
| heureux | heureuse | happy |
| malheureux | malheureuse | unhappy |
| nombreux | nombreuse | numerous |
| dangereux | dangereuse | dangerous |

(2) Adjectives ending in **-er** take a grave accent beside adding **-e:**—

| cher | chère | dear |
|---|---|---|
| premier | première | first |
| dernier | dernière | last |

(3) Adjectives ending in **-f,** change the **f** into **ve** (compare with English "leaf", "leaves", etc.)

| neuf | neuve | new |
|---|---|---|
| actif | active | active |
| vif | vive | lively |

(4) The following adjectives double their last consonants before adding **-e:**

| Masculine | Feminine | |
|---|---|---|
| naturel | naturelle | natural |
| bon | bonne | good |
| européen | européenne | European |
| indien | indienne | Indian |
| gentil | gentille | nice |
| gros | grosse | big |
| gras | grasse | fat |
| sot | sotte | stupid |
| bas | basse | low |

(5) Irregular feminines are:

| blanc | blanche | white |
|---|---|---|
| doux | douce | sweet |
| faux | fausse | false |
| frais | fraîche | fresh |
| long | longue | long |
| sec | sèche | dry |
| complet | complète | complete |

Ces vieux messieurs
sont heureux

(6) The following adjectives have two masculine as well as the feminine forms:

| Masculine | | Feminine | |
|---|---|---|---|
| Before a consonant | Before a vowel or h mute | | |
| beau | bel | belle | beautiful |
| fou | fol | folle | foolish, mad |
| nouveau | nouvel | nouvelle | new |
| mou | mol | molle | soft |
| vieux | vieil | vieille | old |
| ce | cet | cette | this, that |

(7) Adjective ending in -x do not add -s in the plural, e.g., **Ces vieux messieurs sont heureux.**

**NEW**

**la nouvelle mode**   the new fashion.

**un nouveau roman**   a new novel.

**un vêtement neuf**   a new garment.

**habillé de neuf**   dressed in new clothes.

**neuf, neuve**   new, i.e., never before used.

**nouveau, nouvel** (before a vowel), **nouvelle** (f.), new, i.e., not previously seen or heard, fresh, another.

In the meaning of "never before seen or heard" it follows the noun.

In the meaning of "fresh" or "another" it precedes the noun, e.g.,

**un nouveau livre**   another book.

**un livre nouveau**   a new book (which has just been published).

**un livre neuf**   a new book (not a second-hand book).

### TO SIT DOWN

**Infinitive: s'asseoir** to sit down

**Present Tense:**

| je m'assieds | nous nous asseyons |
|---|---|
| tu t'assieds | vous vous asseyez |
| il (elle) s'assied | ils (elles) s'asseyent |

| **Imperfect:** | **Future:** |
|---|---|
| je m'asseyais, etc. | je m'assiérai etc. |

| **Perfect:** | **Imperative:** |
|---|---|
| je me suis assis, etc. | assieds-toi |
| | asseyez-vous |
| | asseyons-nous |

*Note.*—The non-reflexive form **asseoir** has the meaning of to seat, to place, to set.

Alternative forms are also used, for the present tense: **assois, assoit, assoyons, assoyez, assoient.** For the Future **assoirai,** etc.

## EXERCISES

### I Translate into English

1. A-t-il un chapeau neuf? 2. Ces jeunes filles étaient heureuses parce qu'elles avaient des robes neuves. 3. Il n'est pas heureux, parce que sa femme a acheté une robe qui coûte très cher. 4. Cette dame avait une

corbeille (basket) pleine de pommes. 5. N'avait-il pas un pardessus noir, des gants bruns et un chapeau gris? 6. Ma vieille grand'mère est très vive pour son âge. 7. Je n'aime pas le porc gras. 8. Grand-père est assis dans son fauteuil qui est devant la fenêtre ouverte. 9. Il fume une grosse pipe. 10. Le petit poulet que tu as acheté est maigre. 11. L'Ecossais est malheureux parce que son verre est vide. 12. Notre rue est étroite et courte.

## II Replace the dashes by suitable adjectives

1. Le poulet est —. 2. Le crayon est —. 3. La fenêtre est —. 4. Les verres sont —. 5. Est-ce que les couteaux sont —? 6. Le pied de la table est —. 7. Le — chien est —. 8. Cette — plume est —. 9. Ces — jeunes filles sont —. 10. Mes souliers — sont —.

## III Translate into French

1. The bus is full up. 2. There are numerous buses. 3. The next one will be empty. 4. Let us get in quickly. 5. The bottle is full. 6. Is there no seat for that old lady? 7. That is a good system. 8. Your new sideboard is very expensive. 9. Have you seen the new maid? 10. Isn't she pretty? 11. Are you happy, (my) boys? 12. This is our new house. (*Key on pages* 252 *and* 253.)

UN CHÂTEAU DE L'ALLIER

Ce château du Département de l'Allier au Centre de la France, juché sur une hauteur boisée et entouré par des chaumières, nous porte à l'esprit une communauté moyenâgeuse —la demeure seigneuriale dominant les taudis des vilains, pour donner protection contre l'ennemi. Est-ce moins banal que la vérité? L'on aime bien les effets de l'imagination quelquefois!

| | | | |
|---|---|---|---|
| **Juché-e** (p.p.) | **hauteur** (f.) | **boisé-e** (adj.) | **entourer** | **communauté** (f.) |
| Perched | height | wooded | to surround | community |
| **Demeure** (f.) **seigneuriale** | **taudis** (m.) | **vilain-e** (m.f.) | **la vérité** |
| Baronial hall | hovel | villein, serf | truth |

# VINGT ET UNIÈME LEÇON

### THE ROBERTS GO VISITING

In this drawing of the Roberts family calling on French friends, there are shown the objects listed on page 245. But below we give some other terms connected with the illustration.

| **Un chat pie** | **un tapis d'escalier** | **des tringles d'escalier** | **la maîtresse de maison** |
|---|---|---|---|
| cat (black and white) | stair carpet | stair-rods | mistress of the house |

### UNE VISITE—A VISIT

**M. et Mme Roberts, avec leurs enfants Charles et Madeleine, sont**
Mr. and Mrs. Roberts, with their children Charles and Madeleine, have been

**invités chez des amis. Après être montés au deuxième étage, ils**
invited to the house of some friends. After having gone up to the second floor, they

**s'arrêtent devant une porte et sonnent. Une charmante jeune**
stop before a door and ring the bell. A charming young

**femme ouvre.**
woman opens (the door).

**La jeune femme : Bonjour, M. Roberts, bonjour, chère Madame,**
Good day, Mr. Roberts, good day, Madam,

**bonjour, les enfants. Comment allez-vous?**
good day, children. How are you?

### SUR L'ESCALIER—ON THE STAIRCASE

| l'escalier (m.) | la rampe | le palier | la porte d'entrée | la clef |
|---|---|---|---|---|
| stairs | banisters | landing | hall-door | key |

| le trou de la serrure | la serrure | la clef de sûreté | l'éclairage |
|---|---|---|---|
| key-hole | lock | latch-key | light |

| la poignée | la sonnette | le guichet de la boîte aux lettres |
|---|---|---|
| door-handle | bell | letter-box slit |

| le commutateur | le visiteur | la visiteuse |
|---|---|---|
| switch | visitor (man) | visitor (woman) |

**Mme Roberts :** **Comment allez-vous vous-même?  Je suis très heureuse de vous**
How are you yourself?   I am very happy to see you

**retrouver à Paris.  Et votre mari, comment va-t-il?**
again in Paris.   And your husband, how is he?

**La jeune femme :** **Je vous remercie, madame, nous allons tous bien.  Mon mari**
I thank you madame, we are all well.   My husband

**vous attend déjà.  Voulez-vous avoir l'amabilité de me suivre?**
is expecting you already.   Will you have the kindness to follow me?

**Le mari :** **Ah, voilà nos invités.  Je suis heureux, monsieur, de faire**
Ah, here are our guests.   I am delighted, sir, to make

**votre connaissance.  Enchanté, madame.  Ma femme m'a beaucoup**
your acquaintance. Delighted, madam.  My wife has spoken to me

**parlé de vous.  La jeune femme :  Mais asseyez-vous donc,**
a lot about you.                      But do sit down,

**je vous en prie.  Vous êtes sans doute très fatigués.  Veuillez**
please (lit., I beg you).   You are no doubt very tired.  Will you please

**m'excuser quelques instants.  Je vais vous préparer un**
excuse me a few moments.   I will get ready a

**petit rafraîchissement.**
little refreshment.

**Mme Roberts :** **Vous êtes trop aimable, mais il ne faut pas vous déranger, madame.**
You are too kind, but please do not trouble, madam.

**Le mari :** **Vous ne refuserez pourtant pas une tasse de thé et**
You won't, however, refuse a cup of tea and

quelques petits gâteaux, n'est-ce pas?
some little cakes, will you?

M. Roberts :   Comment pourrions-nous refuser, puisque vous insistez avec
How could we refuse, since you insist with

tant de bonne grâce?
so much charm?

Le mari :   Vous nous faites plaisir en acceptant.[1]
You make us happy by accepting.

M. Roberts :   Comme vous êtes charmants, vous autres Français.
How charming you are, you French people.

Le mari :   Je suis très flatté, M. Roberts.   Je trouve d'ailleurs que nous
I am very flattered, Mr. Roberts.   Besides, I find that we

sommes comme les autres; seulement nous nous exprimons d'une
are like others; only we express ourselves in a

façon différente.   Aimez-vous la pêche, M. Roberts?
different way.   Are you fond of fishing, Mr. Roberts?

M. Roberts :   J'aime tous les sports, mais je ne suis jamais allé à la pêche.
I like all (the) sports, but I have never gone fishing.

Je préfère le golf; je trouve qu'il est plus intéressant
Personally I prefer golf; I find that it is more interesting

que la pêche, qui m'ennuierait.
than fishing, which would bore me.

Le mari :   (riant) Quel dommage!   Nos goûts sont donc tout à fait
(laughing) What a pity!   Our tastes are therefore entirely

différents.   Moi, j'aime tant la tranquillité.   Je peux passer
different.   Personally I like so much peacefulness.   I can spend

des heures et des heures au bord d'une rivière ou d'un lac,
hours and hours on the bank of a river or of a lake,

sans bouger, dans l'attente patiente de . . .
without moving, in the patient expectation of . . .

La jeune femme (rentrant) : Voilà, le thé est servi.
There we are, tea is ready.

---

[1] Although the use of such expressions may seem somewhat profuse to us, among French people similar terms are part of the usual conversation on such occasions.

## MÊME DANS PARIS, L'ON PÊCHE

L'ami français de M. Roberts n'est pas le seul amateur de pêche en France. Ici, même en plein centre de Paris, les fervents s'adonnent à leur sport favori. Les uns, de la berge, les autres, de bateaux amarrés dans le fleuve, jettent leurs lignes et attendent que la plongée du flotteur indique la présence d'un poisson trop téméraire attiré par l'appât.

| Fervent-e (m.f.) | s'adonner | flotteur (m.) | téméraire (adj. inv.) | appât (m.) |
|---|---|---|---|---|
| Enthusiast | to devote oneself | float | rash | bait |

*Note.*—Fishing is a passion among Frenchmen to a degree unknown elsewhere. During the coarse-fishing season which commences on June 15, visitors can observe for themselves how every stretch of water is utilised.

**Mme Roberts :** Je me suis permis de vous apporter un petit souvenir de
I permitted myself to bring you a little souvenir from

Londres.   Faites-moi le plaisir d'accepter ce petit cadeau,
London.   Make me the pleasure to accept this little present,

chère Madame.   La jeune femme : Oh, comme vous êtes gentillle,
dear madam.                      Oh, how charming of you,

chère Madame Roberts. En le regardant, je penserai toujours à vous.
dear Mrs. Roberts.  When looking at it I shall always think of you.

Oh, comme c'est mignon!
Oh, how dainty it is!

**Charles :**      Maman, veux-tu me passer le sucre, s'il te plaît.
Mummy, will you pass me the sugar, please.

**Mme Roberts :** Le voilà, mon chéri.   Charles : Merci, maman.
There you are, my darling.      Thank you, mother.

**La jeune femme :** Quel beau temps après tant de jours de pluie!
What beautiful weather after so many rainy days!

**Mme Roberts :** Oui, il fait beau aujourd'hui.   Quand nous étions à Versailles
Yes, it is fine to-day.   When we were at Versailles

il pleuvait tout le temps.
it was raining all the time.

**Le mari :**      C'est vraiment dommage.   Mais Versailles n'est pas loin;
That's really too bad.   But Versailles is not far;

ne voudriez-vous pas y retourner?
wouldn't you like to go there again?

**M. Roberts :**   Pourquoi pas?   Nous restons encore plusieurs semaines à Paris.
Why not?   We still remain several weeks in Paris.

**Le mari :**      C'est plus intéressant d'y aller par beau temps.   Il y a de
It is more interesting to go there in fine weather.   There are

belles forêts tout près.   N'oubliez surtout pas de visiter
beautiful woods quite near.   Above all, don't forget to visit

Fontainebleau.   C'est un peu plus loin, mais là vous serez au
Fontainebleau.   It is a bit farther, but there you will be in the

grand air.   Mme Roberts : Nous pensons y aller avec
open air.               We are thinking of going there with

**nos parents français qui connaissent bien le pays, et qui**
our French relations who know well the country, and who will

**ne manqueront pas de nous montrer toutes les beautés aux environs**
not fail to show us all the beauties in the surroundings

**de Paris.**     **M. Roberts : Chers amis, veuillez bien nous excuser,**
of Paris.          Dear friends, will you please excuse us,

**mais nous sommes obligés de vous quitter pour aujourd'hui.**
but we have to leave you for to-day.

**Nous avons encore un tas de choses à faire.**
We still have a lot of things to do.

**Mme Roberts : Mille fois merci pour votre aimable accueil.   N'oubliez pas de**
A thousand thanks for your charming welcome.   Don't forget to

**nous rendre visite un de ces jours.   Quand viendrez-vous**
pay us a visit one of these days.   When will you

### LE PALAIS DE FONTAINEBLEAU

L'étang qui entoure cette maison royale de campagne fourmille de carpes séculaires tellement apprivoisées qu'elles mangent sans peur de la main du visiteur.

| **Étang** (m.) | **fourmiller** | **séculaire** (adj. inv.) | **apprivoiser** |
|---|---|---|---|
| Pond | to swarm | century-old | to tame |

nous voir?   Samedi vous conviendrait-il?
come to see us?   Would Saturday suit you?

**La jeune femme :** **Oui, mes amis, nous aurons le plaisir de vous voir samedi.**
Yes, my friends, we shall have the pleasure to see you on Saturday.

**Mme Roberts :** **À quelle heure pourrions-nous vous attendre?**
At what time could we expect you?

**La jeune femme :** **Disons, à quatre heures de l'après-midi, si cela vous convient.**
Let us say at four o'clock in the afternoon, if that suits you.

**Mme Roberts : C'est entendu.   Au revoir!     Tous : Au revoir!**
That's all right.   Good-bye!     All :   Good-bye!

### THE TEA TABLE

You should now be able to name practically everything on this table without looking at the list below. Glance at it only to check that you are word-perfect before continuing with the Course. If necessary, look back to earlier lessons, which give most of the words.

### LA TABLE MISE POUR LE THÉ—THE TABLE LAID FOR TEA

| | | | |
|---|---|---|---|
| la table à thé<br>tea table | du pain grillé<br>toast | des gâteaux<br>assorted pastries | de la confiture<br>jam |
| du beurre<br>butter | des tartines de beurre<br>slices of bread and butter | un gâteau<br>cake | la théière<br>tea-pot |
| la tasse<br>cup | le sucrier<br>sugar basin | des petits-fours<br>fancy biscuits | la soucoupe<br>saucer |
| une assiette<br>plate | le couteau<br>knife | la cuillère<br>spoon | le plateau<br>tray | un vase de fleurs<br>vase with flowers |

## TO BE CALLED

### APPELER = to call

**Present**

J'appelle   I call, I am calling
tu appelles
il appelle
nous appelons
vous appelez
ils appellent

**Imperfect:** j'appelais, etc.

**Future:** j'appellerai, etc.

### S'APPELER = to be called

Je m'appelle   I am called, my name is, I
  call myself
tu t'appelles
il s'appelle
nous nous appelons
vous vous appelez
ils s'appellent

**Imperfect:** je m'appelais, etc.

**Future:** je m'appellerai, etc.

### Should, would, the Conditional tense

Je donnerais   I should (would) give
tu donnerais
il donnerait
nous donnerions
vous donneriez
ils donneraient

**Similarly :**

| | | |
|---|---|---|
| je prendrais | I should (would) | take |
| je serais | ,, | ,, | be |
| j'aurais | ,, | ,, | have |
| j'irais | ,, | ,, | go |
| je ferais | ,, | ,, | do |
| je viendrais | ,, | ,, | come |
| je m'appellerais | ,, | ,, | call myself |

The Conditional Tense is formed by adding -ais, -ait, -ions, -iez, -aient, to the Infinitive. Note that the Conditional has exactly the same endings as the Imperfect.

If the Future of the verb shows some irregularity, the same irregularity appears in the Conditional, e.g.,

**Future:**

j'irai   I shall (will) go
je pourrai   I shall (will) be able
j'aurai   I shall (will) have

**Conditional:**

j'irais   I should (would) go
je pourrais   I should (would) be able; I
  could
j'aurais   I should (would) have

*Note.*—In English "I could" may be either Imperfect as in " I could not come last night," or Conditional as in "Couldn't you lend me this book?" In French the two "could's" must be translated differently; "I could not come last night"—Je ne pouvais pas venir hier soir; "Couldn't you lend me this book?"—Ne pourriez-vous pas me prêter ce livre?

## EXERCISES

### I   Translate into English

1. Charles ne se couche pas tard. 2. Il se lève de bonne heure. 3. Il se lave et met vite ses vêtements (=clothes). 4. Après le petit déjeuner il va se promener avec sa sœur. 5. Dans la rue ils rencontrent une dame anglaise avec son petit chien. 6. Quel beau chien! s'écrie-t-il. 7. Comment s'appelle-t-il? 8. Quel âge a-t-il? 9. Les enfants s'en vont. 10. Ils vont se promener. 11. Ils se promènent dans les grandes rues. 12. Le temps est si beau; sinon nous rentrerions plus tôt.

### II   Answer in French

1. Comment s'appelle le père de Charles? 2. Comment vous appelez-vous? 3. Comment s'appelle votre tante? 4. Vous promenez-vous à cinq heures du matin? 5. Te lèves-tu de bonne heure? 6. Te couches-tu après le dîner? 7. Auriez-vous beaucoup de voitures si vous aviez beaucoup d'argent? 8. Feriez-vous beaucoup de voyages si vous aviez un million? 9. Vous coucheriez-vous si vous étiez fatigué? 10. Êtes-vous plus âgé que Charles? 11. Quel âge a-t-il? 12. Allez-vous vous promener avant le petit déjeuner?

**III  Give the French opposite of**

1. noir.  2. large.  3. gras.  4. long.  5. ouvert. 6. plein.  7. le premier jour.  8. un paquet lourd.  9. un couteau tranchant.  10. la poule grasse.  11. la rue étroite.  12. la tour haute.  13. le vieux chapeau.  14. l'année prochaine.  15. la petite fille heureuse.

(*Key on page* 253.)

# KEY TO THE EXERCISES

## Lesson Eighteen

### I

1. Je (ne) suis (pas) plus grand que mon père.  2. J'en écris beaucoup (je n'en écris pas ...)  3. Oui, j'ai (non, je n'ai pas) parlé français hier.  4. Oui, j'en mange.  5. J'ai mangé du pain bis et du beurre.  6. Oui, j'en prends.  7. Je (ne) t'ai (pas) vu.  8. J'en bois (je n'en bois pas).  9. J'en ai bu (je n'en ai pas bu).  10. Je lis un roman de Galsworthy.  11. Je (ne) l'ai (pas) lu.  12. Je (ne) me suis (pas) levé de bonne heure aujourd'hui.

### II

1. Tu mets les fruits sur la table.  2. Ne prends-tu pas . . .  3. N'écris-tu pas . . .?  4. Tu es . . .  5. As-tu tes . . .?  6. Regardes-tu ton . . .?  7. Tu peux venir avec ton . . .  8. Tu te couches tard.  9. Il te voit. 10. Ne te laves-tu pas?  11. Pars-tu avec ta . . .?  12. Tu t'en vas.

### III

1. Voulez-vous aller vous promener?  2. Je ne pourrai pas sortir aujourd'hui.  3. Ne voulez-vous pas voir votre sœur?  4. Ne pourrez-vous pas la voir?  5. Avez-vous vu vos amis?  6. Pouvez-vous me dire, quel chemin je dois prendre pour aller à la Rue Montmartre, s'il vous plaît?  7. Je regrette, je ne peux pas vous le dire.  8. Voilà un agent qui pourra vous le dire.  9. Je vous ai vu hier soir.  10. M'avez-vous vu aussi? 11. J'ai vu votre frère et vos parents, mais je n'ai pas vu votre sœur.  12. Ne faites pas cela.  13. Ne parlez pas si vite!  14. Ne vous en allez pas (ne t'en va pas).  15. Attendez, s'il vous plaît (attends, s'il te plaît).

## Lesson Nineteen

### I

1. Il en achète.  2. Je les y mets.  3. Il le regarde.  4. Elle les a vendues.  5. Nous irons la voir.  6. Il l'y achète.  7. Il y en achète.  8. Elle les y achète.  9. Il les y a achetés.  10. Il y en a acheté.

### II

1. Oui, elle était fatiguée.  2. Ils sont allés dans des magasins pour faire des achats. 3. Non, ils n'y sont pas restés longtemps. 4. Le rayon de maroquinerie l'intéresse. 5. Il veut avoir un jeu de ping-pong.  6. Il en parle toujours.  7. Il veut jouer avec son cousin.  8. Il n'en vend pas.  9. Elle parle à une vendeuse.  10. Ils vont prendre un rafraîchissement.  11. Il ne l'y accompagne pas.  12. Il va acheter des cigarettes.

### III

1. Voilà un crayon.  Où est-il?  Le voilà. 2. Voilà les livres.  Où sont-ils.  Les voilà. 3. Avez-vous du papier?  4. En avez-vous? 5. J'en ai.  6. Il y en a dans la bibliothèque. 7. En voilà.  8. N'avez-vous pas d'enveloppes?  9. Il y en a dans le tiroir.  10. Il n'y en a pas.  11. Il n'y a pas de glace.  12. Il n'y a pas de pain.  13. Il n'y en a pas.  14. N'y en a-t-il pas?  15. Y allez-vous?  16. Y est-il allé?  17. Je n'y vais pas.  18. Il n'y est pas allé.  19. Ils n'y vont plus.  20. Voilà votre billet.  Où est-il?  Là sur la table et en voilà un à la caisse.

## Lesson Twenty

### I

1. Has he got a new hat?  2. These girls were happy because they had new dresses

3. He is not happy, because his wife has bought a dress which is very dear. 4. That woman had a basket full of apples. 5. Didn't he have a black overcoat, brown shoes and a grey hat? 6. My old grandmother is very lively for her age. 7. I don't like fat pork. 8. Grandfather is sitting in his easy chair, which is in front of the open window. 9. He smokes a big pipe. 10. The small chicken you bought is lean. 11. The Scotsman is unhappy, because his glass is empty. 12. Our street is narrow and short.

## II

1. gras. 2. long. 3. fermée. 4. vides. 5. tranchants. 6. courbe. 7. petit — gris. 8. nouvelle — jaune. 9. petites — anglaises. 10. neufs—étroits.

## III

1. L'autobus est complet. 2. Il y a de nombreux autobus. 3. Le prochain sera vide. 4. Montons vite! 5. La bouteille est pleine. 6. N'y a-t-il pas de place pour cette vieille dame? 7. C'est un bon système. 8. Votre nouveau buffet est très cher. 9. Avez-vous vu la nouvelle bonne? 10. N'est-elle pas jolie? 11. Êtes-vous heureux, mes garçons? 12. Ceci est notre nouvelle maison.

## Lesson Twenty-one

### I

1. Charles does not go to bed late. 2. He gets up early. 3. He washes and puts on his clothes quickly. 4. After breakfast he goes for a walk with his sister. 5. In the street they meet an English lady with her little dog. 6. What a beautiful dog! he exclaims. 7. What's his name? 8. How old is he? 9. The children are going away. 10. They are going for a walk. 11. They are walking in the streets. 12. The weather is so beautiful; otherwise we would go back earlier.

### II

1. Il s'appelle M. Roberts. 2. Je m'appelle . . . 3. Elle s'appelle . . . 4. Je ne me promène pas si tôt. 5. Je (ne) me lève (pas) de bonne heure. 6. Je (ne) me couche (pas) après le dîner. 7. Je (ne) les aurais (pas). 8. J'en ferais beaucoup. 9. Je me coucherais. 10. Je (ne) suis (pas) plus âgé que lui. 11. Il a douze ans. 12. Je (ne) vais (pas) me promener avant le petit déjeuner.

### III

1. blanc. 2. étroit. 3. maigre. 4. court. 5. fermé. 6. vide. 7. le dernier jour. 8. un paquet léger. 9. un couteau émoussé. 10. la poule maigre. 11. la rue large. 12. la tour basse. 13. le chapeau neuf. 14. l'année dernière. 15. La grande fille malheureuse.

## ROUND THE TOWN

### Quand on Voyage en France

N'oubliez pas, quand vous voyagez en France, que tous les bagages doivent être enregistrés, et que par conséquent vous devez arriver à la gare assez à l'avance du départ du train, pour accomplir cette tâche.

Si vous voyagez en auto, il vaut la peine de vous fournir avant votre départ de la liste d'hôtels et de restaurants approuvés par l'Auto Club. Comme ça, vous pouvez bien manger dans n'importe quelle ville en France. Et surtout, n'oubliez jamais de demander la spécialité locale, en viande ou en vin, dans chaque ville.

### When Travelling in France

Don't forget, when travelling in France, that all luggage except hand luggage must be registered, and that in consequence you should arrive at the station in sufficient time before the departure of the train, to accomplish this task.

If you are travelling by car, it's worth while to obtain a copy of the (French) Automobile Club's list of approved hotels and restaurants before you start. In that way, you can have a good meal anywhere in France. And, above all, never forget to ask for the local speciality, in meat or in wine, in each town.

# VINGT-DEUXIÈME LEÇON

### MR. ROBERTS AT THE POST OFFICE

Your exercise here is to translate the notices and describe in French the actions of the persons in the post-office, before reading the text in the pages which follow. Use these later to fill in any gaps in the lists which you have made in English and French.

### AU BUREAU DE POSTE—AT THE POST-OFFICE

**M. Roberts avec plusieurs lettres dans la poche et un petit paquet sous**
Mr. Roberts with several letters in his pocket and a small parcel under

**le bras se rend dans un bureau de poste. Il entre et s'adresse à**
his arm is on his way to a post-office. He goes in and addresses himself to

**un employé qui est assis derrière le guichet.**
an employee who is sitting behind the counter.

**M. Roberts :**   **Un timbre de 2 francs 25, s'il vous plaît.**
A 2 francs 25 stamp, please.

**L'employé :**   **Veuillez vous adresser au guichet No. 5.**
Please address yourself to counter No. 5.

**M. Roberts :**   **(à l'employé du guichet 5) Voici trois lettres.   Voulez-vous**
Here are three letters.   Will you

avoir l'amabilité de les affranchir?    Ce sont des lettres pour
have the kindness to put stamps on them.    They are letters for

l'étranger; celle-ci je voudrais bien l'envoyer comme
abroad; this one I should like to send (it) as (a)

lettre recommandée, celle-là comme lettre ordinaire, et celle-là
registered letter, that one as an ordinary letter, and that one

comme imprimé ou échantillon sans valeur.
as printed matter or sample without value.

L'employé :    Je veux bien mettre des timbres sur ces lettres, mais pour
I will put stamps on these letters, but for

la lettre recommandée il faut d'abord remplir cette
the registered letter one has first to fill in this

petite feuille jaune—ah, je vois que vous êtes étranger . . . alors
little yellow form—oh, I see that you are a foreigner . . . well

mettez là le nom et l'adresse du destinataire, et ici
put there the name and the address of the addressee and here

le vôtre.    C'est bien, comme ça . . . voilà le reçu.
yours.    That's right, like this . . . here is the receipt.

M. Roberts :    C'est bien aimable à vous, monsieur; permettez-moi encore une
That is very kind of you, sir; allow me another

question.    Où se trouve le guichet pour les colis?
question.    Where is (to be found) the counter for parcels?

L'employé :    Là-bas, au guichet trois.    Il faudra[1] faire la queue . . . il y a
There, on counter three.    You will have to queue up . . . there are

beaucoup de monde . . . attendez . . . donnez-moi votre colis, je ferai
lots of people . . . wait (a minute) . . . give me your parcel, I'll make

une exception pour vous.
an exception for you.

M. Roberts :    Mais, j'ai vraiment de la chance . . . le voici . . . Dites, monsieur,
But I am really lucky . . . here it is . . . Tell me, sir,

les lettres qu'on met dans la boîte aux lettres
the letters which one puts into the letter-box

---

[1] Lit.  it will be necessary.

aujourd'hui, seront-elles en Angleterre demain?
to-day, will they be in England to-morrow?

**L'employé :**    **Certainement, monsieur, elles seront distribuées demain.**
Certainly, sir, they will be delivered to-morrow.

### VOCABULAIRE

**la cabine téléphonique**
telephone box

**le pèse-lettres**
letter-scales

**le guichet des timbres-poste**
stamp-counter

**l'employé du guichet**
official at counter

**le guichet des versements**
payment counter

**la boîte de la poste aérienne**
air-mail box

**le tarif postal**
postage rate

**l'entrée**
entrance

**le guichet des colis postaux**
parcels counter

**la bascule**
scales

**le colis postal**
parcel

**le pupitre**
desk

**un monsieur écrivant une lettre**
gentleman writing a letter

**une petite fille achetant des timbres**
little girl buying stamps

**une dame envoyant un télégramme**
lady sending a telegram

**la boîte aux lettres**
letter-box

**CABINE TÉLÉPHONIQUE**
Sign over telephone box

**TIMBRES-POSTE**
Sign over stamp counter

**VERSEMENTS**
Sign over payment counter

**TÉLÉGRAMMES**
Sign over telegram counter

**LETTRES RECOMMANDÉES**
Sign over registered letters counter

**POSTE RESTANTE**
"To be called for" counter

**COLIS POSTAUX**
Sign over parcels counter

**TARIF POSTAL**
Headline of poste

**TELEPHONE EXPRESSIONS**

| | |
|---|---|
| **Un coup de téléphone** | a telephone call |
| **Demander interurbain** | to ask for "trunks" |
| **Poste 123** | extension 123 |
| **On nous a coupés** | We've been cut off |

## PARIS QUI JOUE

En haut, les Courses de Nuit à Longchamp attirent un monde chic. En bas, c'est également le hasard qui tente ces habitués d'un café louche.

| **Attirer** | **également** (adv.) | **hasard** (m.) | **tenter** | **louche** (adj.) |
|---|---|---|---|---|
| To attract | likewise | chance, luck | to tempt | doubtful |

| | |
|---|---|
| **LA LETTRE—LETTER** | la **signature**   signature |
| le **papier à lettre**   notepaper | une **enveloppe**   envelope |
| la **date**   date | le **timbre-poste**   postage stamp |
| la **suscription**   opening greeting | l'**adresse**   address |
| le **texte de la lettre**   text of the letter | une **carte postale**   postcard |
| la **salutation finale**   final greeting | un **télégramme (une dépêche)**   telegram |

### THIS ONE, THAT ONE, THESE, THOSE

**Quel gâteau prenez-vous?**   Which cake are you taking?
**Celui-ci est meilleur marché que celui-là.**   This one is cheaper than that one.

**Quelle chaise voulez-vous?**   Which chair do you want?
**Celle-ci ou celle-là?**   This one or that?

**Quels gâteaux prenez-vous?**   Which cakes are you taking?
**Ceux-ci ou ceux-là?**   These or those?

**Quelles chaises voulez-vous?**   Which chairs do you want?
**Celles-ci ou celles-là?**   These or those?

| | | |
|---|---|---|
| "This one" when replacing a masculine noun | = | **Celui-ci** |
| "That one" when replacing a masculine noun | = | **Celui-là** |
| "This one" when replacing a feminine noun | = | **Celle-ci** |
| "That one" when replacing a feminine noun | = | **Celle-là** |
| "These" when replacing masculine nouns | = | **Ceux-ci** |
| "Those" when replacing masculine nouns | = | **Ceux-là** |
| "These" when replacing feminine nouns | = | **Celles-ci** |
| "Those" when replacing feminine nouns | = | **Celles-là** |

Note that the above expressions are used only when replacing nouns.

(1) Followed by a noun **ce (cet)** and **cette** are used for "this" and "that", **ces** for "these" and "those".

(2) "This", "that", "these", "those" are translated by **ce (c')** if employed with a tense of "to be": **C'est mon journal**=This (that) is my newspaper. **Ce sont mes livres**=These (those) are my books. **N'est-ce pas votre chaise?**=Is this not your chair?

(3) "This" when not replacing a noun is **ceci**. "That" when not replacing a noun is **cela**, or **ça**. **Voulez-vous ceci ou cela?**=Do you want this or that? **Ceci est pour vous**=This is for you. **Ne faites pas ça**=Don't do that. **C'est ça**=That's it.

### IL FAUT—IT IS NECESSARY, IT MUST

**il faut travailler**=one must work.
**il me faut y aller**=I must go there (lit., it is necessary for me to go there).

**il vous faut y aller**=you must go there (lit., it is necessary for you to go there).

**il faut le faire**=it must be done.
**il fallait le faire**=it had to be done.
**il faudra le faire**=it will have to be done.
**il ne faut pas fumer trop**=one must not smoke too much.
**il faut lire ce livre**=you must read this book.

The verb **falloir** means "to be necessary"; it is also translated by "must" and "to have to". While the English "must" can be used with any person, the French **falloir** can only be used in connection with the prefix **il**:

**il faut**=it is necessary
(I, you, he, she, it, we, **they** must).
**il fallait**=it was necessary
(I, you, he, she, it, we, they had to).
**il faudra**=it will be necessary
(I, you, etc., will have to).
**il faudrait**=it would be necessary
(I, you, etc., would have to).

## SUMMARY

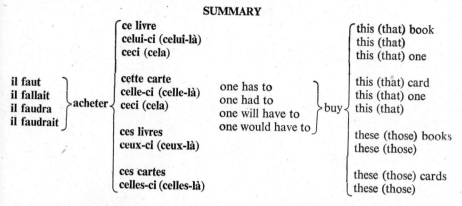

| | | |
|---|---|---|
| | ce livre<br>celui-ci (celui-là)<br>ceci (cela) | this (that) book<br>this (that)<br>this (that) one |
| il faut<br>il fallait — acheter<br>il faudra<br>il faudrait | cette carte<br>celle-ci (celle-là)<br>ceci (cela) — one has to<br>one had to — buy<br>one will have to<br>one would have to | this (that) card<br>this (that) one<br>this (that) |
| | ces livres<br>ceux-ci (ceux-là) | these (those) books<br>these (those) |
| | ces cartes<br>celles-ci (celles-là) | these (those) cards<br>these (those) |

## EXERCISES

### I Translate into English

1. Je vais à la poste. 2. Il me faut des timbres. 3. Où est le bureau de poste? 4. Y a-t-il des lettres pour moi? 5. En voilà une. 6. De qui est-elle? 7. Elle est de mon ami. 8. Qu'est-ce qu'il écrit? 9. Pas grand'chose. 10. Donnez-moi trois timbres de quatre-vingt-dix centimes. 11. Veuillez recommander cette lettre. 12. Voulez-vous envoyer ce télégramme? 13. Avez-vous mis votre lettre à la boîte? 14. Quand pensez-vous que cette lettre arrivera? 15. Il faut l'envoyer poste-restante.

### II Replace the nouns by pronouns

1. Voilà deux lettres; cette lettre-ci est pour moi, cette lettre-là est pour vous. 2. Ce colis est pour vous. 3. Je n'aime pas ces cigarettes. 4. Prenez-vous ce vin blanc ou ce vin rouge? 5. Sa maison est dans cette rue. 6. J'ai acheté cette cravate dans ce magasin-là. 7. Voulez-vous ce melon? 8. Merci, je préfère ce melon-ci. 9. Ces fleurs sont très belles. 10. Cette chaise n'est pas confortable, prenez ce fauteuil. 11. Prenez-vous ces gants-là? 12. Donnez-moi ce pain, s'il vous plaît.

### III Translate into French

1. Do you know these ladies? 2. Are you reading this book? 3. Did they buy this house? 4. Which wine do you want, this one or that one? 5. Do you want these cigarettes? No, thanks, I prefer those. 6. In which store did you buy your gloves, in this one or in that one? 7. You must read this book; it is very interesting. 8. We must speak French now. 9. Where is the post-office? 10. I want some stamps. 11. Two ninety centimes stamps and five post-cards, please. 12. Have you got a one franc twenty-five centimes stamp?

(*Key on pages* 288 *and* 289)

## THE TWENTY-FOUR HOUR CLOCK

All over France you will find the twenty-four hour clock in use, both on the radio and in railway time-tables. For English people there is a very simple way of calculating it in terms of pence. Thus, 19 pence is 1/7 and 19 hours is 7 o'clock (p.m.).

## L'HORLOGE DES VINGT-QUATRE HEURES

Partout en France le système horaire de vingt-quatre heures est d'usage, soit à la radio, soit dans les indicateurs des chemins de fer. Les Anglais, habitués à leur système monétaire duodécimal, n'ont qu'à se dire que 19 " pence " équivalent à 1 shilling et 7 pence, ce dernier chiffre donnant la traduction de " 19 heures."

# VINGT-TROISIÈME LEÇON

### LAUNDRY FOR GRANDMOTHER LESAGE

You ought now to be able to name in French practically every object shown in this drawing. Make a list, and to correct yourself consult the text below—and look back to previous lessons. The washerwoman's basket is called **un panier à linge.**

### LA BLANCHISSEUSE—THE LAUNDRY-WOMAN

**La blanchisseuse rapporte le linge chez grand'mère Lesage. Elle lui remet**
The laundry woman brings back the washing to grandmother Lesage. She hands her

**la note et Mme Lesage commence à compter.**
the bill and Mrs. Lesage begins to count.

**Mme Lesage : 3 chemises d'hommes, 3 chemises de femme, 5 chemises de nuit.**
3 men's shirts, 3 women's chemises, 5 night shirts.

**7 cols mous et 4 cols durs, 12 mouchoirs, 2 caleçons.**
7 soft collars and 4 stiff collars, 12 handkerchiefs, 2 pairs of pants.

**8 paires de bas et 10 paires de chaussettes, un soutien-gorge.**
8 pairs of stockings and 10 pairs of socks, a brassière.

**5 culottes, 3 pyjamas, 2 jupons, un tablier, 14 serviettes. En**
5 knickers, 3 pyjamas, 2 petticoats, 1 apron, 14 napkins. Here

**voici une qui n'est pas à moi, tout le reste est en ordre.**
is one which is not mine, everything else is correct.

**Voici la liste de mon linge sale; il me le faut**
Here is the list of my soiled linen; I must have it

**mardi au plus tard.**     **La blanchisseuse : Bien, madame.**
on Tuesday at the latest.     All right, madam.

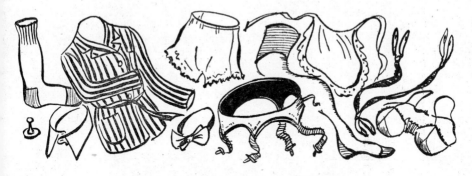

## LES SOUS-VÊTEMENTS—UNDERWEAR

| | | | | |
|---|---|---|---|---|
| **le cache-corset** | **la chemise** | **la chemise de nuit** | **le pyjama** | **la veste** |
| slip-bodice | camisole; vest | night dress | pyjama | jacket |
| **le pantalon** | **le peignoir** | **le soutien-gorge** | **la combinaison** | **la culotte** |
| trousers | dressing gown | "brassière" | combinations | knickers |
| **le jupon** | **la ceinture sport** | **la jarretelle** | **le bas** | **le mouchoir** |
| petticoat | sports-corset | sock suspenders | stocking | handkerchief |
| **le tablier** | **le caleçon** | **le tricot** | **le faux-col** | **le bouton de faux-col** |
| apron | pants | vest; pullover | collar | collar-stud |
| **la manchette** | **le fixe-manche** | **les bretelles** | **la ceinture** | **la cravate** |
| cuff | sleeve-suspenders | braces | belt | tie |
| **le fixe-cravate** | **le nœud papillon** | **la chaussette** | **le fixe-chaussette** | |
| tie-clip | bow-tie | sock | sock-suspenders | |
| **la blanchisserie** | **le linge** | **la lingerie** | **faire blanchir** | **nettoyer** |
| laundry | linen | underwear | to have washed | to clean |
| **raccommoder** | **repriser** | **coudre** | **recoudre** | **le bouton** | **repasser** |
| to mend | to darn | to sew | to sew on | button | to iron |

## THE INDIRECT OBJECT (TO HIM, TO HER, TO THEM, ETC.)

**Il m'écrit**=He writes to me.
**Il lui écrit**=He writes to him (*or* to her).
**Je leur écris**=I write to them.
**Ils nous écrivent**=They write to us.
**Nous vous écrivons**=We write to you.
**Je vous donne le livre**=I give you the book.

**Vous me donnez trop**=You give me too much.
**Il lui donne de l'argent**=He gives him (*or* her) money.
**Elle leur donne des leçons**=She gives them lessons.

**Ils ne nous donnent pas de viande**=They don't give us meat.

**Je lui donne le livre**=I give him the book.

**Je donne le livre à mon père**=I give my father the book.

Let us look at the last example. Here we have two objects, "father" and "book". But clearly "book" is more directly an object than "father", we do not really give the father, we give to the father. "Book" is accordingly the Direct Object, "father" the Indirect Object. In English the Indirect Object is shown by the word *to*, which, however, can frequently be omitted. In French the Indirect Object is indicated by the use of **à**, which may be contracted with **le** to **au** and with **les** to **aux**.

The following are the Indirect Object Pronouns:—

**me**=to me, **te**=to thee, **lui**=to him or to her, **nous**=to us, **vous**=to you, **leur**=to them.

Note that with the exception of **lui** and **leur** the Indirect Object pronouns are the same as the Direct Object pronouns.

With regard to word order, the following rules apply:—

(1) Both Direct and Indirect Object pronouns are placed before the verb, except in the Imperative Affirmative (**je lui donne,** but **donnez-lui**).

(2) In negative sentences these pronouns must come between **ne** and the verb (**je ne lui écris pas**=I don't write to him; **ne lui écrivez pas!**=don't write to him!)

Further examples:—

**Je lui donne un cadeau**=I give him (*or* her) a present.

**Nous leur achetons des bonbons**=We buy them sweets.

**Ils me vendent leur maison**=They sell me their house.

**Parlez-lui**=Speak to him (*or* her).

**Ne lui parlez pas**=Don't speak to him (*or* her).

**Écrivez-nous**=Write to us.

**Ne leur écrivez pas**=Don't write to them.

**Écrivez-moi**=Write to me.

**Ne m'écrivez pas**=Don't write to me.

**Apportez-nous du café**=Bring us some coffee.

**Ne leur apportez pas de thé**=Don't bring them tea.

**Je lui ai téléphoné**=I telephoned to him (*or* her).

**Leur avez-vous téléphoné?**=Did you ring them up?

**Ils ne nous ont pas écrit**=They did not write to us.

**Je l'ai vu hier**=I saw him yesterday.

**Réveillez-les**=Wake them up.

**Ne les réveillez pas**=Don't wake them up.

**Lève-toi**
**Levez-vous** } =Get up.

**Ne te lève pas**
**Ne vous levez pas** } =Don't get up.

Note from the above examples that **me** and **te** become **moi** and **toi** when used with the Imperative Affirmative.

**Le professeur donne un livre à l'élève**=The teacher gives a book to the pupil.

**Il lui donne un livre**=He gives him a book.

**Il le lui donne**=He gives it to him.

---

## ROUND THE TOWN
### En France

La circulation prend toujours le côté droit de la rue.

Un monsieur accompagnant une dame marche toujours à sa gauche.

Le fromage se mange avant le fruit.

On boit souvent le porto comme apéritif.

Le champagne se boit seulement à la fin du repas.

On serre la main, même si on se voit tous les jours.

### In France

Traffic goes always on the right of the road.

A gentleman accompanying a lady walks always on her left.

Cheese is eaten before fruit.

Port is often drunk as an appetiser.

Champagne is drunk only at the end of a meal.

People shake hands, although they see each other every day.

**La petite fille montre sa langue au médecin.**
The little girl shows her tongue to the doctor.

**Elle lui montre sa langue.**
She shows him her tongue.

**Elle la lui montre.**
She shows it to him.

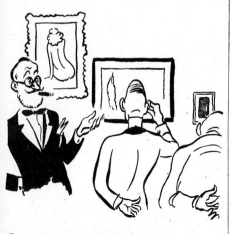

**Je montre mes tableaux à mes amis.**
I show my pictures to my friends.
**Je leur montre mes tableaux.**
I show them my pictures.

**Avez-vous le paquet?**
Have you got the parcel?
**Donnez-le-lui.**
Give it to him (*or* her).
**Ne le lui donnez pas.**
Don't give it to him (*or* her).

**Avez-vous la valise?**
Have you got the suitcase?
**Montrez-la-lui.**
Show it to him (*or* her).
**Ne la lui montrez pas.**
Don't show it to him (*or* her).

**Avez-vous les allumettes?**
Have you got the matches?
**Donnez-les-lui.**
Give them to him (*or* her).
**Donnez-les-leur.**
Give them to them.

**Voici le jardin.**
Here is the garden.
**Montrez-le-leur.**
Show it to them.
**Ne le leur montrez pas.**
Don't show it to them.

**Voilà la maison.**
There is the house.
**Montrez-la-leur.**
Show it to them.
**Ne la leur montrez pas.**
Don't show it to them.

**Voilà les bouteilles.**
There are the bottles.
**Apportez-les-leur.**
Bring them to them.
**Ne les leur apportez pas.**
Don't bring them to them.

Note that **le, la** and **les** precede **lui** and **leur.**

**Je vous donne la pomme.**
I give you the apple.

**Je vous la donne.**
I give it to you.

**YOU SHOULD BE ABLE TO TRANSLATE THIS**

Le cidre est une boisson populaire en Normandie, et la liqueur normande Calvados est également extraite de la pomme.

### LA CONCIERGE EST BIEN LOGÉE!

C'est un gîte confortable, encadré d'arbustes, qu'a trouvé cette concierge! Même Mimi et Minou semblent approuver ce domicile si coquet et si parisien.

| | | | | |
|---|---|---|---|---|
| **Gîte** (m.) | **encadré-e** (p.p.) | **arbuste** (m.) | **Mimi, Minou** | **coquet** (adj.) |
| Lodging | framed | shrub | names for cats | trim, neat |

Je vous donne le journal.
I give (or am giving) you the newspaper.

Je vous le donne.
I give it to you.

Je vous donne les livres.
I give you the books.

Je vous les donne.
I give them to you.

Il me montre son tableau.
He shows me his picture.

Il me le montre.
He shows it to me.

Il me vend sa maison.
He sells me his house.

Il me la vend.
He sells it to me.

Il m'apporte les journaux.
He brings me the newspapers.

Il me les apporte.
He brings them to me.

Nous vous donnons ces livres.
We give you these books.

Nous vous les donnons.
We give them to you.

Il nous envoie l'argent.
He sends us the money.

Il nous l'envoie.
He sends it to us.

Ils te donnent leurs tableaux.
They give you their pictures.

Ils te les donnent.
They give them to you.

Note that **me, te, nous** and **vous** precede **le, la** and **les**.

### SUMMARY

#### Present tense:

$$
\text{je} \left\{ (\text{ne}) \right\} \left\{ \begin{array}{l} \text{le} \\ \text{la} \\ \text{les} \end{array} \right\} \left\{ \begin{array}{l} \text{lui} \\ \text{leur} \end{array} \right\} \left\{ \begin{array}{l} \text{donne} \\ \text{montre} \\ \text{envoie} \\ \text{apporte} \\ \text{écris} \\ \text{dis} \\ \text{fais} \end{array} \right\} (\text{pas})
$$

$$
\text{vous} \left\{ (\text{ne}) \right\} \left\{ \begin{array}{l} \text{le} \\ \text{la} \\ \text{les} \end{array} \right\} \left\{ \begin{array}{l} \text{lui} \\ \text{leur} \end{array} \right\} \left\{ \begin{array}{l} \text{donnez} \\ \text{montrez} \\ \text{envoyez} \\ \text{apportez} \\ \text{écrivez} \\ \text{dites} \\ \text{faites} \end{array} \right\} (\text{pas})
$$

il / elle { (ne) { le / la / les } { lui / leur } { donne / montre / envoie / apporte / écrit / dit / fait } (pas)

je { (ne) { te / vous } { le / la / l' / les } { donne / montre / envoie / etc. } (pas)

nous { (ne) { le / la / les } leur { donnons / montrons / envoyons / apportons / écrivons / disons / faisons } (pas)

il / elle { (ne) { me / te / nous / vous } { le / la / l' / les } { donne / montre / envoie / etc. } (pas)

ils { (ne) { me / te / nous / vous } { le / la / l' / les } { donnent / montrent / envoient / etc. } (pas)

ils / elles { (ne) { le / la / les } { lui / leur } { donnent / montrent / envoient / apportent / écrivent / disent / font } (pas)

elles { (ne) { me / te / nous / vous } { le / la / l' / les } { donnent / montrent / envoient / etc. } (pas)

nous { (ne) { te / vous } { le / la / l' / les } { donnons / montrons / envoyons / etc. } (pas)

### Imperative:

donnez / montrez / envoyez / apportez / écrivez / dites / faites { -le / -la / -les } { -moi / -lui / -leur / -nous }

vous { (ne) { me / nous } { le / la / l' / les } { donnez / montrez / envoyez / etc. } (pas)

### Perfect:

je (ne) { te / vous } { l' / les } ai { (pas) } { donné (e, s, es) / montré (e, s, es) / envoyé (e, s, es) / etc. }

(ne) { le / la / les } { lui / leur } { donnez / montrez / envoyez / apportez / écrivez / dites / faites } (pas)

## EXERCISES

### I Replace the words in italic type by pronouns

1. Je ne lui donne pas *le couteau*. 2. *Charles* envoie *les livres* à ses amis. 3. *Le garçon* apporte *le café*. 4. Nous envoyons *le linge sale* à *la blanchisseuse*. 5. Ecrivez à *ma tante!* 6. Ne parlez pas à *mes parents*. 7. Elles donnent *les fleurs au professeur*. 8. Je donnerai *ces fleurs à mon amie*. 9. Il y a *trois tasses*. 10. On voit *ces dames* chaque jour. 11. *Mon amie* me

### Perfect:

je { (ne) { le / la / les } { lui / leur } ai (pas) } { donné (e, s, es) / montré (e, s, es) / envoyé (e, s, es) / apporté (e, s, es) / écrit (e, s, es) / dit (e, s, es) / fait (e, s, es) } nontre *ses livres*. 12. *Le professeur* nontre *les timbres-poste* à ses élèves.

## I Answer the following questions, using pronouns instead of the nouns

1. Que donnez-vous à votre frère? 2. Que donne le professeur à ses élèves? 3. Madame Roberts parle-t-elle à Mademoielle Lesage? 4. À qui envoyez-vous cette ettre? 5. Qu'est-ce que vous envoyez à os amis? 6. Qu'est-ce que le boulanger end à ses clients? 7. À qui apportez-vous es fleurs? 8. Me donnez-vous votre rgent? 9. Envoyez-vous la lettre à Mme Roberts? 10. Le professeur donne-t-il les vres aux élèves?

## III Translate into French

1. Write to me. 2. Do not write to him. 3. Did you write to them? 4. The laundress brings her the clean linen. 5. You did not send him the newspapers. 6. You did not send them to him. 7. Wake them up. 8. He sends us three shirts, twelve handkerchiefs and six pairs of socks. 9. She has not given us our laundry-list. 10. I don't want to give them her address. 11. Do it to-morrow. 12. Don't do it. 13. Don't give them to him. 14. Show her your picture. 15. Don't show it to them.

(*Key on page* 289)

## PARIS CAMPAGNARD

Le vieux moulin à vent donne un air de campagne à ce coin de la rue Lepic à Iontmartre. Combien de bonnets ont été jetés par-dessus ce moulin!

| | | |
|---|---|---|
| ampagne (f.) | moulin à vent (m.) | "jeter son bonnet par-dessus les moulins" |
| ountry | windmill | "throw your bonnet over the windmill" |

# VINGT-QUATRIÈME LEÇON

## CHEZ LA COUTURIÈRE—AT THE DRESSMAKER'S

**Mme Roberts est allée voir une couturière qui lui a été recommandée par**
Mrs. Roberts has gone to see a dressmaker who has been recommended to her by

**Madame Lesage.　C'est aujourd'hui qu'a lieu le premier essayage**
Mrs. Lesage.　It's to-day that is taking place the first fitting

**d'une robe d'après-midi, et le deuxième essayage d'un tailleur et**
of an afternoon frock, and the second fitting of a tailor-made and

**d'un manteau d'été.**
of a summer coat.

**Mme Roberts : Pas trop mal pour le premier essayage.　Seulement un peu**
　　　　　　Not too bad for the first fitting.　Only a little

　　　　**trop étroit des hanches.**
　　　　too tight over the hips.

　**Couturière :　En effet, madame.　Je vais l'élargir un peu.　Et comme**
　　　　　　Yes, indeed, madam.　I will let that out a bit.　And how

　　　　**longueur?　　　Mme Roberts : Un tout petit peu trop long,**
　　　　is it for length?　　　　　Just a little bit too long,

　　　　**ne trouvez-vous pas?**
　　　　don't you think?

　**Couturière :　Peut-être bien, madame.　Je la raccourcirai d'un centimètre.**
　　　　　　Perhaps it is, madam.　I'll shorten it by one centimetre.

　　　　**Autrement il n'y a rien à changer.　Voulez-vous avoir la**
　　　　Otherwise there is nothing to alter.　Will you have the

　　　　**bonté d'essayer le tailleur maintenant?**
　　　　kindness to try on the tailor-made now?

**Mme Roberts : Avec plaisir, mademoiselle.　En tout je suis très contente,**
　　　　　　With pleasure, mademoiselle.　In general I am very pleased,

　　　　**seulement la jupe ne tombe pas encore assez bien.**
　　　　only the skirt still does not fall quite well.

　　　　**Par contre, les poches et le col peuvent rester comme**
　　　　On the other hand, the pockets and the collar can remain as

ils sont maintenant.      Couturière : Il faudra un nouvel
they are at present.           Another fitting will be

essayage pour le tailleur, madame.   Je vais rectifier
necessary for the tailor-made, madam.   I will put the

la jupe.   Est-ce qu'il vous conviendrait de revenir demain
skirt right.   Would it suit you to come back to-morrow

dans l'après-midi?      Mme Roberts : C'est entendu.
in the afternoon?                    That's all right.

Couturière :   Voilà l'échantillon du drap que vous avez voulu voir
Here is the sample of the cloth which you wanted to see

l'autre jour, madame.
the other day, madam.

Mme Roberts : J'ai changé d'idée.   Je crois que je choisirai une robe de
I've changed my mind.   I think that I'll choose a frock of

velours de soie, mais nous en parlerons plus tard.
chiffon velvet, but we shall discuss that later.

Couturière :   Est-ce que vous verrez Mademoiselle Lesage ces jours-ci, madame?
Will you see Miss Lesage one of these days, madam?

Mme Roberts : Oui, je la verrai demain ou après-demain; avez-vous
Yes, I shall see her to-morrow or the day after to-morrow; have you

quelque chose à lui faire dire?
any message to give to her?

Couturière :   Oui, madame, si cela ne vous dérange pas trop, voulez-vous
Yes, madam, if it is not too much trouble for you, will you

avoir la gentillesse de dire à mademoiselle que je l'attends
have the kindness to tell mademoiselle that I expect her

pour l'essayage de la robe qu'elle a commandée
for the fitting of the dress which she ordered

il y a une quinzaine de jours?
a fortnight ago?

Mme Roberts : Bien, je le lui dirai.      Couturière : Je vous remercie, madame.
Good, I'll tell her.                     Thank you, madam.

## THE TAILOR—LE TAILLEUR

**English.**—1. Dinner jacket; 2. Lounge suit; 3. Rain-coat; 4. Riding breeches; 5. Rolls of cloth; 6. Suit length; 7. Overcoat; 8, 9 and 10. Coat, white waistcoat and trousers of evening dress; 11. Measuring tape; 12. Morning coat; 13. Striped trousers; 14. Patent leather shoes; 15, 16 and 17. Lapels, sleeve and jacket of lounge suit; 18. Norfolk jacket.

**French.**—1. Smoking (m.); 2. Complet veston (m.); 3. Imperméable; 4. Culotte (f.) de cheval; 5. Pièce (f.) d'étoffe; 6. Coupon (m.) de complet; 7. Pardessus (m.); 8, 9, 10, Jaquette (f.) *or* frac (m.), gilet blanc et pantalon d'habit (*or* de tenue de soirée); 11. Centimètre (m.); 12. Jaquette (f.); 13. Pantalon (m.) rayé; 14. Souliers (m. pl.) vernis; 15, 16, 17, Revers (m.), manche (f.) et veston (m.); 18. Veston Norfolk.

| Further Useful Expressions | Un tailleur en vogue<br>A fashionable tailor | un pardessus de facture soignée<br>a well-tailored overcoat |
| --- | --- | --- |
| | Un vêtement confectionné<br>A ready-made garment | un vêtement sur commande<br>a bespoke garment |

## THE DRESSMAKER—LA COUTURIÈRE

**English**—1. Evening dress; 2. Rain-coat; 3. Sports coat; 4. Mirror wardrobe; 5. Sleeve; 6. Collar; 7. Dress (frock); 8. Pullover; 9. Belt; 10. Fur collar; 11. Winter coat; 12. Muff; 13. Pin-cushion; 14. Skirt; 15. Blouse; 16. Tailor-made jacket; 17. Sweater; 18. Tailor-made skirt.

**French**—1. Tenue (f.) de soirée; 2. manteau (m.) de pluie; 3. Manteau de sport; 4. Armoire (f.) à glace; 5. Manche (f.); 6. Col (m.); 7. Robe (f.); 8. Pull-over (m.); 9. Ceinture (f.); 10. Col de fourrure; 11. Manteau d'hiver; 12. Manchon (m.); 13. Pelote (f.) à épingles; 14. Jupe (f.); 15. Blouse (f.); 16. Jaquette (f.) tailleur; 17. Tricot (m.); 18. Jupe tailleur.

---

| | |
|---|---|
| **Être élégante sans recherche** | **une coiffure bien seyante** (from **seoir**) |
| To be faultlessly but simply dressed | a very becoming hat or hair style |

| | | |
|---|---|---|
| **Être affreusement affublée** | **à la mode** | **démodé (e)** |
| To be got up like a scarecrow | in the fashion | out of fashion |

## VÊTEMENTS (ACCESSOIRES)—CLOTHING (ACCESSORIES)

| | |
|---|---|
| **le mouchoir**   handkerchief | **une épingle**   pin |
| **le monogramme**   initials | **une épingle de sûreté**   safety-pin |
| **le foulard**   scarf | **les ciseaux**   scissors |
| **la ceinture**   belt | **la fermeture éclair**   zip-fastener |
| **une aiguille**   needle | **le gant**   glove |
| **le bouton**   button | **le sac à main**   handbag |
| **le fil**   cotton (thread) | **une agrafe**   clasp |
| **la ruche**   frill | **le manchon**   muff |
| **le bouton pression**   press button | **la manchette**   gauntlet cuff |
| **une agrafe et un œillet**   hook and eye | **la dentelle**   lace |

### IDIOMATIC EXPRESSIONS

| | |
|---|---|
| **Avoir lieu**=to take place | **il y a une quinzaine**=a fortnight ago |
| **en effet**=indeed | **il y a quelques semaines (mois)**=a few weeks (months) ago |
| **par contre**=on the other hand | |
| **un tout petit peu**=a tiny little bit | **dans un jour**=in one day |
| **changer d'idée**=to change one's mind | **dans une quinzaine**=in a fortnight |
| **ces jours-ci**=one of these days | **dans quelques jours (semaines)**=in a few days (weeks) |
| **pas du tout**=not at all | |

### POSITION OF EN AND Y

**Il laisse sa femme à la maison.**
  He leaves his wife at home.
**Il l'y laisse.**
  He leaves her there.

**Elle met les fourchettes sur la table.**
  She puts the forks on the table.
**Elle les y met.**
  She puts them there.

**Vous avez des cigarettes.**
  You have got cigarettes.
**Donnez-m'en.**
  Give me some.
**Ne lui en donnez pas.**
  Don't give him any.

**Nous leur parlons de notre jardin.**
  We speak to them about our garden.
**Nous leur en parlons.**
  We speak to them about it.

**Je vous quitte à la gare.**
  I leave you at the station.
**Je vous y quitte.**
  I leave you there.

**Ils nous donnent des pommes.**
  They give us apples.
**Ils nous en donnent.**
  They give us some.

**Il n'y a pas de vin.**
There isn't any wine.

**Il n'y en a pas.**
There isn't any.

**Il n'y a pas d'allumettes.**
There aren't any matches.

**Il n'y en a pas.**
There aren't any.

Note.—(1) When **y** or **en** is used with any other object pronoun the **y** or **en** is always put last; (2) **y** precedes **en**.

### SUMMARY

The order of pronoun objects preceding a verb is this:—

| me | | | | |
|----|----|----|----|----|
| te | le | | | |
| se | la | lui | y | en |
| nous | les | leur | | |
| vous | | | | |

## EXERCISES

### I Replace the words in italic type by pronouns

1. Charles n'écrit pas *ses lettres* dans la cuisine. 2. Elle vous donnera *du pain*. 3. Elles m'ont donné *de la viande*. 4. Ne nous donnez-vous pas *de pommes*? 5. Nous mangeons souvent *du chocolat dans la chambre à coucher*. 6. Nous donnons *des fleurs à Madame X*. 7. Il apporte *des roses à Mesdames X. et Y*. 8. On trouve de jolies *fleurs dans son jardin*. 9. *La tante* a envoyé *des bonbons aux enfants*. 10. J'enverrai *mes enfants à la campagne*.

### II Answer the following questions using pronouns instead of nouns

1. Avez-vous beaucoup de travail à faire aujourd'hui? 2. Donnez-vous du pain aux chiens? 3. Est-ce que vous donnez du vin à un chat? 4. Est-ce que votre père est en Amérique? 5. Est-ce que vous allez souvent au cinéma? 6. Me donnez-vous des pommes? 7. Est-ce que je vous donne de l'argent? 8. Pouvez-vous envoyer des lettres à M. Roberts? 9. Est-ce que la couturière vous fait beaucoup de robes? 10. Voulez-vous m'envoyer des bonbons? 11. Écrivez-vous beaucoup de lettres à vos amis? 12. À qui envoyez-vous des colis?

### III Translate into French

1. What will you give us? 2. I will give you a French lesson. 3. What do you send us? 4. I send you shirts, handkerchiefs and socks. 5. To whom do you send this parcel? 6. I send it to my sister, who is at present in France. 7. I can send you some underwear. 8. Did you write to him about it? 9. I shall give you some chocolate; but don't give any to my brother; I gave him enough. 10. Where are my handkerchiefs? There are some in that box.

(*Key on page* 289)

## AROUND THE TOWN

### Les Midinettes de Paris

Derrière la façade fastueuse des grands établissements de mode, où des dames élégantes viennent choisir des toilettes du dernier chic parisien qui font l'envie de leurs amies, se trouve une personne de grande importance dans l'organisation. C'est la petite "arpète" (apprentie) qui coud dans les ateliers du sous-sol et qui met dans son travail la vraie délicatesse parisienne. Paris la connaît sous le sobriquet de "midinette", parce qu'elle rentre d'habitude dîner chez elle à midi. Elle est facile à reconnaître dans la rue par le chic qu'elle parvient à atteindre malgré son budget restreint.

### Paris "Midinettes"

Behind the sumptuous façade of the great houses of fashion, hidden from the elegant ladies who come to choose frocks— the last word in Paris smartness—which arouse the envy of their friends, is a person of the first importance in the organization. This is the little "arpète" (apprentice) who sews in the basement work-rooms and puts the true Parisian touch into her work. Paris knows her under the nickname of "midinette", because she usually goes home to lunch at midday, easy to recognize in the street by the elegance which she succeeds in achieving, despite her restricted budget.

## LE PALAIS BOURBON

Construit en 1722 sur l'ordre de la duchesse douairière de Bourbon, le Palais Bourbon fait partie aujourd'hui de la Chambre des Députés.  Ici nous voyons l'entrée de derrière.

| | | |
|---|---|---|
| **Douairière** | **faire partie** | **Chambre des Députés** |
| Dowager | form part | Chamber of Deputies (French Parliament) |

# VINGT-CINQUIÈME LEÇON

### LE TAILLEUR—THE TAILOR

**M. Roberts attend le tailleur avec lequel il a fixé un**
Mr. Roberts waits for the tailor with whom he has made an

**rendez-vous pour cet après-midi.  On sonne.  M. Roberts va**
appointment for this afternoon.  The bell is ringing.  Mr. Roberts goes

**lui-même ouvrir la porte, et le tailleur entre.**
himself to open the door, and the tailor comes in.

**M. Roberts :  Je suis très pressé.  Prenez vite mes mesures,**
I am in a great hurry.  Take my measurements quickly,

**s'il vous plaît, monsieur.  Je vous ai déjà dit qu'il me**
please.  I have already told you that I

**faut un complet-veston.  Voilà l'échantillon de l'étoffe**
need a lounge suit.  This is the sample of the material

**que j'ai choisie.**
which I have chosen.

**Le tailleur (en prenant les mesures) : Quelle sorte de doublure désirez-vous,**
(taking the measurements) : What sort of lining do you want,

**monsieur?      M. Roberts :  Je la désire en soie.   Quand**
sir?                          I want it in silk.  When

**pourrons-nous essayer?**
shall we be able to have a fitting?

**Le tailleur :  Après-demain, monsieur.  Je pourrai venir chez vous, si cela**
The day after to-morrow, sir.  I could call on you, if it

**vous convient.  M. Roberts : Non, je passerai chez vous.**
suits you.                    No, I shall come along to your place.

### L'ESSAYAGE—THE FITTING

**Le tailleur :  Bonjour, M. Roberts, quel beau temps nous avons aujourd'hui!**
Good day, Mr. Roberts, what fine weather we have to-day!

**Votre complet est prêt.  Si vous voulez bien l'essayer,**
Your suit is ready.  If you will be good enough to try it on,

nous allons voir comment il va.
we shall see how it fits.

**M. Roberts a mis le complet, et le tailleur voit son client**
Mr. Roberts has put on the suit, and the tailor sees his customer

**froncer les sourcils.**
frowning.

**Le tailleur :**  **Est-ce que vous êtes content, M. Roberts?**
Are you satisfied, Mr. Roberts?

**M. Roberts :**  **Comme-ci comme-ça.   Le veston me gêne sous les bras.**
So so.   The coat is too tight under the arms.

**Le tailleur :**  **Ce n'est rien; au premier essayage il y a toujours**
That's nothing; at the first fitting there are always

**quelques retouches à faire.   Je vais faire le nécessaire.**
a few alterations to be made.   I will see to it.

**Que pensez-vous de la coupe, monsieur?**
What do you think of the cut, sir?

**M. Roberts :**  **La coupe est très bonne, mais le pantalon est trop long.**
The cut is very good, but the trousers are too long.

**J'aime les pantalons un peu courts, car ils ne ramassent pas**
I like trousers rather short, because they do not pick up

**la boue quand il pleut, ni la poussière quand il fait sec. J'ai**
mud when it rains, nor dust when it is dry.   I have

**aussi remarqué qu'ils ne s'usent pas si vite aux bords.**
also noticed that they do not wear out so quickly at the edges.

**Le tailleur :**  **Vous avez raison, monsieur.**
You are right, sir.

**M. Roberts :**  **Je pense que ce beau temps ne va pas durer, et que**
I think that the fine weather is not going to last, and that

**bientôt nous aurons le grand froid.   Prenez mes**
soon we shall have severe cold.   Take my

**mesures pour un pardessus.**
measurements for an overcoat.

**Le tailleur :**  **Certainement, monsieur, et quel genre d'étoffe désirez-vous?**
Certainly, sir, and what kind of cloth do you want?

## LA PLACE DE LA BASTILLE

Le monument actuel s'élève sur l'emplacement où jadis se trouvait la forteresse de la Bastille. La destruction de celle-ci par les émeutiers de 1789 fut le premier pas vers la Révolution, qui entraîna plus tard l'exécution de Louis XVI et de Marie Antoinette.

| | | | |
|---|---|---|---|
| **Emplacement** (m.) | **jadis** (adv.) | **émeutier-ère** (m.f.) | **entraîner** |
| ite | formerly | rioter | to entail, involve |

**M. Roberts :**   Je voudrais un tissu doux, assez épais et d'une
I should like a soft cloth, rather thick and of a
**couleur sombre. C'est un pardessus d'hiver dont j'ai besoin.**
dark colour. It is a winter overcoat I need.

### LES CHAPEAUX—HATS

| | |
|---|---|
| **le chapeau haut-de-forme** top hat | **la coiffe** bonnet |
| **le chapeau melon** bowler hat | **le béret** beret |
| **le chapeau mou** soft hat | **la voilette** veil |
| **le bord** brim | **le chapeau tyrolien** sports hat (Tyrol shape) |
| **le ruban** ribbon | **le chapeau cloche** sports hat (with turned |
| **le panama** Panama | down brim) |
| **la casquette** cap | **le chapeau de paille** straw hat (wide brim) |
| **le capuchon** hood | **le chapeau relevé** hat with turned up brim |

### CHAUSSURES—BOOTS AND SHOES

| | |
|---|---|
| **le magasin de chaussures** shoe-shop | **la bottine** boot |
| **la pantoufle** slipper | **la botte** high boot |
| **la sandale** sandal | **le soulier verni** patent leather shoe |
| **le soulier à bride** shoe with strap | **le talon** heel |
| **le soulier à lacets** tie shoe | **la semelle** sole |
| **l'escarpin** court shoe | **le bout** cap |
| **la guêtre** (man's) spats | **la languette** tongue |
| **le soulier** shoe | **les lacets** (m.) laces |

### AROUND THE TOWN

#### La Mode Masculine à Paris

Pour l'Anglais moyen il peut sembler drôle que M. Roberts, notre "héros", qui doit rentrer en Angleterre dans quelques mois, se soit avisé de se faire faire des vêtements par un tailleur français. Mais de nos jours, la mode masculine européenne tend à se rationaliser, et c'est ainsi que des vêtements faits sur mesure par un bon tailleur parisien, ne sembleraient plus extraordinaires aux amis londoniens de M. Roberts. Il existe à Paris beaucoup de firmes spécialisées dans la coupe anglaise, et plusieurs tailleurs français qui ont fait leur apprentissage à Londres.

#### Paris Men's Fashions

It may seem strange to the average Briton that Mr. Roberts, our "hero," who has to return to England in a few months, should have got the idea of having clothes made by a French tailor. But in these days European men's fashions tend to become rationalized, so that clothes made to measure by a good Paris tailor would no longer seem strange to Mr. Roberts's London friends. There exist in Paris many tailors specializing in English cut, and several French tailors have served their apprenticeship in London.

## ON DÉMÉNAGE

.  Quoique prise près de Paris, cette photographie d'un déménagement villageois offre
toute l'ambiance de la vie champêtre loin de la métropole et de sa vie turbulente.

| **Déménager** | **villageois-e (adj.)** | **ambiance (f).** | **métropole (f.)** |
|---|---|---|---|
| To move (house) | rustic, village | atmosphere, environment | metropolis |

## PERSONAL PRONOUNS USED APART FROM VERBS

**Qui vient?** = Who is coming?

**Moi** = I (am)
**Lui** = He (is)
**Elle** = She (is)
**Nous** = We (are)
**Vous** = You (are)
**Eux** = They (are) (m.)
**Elles** = They (are) (f.)
**Toi** = You (are) (familiar form)

**Qui veut aller à la gare?** = Who wants to go to the station?

**Moi, monsieur** = I, sir

**Qui a pris mon stylo?** = Who has taken my fountain-pen?

**Lui, madame** = He (has), madam

**Je viendrai ⎱ vous**
**avec ⎰ toi** = I shall come with you

**Qui fait tant de bruit?** = Who is making so much noise?

**Ce sont eux** = They are

**Viendras-tu avec moi?** = Will you come with me?

**N'allez pas sans lui** = Don't go without him

**Ne sortez pas sans eux** = Don't go out without them (men or boys)

**Ne sortez pas sans elles** = Don't go out without them (women or girls)

**C'est moi qui ai fait cela** = It is I, who have done it

**C'est lui qui a acheté le couteau** = It is he who has bought the knife

**C'est elle qui a fait la cuisine** = It is she who has done the cooking

**Ce sont eux qui n'ont pas encore mangé** = It is they who have not eaten yet

All the personal pronouns which have occurred so far have been used with verbs only.

e.g. **Vous parlez très bien. Il me donne de l'argent. Elle lui écrit souvent. Il me l'a dit. Il n'y en a pas.**

They are called weak pronouns, because they cannot stand alone and are used in connection with verbs only. In this lesson we met various strong pronouns, i.e., those used apart from verbs.

You must distinguish between:

| WEAK PRONOUNS (*used in connection with verbs*) | STRONG PRONOUNS (*used apart from verbs*) | |
|---|---|---|
| je | moi | I |
| tu | toi | thou |
| vous | vous | you |
| il | lui | he |
| elle | elle | she |
| nous | nous | we |
| ils | eux | they (m.) |
| elles | elles | they (f.) |

Four of the pronouns are the same in both lists above; there are special words only for I, thou, he and they (masc.).

The strong pronouns are more emphatic than the weak ones. The following constructions are therefore used to throw more emphasis on to the pronoun. In English this emphasis is usually shown by the voice only.

e.g., **Moi, je l'ai trouvé** = I have found it

**Ce n'est pas moi qui l'ai fait, c'est lui** = I did not do it, he did

**Lui et moi l'avons apporté** = He and I have brought it

**Charles et moi le ferons** = Charles and I will do it

**Lui et moi, nous allons** = (He and I) we go

**Vous et lui, vous jouez** = (You and he) you play

**Vous, allez-vous-en!** = You (emphatic) go away from here!

Note that strong pronouns are used when the subject consists of two pronouns, or a noun and a pronoun.

## AT HOME

**Je suis chez moi** = I am at home
**Il est chez lui** = He is at home
**Elle est chez elle** = She is at home

**Nous sommes chez nous** = We are at home
**Ils sont chez eux** ⎱
**Elles sont chez elles** ⎰ They are at home
**Êtes-vous chez vous?** ⎱
**Es-tu chez toi?** ⎰ Are you at home?

## MINE, THINE, YOURS, HIS, HERS, ETC.

C'est à moi=That is mine
C'est à lui=That is his
C'est à elle=That is hers
C'est à nous=That is ours
C'est à vous ⎱
C'est à toi ⎰ =That is yours
C'est à eux ⎱
C'est à elles ⎰ =That is theirs
Ce chapeau est à Charles=This hat is Charles's (belongs to Charles)
Il est à lui=It is his (it belongs to him)

### MYSELF, YOURSELF, HIMSELF, HERSELF, ETC.

Je le ferai moi-même=I shall do it myself.
L'a-t-il fait lui-même?=Did he do it himself?
Elle me l'a dit elle-même=She told me herself.
Vous n'avez que vous-même à blâmer=You have only yourself to blame.

Ils le font eux-mêmes ⎱ They are doing
Elles le font elles-mêmes ⎰ it themselves.
Nous ne le savons pas nous-mêmes=We don't know it ourselves.

Note.—moi-même=myself; toi-même= yourself; lui-même=himself; elle-même= herself; nous-mêmes=ourselves; eux-mêmes=themselves (m.); elles-mêmes= themselves (f.); vous-même=yourself; vous-mêmes=yourselves.

### RIRE—TO LAUGH

Present:

| | |
|---|---|
| Je ris | nous rions |
| tu ris | vous riez |
| il rit | ils rient |

Imperfect: je riais, etc.
Future: je rirai, etc.
Conditional: je rirais, etc.
Perfect: j'ai ri, etc.

## EXERCISES

### I Translate into English

1. Je pense à lui. 2. Ne pensez pas à elle. 3. Ce crayon est à moi. 4. Ce journal est-il à vous? 5. Non, il n'est pas à moi. 6. Cette maison est-elle à lui? 7. Ce parapluie est-il à elle? 8. Je n'ai pas discuté (=discussed) la question avec eux. 9. Vous pouvez compter (=count) sur lui. 10. Avez-vous des lettres pour moi? 11. Elle n'est pas chez elle. 12. Il l'a acheté chez Woolworth. 13. Il l'a fait lui-même. 14. Vous me l'avez dit vous-même. 15. Ils ne se savent pas eux-mêmes.

### II Translate into French

1. Can you recommend her to me? 2. Are you thinking of her? 3. Does this umbrella belong to him? 4. Does this belong to her? 5. Is he satisfied with them? 6. Did he speak of me? 7. Are you dissatisfied with him? 8. What does she think of them. 9. Is he at home? 10. Is Miss Smith at home? 11. No, she went to her dressmaker. 12. Did you come from home? 13. I did it myself. 14. Did you do it yourself? 15. Tell him to do it himself. 16. Have you anything for them? 17. My friend and I. 18. Who is hungry? I am. 19. Whom have you seen? Him. 20. Those pencils are not yours; they are Madeleine's. (*Key on pages* 289 *and* 290.)

## LA CHOSE SE PASSE AU CAFÉ

*Premier consommateur:* Monsieur, je crois que nous nous sommes déjà rencontrés, l'année dernière, à ce café.

*Deuxième consommateur:* Vous croyez me reconnaître?

*Premier:* Vous pas, mais votre parapluie.

*Deuxième:* Mon parapluie? Mais je ne l'avais pas à cette époque.

*Premier:* En effet, mais moi, je l'avais.

———

**La chose,** thing; **se passer,** to happen; **consommateur,** customer; **croire,** to believe; **se rencontrer,** to meet; **reconnaître,** to recognize; **le parapluie,** umbrella; **à cette époque,** at that time; **en effet,** that's right.

# VINGT-SIXIÈME  LEÇON

## AU THÉÂTRE—AT THE THEATRE

**Pour célébrer l'anniversaire de sa fille Mme Roberts amena ses**
To celebrate her daughter's birthday Mrs. Roberts took her

**enfants au théâtre.   Après avoir consulté les affiches dans les**
children to the theatre.   After having studied the posters in the

**rues et les colonnes des spectacles dans les journaux Mme Roberts**
streets and the play-columns in the newspapers Mrs. Roberts

**avait décidé de les amener à la Comédie Française où**
decided to take them to the Comédie Française where

**l'on jouait "Le Malade Imaginaire" de Molière.   Quand elle était en**
Molière's "Le Malade Imaginaire" was being played.   When she was in

**ville pour faire des achats elle avait retenu trois places au**
town to do some shopping she had booked three seats in the

**parterre.   Le soir de la représentation, quand ils arrivèrent**
pit-stalls.   On the evening of the performance, when they arrived

**au théâtre Mme Roberts alla d'abord au vestiaire pour y**
at the theatre Mrs. Roberts went first to the cloakroom to

**laisser son manteau et son chapeau.   Puis ils donnèrent leurs**
leave her coat and her hat there.   Then they gave their

**billets à l'ouvreuse, qui les conduisit à leurs places.   Charles**
tickets to the usherette, who led them to their seats.   Charles

**acheta un programme et donna un pourboire à l'ouvreuse.**
bought a programme and gave a tip to the usherette.[1]

**Charles (à l'ouvreuse): Pouvez-vous nous louer des jumelles?**
   (to the usherette): Can you hire us a pair of opera-glasses?

**L'ouvreuse :   Certainement, monsieur, c'est trois francs cinquante.**
   Certainly, sir, it's three francs fifty.

**Charles :   Voici dix francs; avez-vous de la monnaie?   (Il est très**
   Here is ten francs; have you any change?   (He is very

---

[1] It is customary in France to tip ouvreuses, and they expect it.

**fier, parce que c'est la première fois qu'on**
proud, because it is the first time that he has been

**l'a appelé "monsieur".)**
called "sir".)

L'ouvreuse :   **Non, monsieur, mais je vais aller vous en chercher.**
No, sir, but I'll go to get you some.

**Charles ajuste ses jumelles et regarde autour de lui.)**
Charles adjusts his opera-glasses and looks round.)

### LE THÉÂTRE FRANÇAIS (COMÉDIE FRANÇAISE)

L'eau étincelante forme une espèce de rideau devant le foyer des "Sociétaires".

| **étincelant-e** (adj.) | **rideau** (m.) | **"Sociétaires"** |
|---|---|---|
| sparkling | curtain | designation of Comédie Française players |

**Charles :**     **Le théâtre est bondé.**
The theatre is crowded.

**Madeleine :**    **Il n'y a pas une place de libre.**
There is not one seat free.

**L'ouvreuse (à Charles) : Voici votre monnaie, monsieur.**
(to Charles) : Here is your change, sir.

**Mme Roberts : Attention, on frappe les trois coups.   C'est comme cela**
Listen, there are the three knocks.   That is how the

**qu'on annonce en France le commencement du spectacle.**
beginning of the play is announced in France.

**Charles :**     **Quel drôle de coutume.**
What a funny custom.

**Mme Roberts : Chut! on commence.**
Quiet! it's starting.

**(Le rideau se lève et on joue la première scène du "Malade Imaginaire",**
(The curtain rises on the first scene of "Le Malade Imaginaire",

**comédie brillante d'un fou qui n'est point malade et qui**
brilliant comedy of a hypochondriac who is not ill and who

**s'entoure de médecins.)**
surrounds himself with doctors.)

## PAST TENSES

(1) **Il a visité le cinéma deux fois cette semaine**=He has visited the cinema twice this week.

(2) (*a*) **Le cinéma était bondé**=the cinema was crowded.

(*b*) **Il visitait le cinéma deux fois par semaine**=He visited (used to visit) the cinema twice a week.

(*c*) **Nous demeurions à Paris pendant six mois**=We lived in Paris for six months.

(3) **Il entra, acheta un billet et le donna à l'ouvreuse**=He entered, bought a ticket and gave it to the usherette.

## AROUND THE TOWN

### Les "Girls" de Paris

La plupart des touristes anglais font au moins une visite dans un des grands music-halls où le genre de spectacle n'exige pas une grande connaissance de la langue française. Là ils voient parmi les troupes de danseuses beaucoup de leurs compatriotes. Les "Girls" de Paris sont renommées, et il y avait longtemps à Paris un pasteur anglais, le Révérend Basil Cardew, qui se dévouait à leurs besoins.

### The "Girls" of Paris

Most English tourists make at least one visit to one of the big music-halls where the type of entertainment does not require any great knowledge of French. There they see among the troupes of dancing girls many of their fellow-countrywomen. The "Girls" of Paris are famous, and for a long time in Paris there was an English parson, the Rev. Basil Cardew, who ministered to their needs.

(4) **Quand il entra la représentation avait déjà commencé**=When he entered the performance had already begun.

In the last two foregoing sentences a new tense makes its appearance, which is called the Preterite. It is used in narratives of a historic or literary nature, in telling of past actions that happened once, as distinct from habitual or continuous actions (compare the last two sentences with sentence 1). For descriptions (see sentence 2*a*), and habitual (2*b*) or continuous action (2*c*), the Imperfect is used. In French conversation, however, past incidents are given in the Perfect (see sentence 1).

The imperfect may be translated in three different ways.

**je donnais** $\begin{cases} \text{I gave} \\ \text{I was giving} \\ \text{I used to give} \end{cases}$

Students who are learning French for conversational purposes only may ignore the Preterite, which is never used in conversation.

### THE PRETERITE

| donner=to give | finir=to finish |
|---|---|
| je donnai | je finis |
| tu donnas | tu finis |
| il donna | il finit |
| nous donnâmes | nous finîmes |
| vous donnâtes | vous finîtes |
| ils donnèrent | ils finirent |

| perdre=to lose | recevoir=to receive |
|---|---|
| je perdis | je reçus |
| tu perdis | tu reçus |
| il perdit | il reçut |
| nous perdîmes | nous reçûmes |
| vous perdîtes | vous reçûtes |
| ils perdirent | ils reçurent |

Note that the regular endings of the Preterite are:

| -er verbs | -ir and -re verbs | -oir verbs |
|---|---|---|
| -ai | -is | -us |
| -as | -is | -us |

| -a | -it | -ut |
|---|---|---|
| -âmes | -îmes | -ûmes |
| -âtes | -îtes | -ûtes |
| -èrent | -irent | -urent |

| avoir=to have | être=to be |
|---|---|
| j'eus =I had | je fus=I was |
| tu eus | tu fus |
| il eut | il fut |
| nous eûmes | nous fûmes |
| vous eûtes | vous fûtes |
| ils eurent | ils furent |

**venir**=to come

je vins=I came
tu vins
il vint
nous vînmes
vous vîntes
ils vinrent

aller=to go, same as **donner** (**j'allai**, etc.)
tenir=to hold, same as **venir** (**je tins**, etc.)
faire=to make—**je fis**, etc.
prendre=to take—**je pris**, etc.
mettre=to put—**je mis**, etc.
dire=to say—**je dis**, etc.
boire=to drink—**je bus**, etc.
lire=to read—**je lus**, etc.
écrire=to write—**j'écrivis**, etc.
connaître=to know—**je connus**, etc.
courir=to run—**je courus**, etc.
mourir=to die—**je mourus**, etc.
voir=to see—**je vis**, etc.
pouvoir=to be able—**je pus**, etc.
croire=to believe—**je crus**, etc.
savoir=to know—**je sus**, etc.
s'asseoir=to sit down — **je m'assis, tu t'assis, il s'assit**, etc.
pleuvoir=to rain—**il plut**

The Preterite is used in the literary language only. It expresses a particular fact or event which took place (once) at some definite past time (there must be an interval of at least one day).

### English

1. Stage door; 2. Dress circle; 3. Upper circle; 4. Box; 5. Spotlight; 6. Curtain; 7. Limelights; 8. Proscenium; 9. Safety-curtain; 10. Scenery; 11. Stage-hands; 12. Stage-manager; 13. Star (male); 14. Star (feminine); 15. Supporting cast; 16. Foot-lights; 17, 18. Prompter and prompter's box; 19, 20. Orchestra and orchestra pit; 21. Conductor; 22. Emergency exit; 23. Opera-glasses; 24. Sweets-seller; 25. Seating attendant; 26. Orchestra stalls; 27. Programme-girl; 28. Box office; 29. Foyer; 30. Bar.

### French

1. Entrée (f.) des artistes; 2. Premier

| Further Useful Expressions | Faire fureur To be a " riot " | faire four to be a "flop" | costumière (f.) wardrobe-mistress |
|---|---|---|---|
| | Effets sonores (m.pl.) Sound effects | coulisses (f.pl.) wings | metteur (m.) en scène producer |

# LE THÉÂTRE

balcon (m.); 3. Seconde galerie (f.); 4. Loge (f.); 5. Projecteur (m.); 6. Rideau (m.); 7. Lumière (f.) oxhydrique; 8. Avant-scène; 9. Rideau métallique; 10. Décors (m. pl.); mise (f.) en scène; 11. Machinistes (m. pl.); 12. Régisseur (m.) 13. Acteur de premier rôle; vedette; 14. Actrice de premier rôle; vedette; 15. Troupe (f.); 16. Rampe (f.); 17, 18. Souffleur-euse (m. f.); trou du souffleur; 19, 20. Orchestre (m.); fosse (f.) d'orchestre; 21. Chef (m.) d'orchestre; 22. Sortie (f.) de secours; 23. Jumelles (f. pl.) (when hired from theatre) en location; 24. Vendeuse de bonbons; 25. Ouvreuse (f.); 26. Fauteuils (m. pl.) d'orchestre; 27. Vendeuse de programmes; 28. Location (f.); 29. Foyer (m.); 30. Buffet (m.).

| | | | |
|---|---|---|---|
| **Nom** (m.) de théâtre | spectateur-trice (m.f.) | **habilleuse** (f.) | **effets scéniques** (m.pl.) |
| Stage-name | theatre-goer | dresser | effects |
| **Se faire acteur-actrice** | **droits** (m.pl.) **de production** | trac (m.) | **aparté** (m.) |
| To go on the stage | stage-rights | stage-fright | stage-whisper, aside |

| Il eut une entrevue | He had an interview |
|---|---|
| hier | yesterday |
| la semaine dernière | last week |
| le mois passé | last month |
| l'année dernière | last year |

but: **il a eu une entrevue aujourd'hui** = he had an interview to-day (lit., he has had)

Learn this tongue-twister by heart:

**Didon dîna, dit-on, du dos d'un dodu dindon**
Queen Dido dined, they say, off the back of a fat turkey.

**conduire** = to lead, to drive
**je conduis, tu conduis, il conduit**
**nous conduisons, vous conduisez**
**ils conduisent**
Imperfect: **je conduisais,** etc.
Preterite: **je conduisis,** etc.
Future: **je conduirai,** etc.
Perfect: **j'ai conduit,** etc.

**paraître** = to appear
**je parais, tu parais, il paraît**
**nous paraissons, vous paraissez**
**ils paraissent**
Imperfect: **je paraissais,** etc.
Preterite: **je parus,** etc.
Future: **je paraîtrai,** etc.
Perfect: **j'ai paru,** etc.

## EXERCISES

### I Write these sentences using the Preterite Tense

1. Je (recevoir) la lettre hier soir.  2. Il (venir) à Paris.  3. Ils ne nous (répondre) pas.  4. Ils (visiter) le musée.  5. Nous (aller) chez lui.  6. Quand on (ouvrir) la porte je (entrer).  7. Elle (faire) venir le médecin.  8. Ils (écrire) des lettres.  9. Elle (répondre) à sa question.  10. Il (finir) sa leçon.

### II Translate into English

1. Ils ne nous répondirent pas.  2. Il arriva le soir.  3. Elle me donna son billet.  4. Elles choisirent des robes élégantes.  5. Il coupa le pain.  6. Elle chantait pendant que je jouais.  7. Elle chantait quand il entra.  8. Quand je fus à Paris je visitai l'Opéra.  9. Elles donnèrent de l'argent à la pauvre femme.  10. La porte de la chambre fut ouverte.

### III

Re-write the sentences from Exercise II in conversational language (using the perfect instead of the preterite).

1. Ils ne nous ont pas répondu, etc.

### IV. Answer these Questions in French

1. Y a-t-il beaucoup de théâtres à Paris?  2. Avez-vous déjà été dans un théâtre français?  3. Quelle comédie Charles et Madeleine vont-ils voir?  4. Dans quel théâtre la joue-t-on?  5. Quelles places ont-ils?  6. Leur mère laisse-t-elle son chapeau au vestiaire?  7. Qui les conduit à leurs places?  8. Pourquoi Charles est-il fier?  9. Qu'est-ce qu'ils pensaient de la représentation?  10. Qu'est-ce qu'ils ont fait pendant l'entr'acte?

*(Key on page 290)*

# KEY TO THE EXERCISES

## Lesson Twenty-two

### I

1. I am going to the post-office.  2. I must have some stamps.  3. Where is the post-office?  4. Are there any letters for me?  5. There is one.  6. Whom is it from?  7. It is from my friend.  8. What is he writing?  9. Nothing important.  10. Give me three 90-centime stamps.  11. Will you register this letter.  12. Do you want to send this telegram?  13. Did you post your letter?  14. When do you think this letter will arrive?  15. You will have to send it poste restante (or "I'll have", "We'll have", etc., according to the context).

### II

1. Les voilà; celle-ci est pour moi; celle-là est pour vous.  2. Ceci est pour vous.  3. Je n'aime pas celles-ci.  4. Prenez-vous celui-ci ou celui-là?  5. Elle y

est. 6. Je l'y ai achetée. 7. Le voulez-vous? 8. Je préfère celui-ci. 9. Elles (celles-ci) sont très belles. 10. Celle-ci n'est pas confortable, prenez celui-là. 11. Prenez-vous ceux-là? 12. Donnez-moi celui-ci (celui-là), s'il vous plaît.

### III

1. Connaissez-vous ces dames? 2. Lisez-vous ce livre? 3. Ont-ils acheté cette maison? 4. Quel vin voulez-vous, celui-ci ou celui-là? 5. Voulez-vous ces cigarettes? Non, merci, je préfère celles-là. 6. Dans quel magasin avez-vous acheté vos gants, dans celui-ci ou dans celui-là? 7. Il faut lire ce livre; il est très intéressant. 8. Il faut parler français maintenant. 9. Où est la poste? 10. Il me faut des timbres. 11. Deux timbres de quatre-vingt dix centimes et cinq cartes postales, s'il vous plaît. 12. Avez-vous un timbre d'un franc vingt-cinq?

## Lesson Twenty-three

### I

1. Je ne le lui donne pas. 2. Il les leur envoie. 3. Il l'apporte. 4. Nous le lui envoyons. 5. Écrivez-lui! 6. Ne leur parlez pas. 7. Elles les lui donnent. 8. Je les lui donnerai. 9. Il y en a trois. 10. On les voit chaque jour. 11. Elle me les montre. 12. Il les leur montre.

### II

1. Je lui donne une cravate. 2. Il leur donne une leçon. 3. Elle lui parle. 4. Je l'envoie à mon ami. 5. Je leur envoie des lettres. 6. Il leur vend du pain. 7. Je les apporte à ma mère. 8. Je ne vous le donne pas. 9. Je la lui envoie. 10. Il les leur donne.

### III

1. Écrivez-moi. 2. Ne lui écrivez pas. 3. Leur avez-vous écrit? 4. La blanchisseuse lui apporte le linge propre. 5. Vous ne lui avez pas envoyé les journaux. 6. Vous ne les lui avez pas envoyés. 7. Réveillez-les. 8. Il nous envoie trois chemises, douze mouchoirs, et six paires de chaussettes. 9. Elle ne nous a pas donné notre liste de blanchissage. 10. Je ne veux

pas leur donner son adresse. 11. Faites-le demain. 12. Ne le faites pas. 13. Ne les lui donnez pas. 14. Montrez-lui votre tableau. 15. Ne le leur montrez pas.

## Lesson Twenty-four

### I

1. Charles ne les écrit pas dans la cuisine. 2. Elle vous en donnera. 3. Elles m'en ont donné. 4. Ne nous en donnez-vous pas? 5. Nous y en mangeons souvent. 6. Nous lui en donnons. 7. Il leur en apporte. 8. On y en trouve de jolies. 9. Elle leur en a envoyé. 10. Je les y enverrai.

### II

1. Je n'en ai pas beaucoup à faire aujourd'hui. 2. Je leur en donne. 3. Je ne lui en donne pas. 4. Non, il n'y est pas. 5. Non, je n'y vais pas souvent. 6. Je vous en donne. 7. Vous ne m'en donnez pas. 8. Je peux lui en envoyer. 9. Elle m'en fait beaucoup. 10. Je vous en enverrai demain. 11. Je leur en écris tous les jours. 12. J'en envoie à ma cousine.

### III

1. Que nous donnerez-vous? 2. Je vous donnerai une leçon de français. 3. Que nous envoyez-vous? 4. Je vous envoie des chemises, des mouchoirs et des chaussettes. 5. À qui envoyez-vous ce colis? 6. Je l'envoie à ma sœur qui est maintenant en France. 7. Je peux vous envoyer des sous-vêtements. 8. Lui avez-vous écrit à ce sujet? 9. Je vous donnerai du chocolat; mais n'en donnez pas à mon frère; je lui en ai assez donné. 10. Où sont mes mouchoirs? Il y en a dans cette boîte.

## Lesson Twenty-five

### I

1. I am thinking of him. 2. Don't think of her. 3. This pencil is mine. 4. Is this paper yours? 5. No, it is not mine. 6. Does this house belong to him? 7. Does this umbrella belong to her? 8. I haven't discussed the question with them. 9. You can count on him. 10. Have you any letters

for me? 11. She is not at home. 12. He bought it at Woolworth's. 13. He did it himself. 14. You told me yourself. 15. They don't know themselves.

## II

1. Pouvez-vous me la recommander? 2. Pensez-vous à elle? 3. Est-ce que ce parapluie est à lui? 4. Est-ce que ceci est à elle? 5. Est-il content d'eux (or d'elles). 6. A-t-il parlé de moi? 7. Êtes-vous mécontent de lui? 8. Qu'est-ce qu'elle pense d'eux? 9. Est-il chez lui? 10. Miss Smith est-elle chez elle? 11. Non, elle est allée chez sa couturière. 12. Est-ce que vous êtes venu de chez vous? 13. Je l'ai fait moi-même. 14. L'avez-vous fait vous-même? 15. Dites-lui de le faire lui-même. 16. Avez-vous quelque chose pour eux (or elles)? 17. Mon ami et moi. 18. Qui a faim? Moi. 19. Qui avez-vous vu? Lui. 20. Ces crayons ne sont pas à vous; ils sont à Madeleine.

### Lesson Twenty-six

#### I

1. reçus. 2. vint. 3. répondirent. 4. visitèrent. 5. allâmes. 6. ouvrit, j'entrai. 7. fit. 8. écrivirent. 9. répondit. 10. finit.

#### II

1. They did not answer us. 2. He arrived in the evening. 3. She gave me her ticket. 4. They selected some elegant frocks. 5. He cut the bread. 6. She sang while I played. 7. She was singing when he entered. 8. When I was in Paris I visited the Opera. 9. They gave the poor woman money. 10. The door of the room was opened.

#### III

1. Ils ne nous ont pas répondu. 2. Il est arrivé le soir. 3. Elle m'a donné son billet. 4. Elles ont choisi des robes élégantes. 5. Il a coupé le pain. 6. Elle a chanté pendant que j'ai joué. 7. Elle chantait quand je suis entré. 8. Quand j'étais à Paris j'ai visité l'Opéra. 9. Elles ont donné de l'argent à la pauvre femme. 10. La porte de la chambre a été ouverte.

#### IV

1. Il y en a beaucoup. 2. Je n'y ai pas encore été, or je n'y suis pas encore allé. 3. Ils vont voir " Le Malade Imaginaire." 4. On la joue à la Comédie Française. 5. Ils ont des places au parterre. 6. Elle l'y laisse. 7. Une ouvreuse les y conduit. 8. Parce qu'on l'appelle "Monsieur". 9. Ils en étaient très contents. 10. Ils se sont promenés au foyer.

---

### AROUND THE TOWN

#### Les Halles Centrales

Les Halles Centrales de Paris, où l'on vend en gros (wholesale) presque tout ce qui est mangeable, offrent du crépuscule jusqu'à l'aube, un spectacle des plus pittoresques. Ce qui attire surtout les curieux, ce sont les restaurants du marché qui restent ouverts toute la nuit. On ne peut pas s'appeler un vrai parisien, si l'on n'a pas mangé une soupe à l'oignon chez le Père Tranquille, à quatre heures du matin.

#### Paris Central Markets

The Halles Centrales or Central Markets of Paris, which deal in pretty nearly everything eatable, offer a lively picture from dusk till dawn. The attraction for many visitors is the market restaurants, which remain open all night. You cannot call yourself a real Parisian unless you have eaten a soupe à l'oignon at the Père Tranquille, at four o'clock in the morning.

---

#### JEU DE MOTS

*Réflexion mélancolique d'un mari :*— Avant mon mariage, ma femme m'était chère et j'étais son trésor. . . . Mais, maintenant, elle m'est plus chère encore, et je suis son trésorier.

**Jeu de mots,** play with words, pun ; un **mari,** husband; **un trésor,** treasure; un **trésorier,** treasurer.

# VINGT-SEPTIÈME LEÇON

### READY FOR THE JOURNEY

When you know that Grandpa Lesage can be called **un vieillard** (old man), what you have learned in previous lessons should enable you to describe everything and everybody in this picture. If not, you should regard it as a "Stop!" notice, and go back for further study to earlier lessons where these words are encountered.

### PROJETS DE VOYAGE—TRAVELLING PLANS

**Monsieur et Madame Lesage ont décidé d'aller passer les vacances au bord de la mer,**
M. and Mme Lesage have decided to spend the holidays at the seaside,

**et pour que tout marche bien ils arrangent tous les**
and in order that everything may go well, they arrange all the

**détails à l'avance.**
details beforehand.

**Mme Lesage :** **Puisque grand-père et grand'mère Lesage veulent bien nous**
As grandfather and grandmother Lesage wish to come with us,

    **accompagner, nous serons six.**
    we shall be six.

**M. Lesage :** **Ce qui nous permettra d'obtenir un billet de famille, et de**
This will enable us to obtain a family ticket, and to

    **voyager à prix réduit et aussi plus confortablement, puisque nous**
    travel at a reduced price, and also more comfortably, as we

ROUEN: RUE DE LA GROSSE HORLOGE

Cette ancienne horloge, chef-d'œuvre de l'art horloger, surmonte l'arche de la rue à laquelle elle donne son nom. Jeanne d'Arc fut brûlée près de là.

| **Chef-d'œuvre** (m.) (pron. sheh-dâyvr) | **surmonter** | **arche** (f.) | **brûler** |
|---|---|---|---|
| Masterpiece; outstanding achievement | to surmount | arch | to burn |

**aurons un compartiment pour nous seuls.**
shall have a compartment entirely to ourselves.

Georges :   **Et notre oncle, notre tante et nos deux cousins, que vont-**
And uncle, aunt and our two cousins—what are they

**ils faire?  Je crois qu'ils aimeraient aussi aller au bord**
going to do?  I think they would also like to go to the seaside

**de la mer durant leur séjour en France.  Cela me ferait**
during their stay in France.  It would give me great

**plaisir de les conduire en auto à Dieppe.  J'aurais pu emmener**
pleasure to drive them by car to Dieppe.  I could take at

**au moins cinq personnes.  Je pensais que nous pourrions passer**
least five persons.  I thought we could go

**par Rouen afin de visiter la magnifique**
via Rouen so that we could visit the beautiful

**cathédrale gothique.**
Gothic cathedral.

Mme Lesage :  **En voilà une bonne idée.  Et quand ils reviendront avec Lucie**
That's a very good idea.  And when they return with Lucie

**de leur visite au Jardin Zoologique nous discuterons**
from their visit to the Zoological Gardens we will discuss

**le projet avec eux.**
the plan with them.

Grand'mère :  **Je crois les entendre maintenant.**
I think I hear them coming now.

**(La porte s'ouvre, et Mme Roberts, Madeleine, Charles, et Lucie Lesage entrent.)**
(The door opens, and Mrs. Roberts, Madeleine, Charles, and Lucie Lesage enter
the room.)

Charles :  **Nous voilà, grand'maman.  Nous nous sommes amusés follement.**
Here we are, grandmama.  We have had such a marvellous time.

**Ma sœur et moi, nous sommes montés sur un éléphant.**
My sister and I, we mounted an elephant.

**Madeleine avait très peur comme toutes les petites filles,**
Madeleine was very frightened like all little girls,

**mais pas moi!**
but not me!

## PARIS: LE JARDIN D'ACCLIMATATION

En haut, la cacahuète qu'offre le petit garçon ne constitue guère une ripaille pour le grand pachyderme. En bas, les lions ont l'air d'écouter comme des écoliers sages le discours du dompteur. Les spectateurs peuvent bien sourire parce qu'un fossé les sépare des lions.

| Cacahuète (f.) | ripaille (f.) | pachyderme (m.) | écolier | dompteur-euse (m.f.) |
|---|---|---|---|---|
| Peanut; monkey-nut | feast | pachyderm, elephant | pupil | tamer |

**Mme Roberts :** Tais-toi, Charles!   Si tu te vantes comme ça, je ne te sortirai
Be quiet, Charles!  If you boast like that, I shall not take you out

plus.   .   **Georges :** Écoutez bien, ma tante.   Cela vous ferait-il
again.                Listen, auntie.   Would you like to go to

**plaisir d'aller tous en auto à Dieppe en passant par**
Dieppe by car by way of Rouen where we could

**Rouen où nous pourrions visiter la cathédrale?   La voiture peut**
visit the Cathedral?   The car can

**contenir cinq personnes, y compris moi, si cela ne vous fait rien**
take five people, including myself, if you don't mind being

**d'être un peu serrés à l'arrière.   Les autres pourront prendre**
rather squashed at the back.   The rest can go by

**le train, et comme vous êtes si nombreux, vous pouvez**
train, and as there are so many of you, you will be able to

**voyager à prix réduit.**
travel at a reduced rate.

**M. Roberts :**   **Très bonne idée, et je propose que les grand-parents, vos**
That is a very good idea, and I suggest that your grandparents,

**parents et moi voyagions par chemin de fer et que les autres**
your father and mother and I, travel by rail, and the rest

**partent en auto avec Georges demain.   (Tous sont d'accord.)**
go with George by car to-morrow.   (All agree.)

### PETITES HISTOIRES
These little stories in French are intended to test your knowledge.   Words which you cannot be expected to know are translated.   Other examples are given elsewhere.

### IL CHERCHAIT UN GRATTE-CIEL!
Quel est le prix de vos chambres, monsieur le gérant?
Cent vingt francs au premier étage, cent au second, quatre-vingts au troisième et cinquante au quatrième.
Merci, et excusez-moi de vous avoir dérangé inutilement, mais votre hôtel n'est pas assez haut pour moi.

### AUX TROPIQUES
Et qu'est-ce que vous faites contre les microbes?
Eh bien, d'abord je fais bouillir l'eau.
Ah! et puis?
Et puis je la stérilise.
Très bien, et puis?
Et puis je bois de la bière!

### IL ENTRAIT EN FRAPPANT
Comment avez-vous connu votre second mari?
Il a écrasé mon premier dans un accident d'auto.

Aux Tropiques means "In the Tropics"; écraser (in this sense) means "to run over," and stériliser you can guess from the English word, which is spelt like it.

### English

1. Two-seater open tourer with dickey; 2. Studded pedestrian crossing; 3. Bicycle carrier; 4. Lorry; 5. Cyclist; 6. "No Parking" sign; 7. Limousine with sliding roof; 8. Driver's mirror; 9. Windscreen wiper; 10. Headlights; 11. Bumpers; 12. Number-plate; 13. Motor-cyclist; 14. Drophead coupé; 15. Spare wheel; 16. Mudguard; 17. Running board; 18. Back wheel; 19. Window; 20. Bonnet; 21. Petrol pump; 22. "Have Your Air Tested"; 23. Garage hand; 24. Front wheel; 25. Tyre; 26. Radiator; 27. Radiator fan; 28. Distributor; 29. Cylinder head; 30. Carburettor; 31. Air filter; 32. Jack; 33. Valves; 34. Steering column; 35. Gear box; 36. Gear lever; 37. Steering wheel; 38. Front seat; 39. Door; 40. Back seat.

### French

1. Torpédo (f.) à deux places avec spider; 2. Passage (m.) clouté; 3. Bicyclette (f.) de livreur; 4. Camion (m.); 5. Cycliste (m. or

## LA RUE ET L'AUTO

); 6. "Stationnement (m.) Défendu"[1];
7. Limousine (f.) à toit découvrable; 8.
Miroir (m.) rétroviseur; 9. Essuie-glaces
(m.); 10. Phares (m.); projecteurs (m.);
11. Pare-chocs (m.); 12. Numéro (m.) de
police; 13. Motocycliste (m. or f.); 14.
Coupé (m.) à capote rabattable; 15. Roue
(f.) de secours; 16. Pare-boue (m.); 17.
Marchepied (m.); 18. Roue arrière (or
d'arrière); 19. Glace (f.); 20. Capot (m.);

21. Pompe (f.) à essence; 22. "Vérifiez la
pression de vos pneus"; 23. Garagiste (m.);
employé (m.) de garage; 24. Roue d'avant;
25. Pneumatique (m.); 26. Radiateur (m);
27. Ventilateur (m.); 28. Distributeur (m.)
d'allumage; 29. Culasse (f.); 30. Carburateur (m.); 31. Épurateur (m.) d'air; 32.
Lève-auto (m.); 33. Soupapes (f. pl.); 34.
Colonne (f.) de direction; 35. Boîte (f.) de
vitesses; 36. Levier (m.) des vitesses; 37.
Volant (m.); 38. Siège (m.) d'avant;
39. Portière (f.); 40. Siège d'arrière.

---

Indicated by letter "P" with stroke through it.

## MOTORING TERMS

| | |
|---|---|
| **la corne**   hooter | **un parc à autos**   parking-place |
| **corner**   to hoot | **le garage**   garage |
| **allumer**   to switch on (*lights*) | **remiser**   to garage |
| **éteindre**   to switch off | **la panne**   breakdown |
| **doubler**   to overtake | **la réparation**   repair |
| **croiser**   to pass (*in opposite direction*) | **la carrosserie**   body |
| **parquer**   to park | **le châssis**   chassis |
| **glisser, déraper**   to skid | **le moteur**   engine |

## ADVERBS

**Il fait terriblement froid**
    It is terribly cold
**C'est certainement une erreur**
    That is certainly an error
**Il travaille énormément**
    He works very hard
**Elle joue rarement**
    She rarely plays
**Je l'ai totalement oublié**
    I completely forgot it
**Ils viendront immédiatement**
    They will come immediately
**Je l'ai trouvé, heureusement**
    I found it, fortunately
**Je l'ai perdu, malheureusement**
    I lost it, unfortunately
**Il me l'a dit distinctement**
    He clearly said it to me
**Elle marche gracieusement**
    She walks gracefully
**Il parle sérieusement**
    He speaks seriously

The ending **-ment** corresponds to the English adverbial ending "-*ly*"; it is added to the feminine of the adjective. If the masculine adjective ends with a vowel **-ment** is added to the masculine.

**Le professeur est distrait**
    The professor is absent-minded

**Il traverse la rue distraitement**
    He crosses the road absent-mindedl

---

## LES ENFANTS ! . . .

Un dîner de cérémonie. La petite Sophie, huit ans, interpelle son grand-père:
Grand-papa . . .

Mais le grand-papa interrompt:
Les petites filles doivent se taire et écouter.

A la fin du repas le grand-père, devenu bienveillant, interroge l'enfant:

Que me voulais-tu, mon enfant? Parl maintenant.

Trop tard: il y avait une mouche dans votr salade et vous l'avez mangée.

**Interpeller** means "to address", **inter rompre** "to interrupt", **se taire** "to b silent", **bienveillant** "kind, benignant", an **interroger** "to question".

| Masculine | Feminine | | Adverb | |
|---|---|---|---|---|
| heureux | heureuse | happy, fortunate | heureusement | happily, fortunately |
| malheureux | malheureuse | unhappy, unfortunate | malheureusement | unfortunately |
| poli | polie | polite | poliment | politely |
| fier | fière | proud | fièrement | proudly |
| distrait | distraite | absent-minded | distraitement | absent-mindedly |
| sage | sage | wise | sagement | wisely |
| franc | franche | frank | franchement | frankly |
| lent | lente | slow | lentement | slowly |
| doux | douce | sweet | doucement | sweetly |
| triste | triste | sad | tristement | sadly |
| énorme | énorme | enormous | énormément | enormously |
| patient | patiente | patient | patiemment | patiently |
| constant | constante | constant | constamment | constantly |
| évident | évidente | evident | évidemment | evidently |

Note that the last four of these adverbs are formed slightly irregularly.

### Comparison of Adverbs:

| Poliment | plus poliment |
|---|---|
| Politely | more politely |

le plus poliment
most politely

For the comparative, prefix **plus**, for the superlative, **le plus** (same as the comparison of Adjectives ; see page 130).

### Irregular Comparison:

| bien = well | mieux = better |
|---|---|
| peu = little | moins = less |
| beaucoup = much | plus = more |
| mal = ill, badly | pis or plus mal = worse |

le mieux = best
le moins = least
le plus = most
le pis or le plus mal = worst

Distinguish carefully between these irregular adverbs and the irregular adjectives :

### Adverb:

il parle bien = he speaks well
il parle mieux = he speaks better
il parle le mieux = he speaks best

### Adjective:

un bon vin = a good wine
un meilleur vin = a better wine
le meilleur vin = the best wine

### Adverb:

il parle mal = he speaks badly
il parle plus mal = he speaks worse
il parle le plus mal = he speaks worst

### Adjective:

une mauvaise organisation
        a bad organisation
une plus mauvaise organisation
        a worse organisation
la plus mauvaise organisation
        the worst organisation

### Position of Adverbs:

il neige souvent = it often snows
il a souvent neigé = it has often snowed

Adverbs are usually placed just after the verb, or in compound tenses after the auxiliary.

For emphasis, however, the adverb frequently stands at the beginning or end of the sentence, e.g. fièrement il me l'a montré or il me l'a montré fièrement = proudly he showed it to me.

## EXERCISES

**I Form adverbs from the following adjectives :**

1. joli. 2. premier. 3. long. 4. bon.
5. mauvais. 6. curieux. 7. général.
8. complet. 9. meilleur. 10. absolu.

### ROUEN: LA RUE DAMIETTE

Les façades, les toitures, les pignons—tout évoque le passé dans cette rue ancienne.

| **Façade** (f.) | **toiture** (f.) | **pignon** (m.) | **évoquer** |
|---|---|---|---|
| Front | roof, roofing | gable, gable-end | to evoke, to recall |

## II Translate into English

1. C'est un bon homme. 2. C'est le meilleur homme du monde. 3. Ce dîner est bien fait. 4. Il est mieux que celui d'hier. 5. Votre hôtel est meilleur que le mien. 6. Vous le faites mieux que lui. 7. C'est mon meilleur ami. 8. Il parle mieux le français que moi. 9. Elle parle très mal. 10. Il va plus mal ce matin. 11. Il est moins intelligent que son père. 12. J'ai extrêmement faim. 13. Il fait terriblement chaud. 14. Malheureusement je ne pouvais pas le trouver. 15. Évidemment il est gravement malade. 16. J'aime beaucoup le tennis, mais j'aime mieux le golf. 17. Hier elle se portait bien, mais aujourd'hui elle se porte plus mal. 18. Il parle peu, mais sa femme parle beaucoup moins. 19. J'ai fini mon travail. Tant mieux (so much the better) pour vous. 20. Il faut partir immédiatement.

## III Translate into French

1. I like this picture very much. 2. They are enormously rich. 3. She speaks better than her sister. 4. She is a very good girl; she always works well. 5. Unfortunately he has lost the book. So much the worse (tant pis) for him. 6. This is not his best book. 7. Do you like him better than her? 8. Did you sleep well? 9. You have written this letter badly. 10. Worse than ever. 11. Is your father better? 12. No, he is much worse than yesterday. 13. I am terribly thirsty. 14. Can you do it immediately? 15. Fortunately I am free at present. 16. He is generally at home from five to six. 17. Please speak more distinctly. 18. Unfortunately I did not find her at home. 19. He naturally thinks that you will come. 20. That is exactly my opinion. (*Key on pages* 334 *and* 335).

## CHAMONIX EN HIVER

À une allure vertigineuse, leurs bâtons de ski en l'air, les skieurs descendent la piste.

| | | | |
|---|---|---|---|
| **Allure** (f.) | **vertigineux-euse (adj.)** | **bâton** (m.) **de ski** | **piste** (f.) |
| Speed, gait, bearing | giddy, dizzy | skiing-stick | skiing-slope |

# VINGT-HUITIÈME LEÇON

## OFF TO THE SEASIDE

In this picture you see the Lesage children leaving by car for their visit to Rouen. You should now be able to describe in French other features shown in the illustration.

| **Encaisseur** | **bouche d'égout** | **bouche d'incendie** | **bébé** | **voiture d'enfant** |
|---|---|---|---|---|
| Bank messenger | drain cover | hydrant | baby | perambulator |

### A JOURNEY BY CAR

**(Les portières claquent; les autres Lesage et M. Roberts agitent des mouchoirs,**
(The doors slam; the other Lesages and Mr. Roberts wave their handkerchiefs,

**et voilà les enfants partis.   Charles est très intrigué par la voiture.**
and away the children go.   Charles is very much interested in the car.

**Il ne connaît jusqu'à présent que les automobiles anglaises.)**
Up to now he only knows English cars.)

**Charles :**     **Quelle est la marque de cette voiture?**
              What make is this car?

**Georges :**     **C'est une Renage.   Elle tient très bien la route, et les freins sont**
              It is a Renage.   It holds the road well, and the brakes are

              **très bons.   Regardez cette reprise.**
              very good.   Look how she responds.

**(Le compteur de vitesse commence à grimper d'une façon impressionnante:**
(The speedometer begins to mount in an alarming manner:

90—100—110—115 kilomètres par heure.)
approximately 56—63—69—72 miles an hour.)

**Mme Roberts :** Georges, pas si vite; vous savez que votre mère vous a demandé
Not so fast, George.  You know your mother asked you not

de ne pas dépasser le 100.
to exceed 100 (63 m.p.h.).

(Georges, jetant un coup d'œil dans le rétroviseur et s'apercevant
(George, giving a glance in the mirror and noticing that the three

que les trois passagers n'avaient pas l'air à l'aise, ralentit.  Il
passengers did not look very happy, slows down.   The

faisait très beau; on avait glissé le toit ouvrant vers l'arrière, et toutes
weather was very fine; they had pushed back the sunshine roof, and all

les glaces étaient baissées.  Mais voilà qu'en montant une côte un peu
the windows were down.   But just as they are climbing a rather

raide le moteur a une panne.  Georges descend et ouvre le capot.)
steep hill, the engine gives out.   Georges gets out and opens the bonnet.)

**Georges :**       Il doit y avoir une saleté dans le carburateur;
There must be some dirt in the carburettor;

je vais le démonter.
I shall take it to pieces.

(Georges sort un tournevis de la boîte à outils, et se met au travail.  Les deux
(George takes out a screwdriver from the tool-box, and sets to work.)   The two

garçons, appuyés côte à côte sur le garde-boue, nettoient bien vite les
boys, leaning side by side on the mudguard, quickly clean the different

différents gicleurs.  Georges vérifie le niveau de l'eau et essaie de mettre en marche;
jets.   George tests the water in the radiator and tries to get going;

enfin le moteur démarre.  Arrivant dans une petite ville, Georges
in the end the engine starts.   Arriving at a small town, George

hésite; la route n'est pas bien indiquée.  Il hèle une vieille dame.)
hesitates; the route is not very clearly indicated.   He hails an old lady.)

**Georges :**       Pour Rouen, s'il vous plaît, Madame?
Which is the way to Rouen, please?

**La vieille dame :** C'est tout droit, mon bon ami; et puis vous prendrez
Straight on, my boy; and then you take

**la deuxième à droite.**
the second to the right.

**Georges : Merci bien, madame.**
Thanks so much.

**(Le voyage se poursuit sans**
(The journey continues without

**autre encombre jusqu'à la tombée**
further hindrance until

**de la nuit. Ils arrivent à Rouen sans avoir**
nightfall. They arrive at Rouen without having

**besoin d'allumer les phares. C'est assez heureux,**
to use their headlights. This is rather lucky,

**car Georges s'aperçoit le lendemain que le feu rouge et la plaque**
as George notices next day that the red light and back number plate

**ne marchent pas. Ils se dirigent vers un très bon hôtel que leur avaient**
are not working. They make their way to a very good hotel which had been

**recommandé des amis. C'est là qu'ils passent la nuit.)**
recommended by their friends. There they pass the night.)

## MORE MOTORING TERMS

| | |
|---|---|
| **conduire** (*je conduis, il conduit, nous conduisons, j'ai conduit*) to drive | **mettre en marche** to start the engine |
| **tenir le volant** to take the wheel | **mettre en première (deuxième) vitesse** to put in first (*second*) gear |
| **le conducteur** the driver | **la vitesse** speed |
| **le permis de conduire** driving licence | **accélérer** to accelerate |
| **le permis de circulation** car licence | **ralentir** to slow down |
| **l'essence** petrol | **freiner** to brake |

### TO, AT, IN (A PLACE, ETC.)

| | | | | |
|---|---|---|---|---|
| **La France** | = France | **en France** | = | to *or* in France |
| **La Grande-Bretagne** | = Great Britain | **en Grande-Bretagne** | = | to *or* in Great Britain |
| **l'Angleterre** | = England | **en Angleterre** | = | to *or* in England |
| **La Belgique** | = Belgium | **en Belgique** | = | to *or* in Belgium |
| **La Suisse** | = Switzerland | **en Suisse** | = | to *or* in Switzerland |
| **La Russie** | = Russia | **en Russie** | = | to *or* in Russia |
| **La Bretagne** | = Britanny | **en Bretagne** | = | to *or* in Britanny |
| **La Normandie** | = Normandy | **en Normandie** | = | to *or* in Normandy |
| **L'Écosse** | = Scotland | **en Écosse** | = | to *or* in Scotland |
| **L'Irlande** | = Ireland | **en Irlande** | = | to *or* in Ireland |
| **L'Allemagne** | = Germany | **en Allemagne** | = | to *or* in Germany |
| **L'Italie** | = Italy | **en Italie** | = | to *or* in Italy |
| **L'Europe** | = Europe | **en Europe** | = | to *or* in Europe |

| | | | | |
|---|---|---|---|---|
| L'Amérique | = America | en Amérique | = to *or* in America |
| L'Asie | = Asia | en Asie | = to *or* in Asia |
| Le Japon | = Japan | au Japon | = to *or* in Japan |
| Le Danemark | = Denmark | au Danemark | = to *or* in Denmark |
| Le Portugal | = Portugal | au Portugal | = to *or* in Portugal |
| Le Brésil | = Brazil | au Brésil | = to *or* in Brazil |
| Les États-Unis | = United States | aux États-Unis | = to *or* in the U.S.A. |
| Les Indes | = India | aux Indes | = to *or* in India |

The names of all the continents and of most countries are Feminine. . . . With the names of countries and continents, **en** is used for "*in*" or "*to*"; but if the name is Masculine, **au** (or **aux**) is used.

| | | |
|---|---|---|
| à Paris | = | in, to *or* at Paris |
| à Londres | = | in, to *or* at London |
| à Douvres | = | in, to *or* at Dover |
| au Havre | = | in, to *or* at Le Havre |
| à La Haye | = | in, to *or* at The Hague |

With the names of towns, **à** = "*in*", "*to*", or "*at*". In some cases (e.g. **Le Havre**, **La Haye**) the definite article forms part of the name of the town.

**à l'école** =
   at school *or* to school

**à la campagne** =
   in the country *or* to the country

**à l'Hôtel de Ville** =
   at the Town Hall *or* to the Town Hall

**dans le nord de l'Angleterre** =
   in the north of England

**dans tous les pays** =
   in all countries

**dans la pharmacie** =
   in the chemist's shop (comp. **chez le pharmacien** = at the chemist's)

**je partirai dans trois minutes** =
   I shall leave in three minutes

**Dans**, meaning "*within*" or "*inside*", is more definite than **en** or **à**.

**Ils vont au théâtre**          **Ils sont au théâtre**

Note that **à** is equivalent to "*on*" in the following expressions:—

**aller à pied**=to go on foot
**aller à cheval**=to go on horseback
**aller à bicyclette**=to ride on a bicycle, etc.

Note also:—

| | |
|---|---|
| **aller en auto** | = to go by car |
| **aller en chemin de fer** | = to go by rail |
| **aller en bateau** | = to go by boat |
| **aller en autocar** | = to go by coach |

Elles vont à l'église

Elles sont à l'église

Il est à la poste

Il est dans (or à) la poste

## EXERCISES

### I   Translate into English

Versailles est près de Paris. De Paris à Versailles il y a dix-huit kilomètres. Quelle est la distance de Paris au Havre? Le Havre est à 288 kilomètres de Paris. Du Havre on peut aller en bateau à New York. Combien de jours faut-il pour aller d'Europe en Amérique? Environ (=about) cinq ou six jours. Combien d'heures faut-il pour aller de Paris au Havre? De trois à quatre heures. Voici un indicateur. Il y a un express qui part à midi trente. Un rapide part de Paris à sept heures. A cinq heures de l'après-midi il y a un train omnibus (slow train). Mais il est très lent (slow); il s'arrête à toutes les gares.

## II Translate into French

1. Is Versailles far from Paris? 2. Do you live far from here? 3. Our house is five minutes from here; we live near the church. 4. How far is it from here to the station? 5. About three kilometres; half an hour on foot. 6. Will you go by boat or by train? 7. How many hours does it take to go from here to the seaside? 8. Is there an express train in the morning? 9. There is only a slow train. It stops at all stations. 10. Are there no fast trains? 11. The best train is a fast train which leaves at noon and arrives at 8.35 p.m. 12. It stops only twice. (*Key on page* 335.)

## DIEPPE: ANCIENNE ET MODERNE

Tout change dans ce monde-ci, et la forteresse sur la colline fut érigée en 1435 comme défense contre les Anglais, qui luttaient à cette époque sous le commandement du duc de Bedford pour établir les droits de succession de leur roi Henri VI au trône de France.

De nos jours les ennemis d'autrefois sont devenus de bons amis et c'est une invasion d'une autre sorte qui menace Dieppe, puisque des milliers d'Anglais vont chaque année en pélerinage à Dieppe. Les hôtels qui longent la plage sont pour la plupart occupés par des touristes anglais, venant chercher la santé et le repos.

Derrière les hôtels modernes, on entrevoit la vieille ville avec sa cathédrale.

| Colline (f.) | ériger | lutter | pélerinage (m.) | longer | santé (f.) | repos (m.) |
|---|---|---|---|---|---|---|
| Hillock | to erect | to struggle | pilgrimage | to lie along | health | rest |

# VINGT-NEUVIÈME LEÇON

## AT THE SWIMMING POOL

A swimming pool vocabulary is on page 314.   Study this in conjunction with the other vocabularies contained in this lesson, until you are able to make out your own list in French of the things shown and what everyone in this picture is wearing or doing.

### AU BORD DE LA MER—AT THE SEASIDE

**Les Lesage avaient décidé avec les Roberts de prendre un appartement**
The Lesages had decided with the Roberts to take furnished rooms

**meublé à Dieppe.   Cela revient bien meilleur marché que d'aller à l'hôtel.**
at Dieppe.   This comes much cheaper than going to a hotel.

**Le premier jour, tandis que Mme Roberts est occupée à déballer les vêtements et**
On the first day, while Mrs. Roberts is busy unpacking their clothes and

**à les ranger, la jeunesse va faire un tour du côté de**
putting them away, the youngsters go off to take a turn in the direction of

**la plage.**
the beach.

**Madeleine :**     **Quel dommage!   Nous n'avons pas encore nos maillots de bain.**
                 What a pity!   We have not got our bathing costumes yet.

                 **Nous aurions pu aller jouer sur la plage et nous baigner.**
                 We should have been able to play on the beach and to bathe.

**Lucie :**  **Nous irons cet après-midi.   Il y aura plus de place, car la**
We will go this afternoon.   There will be more room, as the

**marée sera basse.**
tide will be low.

**Charles :**  **Regardez le grand bateau tout là-bas à l'horizon.   Je me**
Look at the big boat right over there on the horizon.   I

**demande où il va.**
wonder where she is going.

**Georges :**  **Ce doit être le bateau qui vient d'Angleterre.   Il y a un**
It must be the boat coming from England.   There is a

**service de jour et un service de nuit.**
day and night service.

**Charles :**  **Moi, j'aime mieux aller de jour.   On peut au moins se promener**
I prefer to go by day.   One can at least walk about

**sur le pont et voir ce qui se passe.**
on the deck and see what is going on.

**Madeleine :**  **Oh, regardez le petit chalutier qui sort du port.**
Oh, look at the little trawler going out of the harbour.

**Lucie :**  **Il est d'une jolie couleur brune.   Je pense qu'il part**
It is a very pretty brown colour.   I think it is going

**à la pêche.**    **Georges : Demandons à ce vieux pêcheur quels**
fishing.                    Let us ask this old fisherman what

## AT THE BATHING BEACH

By carefully memorising the French names of everything shown in this picture, as set out on page 313, in conjunction with the Swimming Pool vocabulary on page 314, you can equip yourself for your next seaside holiday in France. Now that you are at an advanced stage of the Course, and should be in possession of a sound knowledge of colloquial French, this seems an object well worth while. Therefore, we leave it to you to study the vocabularies until you feel that you could name anything here in French, and become a happy (and vocal) member of the cheerful crowd on the sea front of this typical holiday resort.

**poissons on prend ici.**
fish they catch here.

**(Le vieil homme était assis sur le rebord de pierre de la promenade et**
(The old man was seated on the stone edge of the esplanade and

**reparait des filets.)**
was mending some nets.)

Georges :     **Pardon, monsieur.   Quels sont les poissons que l'on pêche**
Excuse me.   What fish are caught in this

**par ici?        Le vieux pêcheur (souriant) : Vous voulez donc**
neighbourhood?                (smiling) : So you want to

**devenir pêcheurs.   C'est un rude métier.   Eh bien, il y a des bateaux**
become fishermen.   It is a hard calling.   Well, some boats are

**qui vont pêcher le hareng dans la mer du Nord, et**
going to fish for herring in the North Sea, and

**d'autres la morue du côté de Terre-Neuve.**
others to catch cod near Newfoundland.

Madeleine :     **C'est loin cela!**
That is a long way!

Le pêcheur :     **Mais oui, c'est loin, ma petite fille.   Je vois que tu**
Yes, it is a long way, my little lass.   I see that you

**sais déjà bien ta géographie.**
know your geography well already.

Georges :     **Nous, nous nous contenterons de pêcher la crevette et**
Well, we will content ourselves with catching shrimps and

**la moule, si toutefois il y en a.**
mussels, if there happen to be any.

Le pêcheur :     **Oui, vous en trouverez facilement.**
Yes, you'll find some easily.

Lucie :     **Il y en a même à déjeuner aujourd'hui.**
There are even some for lunch to-day.

Georges :     **Et comme les autres seront probablement déjà arrivés,**
And as the others will have probably arrived by now,

**rentrons vite.**                **Charles : Ça c'est une bonne idée, car**
let's go back quickly.                That is a good idea, for

**j'ai une faim de loup.**
I am famishing.

**Ils restaient deux semaines au bord de la mer.**    **Deux fois par jour,**
They stayed for two weeks at the seaside.    Twice a day

**ils se baignaient.**    **Après le deuxième bain ils jouaient au tennis ou**
they bathed.    After the second bathe they played tennis or

**allaient sur la jetée pour voir le départ des pêcheurs.**    **Charles s'amusait**
went on the pier to see the departure of the fishermen.    Charles amused himself

**à construire des châteaux de sable.**    **Le soir on admirait le coucher du soleil,**
by building sand-castles.    In the evening they admired the sunset,

**ou dansait tandis que leurs parents risquaient quelques francs**
or danced while their parents risked some francs

**dans les salles de jeu du casino.**
in the gaming room of the casino.

### AU CASINO

En plein ou à cheval, pair ou impair?    Madame semble trouver le choix difficile.

| **En plein** | **à cheval** | **pair, impair** (adj.) |
|---|---|---|
| All out on one number | stake divided between two numbers | even, odd |

## CÔTÉ

**le côté** side, direction, way, part

**d'un côté, de l'autre côté** on the one hand, on the other hand

**à côté** close by, beside

**de ce côté-ci** on this side

**de ce côté-là** on that side

**de quel côté est la gare?** whereabout is the station?

**du côté de Paris** towards (*in the direction of*) Paris

**venez de ce côté** come this way; come on this side

**la maison est tout à côté** the house is quite near

**à côté de** by the side of, next to

**il habite à côté de nous** he lives next door to us

**de mon côté** on my side; for my part

N.B.—la côte (koht)=the coast or the rib, or the hill.

### AU BORD DE LA MER—AT THE SEASIDE

**la mer** sea

**la plage** beach

**le brise-lames** breakwater

**la jetée** pier

**la tente** tent

**la cabine de plage** bathing cabin

**la cabine roulante** bathing machine

**le poste de sauvetage** life-saving station

**la bouée de sauvetage** life-buoy

**la ceinture de natation** cork-jacket

**le canot** rowing-boat

**l'ombrelle (f.)** sunshade

**le peignoir de bain** bathing wrap

**le maillot de bain** bathing suit

**la serviette de bain** bathing towel

**le soulier de bain** bathing shoe

**le bonnet de bain** bathing cap

**le caleçon de bain** bathing slip

**la vague** wave

**le banc de sable** sandbank

**la mouette** sea-gull

**la promenade (le quai)** promenade (front)

**le kiosque à musique** bandstand

**un hôtel** hotel

**le casino** casino

### LA NAGE—SWIMMING

**le crawl** crawl (free style)

**la nage sur le côté** overarm stroke

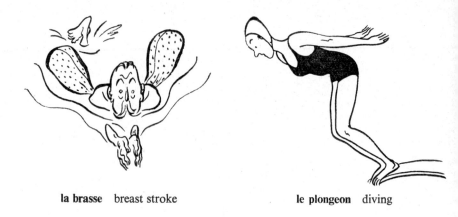

**la brasse**   breast stroke      **le plongeon**   diving

**la nage sur le dos**   back stroke

## LA PISCINE—SWIMMING BATH

**le bain de soleil**   sun-bathing
**la cabine de bain**   dressing cubicle
**la douche**   shower-bath
**le bassin de natation**   swimming pool
**le professeur de natation** swimming instructor
**le tremplin**   diving board
**la glissoire**   water-chute

**la bête en caoutchouc**   rubber animal
**le nageur**   swimmer
**le caleçon de bain**   bathing-slip
**la nageuse**   swimmer (*woman*)
**le costume de bain**   bathing costume
**le bonnet de bain**   bathing cap
**le peignoir de bain**   bathing wrap

### ON

**On dit qu'il est riche**=They say he is rich.
**On vous demande au téléphone**=
     You are wanted on the phone.
**On frappe**=Someone is knocking.
**On sonne**=The bell is ringing.
**On voit la mer d'ici**=
     The sea can be seen from here.

**Où peut-on trouver cela?**=
     Where can one find that?

**On cultive beaucoup de vignes en France**=
     Vines are much grown in France

**Que dit-on dans le journal?**
     What do they say in the paper?

**DIEPPE: ARRIVEE DU PAQUEBOT**

Dans ce tohu-bohu, les stewards arrivent quand même à dénicher les bagages de leurs patrons de passage.

| | | | |
|---|---|---|---|
| **Tohu-bohu (m.)** | **arriver à (faire quelque chose)** | **dénicher** | **de passage** |
| Hurly-burly, muddle | to succeed in (doing something). | to ferret out | temporary |

**On** is much more widely used than its English equivalent *"one"*. It is employed as a general term meaning *"people"*, *"some one"*, *"you and I"*; it is also used instead of the English passive voice. The sentence *"French is spoken here"* is in the so-called Passive Voice. In French this is rendered in the Active Voice, by using **on: Ici on parle français.** There is also a Passive form of French verbs, but it is used less frequently than the English Passive, so that we can deal with it at a later stage of this course. In the meantime use **on** and the Active Voice.

## WORDS DENOTING A QUANTITY

**Un peu d'eau**=a little water
**beaucoup de viande**=much meat
**peu de chiens**=few dogs
**beaucoup de Français**=many Frenchmen
**combien d'argent**=how much money
**combien de chevaux**=how many horses
**trop de sucre**=too much sugar
**trop de gens**=too many people
**plus de café**=more coffee
**moins de chocolat**=less chocolate
**moins de cigarettes**=fewer cigarettes
**Je n'ai pas autant d'argent que lui**=I have not so much money as he.

**J'ai autant de cartes que lui**=I have as many cards as he.
**Vous avez eu assez de vin**=You have had enough wine.
**C'est quelque chose de nouveau**=That is something new.
**Il a bu plus de six verres**=He has drunk more than six glasses.
**Vous avez travaillé moins de trois heures**= You worked less than three hours.

Note that words denoting a quantity, like *"much"*, *"little"*, *"more"*, *"less"*, etc., are followed by **de.**

## ADVERBS OF QUANTITY

**beaucoup de**=much, many, a great deal of;    **peu de**=little, few;

**trop de**=too much, too many;    **beaucoup trop de**=far too much (many);

**plus de**=more;    **beaucoup plus de**=much more;    **moins de**=less;

**beaucoup moins de**=much less, far less; **assez de**=enough; **tant** or **autant de**=so much, so many.

## ADVERBS IN COMPARISON

**aussi . . . que**=as . . . as . . . (**si . . . que**, often used in negative sentences instead of **aussi . . . que**); **autant que**=as much as, so much as; **plus que**=more than; **moins que**=less than.

When there is no Comparison:
**J'ai lu plus de vingt pages**=I read more than twenty pages.
**Il a écrit moins de deux pages**=He wrote less than two pages.

## ADVERBS OF MANNER

**bien**=well
**très bien, fort bien**=very well
**assez bien**=fairly well

**mieux**=better
**bien mieux**=rather better
**beaucoup mieux**=much better

**mal**=badly
**assez mal**=rather badly
**beaucoup plus mal**=much worse

**vite**=fast, quickly
**presque**=almost
**davantage**=more

## LA GLACE À LA FRAISE (VANILLE)—STRAWBERRY (VANILLA) ICECREAM

1. Paul a beaucoup de glace.
2. Gustave a moins de glace que Paul, mais il en a assez.
3. Richard a assez de glace.
4. Gaston n'a pas autant de glace que Richard.
5. Robert a peu de glace.
6. André n'a pas de glace du tout (*at all*).
7. Charles a trop de glace.
8. Georges a autant de glace que Paul.

### SI

1. Il n'est pas venu?=He has not come?
   Si, monsieur=Yes, sir, he has.
   N'est-il pas venu?=Has he not come?
   Si! il est venu=Yes, he has come.
   si="Yes" in answer to a negative or interrogative negative.

2. Je suis si heureux de vous voir=I am so glad to see you.
   Il n'est pas si intelligent que son frère= He is not so intelligent as his brother
   si=so

3. Si vous le cherchez, vous le trouverez=If you look for it you will find it.
   Si je l'avais su, je vous l'aurais dit=If I had known it, I would have told it to you.
   Je le ferai, si j'ai le temps=I shall do it, if I have time.
   S'il fait beau demain, nous irons au bord de la mer=If it's fine to-morrow we shall go to the seaside.

S'il vient vous lui direz de m'attendre= If he comes, tell him to wait for me.

Si vous étiez à ma place, le feriez-vous?= If you were in my place, would you do it?

Si vous me donniez le livre, je serais très heureux=If you gave me the book, I should be very glad.

## *EXERCISES*

**I Answer the following questions in French (referring to the top of this page)**

1. Paul a-t-il de la glace? 2. Gustave a-t-il autant de glace que Paul? 3. Richard a-t-il beaucoup de glace? 4. Robert en a-t-il assez? 5. André a-t-il de la glace? 6. Charles a-t-il autant de glace que Paul? 7. Qui en a le plus? 8. Qui en a le moins? 9. Qui n'en a pas? 10. Qui a trop de glace?

## II Translate into English

1. Combien de personnes y aura-t-il chez vous? 2. Avez-vous autant d'argent que Rockefeller? 3. Je n'ai pas assez d'argent. 4. Voulez-vous donner un peu d'argent à ce pauvre garçon? 5. Il y avait trop de personnes chez lui. 6. J'ai bu autant que lui. 7. J'ai tant travaillé que je suis fatigué. 8. Vous ne travaillez pas assez. 9. Il ne parle pas autant qu'elle. 10. Ne fumez pas tant. 11. Il ne fume pas beaucoup. Si, il fume beaucoup. 12. Est-ce qu'ils boivent beaucoup? 13. Non, pas beaucoup. 14. Ces moules (=mussels) sont-elles fraîches? Je pense bien (=I should say so).

## III Translate into French

1. You are not eating enough vegetables. 2. There will be too many people. 3. You are drinking too much beer. 4. You have given too much meat to my son. 5. Will there be enough wine? 6. He is not reading enough. 7. I read more than three hours. 8. How many letters have you written? 9. You had not so much appetite as your brother. 10. You did not work? Why yes, I did. 11. She does not smoke very much. 12. You are not writing enough exercises. 13. If you will go to bed now I shall leave. 14. If he pays me, I shall pay you. 15. If he comes, tell him that I am waiting for him. (*Key on pages* 335 *and* 336.)

## LYON: HÔTEL DE VILLE ET FONTAINE

Lyon, deuxième cité de France et chef-lieu du Département du Rhône, est le centre d'une région industrielle. La ville, renommée pour ses soieries et notoire par son climat pluvieux, est située au confluent du Rhône avec la Saône.

| Chef-lieu (m.) | renommé -e(adj.) | soierie (f.) | notoire (adj.) |
|---|---|---|---|
| Chief town of Dept. | famous, celebrated | silk-trade | notorious |

Note that Lyon is spelt in French without final "s."

# TRENTIÈME LEÇON

### CHARLES HAS AN ACCIDENT

When you have studied the lesson, you will find out the why and the wherefore of the accident. Charles has ignored an important French traffic rule. In case you think of taking your bike to France, you must regard this picture as a warning.

### CHEZ LE PHARMACIEN—AT THE CHEMIST'S

**Monsieur Roberts n'a pas pu passer toutes les vacances avec sa famille. Il**
Mr. Roberts was not able to spend all the holidays with his family. He

**a dû rentrer pour affaires à Londres. Bonne aubaine pour Charles,**
was obliged to return to London on business. This was great luck for Charles,

**qui n'ose pas faire trop de bêtises en présence de son père.**
who does not dare to do so many stupid things in his father's presence.

**Charles a en effet très envie d'emprunter la bicyclette de Jean,**
Charles is in fact very keen on borrowing the bicycle of Jean,

**fils du concierge, pour aller faire un petit tour. Dès le départ de son père,**
the porter's son, to go for a little ride. As soon as his father has gone,

**il va trouver Jean, qui consent à lui prêter son vélo moyennant**
he goes to find Jean, who consents to lend him his bike in exchange for

**quelques billes. Charles, au comble de la joie, grimpe sur la**
some marbles. Charles, very thrilled, jumps on the

**machine et se met à pédaler de toutes ses forces.    Malheureusement, au détour**
machine, and goes pedalling off at a great rate.    Unfortunately, at a turn

**du chemin, il voit une automobile se diriger droit sur lui.    Les freins ne sont**
of the road, he sees a car coming straight for him.    The brakes are not

**pas assez bons, et sa machine s'écrase contre le pare-chocs de la voiture;**
good enough, and his machine crashes against the bumper of the car;

**il fait un vol-plané par-dessus le capot de l'automobile, atterrissant**
he flies over the bonnet of the car; landing

**fort brutalement sur le gravier de la route.    Voilà ce que c'est d'oublier que**
heavily on the gravel of the road.    This is what happens if one forgets

**l'on conduit à droite en France.**
to ride on the right in France.

**L'automobiliste (accourant vers Charles) : T'es-tu fait mal, petit bandit?**
             (running towards Charles) : Are you hurt, you little scamp?

**Charles (les genoux et les mains en sang, et s'efforçant de ne pas**
         (his knees and hands covered with blood, and trying not

         **pleurer) : Oui, un peu, monsieur.**
         to cry) : Yes, a little.

**L'automobiliste : Tu as de la chance; il y a une pharmacie tout près.**
         You are lucky; there happens to be a chemist's shop quite close.

         **(À un passant).    Pourriez-vous m'aider à porter ce chenapan**
         (To a passer-by).    Would you mind helping me to

         **jusqu'à cette pharmacie, s'il vous plaît, monsieur?**
         carry this little rascal to that chemist's, please?

**(Quelques instants après, le pharmacien tâte Charles pour voir s'il n'a rien**
(A few minutes later, the chemist feels Charles to see if he has broken

**de cassé, tandis que son aide lui nettoie ses plaies.    Charles a bien**
anything, while his assistant cleans his wounds.    Charles is very much

**envie de crier quand on lui touche le genou avec un tampon d'alcool.)**
inclined to cry out when they touch his knee with a spirit dressing.)

**Le pharmacien : Tiens, tu t'es cogné la tête aussi.    Tu as un peu de sang**
         Well, you've bumped your head, too.    You have a little blood

         **dans les cheveux.    Il va falloir t'en couper quelques-uns et**
         in your hair.    We shall have to cut some off and

**te nettoyer la tempe avec de l'eau oxygénée.**
clean your temple with peroxide.

**(Le lendemain Charles est dans sa chambre, allongé sur un divan; sa mère est**
(The next day Charles is in his room, lying on a sofa ; his mother is

**auprès de lui et coud.   La sonnette retentit.)**
beside him, sewing.   The bell rings.)

**Mme Roberts : Le médecin!**
The doctor!

**Charles :      J'espère qu'il ne me fera pas mal.**
I hope he won't hurt me.

**Le Médecin (entrant) :   Alors voilà notre cycliste.   Il paraît qu'il a**
(entering) : Well, and how's our cyclist?   It seems that he has

**une côte cassée, un oeil au beurre noir, une épaule démise, une**
a broken rib, a black eye, a dislocated shoulder, a

**cheville foulée, etc., etc. . . .!**
sprained ankle, and so on and so forth!

**Mme Roberts (riant) :  Non, Docteur, heureusement, ce n'est pas si grave**
(laughing) : No, Doctor, it is fortunately not so bad

**que cela — quelques petites écorchures seulement.**
as that—only a few slight grazes.

**Le Médecin (défaisant le bandage du genou de Charles) :  Voyons cette**
(undoing the bandage on Charles's knee) : Let's see how this

**plaie, si elle se referme bien.  Ah, très bien, mon petit.  Mais**
wound is healing.  Well, very good, my boy.  But

**plus de vélo pour quelques semaines, n'est-ce pas!**
no more bikes for some weeks!

**(Quelques jours après, Charles était tout-à-fait guéri.)**
(A few days later, Charles was entirely cured.)

### LE CORPS HUMAIN—THE HUMAN BODY

| | | | |
|---|---|---|---|
| **la tête** head | | **le ventre** stomach |
| **les cheveux** hair | | **le nombril** navel |
| **le front** forehead | | **le bras** arm |
| **un œil (pl. les yeux)** eye | | **le coude** elbow |
| **une oreille** ear | | **la main** hand |
| **la joue** cheek | | **la jambe** leg |
| **la bouche** mouth | | **la cuisse** thigh |
| **la gorge** throat | | **le genou** knee |
| **le cou** neck | | **le mollet** calf |
| **le tronc** trunk | | **le pied** foot |
| **une épaule** shoulder | | **l'orteil (m.)** toe |
| **la poitrine** chest | | **le talon** heel |

### LA MAIN—THE HAND

**les doigts (m. pl.)** fingers
**le pouce** thumb
**l'index (m.)** index finger, forefinger
**le majeur** middle finger
**l'annulaire (m.)** ring finger
**l'auriculaire (m.)** little finger
**le poignet** wrist
**la paume** palm of the hand
**le pouls** pulse

### MEDICAL VOCABULARY

| | |
|---|---|
| **le médecin** doctor | **la grippe** influenza |
| **le chirurgien** surgeon | **la blessure** wound |
| **un hôpital** hospital | **blessé** wounded |
| **malade** ill | **une ambulance** ambulance |
| **la maladie** illness | **écrasé** run over |
| **le mal** complaint; pain | **renversé** knocked down |
| **le mal de tête** headache | **faire venir un médecin** to send for a doctor |
| **le mal de cœur** sickness | **une ordonnance** prescription |
| **le mal de gorge** sore throat | **une opération** operation |
| **le malaise** indisposition | **opérer** to operate |
| **un rhume** cold | **aller mieux** to be getting better |
| **la fièvre** temperature | **aller plus mal** to be getting worse |
| **la douleur** pain | **être guéri** to be healed; to be well again |

mourir  to die
mort  dead
le pharmacien  chemist
la pharmacie  chemist's
le remède (contre)  remedy (for)
préparer une ordonnance  to make up a
  prescription
le poison  poison
le bandage  bandage
le coton  cotton wool
une lotion  lotion
une pastille  lozenge
une potion  draught
un onguent  ointment
une pilule  pill
un emplâtre  plaster
une poudre  powder

Une cuillerée à bouche
A tablespoonful

toutes les trois heures
every three hours

Agiter avant de s'en servir
Shake before use

## CHEZ LE MÉDECIN—AT THE DOCTOR'S

Monsieur a mal à la tête
    The man has a headache
Madame a mal aux yeux
    The lady has eye trouble
Le vieux monsieur a mal au dos
    The old man has the back-ache
Le petit garçon a mal au nez
    The little boy has nose trouble

La petite a mal au bras gauche
    The little girl has a bad left arm
Mademoiselle a mal au pied droit
    The young lady has a bad right foot
Monsieur a mal à la gorge
    The man has throat trouble
Madame a mal aux oreilles
    The lady has ear trouble

## MINE, THINE, HIS, ETC.
### Singular

|  | *masculine* | *feminine* |
|---|---|---|
| mine | le mien | la mienne |
| thine | le tien | la tienne |
| his, hers | le sien | la sienne |
| ours | le nôtre | la nôtre |
| yours | le vôtre | la vôtre |
| theirs | le leur | la leur |

### Plural

|  | *masculine* | *feminine* |
|---|---|---|
| mine | les miens | les miennes |
| thine | les tiens | les tiennes |
| his, hers | les siens | les siennes |
| ours | les nôtres | les nôtres |
| yours | les vôtres | les vôtres |
| theirs | les leurs | les leurs |

**mon jardin et le sien**
my garden and his (or hers)
**ma maison et la sienne**
my house and his (or hers)
**mes chiens et les siens**
my dogs and his (or hers)
**mes pommes et les siennes**
my apples and his (or hers)

Note. Possessive Pronouns agree with the nouns they refer to in number and gender.

**Further examples:**

**Ma mère et la sienne**=My mother and his (or hers)

**Sa chambre est plus petite que la vôtre**= His room is smaller than yours.

**Son appartement est plus luxueux que le mien**=His flat is more luxurious than mine.

**Il a reçu des cadeaux de ma mère et de la tienne**=He has received presents from my mother and yours.

**Son auto est plus chère que la mienne**= His car is more expensive than mine.

**Le pardessus de votre frère ressemble au mien**=Your brother's overcoat is similar to mine.

**Je ne parle pas de votre gramophone, je parle du sien**=I am not speaking of your gramophone, I am speaking of his.

**À qui est cette chaise? C'est la mienne**= Whose chair is this? It is mine.

N.B.—Mine, yours, his, etc., when used in connection with *is* or *are* are generally translated by **à moi, à vous, à lui,** etc. (see page 281).

### DANS—OUT OF

Note the following expressions:
**Je bois dans une tasse**=
I drink out of a cup.
**Je lis dans un livre**=
I read out of a book.
**Je mange dans une assiette**=
I eat out of a plate.
**Je prends la clef dans ma poche**=
I take the key out of my pocket.

### FRACTIONS

$1/2$=**un** (or **une**) **demi(e)** or **la moitié**
$1/4$=**un quart**
$3/4$=**trois quarts**
$1/3$=**un tiers**
$2/3$=**deux tiers**
$1/5$=**un cinquième**
$2/5$=**deux cinquièmes**
$1/6$=**un sixième**
$5/6$=**cinq sixièmes,** etc.

**Une livre et demie de beurre**=
A pound and a half of butter
**Une demi-heure de récréation**=
Half an hour's recreation
**Une heure et demie**=
An hour and a half
**Un demi-siècle**=
Half a century
**La moitié de six est trois**=
Half of six is three.
**Il m'a donné la moitié de sa poire**=
He gave me half his pear.
**Je vous en donnerai la moitié**=
I shall give you half (*of it*).

### Note on the word "half"

From the above examples it should be noted that
(1) When **demi** is used after et it takes the gender of the noun to which it refers.
(2) When used before a noun **demi** forms a compound word and is invariable.
(3) When *half* is a noun it must be translated by **la moitié.**

## COLLECTIVE NUMBERS

**Une dizaine de verres**=
    About ten glasses
**Une douzaine d'oranges**=
    A dozen oranges
**Une quinzaine**=
    A fortnight (*first and last days being included*)
**Une quinzaine d'enfants**=
    About fifteen children
**Une vingtaine d'huîtres**=
    About twenty oysters
**Une trentaine de personnes**=
    About thirty persons
**Une centaine d'hommes**=
    About a hundred men
**Des centaines d'hommes**=
    Hundreds of men
**Un millier de bouteilles**=
    About a thousand bottles
**Des milliers de bouteilles**=
    Thousands of bottles
**Cela m'a coûté une centaine**=
    That has cost me about a hundred francs.

## ONCE, TWICE, ETC.

**Une fois**=Once
**Deux fois**=Twice
**Trois fois**=Three times
**Quatre fois**=Four times
**Cinq fois**=Five times, etc.

**Deux fois six font douze**=2x6=12
**Sept fois trois font vingt et un**=7x3=21
**La première fois**=The first time
**La dernière fois**=The last time
**Une fois pour toutes**=Once for all

**Je ne peux pas vous comprendre, si vous parlez tous à la fois**=I can't understand you if you all speak at the same time.

## SANS—WITHOUT

**Ne sortez pas sans parapluie**=Don't go out without an umbrella.
**Prenez vous le café avec ou sans lait?**=Do you drink coffee with or without milk?
**Avec du lait, mais sans sucre**=With milk, but with no sugar.
**On ne peut pas y entrer sans billet**=You can't go in there without a ticket.

**On peut y aller sans passeport**=You can go there without a passport.

Note that **sans,** when used before a noun, is not followed by an article.

# EXERCISES

## I   Translate into English

1. Deux et trois font cinq. 2. Combien font seize et onze? 3. Je le lui ai dit cent fois. 4. Ce monsieur va à l'église tous les jours à dix heures et demie. 5. Il part pour Paris dans une demi-heure. 6. Combien de fois leur a-t-il écrit? 7. Ils partent pour l'Amérique dans un quart d'heure. 8. Il dort la moitié du temps. 9. Donnez-lui la moitié de cette pomme. 10. Donnez-lui le tiers de cela. 11. Combien d'oranges désirez-vous? 12. Donnez m'en une douzaine, s'il vous plaît. 13. Charles a perdu son crayon. En voici un; est-ce le sien? 14. Vos parents sont avec les miens. 15. À qui est ce gâteau? C'est le leur.

## II   Translate into French

1. This chair is his, but this armchair is yours. 2. What a beautiful picture! Is it yours? 3. Our garden is smaller than yours. 4. Whose are those flowers? These are mine; yours are in the other room. 5. Would you like some of this cake? I can give you half of it. 6. How many pages of this book have you read? I have read about twenty. 7. I paid about a thousand francs for it. 8. What time is it? 9. It is a quarter past five. 10. It is half past nine p.m. 11. Seven and six are thirteen. 12. How much are five times eight? 13. I have no pencils. 14. Here are about ten. 15. I forgot my pen. Here is mine. 16. Do not take his (hat). 17. You are taking hers (hat). 18. Have you found his (box)? 19. I haven't got hers (box). 20. How many oranges do you want? Give me half a dozen.

## III   Give the following times in French

1. 6.30 a.m. 2. 9.00 a.m. 3. 10.45 a.m. 4. 12.15 p.m. 5. 1.30 p.m. 6. 6.50 p.m. 7. 8.05 p.m. 8. 0.03 a.m.

(*Key on page* 336).

# TRENTE-ET-UNIÈME LEÇON

### CHEZ LE COIFFEUR—AT THE HAIRDRESSER'S

**Mme Roberts et Madeleine sont allées chez un coiffeur. Il y a un salon**
Mrs. Roberts and Madeleine have gone to a hairdresser's.   There is a saloon

**pour dames et un salon pour messieurs.   En passant Madeleine aperçoit un gros**
for ladies, and one for gentlemen.   In passing, Madeleine notices a stout

**monsieur, la figure toute couverte de savon à barbe.   Sur l'étagère à côté**
gentleman with his face all covered with shaving soap.   On the stand at the side

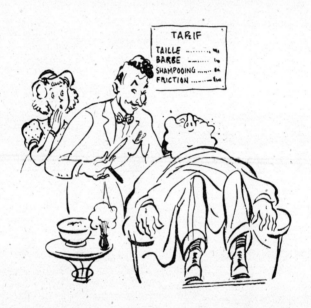

**il y a un blaireau et un bol à savon.   Le barbier est en train de passer**
there is a shaving brush and a soap bowl.   The barber is just sharpening

**le rasoir sur le cuir à aiguiser.   Madeleine frissonne et pense que cela**
the razor on the strop.   Madeleine shivers, and thinks how

**doit être désagréable de se faire raser!   Dans le salon de dames la coiffeuse**
horrid it must be to be shaved!   In the ladies' saloon the assistant

**demande à Mme Roberts ce qu'elle veut.**
asks Mrs. Roberts what she requires.

**Mme Roberts : Une coupe pour la petite, s'il vous plaît.   Dégagez-lui bien**
       A haircut for the little girl, please.   Nice and short on

## PARIS, UN QUATORZE JUILLET

C'est le 14 juillet, anniversaire de la prise de la Bastille en 1789, et Fête Nationale française.  En haut, le feu d'artifice le long des quais jette ses reflets dans la Seine.  En bas, on danse en pleine rue avec le premier venu, à la musique d'un orchestre champêtre.

| **Feu d'artifice (m.)** | **reflet (m.)** | **le premier venu** | **orchestre (m.) champêtre** |
|---|---|---|---|
| Fireworks | reflection | the first comer | rustic band |

le cou.   La raie sur le côté gauche.
the neck.   The parting on the left side.

**La Coiffeuse :** Faut-il lui passer le fer à friser, madame?
Shall I use the curling-tongs, madam?

**Mme Roberts :** Non, inutile, mais faites-lui une friction.
No, it is not necessary, but give her a massage.

**La Coiffeuse :** Pas de shampooing?
No shampoo?

**Mme Roberts :** Non.   (à Madeleine) : Sois bien sage.   Je vais dans
No.   (to Madeleine) :   Be very good.   I am going into

la pièce à côté me faire une mise en plis.   Viens me retrouver
the next cubicle to have a setting.   Come to find me

quand tu auras fini.
when you have finished.

(Madeleine enfile le peignoir et s'assied dans le grand fauteuil.   La
(Madeleine slips on the cape and seats herself in the big armchair.   The

coiffeuse commence par bien la peigner.   Puis elle lui passe la tondeuse
hairdresser begins by thoroughly combing her hair.   Then she passes the clippers

sur la nuque; puis elle fait cliqueter ses ciseaux.
over the back of her neck ; then she clicks her scissors.

Tout en travaillant, elle lui demande si elle se plaît en France,
While she is working, she asks her if she enjoys being in France,

et passe de bonnes vacances.)
and if she is spending nice holidays.)

**La  Coiffeuse :** Avez-vous au moins été à la Fête du 14 juillet quand
Did you at least go to the celebrations on July 14th, when

vous étiez à Paris?
you were in Paris?

**Madeleine :** Oh oui; nous avons été à la Revue.   C'était magnifique, et puis
Oh yes ; we went to the Review.   It was splendid, and then

le soir nous nous sommes promenés dans les rues et nous
in the evening we walked about the streets and we

avons vu tous les Parisiens qui dansaient à la lumière
saw all the Parisians dancing by the light

des lampions.   C'était très joli.
of the lanterns.   It was very pretty.

(La coupe une fois terminée, la coiffeuse donne le miroir à Madeleine
(The haircut being finished, the assistant gives Madeleine a looking-glass

et lui demande si elle est satisfaite.)
and asks if she is satisfied.)

Madeleine :   C'est parfait.
It is quite all right.

La Coiffeuse :  Je vais vous faire la friction maintenant.   Que préférez-vous,
I will give you a friction now.   Which do you prefer,

Eau de Cologne ou de lavande?
Eau de Cologne or Lavender Water?

Madeleine :   Eau de Cologne, s'il vous plaît.   (Après la friction, la
Eau de Cologne, please.   (After the friction, the

coiffeuse peigne soigneusement Madeleine, et donne un coup de brosse à ses vêtements.
hairdresser carefully combs Madeleine's hair, and gives her clothes a brush.

Elle va alors rejoindre sa mère; elle la trouve sous un
Then she (Madeleine) goes to rejoin her mother ; she finds her under an

énorme appareil à ondulations permanentes.   Une manucure est en train de
enormous apparatus for permanent waving.   A manicurist is just

lui faire les ongles.)
doing her nails.)

Mme Roberts :  Je me suis tout de même laissé faire une indéfrisable.   Cela
I am having a permanent wave done after all.   It

va durer encore pas mal de temps, aussi tu ferais bien
will take rather a long time still, so you had better

de rentrer toute seule.   Montre-moi comment tes cheveux sont coupés.
go home alone.   Show me how your hair is cut.

Madeleine, après s'être fait examiner, laisse sa mère en compagnie des
Madeleine, after having shown herself, leaves her mother in the company of the

séchoirs et des bouteilles de lotion et va retrouver ses cousins
hair-drying machines and bottles of lotion, and goes off to find her cousins

à la maison.)
at home.)

CHEZ LE COIFFEUR

## Men's Side

**English.**—1. Hair-lotion; 2. Scent-spray; 3. Wash-basin; 4. Hairdresser's assistant; 5. Hair-clippers; 6. Men's hairdresser; 7. Towels; 8. Razor; 9. Soap-bowl; 10. Shaving-brush; 11. Powder-spray; 12. Strop.

**French.**—1. Lotion (*f.*); 2. Vaporisateur (*m.*); 3. Cuvette (*f.*); 4. Aide-coiffeur (*m.*) 5. Tondeuse (*f.*); 6. Coiffeur (*m.*) pour messieurs; 7. Serviettes (*f.pl.*); 8. Rasoir (*m.*); 9. Bol (*m.*) à savon; 10. Blaireau (*m.*) 11. Pulvérisateur (*m.*); 12. Cuir (*m.*) à aiguiser.

| Further Useful Expressions | **La barbe, s.v.p.** Shave, please | pas trop près not too close | **les cheveux, s.v.p.** haircut, please | **pas trop courts** not too short |
|---|---|---|---|---|

## AT THE HAIRDRESSER'S

### Ladies' Side

**English.**—1. Douche; 2. Wash-basin; 3. Nail-polisher; 4. Manicurist; 5. Permanent-wave apparatus; 6. Perfumes, creams and powders; 7. Face-packs; 8. Drying-hood; 9. Curling-irons; 10. Lipstick; 11. Comb; 12. Hand-mirror.

**French.**—1. Douche (*f.*); 2. Cuvette (*f.*); 3. Polissoir (*m.*); 4. Manucure (*f.*); 5. Appareil (*m.*) à ondulations indéfrisables; 6. Parfums, crèmes et poudres-de-riz; 7. Masques (*m.*) anti-rides; 8. Sèche-cheveux (*m.*); 9. Fer (*m.*) à friser; 10. Bâton (*m.*) de rouge; 11. Peigne (*m.*); 12. Glace (*f.*) à main.

| les bouts seulement | couper | onduler | boucler | rafraîchir | une ondulation indéfrisable |
|---|---|---|---|---|---|
| a trim only | to cut | to wave | to curl | to trim | permanent wave |

## LES CHEVEUX ET LA BARBE—HAIR AND BEARD

**la moustache**　moustache
**les favoris**　whiskers
**les côtelettes**　side-whiskers (*mutton chops*)
**la barbe**　beard
**la barbe en pointe**　pointed beard

**la tête chauve**　bald head
**les cheveux bouclés**　curly head
**les cheveux en brosse**　bristly hair
**la raie médiane**　parting (*in the middle*)
**la raie à gauche**　parting (*on the left*)

MARSEILLE: LE PORT

Notre impression du grand port d'escale montre les bassins à flot et les bassins de radoub.

**Port (m.) d'escale**　　**bassin (m.) à flot**　　　　　　**bassin de radoub**
Port of call　　　　　　wet dock, flooding dock　　　　dry dock, graving dock

la **perruque** wig
les **cheveux longs** long (*loose*) hair
les **cheveux courts** bobbed hair
le **chignon** bun
la **natte** pig-tail
les **macarons** "earphones"
à la **garçonne** shingled
la **frange** fringe
la **tête** head
le **front** forehead
les **tempes** temples
la **nuque** back of the neck
le **sommet** crown of the head
la **joue** cheek

### EACH, EVERY

**Mettez chaque livre à sa place**=Put each book in its place.

**Il rit chaque fois que je le vois**=He laughs every time I see him.

**Donnons du chocolat à chaque enfant**=Let's give chocolate to each of the children.

**Donnons chacun cent francs**=Let's all give a hundred francs.

**Donnons cent francs à chacun**=Let's give a hundred francs to everybody.

**Donnons des fleurs à chacune**=Let's give flowers to every one (*woman*).

 Note that **chaque** is an adjective and has the same form for both masculine and feminine.
 **Chacun** (*masc.*) and **chacune** (*fem.*) are pronouns.

### DONC

**Attendez donc**=Do wait
**Jouez donc**=Do play
**Parlez-lui donc**=Do speak to him
**Montrez-le lui donc**=Do show it to him
**Gardez-en donc**=Do keep some
**Restez-y donc**=Do stay there
**Soyez donc sérieux**=Do be serious
**Asséyez-vous donc**=Do sit down
 **Donc** like English "do" is used for emphasis and is often not translatable.

### WHICH, WHAT

**Quel homme?**=Which man?
**Quels hommes?**=Which men?
**Quelle femme?**=Which woman?
**Quelles femmes?**=Which women?
**Quel homme?**=What man?

**Quels hommes?**=What men?
**Quelle femme?**=What woman?
**Quelles femmes?**=What women?
**Lequel de ces deux?**=Which one of these two (*men*)?
**Laquelle de ces deux?**=Which one of these two (*women*)?
**Lesquels de ces hommes?**=Which of these men?
**Lesquelles de ces femmes?**=Which of these women?
**Quel homme!**=What a man!
**Quels hommes!**=What men!
**Quelle femme!**=What a woman!
**Quelles femmes!**=What women!

### Which (or what)

followed by a masculine noun, singular
        **quel**
followed by a feminine noun, singular
        **quelle**
followed by a masculine noun, plural
        **quels**
followed by a feminine noun, plural
        **quelles**

### Which one

replacing a masculine noun, singular
        **lequel**
replacing a feminine noun, singular
        **laquelle**

### Which

replacing a masculine noun, plural
        **lesquels**
replacing a feminine noun, plural
        **lesquelles**
 In exclamation "what a . . !"=**quel** or **quelle**.
 "What" (followed by a verb)=**que** or **qu'est-ce que**.
**Que faites-vous?**
**Qu'est-ce que vous faites?**
     What are you doing?
**Qu'avez-vous?**
**Qu'est-ce que vous avez?**
     What have you got?
**Que pensez-vous?**
**Qu'est-ce que vous pensez?**
     What do you think?

N.B.—After **de** or **à** or any other preposition or if the verb is omitted, **que** is changed to **quoi.**

**De quoi parlez-vous?** = What are you talking about?

**À quoi cela sert-il?** = What is this for?

**Il n'y a pas de quoi** = Don't mention it (*in answer to an apology*).

**Quoi de nouveau ce matin?** = What is new this morning?

**Il a quelque chose contre moi. Je ne sais quoi** = He has something against me. I don't know what.

**Un je ne sais quoi** = An indefinable something, something or other.

**What** (when the subject of the sentence) = **qu'est-ce qui.**

**Qu'est-ce qui brûle?** = What is burning?

**Qu'est-ce qui vous amuse?** = What is amusing you?

**Qu'est-ce qui est tombé?** = What has fallen?

**Qu'est-ce qui est arrivé?** = What has happened?

**Qu'est-ce qui vous est arrivé?** = What has happened to you?

### OF WHICH, TO WHICH, ETC.

**Auquel de ses livres pensez-vous?** = Which of his books are you thinking of?

**À laquelle de mes sœurs voulez-vous envoyer ces fleurs?** = To which one of my sisters do you want to send these flowers?

**Auxquels de ses amis écrivez-vous?** = To which of his friends are you writing?

**Duquel parlez-vous?** = Of which one are you speaking? (*i.e. of a man*)

**À laquelle pensez-vous?** = Of which one are you thinking? (*i.e. of a woman*)

**Desquels voulez-vous?** = Which do you want? (*i.e. things which are masculine*)

**Desquelles voulez-vous?** = Which do you want? (*i.e. things which are feminine*)

## EXERCISES

### I  Translate into English

1. Veuillez servir le fromage. Duquel désirez-vous, monsieur? 2. Apportez-moi des fruits, s'il vous plaît. 3. Lesquels voulez-vous, madame? Que dire? 4. A quoi cette machine sert-elle? 5. Achetez donc une livre de chaque sorte. 6. Vendez donc une demi-livre à chacun. 7. En quoi pouvez-vous lui être utile (=useful)? 8. Qu'est-ce qui leur est arrivé? 9. Qu'est-ce qui vous intéresse? 10. Qu'est-ce qu'on peut faire? 11. Qu'avez-vous contre moi? 12. Qu'est-ce qu'ils ont? 13. Laquelle des deux est la plus belle? 14. Lequel de ces cigares voulez-vous? 15. Que pensez-vous de son opinion?

### II  Translate into French

1. Do come. 2. Do take it. 3. Do write to her. 4. Do send it to him. 5. Do buy some of each sort (la sorte). 6. What are you saying? 7. What do you think of her? 8. What does he want to tell me? 9. Which of these cigars do you prefer? 10. Which of the two is the more intelligent (woman)? 11. What a beautiful woman! 12. Tell me which one (cheese) you will have. 13. What can you give us? 14. Which of these men is your brother? 15. Which of these girls will play with us? (*Key on page 336*).

## KEY TO THE EXERCISES

### Lesson Twenty-seven

#### I

1. joliment. 2. premièrement. 3. longuement. 4. bien. 5. mal. 6. curieusement. 7. généralement. 8. complètement. 9. mieux. 10. absolument.

#### II

1. He is a good man. 2. He is the best man in the world. 3. This dinner is well done. 4. It is better than yesterday's. 5. Your hotel is better than mine. 6. You are doing it better than he. 7. He is my best friend. 8. He speaks French better

than I. 9. She speaks very badly. 10. He is much worse this morning. 11. He is less intelligent than his father. 12. I am extremely hungry. 13. It is terribly hot. 14. Unfortunately I could not find him (or it). 15. He is evidently seriously ill. 16. I like tennis very much, but I like golf better. 17. Yesterday she was well, but to-day she is much worse. 18. He speaks little, but his wife speaks much less. 19. I finished my work. So much the better for you. 20. You (I, we) have to leave at once.

### III

1. J'aime beaucoup ce tableau. 2. Ils sont énormément riches. 3. Elle parle mieux que sa sœur. 4. C'est une très bonne fille; elle travaille toujours bien. 5. Malheureusement il a perdu le livre. Tant pis pour lui. 6. Ceci n'est pas son meilleur livre. 7. L'aimez-vous mieux qu'elle? 8. Avez-vous bien dormi? 9. Vous avez mal écrit cette lettre. 10. Pire que jamais. 11. Votre père va-t-il mieux? 12. Non, il va pis qu'hier. 13. J'ai terriblement soif. 14. Pouvez-vous le faire immédiatement? 15. Heureusement je suis libre à présent. 16. Généralement il est chez lui de cinq à six. 17. Veuillez parler plus distinctement. 18. Malheureusement je ne l'ai pas trouvée chez elle. 19. Il pense que vous viendrez, naturellement. 20. C'est exactement mon opinion.

## Lesson Twenty-eight

### I

Versailles is near Paris. It is 18 kilometres from Paris to Versailles. What is the distance from Paris to Le Havre? Le Havre is 228 kilometres from Paris. From Le Havre one can go by boat to New York. How many days does one need to go from Europe to America? About five or six days. How many hours does one need to go from Paris to Le Havre? Three to four hours. Here is a time-table. There is an express train which leaves at half past twelve. A fast train leaves Paris at seven o'clock. At five in the afternoon there is a slow train. But it is very slow; it stops at every station.

### II

1. Versailles est-il loin de Paris? 2. Habitez-vous loin d'ici? 3. Notre maison est à cinq minutes d'ici; nous habitons près de l'église. 4. Quelle distance d'ici à la gare? 5. Environ trois kilomètres; une demi-heure à pied. 6. Irez-vous en bateau ou en chemin-de-fer? 7. Combien d'heures faut-il pour aller d'ici au bord de la mer? 8. Est-ce qu'il y a un train express le matin? 9. Il n'y a qu'un train omnibus. Il s'arrête à toutes les gares. 10. N'y a-t-il pas de trains rapides? 11. Le meilleur train est un rapide qui part à midi et arrive à huit heures trente-cinq du soir. 12. Il ne s'arrête que deux fois.

## Lesson Twenty-nine

### I

1. Oui, il y en a. 2. Il n'y en a pas autant. 3. Il n'y en a pas beaucoup, mais il y en a assez. 4. Non, il n'y en a pas assez. 5. Il n'y en a pas du tout. 6. Il en a plus que Paul. 7. Charles en a le plus. 8. Robert à le moins de glace, mais André n'en a pas. 9. André. 10. Charles en a trop.

### II

1. How many persons will there be at your place? 2. Have you got as much money as Rockefeller? 3. I have not enough money. 4. Will you give this poor boy a little money? 5. There were too many people with him. 6. I drank as much as he. 7. I worked so much that I am tired. 8. You are not working enough. 9. He does not speak so much as she. 10. Don't smoke so much. 11. He does not smoke much. Yes, he does. 12. Do they drink a lot? 13. No, not much. 14. Are these mussels fresh? I should say so.

## III

1. Vous ne mangez pas assez de légumes. 2. Il y aura trop de personnes. 3. Vous buvez trop de bière. 4. Vous avez donné trop de viande à mon fils. 5. Y aura-t-il assez de vin? 6. Il ne lit pas assez. 7. Je lis plus de trois heures. 8. Combien de lettres avez-vous écrites? 9. Vous n'aviez pas tant d'appétit que votre frère. 10. Vous n'avez pas travaillé? Si. 11. Elle ne fume pas beaucoup. 12. Vous n'écrivez pas assez d'exercices. 13. Si vous voulez vous coucher maintenant, je partirai. 14. S'il me paie, je vous payerai. 15. S'il vient, dites-lui que je l'attends.

## Lesson Thirty

### I

1. Two and three make five. 2. How much are sixteen and eleven? 3. I told him a hundred times. 4. This gentleman goes to church every day at half past ten. 5. He leaves for Paris in half an hour. 6. How many times did he write to them? 7. They leave for America in a quarter of an hour. 8. He sleeps half the time. 9. Give him half of that apple. 10. Give him a third of this. 11. How many oranges do you want? 12. Please let me have a dozen of them. 13. Charles lost his pencil. Here is one; is it his? 14. Your parents are with mine. 15. Whose cake is this? It is theirs.

### II

1. Cette chaise est la sienne, mais ce fauteuil est le vôtre. 2. Quel beau tableau! Est-ce le vôtre? 3. Notre jardin est plus petit que le vôtre. 4. À qui sont ces fleurs? Elles sont à moi; les vôtres sont dans l'autre chambre. 5. Voudriez-vous un peu de ce gâteau? Je peux vous en donner la moitié. 6. Combien de pages de ce livre avez-vous lues? J'en ai lu une vingtaine. 7. Je l'ai payé un millier de francs. 8. Quelle heure est-il? 9. Il est cinq heures et quart. 10. Il est neuf heures et demie du soir. 11. Sept et six font treize. 12.

Combien font cinq fois huit? 13. Je n'ai pas de crayons. 14. En voici une dizaine. 15. J'ai oublié ma plume. Voici la mienne. 16. Ne prenez pas le sien. 17. Vous prenez le sien. 18. Avez-vous trouvé la sienne? 19. Je n'ai pas la sienne. 20. Combien d'oranges voulez-vous? Donnez-m'en une demi-douzaine.

### III

1. Six heures trente du matin. 2. Neuf heures du matin. 3. Onze heures moins le quart. 4. Midi et quart. 5. Une heure et demie de l'après-midi. 6. Sept heures moins dix du soir (dix-huit heures cinquante). 7. Huit heures cinq du soir (vingt heures cinq). 8. Minuit trois.

## Lesson Thirty-one

### I

1. Will you please serve the cheese. Which do you want, sir? 2. Bring me some fruit, please. 3. What kind do you want, madam? What shall I (we) say? 4. What is this machine for? 5. Do buy one pound from each sort. 6. Do sell half a pound to each. 7. In what way can you be useful to him (her)? 8. What has happened to them? 9. What interests you? 10. What can one do? 11. What have you got against me? 12. What have they got? 13. Which of the two is the more beautiful? 14. Which of these cigars do you want? 15. What do you think of his opinion?

### II

1. Venez donc. 2. Prenez-le donc. 3. Écrivez-lui donc. 4. Envoyez-le lui donc. 5. Achetez-en donc de chaque sorte. 6. Que dites-vous? 7. Que pensez-vous d'elle? 8. Que veut-il me dire? 9. Lequel de ces cigares préférez-vous? 10. Laquelle de ces deux est la plus intelligente? 11. Quelle belle femme! 12. Dites-moi lequel vous voulez. 13. Que pouvez-vous nous donner? 14. Lequel de ces hommes est votre frère? 15. Laquelle de ces jeunes filles va jouer avec nous?

## SUR LA CÔTE D'AZUR

Les mimosas, les pins, les palmiers perchés sur les coteaux et une mer calme et bleue — c'est un pays de rêve où le soleil brille presque toujours dans un ciel pur.

**Pin** (m.)        **palmier** (m.)        **coteau** (m.)        **rêve** (m.)        **ciel** (m.)
Pine tree        palm tree        slope        dream        sky

# TRENTE-DEUXIÈME LEÇON

### M. LESAGE ET SON TRAVAIL—MR. LESAGE AND HIS WORK

**Monsieur Lesage va au bureau par le métro.   Il habite la banlieue.**
Mr. Lesage goes to the office by tube.   He lives in the suburban area.

**Chaque matin il va à la station du métro, qui n'est pas loin de**
Every morning he goes to the Underground station, which is not far from

**chez lui.   Il prend son billet au guichet.   Ensuite il descend**
his house.   He takes his ticket at the booking office.   Then he goes down

**l'escalier et va sur le quai, où il attend le train.   Quand le**
the stairs and goes on to the platform, where he waits for the train.   When the

**train arrive il monte dans un compartiment et il s'assied.   Mais bien**
train arrives he gets into a compartment and sits down.   But quite

**souvent il n'y a pas de place assise et M. Lesage est obligé de rester debout.**
often there is no room to sit down and Mr. Lesage has to stand.

**Pendant le voyage il lit son journal.**
During the journey he reads his paper.

**La politique ne l'intéresse pas.   Il s'intéresse aux sports et au théâtre.**
Politics do not interest him.   He is interested in sport and in the theatre.

**Le matin le train est toujours bondé.   Quand le train arrive à sa**
In the morning the train is always crowded.   When the train arrives at his

**gare il en descend et il remonte l'escalier.   Le bureau est tout près**
station he gets out (of it) and goes up the stairs.   The office is quite near

**de la gare.   Il y va à pied.   Quelquefois quand**
the station.   He walks there (lit., goes there on foot).   Sometimes when

**il pleut il prend l'autobus.   À neuf heures il arrive au bureau de la**
it rains he takes the 'bus.   At nine o'clock he arrives at the office of

**compagnie dont il est propriétaire.   Il est fabricant de jouets.   Le**
the company of which he is the proprietor.   He is a toy manufacturer.   The

**bureau est au centre de la ville.   L'usine n'est pas à Paris; elle est dans**
office is in the centre of the town.   The factory is not in Paris; it is in

**la banlieue.   Dans le bureau il y a beaucoup d'employés.   M. Lesage est leur**
the suburbs.   In the office there are many employees.   Mr. Lesage is their

## M. LESAGE GOES TO THE OFFICE

After studying Lesson 32, make certain, before passing on, that you can name in French everything in this picture—the train itself, the underground station, the passengers seated and those standing, etc. The following words and expressions will help you :—**un compartiment de seconde classe; beaucoup de monde; le contrôleur; les voyageurs; debout; assis; le quai; sont descendus; changer de train; monter l'escalier; sortir du métro.** (The word **Correspondance** means that this is one of the stations where one changes for other connecting lines.)

**patron. Lors qu'il arrive dans le bureau il lit la correspondance. Ensuite il**
employer.   When he arrives in the office he reads the correspondence.   Then he

**dicte quelques lettres à une sténo-dactylo. Elle les écrit à la machine.**
dictates some letters to a shorthand typist.   She writes them on the machine.

**Quand la sténo a fini les lettres M. Lesage les signe. Ensuite un**
When the typist has finished the letters Mr. Lesage signs them.   Then one

**des commis les met à la poste. Voici une des lettres que M. Lesage a**
of the clerks posts them.   Here is one of the letters which Mr. Lesage has

**récemment dictées:—**
recently dictated:—

                                             **Paris, le 6 juin, 194..**
                                             Paris, 6th June, 194..

          **Messieurs,**
          Dear Sirs,

          **Voici bientôt six mois que je n'ai reçu de commande de**
          It will soon be six months since I received an order from

          **vous.   Je ne puis m'expliquer ce silence que par la**
          you.   I can only explain (to myself) this silence by the

          **stagnation générale des affaires.   Désireux de ranimer**
          general business stagnation.   As I should be glad to renew

          **nos rapports, je vous adresse par le même courrier mon**
          our relations, I am sending you by the same post my

          **dernier catalogue, et je m'empresse d'attirer votre**
          latest catalogue, and I especially wish to call your

          **attention sur les prix exceptionnels auxquels je puis**
          attention to the exceptional prices at which I can

          **vous offrir actuellement mes articles.   Je crois donc agir**
          offer you my articles at present.   In this I believe that I am acting

          **dans votre meilleur intérêt en vous conseillant de faire**
          in your best interests by advising you to make

          **dès maintenant vos achats pour la saison d'hiver.   Dans**
          your purchases now for the winter season.   Hoping

          **l'espoir d'une forte commande, je vous prie d'agréer, Messieurs,**
          to have the pleasure of receiving a large order, I remain, Sirs,

**nos salutations distinguées.**
Yours faithfully,

**Paul Lesage.**

**Quelques jours plus tard M. Lesage**
A few days later Mr. Lesage

**reçut la réponse suivante:—**
received the following reply:—

**Bordeaux, le 9 juin 194..**
Bordeaux, 9th June, 194..

**Monsieur,**
Dear Sir,

**Nous vous remercions de l'offre que vous nous avez faite par**
We thank you for the offer which you made us in

**votre lettre du 6 ct. (courant).**
your letter of the 6th inst.

**Nous avons examiné votre prix-courant et les échantillons, et nous**
We have examined your price-list and samples, and we

**sommes heureux de commander à votre maison les**
have the pleasure of ordering from your firm the

**marchandises énumérées sur le bon de commande ci-inclus.**
goods specified in the enclosed order form.

**Nous espérons que vous pourrez exécuter cette commande**
We hope that it will be possible for you to execute this order

**de suite. Nous serons forcés de refuser**
at once. We shall be compelled to refuse

**de prendre livraison de la marchandise, si elle n'est pas**
acceptance of the goods, if they are not

**entre nos mains le 30 courant au plus tard.**
in our hands by the 30th inst. at the latest.

**Recevez, Monsieur, nos sincères salutations,**
Yours faithfully,

**L. Meunier.**

**p.p. Grands Magasins de Bordeaux. L. Meunier.**

## M. LESAGE IN HIS OFFICE

With the exception of M. Lesage, whom you already know to be **le patron** or employer, everybody and everything in this typical office is listed on page 343. When you have studied this list carefully, you should be able to give its French name to any object in the picture. Then, with the assistance of the following expressions, you should be able to write in French a description of the picture, telling the story in your own words. **Le patron; assis à son bureau; objets sur le bureau; appelle sa secrétaire; dicte des lettres; appelle le garçon de bureau; lui dit de mettre les lettres à la poste.**

### LE BUREAU—THE OFFICE

| | |
|---|---|
| **le bureau**  writing-table, desk | **le coffre-fort**  safe |
| **le fauteuil**  easy chair | **le calendrier**  calendar |
| **la chaise**  chair | **la sténo-dactylo(graphe)**  typist |
| **le bloc-notes**  scribbling block | **la machine à écrire**  typewriter |
| **la règle**  ruler | **le tabouret**  revolving chair |
| **un encrier**  inkpot | **une étagère**  bookshelf |
| **le buvard**  blotting paper | **le pèse-lettres**  letter balance |
| **un ouvre-lettres**  letter-opener | **la lampe de table**  desk-lamp |
| **le tiroir**  drawer | **le garçon de bureau**  office-boy |
| **les rayons**  shelves | **le téléphone**  telephone |
| **la corbeille à papier**  wastepaper basket | |

### CE QU'IL FAUT POUR ÉCRIRE—WRITING UTENSILS

| | |
|---|---|
| **la feuille de papier**  sheet of paper | **le stylo(graphe)**  fountain-pen |
| **le papier carbone**  carbon paper | **le porte-mines**  (*propelling*) pencil |
| **la copie**  carbon copy | **le taille-crayon**  pencil sharpener |
| **le porte-plume**  penholder | **le bâton de cire à cacheter**  stick of sealing |
| **la plume**  nib | wax |
| **le crayon**  pencil | **une enveloppe**  envelope |

### HAVE AS AN IMPERATIVE

$\left.\begin{array}{l}\textbf{Ayez}\\\textbf{Aie}\end{array}\right\}$ =have . . .! **Ayons**=let us have . . .!

**Aie (ayez) de la patience!**=have patience!
**Ayons du courage!**=Let us have courage!
**Il faut avoir de la patience**=You (*we*) must have patience
**Il ne faut pas avoir peur**=You (*we*) must not be afraid

### BE AS AN IMPERATIVE

$\left.\begin{array}{l}\textbf{Sois}\ . .!\\\textbf{Soyez}\ . .!\end{array}\right\}$ =Be . . .!   **Soyons . . .!**=Let us be . . .!

**Sois (Soyez) patient(e)!**=Be patient!
**Sois (Soyez) donc sérieux!**=Do be serious!
(sérieuse)
**Ne sois (soyez) pas si impatient!**=Don't be so impatient!

**Soyons exacts (exactes)**=Let us be punctual
**Ne soyons pas en retard**=Don't let us be late

Notice that the adjectives are either masculine or feminine.

### WHO, WHOSE, WHOM, ETC.

**Qui est-ce?**=Who is it?
**Qui l'a?**=Who has got it?
**Qui l'avait?**=Who had it?
**Qui l'a fait?**=Who did it?
**Qui avez-vous vu?**=Whom did you see?
**Avec qui allez-vous?**=With whom are you going?
**À qui l'avez-vous donné?**=To whom did you give it?
**À qui est ce chapeau?**=Whose hat is this?

À qui sont ces gants ?=Whose gloves are these?

De qui parlez-vous ?=Of whom are you speaking?

Qui ?=Who? *or* Whom?

À qui ?=To whom?

De qui ?=Of whom?

Avec qui ?=With whom?

N.B.—À qui est . . . ?=Whose is . . .?

À qui sont . . . ?=Whose are . . .?

## HOW TO TRANSLATE " IT IS " (" IT WAS ")

### 1. c'est . . . (c'était) . . .

| c'est (c'était) | it is (it was) |
|---|---|
| bon | good |
| facile | easy |
| vrai | true |
| amusant | amusing |
| là-bas | over there |
| mon jardin | my garden |
| le mien | mine |

Est-ce ⎫ votre ⎫ Is it ⎫ your hat?
Était-ce ⎰ chapeau ? ⎰ Was it ⎰

"It is"=c'est ("it was"=c'était) if followed by a noun; or by an adjective, provided the word "it" does not refer to a noun.

### 2. il est (était); elle est (était)

Voici mon briquet. Il est joli, n'est-ce pas ? = Here is my petrol-lighter. It is nice, isn't it?

Voici ma montre. Elle est petite, n'est-ce pas ?=Here is my watch. It is small, isn't it?

| Le jardin | The garden |
|---|---|
| Il est à moi | It is mine |
| Il était à moi | It was mine |
| Il sera à moi | It will be mine |
| La maison | The house |
| Elle est à moi | It is mine |
| Elle était à moi | It was mine |
| Elle sera à moi | It will be mine |

"It"=il or elle according to the gender of the noun "it" refers to.

### 3. il est (il était) . . .

| il est (il était) | it is (it was) |
|---|---|
| deux heures | two o'clock |
| tard | late |
| midi | noon |
| minuit | midnight |

"It is"=il est ("it was"=il était) when speaking of time.

### 4. il fait (il faisait) . . .

| il fait (il faisait) | it is (it was) |
|---|---|
| beau | fine |
| mauvais | nasty |
| chaud | hot |
| froid | cold |
| sec | dry |
| humide | wet |
| du vent | windy |
| du brouillard | foggy |

"it is"=il fait ("it was"=il faisait) when speaking about the weather.

### 5. il . . .

| il pleut | It is raining |
|---|---|
| neige | snowing |
| gèle | freezing |
| dégèle | thawing |
| il pleuvait | It was raining |
| neigeait | snowing |
| gelait | freezing |
| dégelait | thawing |

## EXERCISES

### I Répondez en français

1. Où est le bureau? 2. Qui est le propriétaire de la compagnie? 3. Où est l'usine? 4. Qu'est-ce qu'il y a dans le bureau? 5. Qui écrit les lettres? 6. Qui les met à la poste? 7. Avez-vous une machine à écrire? 8. Quel temps fait-il aujourd'hui? 9. Dans quel mois fait-il du brouillard? 10. Est-ce qu'il fait chaud aujourd'hui? 11. Quelle est la date? 12. À qui est ce livre?

### II Traduisez en français

1. The clerk arrives at the office at a quarter to eight. 2. The boss dictates many letters. 3. The typist writes them on the machine. 4. The clerk goes to the office on foot. 5. When it rains he comes by bus. 6. He sits down in the Underground. 7. When the train arrives he gets out. 8. She lives in the suburbs. 9. Don't be late. 10. Whose typewriter is this? 11. To whom are you writing? 12. It is 5 past 7. 13. It is very late. 14. It is a nice day. 15. Whose watch is this? It is mine.

### III  Traduisez en anglais

1. L'usine de M. Lesage est dans la banlieue. 2. Le patron emploie beaucoup de commis. 3. La sténo arrive à neuf heures moins cinq. 4. Le commis descend de l'autobus. 5. Il habite près d'ici. 6. Elle ne veut pas rester debout. 7. Le propriétaire de la compagnie ne voyage pas en troisième classe. 8. La gare n'est pas loin de chez lui. 9. Elles descendent sur le quai et elles attendent le train. 10. Quand le train arrive, elles y montent.

(*Key on page* 369.)

ANNECY : LE VIEUX QUARTIER

Ses canaux, bordés de maisons avec balcons et contrevents, sont une caractéristique pittoresque de cette ville, située parmi les montagnes de la Haute Savoie au sud du lac Léman.

| **Bordé(es)** (p.p.) | **balcon** (m.) | **contrevent** (m.) | **parmi** | le lac Léman |
|---|---|---|---|---|
| Bordered | balcony | shutter | among | Lake of Geneva |

# TRENTE-TROISIÈME LEÇON

## LES SPORTS

**Georges Lesage est un amateur passionné de sports. Il est membre d'une**
George Lesage is an ardent sports amateur.　He is a member of a

**équipe de football et il joue dans des matches contre d'autres équipes.**
football team and plays in matches against other teams.

**Quelquefois il joue comme avant, et quelquefois comme demi. Son équipe est**
Sometimes he plays as a forward and sometimes as a half-back.　His team is

**une des mieux connues; elle a gagné beaucoup de matches importants contre**
one of the best known; it has won many important matches against

**d'autres clubs français et étrangers. Il est aussi membre d'une association**
other clubs, both French and foreign.　He is also a member of a sports

**sportive qui possède un grand terrain de sports; il y a un vélodrome,**
club which possesses a large sports ground; there is a cycling ring,

**une piste, une piscine et plusieurs terrains pour le football et le**
a running track, a swimming pool and several fields for Association and

**rugby, deux sports pour lesquels les Français sont très enthousiastes.**
Rugby, two games about which the French are very enthusiastic.

**En outre il y a plusieurs rings pour les amateurs de boxe et des courts de tennis,**
In addition there are several boxing rings and tennis courts,

**deux sur gazon et six courts durs. L'autre jour Georges a invité son cousin**
two grass and six hard courts.　The other day George invited his English

**anglais à l'accompagner à une grande matinée sportive. Les courses à pied,**
cousin to accompany him to a big sports matinee.　Running,

---

### LES SPORTS=SPORTS

| | |
|---|---|
| **La natation** swimming | **Le football** Association football |
| **La pêche** fishing | **L'athlétisme** (m.) athletics |
| **Le canotage** boating | **Le ski** ski-ing |
| **L'aviron** (m.) rowing | **Le patinage** skating |
| **Le yachting** yachting | **La chasse** hunting |
| **Le tennis** tennis | **Le tir** shooting |
| **La boxe** boxing | **Les courses de chevaux** racing |
| **La lutte** wrestling | **Le cyclisme** cycling |
| **L'escrime** (f.) fencing | **L'équitation** (f.) riding |

**le lancement du disque et du javelot, le saut en longueur et en hauteur,**
discus and javelin throwing, long jump and high jump,

**le saut à la perche, la lutte, la boxe, l'escrime, etc., y sont représentés par**
pole jumping, wrestling, boxing, fencing, etc., are represented there by the

**les meilleurs athlètes parisiens, dont plusieurs champions internationaux.**
best Parisian athletes, among them several international champions.

**Le jour de l'événement les deux cousins arrivent dans une des tribunes,**
On the day of the event the two cousins arrive at one of the stands,

**qui sont bondées.**
which are crowded.

**Charles :** **Nous sommes un peu en retard.**
We are a little late.

**Georges :** **Nous n'avons pas perdu grand'chose. Nous n'avons manqué que**
We have not lost much. We have only missed a few

**quelques épreuves éliminatoires.**
trial heats.

**Charles :** **As-tu un programme?**
Have you a programme?

**Georges :** **Oui, et un crayon pour prendre des notes.**
Yes, and a pencil to take notes.

**Charles :** **Attention, voici l'épreuve finale de la course à obstacles.**
Look, this is the final heat for the hurdle race.

**Georges :** **Mauvais départ.** **Charles : C'est le petit homme portant des**
Bad start. It is the little man wearing

**lunettes qui a gagné.** **Georges : Trop facilement.**
spectacles who has won. Too easily.

**Charles :** **Quel est le concours suivant?**
What is the next event?

**Georges :** **Le saut en longueur. Il sera suivi d'une course plate.**
The long jump. It will be followed by a flat race.

**Charles :** **Le voilà qui saute! Bien sauté! Combien a-t-il**
There he jumps! Well jumped! What distance has he

**sauté?** **Georges : Presque cinq mètres.**
jumped? Nearly 17 feet.

Deux fameux joueurs français de tennis; une course d'obstacles au meeting inter-
universitaire; le départ d'une Course de Sept Jours de cyclisme au Vélodrôme d'Hiver;

| **Sportif-ive (adj.)** | **départ (m.)** | **montrer** | **photomontage (m.)** |
| Sporting | start (of event) | to show | montage photograph |

**PARIS SPORTIF**

et un match de football au Parc des Princes, sont montrés dans ce photomontage représentant la vie sportive de Paris. Ce sont les sports les plus populaires en France.

**Course (f.) de Sept Jours**

A favourite French cycling test which lasts day and night for seven days.

Charles :          **Pas mal du tout.   Voyez cette grande coupe.**
                   Not bad at all.   Look at that large cup.

Georges :          **Je crois que c'est le prix pour la course de cent mètres.**
                   I think that is the prize for the hundred metres flat race.

Charles :          **Assisterons-nous à la distribution des prix?**
                   Shall we be present at the prize-giving?

Georges :          **Bien sûr, elle aura lieu à la fin des**
                   Certainly, it will take place at the end of the

                   **concours de saut.**
                   jumping competitions.

## VOCABULARY

**une course**  race
**un stade**  stadium
**une partie**  game
**une équipe**  team
**une épreuve**  event; race; heat
**une demi-finale**  semi-final
**une finale**  final
**le terrain**  ground
**la piste**  track
**un match amical**  a friendly game
**un match nul**  a drawn game
**gagner**  to win
**perdre**  to lose
**battre**  to beat
**gagné**  won
**battu**  beaten
**perdu**  lost
**disqualifier**  to disqualify
**jouer au tennis**  to play tennis (*golf, etc.*)
**une partie de tennis**  a game of tennis
**la mi-temps**  half-time
**la deuxième mi-temps**  second half
**le concurrent**  competitor

## L'ATHLÉTISME—ATHLETICS

1. **la course**  running
   **le départ**  start
   **le coureur**  runner
   **le but**  finish
   **être léger à la course**  to be a swift runner

2. **la course à obstacles**  hurdle-race
   **la haie**  hurdle

3. **le saut**  jumping
   **le saut en hauteur**  high jump
   **le saut en longueur**  long jump
   **le saut à la perche**  pole jump
   **le sauteur**  jumper
   **la perche**  pole
   **la latte**  bar

4. **le lancement du javelot**  javelin throwing
   **le javelot**  javelin

5. **le lancement du disque**  discus throwing
   **le disque**  discus

## LE FOOTBALL— FOOTBALL (ASSOCIATION

**le terrain de jeu (le stade)**  field
**le but**  goal
**l'arbitre (m.)**  referee
**la balle**  ball
**les spectateurs (le public)**  spectators
**la tribune**  stand
**le gardien**  goalkeeper
**un arrière droit**  a right back
**un arrière gauche**  a left back
**un demi droit**  a right half back
**un demi centre**  a centre half back
**un demi gauche**  a left half back
**un ailier droit**  an outside right
**un ailier gauche**  an outside left
**un inter-droit**  an inside right
**un inter-gauche**  an inside left
**l'avant-centre**  the centre forward

## AUCUN, AUCUNE

**Je ne connais aucun de ses amis**=I know none of his friends.

**Je n'ai aucun plaisir**=I have no pleasure

**Aucun(e) de vous n'est arrivé(e) à l'heure**= None of you have arrived in time.

**Ce livre m'intéresse plus qu'aucun autre**= This book interests me more than any other.

**Cette robe vous va mieux qu'aucune autre**= This frock suits you better than any other.

**Sans aucun doute**=Without any doubt.

**aucun(e)**=any; preceded by **ne** (but not followed by **pas**)=none, no, not any

## AUTRE

**Si vous n'aimez pas ces couteaux je vous en montrerai d'autres**=If you don't like these knives I'll show you others.

**Une autre fourchette s'il vous plaît. Celle-ci n'est pas propre**=Another fork please. This one is not clean.

**Je l'ai rencontré l'autre jour**=I met him the other day.

**C'est une autre affaire**=That is another matter.

**Elle ne parle jamais d'autre chose**=She never speaks of anything else.

**Il est resté, les autres sont partis**=He has stayed, the others have left.

**Vous me demandez du savon et une serviette; je n'ai ni l'un ni l'autre**=You ask me for some soap and a towel; I haven't got either.

**L'un et l'autre sont partis** ⎱ =They have
**L'une et l'autre sont parties** ⎰ both left.

**C'était bien autre chose alors**=It was (*things were*) very different then (*i.e., much better or much worse*).

**Nous autres Anglais**=We English people

**Vous autres Français**=You French people

**À d'autres !**=Tell that to others; don't tell *me* that! (*slang*)

**autre**=other

**l'un** ⎱
**l'une** ⎰ et l'autre=both

**ni l'un ni l'autre**=neither

**l'un ou l'autre**=either

**autrefois**=formerly

**autrement**=otherwise

**autre part**=elsewhere

**d'autre part**=on the other hand

**de temps à autre**=from time to time

## MÊME

**Le même jour**=The same day

**La même année**=The same year

**Le jour même**=The very same day

**L'année même**=The very same year

**Il dit toujours la même chose**=He always says the same (*thing*).

**C'est la même chose qu'en anglais**=It is the same as in English.

**Il est toujours le même**=He is always the same.

**Elle est toujours la même**=She is always the same.

**Il ne m'a même pas répondu**=He has not even answered me.

**Elle ne m'a même pas remercié**=She did not even thank me.

**Je le ferai quand même**=I'll do it all the same.

**Je le ferai moi-même**=I'll do it myself.

**Il est fou de même que son père**=He is mad like his father.

### HOW TO TRANSLATE "ARE YOU"

#### 1. Êtes-vous . . .?

Êtes-vous (étiez-vous) are you (were you)?

| | |
|---|---|
| **le patron ici ?** | the boss here? |
| **Anglais(e) ?** | English? |
| **fatigué(e) ?** | tired? |
| **pressé(e) ?** | in a hurry? |
| **en retard ?** | late? |

Normally "are you"=**êtes-vous** ("were you"=**étiez-vous**). Note, however, that "are you"=**avez-vous** ("were you"=**aviez-vous**) in the following cases:

#### 2. Avez-vous . . .?

Avez-vous (aviez-vous) are you (were you)

| | |
|---|---|
| **chaud ?** | hot? |
| **froid ?** | cold? |
| **faim ?** | hungry? |
| **soif ?** | thirsty? |

| | |
|---|---|
| raison? | right? |
| tort? | wrong? |
| peur? | afraid? |
| honte? | ashamed? |
| pitié de lui? | sorry for him? |
| besoin de cela? | in need of that? |

N.B.—When speaking of *things* and not *persons* use être chaud, être froid.

il a froid = he is cold
il (= le vin) est froid ) it is cold
elle (= l'eau) est froide ) it is cold

### 3. . . . -vous?

| | | | |
|---|---|---|---|
| Venez | | | coming? |
| Allez | | | going? |
| Attendez | }-vous? | are you | waiting? |
| Écoutez | | | listening? |
| Mangez | | | eating? |

| | |
|---|---|
| Allez-vous | are you going to |
| (alliez-vous) | (were you going to) |
| attendre? | wait? |
| jouer? | play? |
| partir? | leave? |
| le faire? | do it? |
| en manger? | eat some? |

No difference is made in French between "*I come*" and "*I am coming*"; "*I wait*" and "*I am waiting*"; "*are you coming?*" and "*do you come?*"; "*are you waiting?*" and "*do you wait?*", etc.

## EXERCISES

### I Traduisez en anglais

1. Cette partie m'intéresse plus qu'aucune autre. 2. Il court plus vite qu'aucun de ses concurrents. 3. Aucun d'eux n'est arrivé à l'heure. 4. Aucun spectateur ne l'a vu. 5. Il y a un autre vélodrome près d'ici. 6. Il ne parle jamais d'autre chose. 7. Je suis resté seul à la maison; les autres sont allés à la piscine. 8. Il a le même handicap que moi. 9. Nous jouons dans la même équipe. 10. Si vous n'aimez pas ces épreuves nous pouvons en voir d'autres. 11. Vous me demandez si je joue au tennis et au football? Je ne joue ni à l'un ni à l'autre.

12. Assisterez-vous à la distribution des prix qui aura lieu demain?

### II Traduisez en français

1. None of your friends was on the sports ground. 2. I have seen neither the one nor the other. 3. They are faster than any of their competitors. 4. Did you play with them the other day? 5. He always plays on the same tennis court. 6. This game interests him more than any other. 7. We had a game of tennis the other day. 8. Are you a member of the sports club? 9. Are you Charles's cousin? 10. Are you warm enough? 11. Are you coming? 12. Are you going to play? (*Key on pages* 369 *and* 370).

### HISTOIRES AMUSANTES

· The words which you cannot be expected to know are translated below. With that help you should be able to read these simple tales.

Deux petites filles se promènent dans la campagne.
Au milieu d'un pré paissent deux vaches, une blanche et une noire.
Tiens, dit l'une des deux petites à sa camarade, tu vois ces deux vaches?
Oui.
Eh bien, c'est la vache blanche qui donne le lait et la vache noire qui donne le café!

————

Jeannette, 7 ans, observe la poussière que l'auto soulève sur une route de campagne.
C'est vrai, maman, que nous ne sommes que poussière?
Oui, ma petite chérie.
Alors les nègres, c'est de la poussière de charbon?

Pré (m.), meadow; paissent (from paître), are grazing; poussière (f.), dust; soulever, to raise; campagne (f.), country; ne . . . que, only; chéri-e, (m. f.), darling; nègres, (m. pl.), negroes; poussière de charbon, coal-dust.

# TRENTE-QUATRIÈME LEÇON

### LES SPORTS (suite)—SPORTS (continued)

**Le football n'est pas le seul sport qui intéresse Georges. Il est aussi**
Football is not the only sport that interests George. He is also

**amateur de boxe. L'autre jour il**
fond of boxing. The other day he

**a été mis knock-out à la fin d'un**
was knocked out at the end of a

**match sur cinq rounds. "Je n'étais**
match of five rounds. "I was not

**pas bien entraîné", c'est ce**
well-trained", is what he

**qu'il dit. Mlle Lesage joue au**
says. Miss Lesage plays

**tennis. Elle est membre d'un club,**
tennis. She belongs to a club,

**et elle joue dans des matches**
and plays in matches

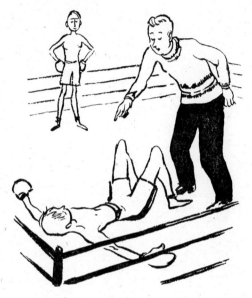

**contre d'autres clubs. Elle est bonne joueuse et gagne beaucoup**
against other clubs. She is a good player and wins many

**de ses parties. Le sport qui intéresse M. Lesage est la course de chevaux.**
of her sets. The sport that interests Mr. Lesage is horse-racing.

**Accompagné de son beau-frère il est allé à Longchamp, l'un des champs**
Accompanied by his brother-in-law he went to Longchamp, one of the

**de course les plus populaires de la région parisienne. Mme Roberts les a**
most popular race-courses near Paris. Mrs. Roberts accompanied

**accompagnés aussi. Elle a dit qu'on y voit de si jolies toilettes.**
them also. She said that one can see such beautiful dresses there.

**Il y avait énormément de monde sur les pelouses. M. Lesage et les**
There was an enormous crowd on the lawns. Mr. Lesage and the

**Roberts se sont installés dans une des tribunes du pesage.**
Roberts got seats in one of the stands of the paddock.

## LONGCHAMP, UN JOUR DE GRAND PRIX

C'est le Derby des Parisiens. Et les tribunes bondées, les mannequins qui font valoir les derniers modèles, le tableau d'affichage entouré d'ardents spéculateurs, la perspective d'une fin serrée—tout nous offre l'impression d'un événement sportif des plus importants. Longchamp est dans le Bois de Boulogne à Paris.

| **Tribune** (f.) | **bonder** | **faire valoir** | **tableau** (m.) **d'affichage** | **fin** (f.) **serrée** |
|---|---|---|---|---|
| Stand | to fill | show to advantage | number board | close finish |

**M. Lesage a risqué cent francs sur un cheval, pour lequel il avait reçu**
Mr. Lesage risked 100 francs on a horse for which he had received

**un bon tuyau. Mme Roberts n'a pas fait attention aux tuyaux qu'on lui avait**
a good tip. Mrs. Roberts did not take any notice of the tips given

**donnés. Elle a mis cinquante francs sur un cheval dont l'air lui plaisait.**
to her. She put fifty francs on a horse, the look of which she liked.

**Elle a eu la veine de le voir gagner. C'était bien son jour de veine.**
She had the luck to see it win. It really was her lucky day.

**Quant à Madeleine, elle va devenir bonne patineuse. Avec sa cousine**
As for Madeleine, she is going to become a good skater. With her cousin

**elle va patiner trois fois par semaine dans un skating qui vient de**
she goes skating three times a week at a skating rink which has

**s'ouvrir dans leur quartier. Le sport favori de Charles (malgré sa**
just been opened in their district. Charles's favourite sport (despite his

**mésaventure infortunée) est toujours le cyclisme, qui est un des**
unfortunate mishap) is still cycling, which is one of the

AT THE SKATING RINK

In this picture Lucie Lesage is showing Madeleine Roberts and the others how easy it is to skate! Try to describe the scene in French, introducing the following words which are new to you:— **accoudoir** (m.)=balustrade; **tricot** (m.)=jumper, knitted-vest; **patins** (m.) **à glace**=skates.

**sports les plus populaires en France.   L'autre jour il s'est égaré en**
most popular sports in France.   The other day he lost his way when

**rentrant d'une randonnée aux environs de Paris.   En outre, l'un**
returning from a trip into the surroundings of Paris.   In addition, one

**de ses pneus a crevé.   Heureusement un monsieur**
of his tyres burst.   Fortunately a gentleman

**est arrivé à qui il a pu**
arrived of whom he was able

**demander son chemin.**
to ask his way.

Charles :       **Pardon, monsieur.**
                Excuse me, sir,

**veuillez me dire où je suis —**
will you please tell me where I am —

**je me suis égaré.**
I have lost my way.

Le monsieur :   **Vous êtes près de Fontainebleau.   Au coin de la rue vous**
                You are near Fontainebleau.   At the corner of the street

                **verrez un poteau-indicateur.**
                you will see a sign-post.

Charles :       **Pourrai-je faire réparer mon pneu à Fontainebleau?**
                Shall I be able to get my tyre repaired at Fontainebleau?

Le monsieur :   **Sans doute; vous y trouverez des garages.**
                Undoubtedly; you will find some garages there.

Charles :       **Bonsoir, monsieur, je vous remercie.**
                Good evening, sir, and thank you.

Le monsieur :   **Il n'y a pas de quoi, mon ami.**
                You are welcome (my friend).

**(Charles continue son chemin, poussant son vélo, lorsqu'un sergent de ville**
(Charles continues his way, pushing his bike, when a policeman

**l'arrête.)**          Le sergent :   **Halte, mon petit, il faut allumer la lanterne.**
stops him.)                          Stop, my little man, you have to light your lamp.

Charles :       **Déjà?   Quelle heure est-il donc?**
                Already?   What is the time then?

Le sergent :  **Il est huit heures**
It is ten

**moins dix.**
to eight.

Charles :  **Mais faut-il allumer**
But do I have to light

**quand je ne suis pas**
when I am not

**sur mon vélo?**
on my bike?

Le sergent :  **Parfaitement,**
You have to

**mon petit.**
(certainly), my little man.

Charles :  **Bien, j'allumerai.**
All right, I shall light up.

**J'ignorais le règlement.**
I did not know the regulations.

## LE TENNIS—TENNIS

le court   tennis court
le filet   net
la raquette   racquet
la palette   table tennis bat
une balle de tennis   tennis ball
le joueur de tennis   tennis player
le ramasseur de balles   ball-boy
la ligne de côté   side line
la ligne de service   service line
la ligne médiane   central line
la ligne du fond   base line
l'arbitre   umpire
le filet   net
la balle   ball

## LA COURSE DE CHEVAUX—HORSE RACING

le champ de course   race-course
les tribunes   stands
la tribune   judge's box
le juge   judge

le pesage   paddock
la pelouse   public enclosures
la piste   course (*track*)
le départ   starting-point
l'arrivée   finish
une haie   hurdle
un cheval de course   race-horse
le jockey   jockey
la casquette   cap
la cravache   whip
un bookmaker   bookmaker
le pari-mutuel   totalisator
l'écurie (f.)   stables

## LA BOXE—BOXING

1. le boxeur   boxer
le ring (*English pronunciation*)   ring
les cordes (f. pl.)   ropes
l'arbitre   referee
le public   public
les seconds   seconds
le commencement d'un match sur 15 rounds
   the beginning of a 15-rounds match

## THE FISTIC ART

Your task here is to study the lists on pages 357 and 359 and then to describe in French everything you see in the picture—ropes, ring, seconds, the various blows exchanged by the boxers, and what is happening to the tired-looking sportsman shown in the lower right-hand portion of the picture. You will note from the vocabularies that in boxing, as in other sports, many English expressions are made use of in French without any alteration, and even the English pronunciation is used in some instances. A description of the above scene in French should, therefore, give you no great difficulty.

2. **Un des boxeurs place un direct gauche, que son adversaire esquive par dessous** One of the boxers delivers a straight left, which his opponent eludes by "ducking."

3. **Un crochet du droit** a right hook

4. **Un coup balancé** a swing

5. **Les deux boxeurs en clinch** The two boxers clinching

6. **L'un des boxeurs est mis knock out (est knock-outé)** One of the boxers is knocked out.

### JUST

**Ils viennent d'arriver**=They have just arrived.

**Maman vient de sortir**=Mother has just gone out.

**Il venait d'envoyer le télégramme**=He had just sent the telegram.

**Nous venions de passer quelques jours à la campagne**=We had just spent a few days in the country.

**Venir de,** followed by an Infinitive, expresses the immediate past.

### TO BE GOING TO

**Je vais écrire des lettres**=I am going to write some letters.

**Qu'est-ce qu'il va faire?**=What is he going to do?

**Nous allons le voir cet après-midi**=We are going to see him this afternoon.

**Il allait jouer du piano**=He was going to play the piano.

**Nous allions sortir**=We were going out.

**Aller,** followed by an Infinitive, indicates the immediate future.

### TO HAVE SOMETHING DONE

**Elle fait faire une robe pour sa petite fille**= She is having a dress made for her little girl.

**Voulez-vous faire réparer cela?**=Will you have this repaired?

**Je le ferai travailler**=I shall make him work.

**Voulez-vous faire nettoyer ma chambre?**= Will you have my room cleaned?

**Je le lui ferai envoyer**=I will get it sent to him.

**Faites frire ce poisson**=Fry this fish; have this fish fried.

**Voulez-vous faire rôtir ce poulet?**=Will you roast this chicken; will you have this chicken roasted?

**Faire,** followed by an Infinitive, means to have (*or to get*) something done. Note also the following expressions:

**faire une promenade**=to take a walk

**faire des emplettes**=to go shopping

**faire la vaisselle**=to wash up

**faire trente kilomètres**=to walk (*or drive*) thirty kilometres.

**quel temps fait-il?**=how is the weather?

**il fait beau**=it is fine

**il fait mauvais**=it is bad

**il fait chaud**=it is hot

**il fait froid**=it is cold

**il fait frais**=it is cool

**il fait vilain**=it is nasty

**il fait clair**=it is light

**il fait sombre**=it is dark

**il fait lourd**=it is sultry

### THE INFINITIVE AFTER VERBS AND PREPOSITIONS

**Avant d'entrer dans la maison**=Before entering the house.

**Il avoue avoir dit cela**=He admits having said this.

**Je n'ai pas besoin d'y aller**=I have no need to go there.

**Je l'ai vu battre le chien**=I saw him beating the dog.

**Au lieu de sonner**=Instead of ringing.

**Finissons cela avant de rentrer**=Let us finish that before going home.

**Après avoir fait cela**=After having done that.

**Après avoir ouvert la fenêtre**=After having opened the window.

**Après avoir fini mon travail**=After having finished my work.

**Après être arrivé**=After having arrived.

**J'aime à faire cela**=I like doing that.

**C'est jouer un jeu dangereux**=That is playing a dangerous game.

When a verb follows another verb or a preposition (except **en**) it must be in the Infinitive. Note the examples above. In English, forms in "*-ing*" are used where in French the Infinitive has to be employed. Notice that **après** takes the Past Infinitive.

Note also the following uses of the Infinitive (*in place of an English subordinate clause or personal mood*):

**Je crois le connaître**=I think I know him.

**Il pense avoir raison**=He thinks that he is right.

**Nous croyions entendre un cri**=We thought we heard a cry.

**Comment savoir si c'est vrai?**=How do I (*do we, does one*) know, if it is true?

**Pourquoi manger quand on n'a pas faim?**=Why eat when you are not hungry?

**Que faire?**=What shall I (*we, one*) do?

**Qui croire?**=Whom am I (*are we, is one*) to believe?

**Je ne sais que faire**=I don't know what to do.

Note further the use of the Infinitive in signs and general notices:

**défense de fumer**=smoking forbidden        **à vendre**=for sale

## EXERCISES

### I Translate into English

1. Venez m'aider. 2. Elle regrette de ne pas pouvoir vous rencontrer (=to meet) ce soir. 3. Je n'ai pas le temps de vous envoyer des lettres. 4. Permettez-moi de vous donner un avis (=advice). 5. Je suis heureux de vous entendre parler ainsi (=like this). 6. Veuillez me faire réveiller à six heures. 7. Je vais faire faire une robe d'après-midi chez ma couturière. 8. Comme il fait froid nous faisons allumer du feu. 9. Je vous ferai envoyer votre valise. 10. Je crois avoir vu ce monsieur. 11. Faites venir la domestique. 12. Je vais mettre ces lettres à la poste. 13. Elles vont finir (=to finish) dans une minute. 14. Il semble (=seems) avoir oublié son rendezvous. 15. Il vient de voir votre père. (*Key on page* 370).

### II Translate into French

1. He has just gone out. 2. They have just arrived. 3. I am going to open the window. 4. Are you going to play now? 5. I believe that I saw your aunt at the concert. 6. They are going to leave to-night. 7. Is it cold? 8. Was it hot yesterday? 9. Have the windows closed; it is too cold. 10. I'll make him work. 11. Have these eggs boiled. 12. I think that I know them. 13. Instead of skating we shall go swimming. 14. After having finished his work he made a trip on his bicycle into the surroundings of the town. 15. I like watching the skaters. 16. He lost his way returning from the race-course. 17. He gave me a good tip. 18. My favourite sport is cycling. 19. The other day he lost fifty francs. 20. It was not his lucky day.

## UN HÔTEL DU VIEUX PARIS

Dans ces petits hôtels bon marché, les gens peu fortunés trouvent un confort restreint. Remarquez les volets que l'on ferme la nuit. Chaque maison en est pourvue en France.

| **Bon marché** | **peu fortuné-e** | **confort** (m.) | **restreint-e** (adj.) | **le volet** |
|---|---|---|---|---|
| Cheap | of slender means | comfort | qualified, limited | shutter |

# TRENTE-CINQUIÈME LEÇON

## À LA CAMPAGNE—IN THE COUNTRY

**La France est un pays agricole. Les petits propriétaires terriens**
France is an agricultural country. Small landed proprietors

**y sont très nombreux. Dans un village presque tous les habitants sont**
are very numerous there. In a village almost all the inhabitants are either

**des cultivateurs ou des vignerons. On y trouve aussi quelques artisans,**
farmers or vine-growers. There are also to be found some artisans,

**un curé, un médecin et un instituteur. Presque chaque maison est entourée**
a priest, a doctor and a schoolmaster. Almost every house is surrounded

**d'une cour et d'un jardin. On y voit aussi des écuries pour les chevaux,**
by a courtyard and a garden. There are also to be seen stables for the horses,

**des étables pour le bétail, des granges pour le blé, des remises pour**
sheds for the cattle, barns for the corn, sheds for the

**les voitures et les chariots. Dans la cour on peut voir des chèvres avec leurs chevreaux,**
carriages and the carts. In the courtyard one can see goats with their kids,

**des poules avec leurs poussins, des dindons, des oies et des pigeons. Les maisons les**
hens and their chicks, turkeys, geese and pigeons. The smallest

**plus petites ont seulement un rez-de-chaussée et sont couvertes de paille. On les appelle**
houses have only a ground-floor and are covered with straw. They are called

**des chaumières. Les autres maisons ont un premier et quelquefois**
"chaumières" (thatched cottages). The other houses have a first and sometimes

**aussi un deuxième étage. Les seuls édifices du village**
also a second floor. The only (public) buildings of the village

**sont l'église et l'école. Le printemps est une saison de grand**
are the church and the school. Spring is a season of hard

**travail pour le cultivateur, car il doit labourer ses terres et semer**
work for the farmer, for he has to plough his lands and to sow

**les différentes espèces de blé. Dans les jardins, les jardiniers**
the different kinds of corn. In the gardens, the gardeners

**aussi ont beaucoup à faire. Ils doivent bêcher le sol pour le préparer**
too have much to do. They must dig the ground to prepare it

à recevoir les plantes qu'ils veulent y planter. Le soleil fait croître l'herbe
to receive the plants which they want to plant there. The sun makes the grass grow

et mûrir le blé. Au commencement de l'été le foin est
and the corn ripen. In the beginning of the summer the hay is

mûr. Il est coupé, séché et transporté à la ferme. À la fin de juillet ou
ripe. It is cut, dried and taken to the farm. At the end of July or

au commencement d'août la moisson commence. Après avoir coupé le blé,
beginning of August the harvest begins. After the corn has been cut,

on le met en gerbes pour le sécher. Puis on le battra pour en sortir les
it is made into sheaves to dry. Then it will be thrashed to get out the

grains, qui seront transportés au moulin pour en faire de la farine.
grain, which will be taken to the mill to be made into flour.

En automne on récolte les pommes de terre et les betteraves; dans les
In autumn potatoes and beetroot are harvested; in the

vignobles c'est le temps des vendanges. Dans le verger on cueille
vineyards it is the time of the grape-harvest. In the orchard the last

les derniers fruits: les pommes, les poires et les prunes. Les pommes poussent
fruits are picked: apples, pears and plums. The apples grow

sur un arbre; c'est le pommier. La poire pousse sur le poirier et la prune
on a tree; it is the apple tree. The pear grows on the pear tree and the plum

sur le prunier. Les cerises, qui poussent sur le cerisier, ont déjà été
on the plum tree. The cherries, which grow on the cherry tree, were already

cueillies en juin. L'été est la période des excursions à pied, à bicyclette ou
picked in June. Summer is the time of excursions on foot, on a bicycle or

en auto, et des promenades dans les bois et dans les forêts. C'est la saison
by car, and of walks in woods and forests. It is the season

des grandes chaleurs et des orages. Les Lesage passent presque tous les
of great heat and of thunderstorms. The Lesages spend almost all the

dimanches à la campagne. Ils se lèvent de bonne heure, montent dans leur
Sundays in the country. They get up early, get into their

auto, et arrivent bientôt en pleine campagne.
car, and soon arrive in the open country.

Quand il fait chaud ils vont dans une forêt. Ils y choisissent un bon endroit
When it is hot they go into the forest. There they choose a good place

## A FRENCH VILLAGE SCENE

You are now getting very near the end of the Course. If you have studied all the lessons carefully you should be well equipped to cope with almost any situation in which a traveller in France might find himself or herself. So far most of the Course has had a more or less urban background, but this picture shows you a very typical section of the sort of village life you may encounter if you go through France by car, by bicycle or on foot. Think of yourself, therefore, as making ready for such a tour, and study the list set out on page 365 until you feel competent to name in French any object in this picture without aid. Write a description of the picture.

**à l'ombre pour faire leur pique-nique.   Mme Lesage leur a préparé**
in the shade to have their picnic.   Mrs. Lesage has prepared them

**un grand panier plein de bonnes choses.   Après le repas ils se promènent**
a large basket full of good things.   After the meal they stroll about

**dans la forêt.   Ainsi ils passent une journée agréable en plein air.**
in the forest.   Thus they spend a pleasant day in the open air.

### LE VILLAGE—VILLAGE

**le poteau indicateur**  sign-post
**une église**  church
**le curé**  parish priest
**le pâturage**  pasture land
**un étang**  pond
**une école**  school
**la ferme**  farm-house
**la pompe à eau**  water-pump
**une étable**  cowshed
**la vache**  cow
**le veau**  calf
**une écurie**  stable
· **le cheval**  horse
**la herse**  harrow
**le seau à lait**  milk-pail
**la meule de foin**  hay-rick
**la fourche à foin**  pitchfork
**le poulailler**  chicken-house
**le coq**  cock
**la poule**  hen
**le poussin**  chick
**la grange**  barn
**une oie**  goose
**le dindon**  turkey
**la voiture**  carriage
**le chariot**  cart
**le moulin à vent**  windmill
**le pigeon**  pigeon
**la colombe**  dove

### TO GROW

**pousser** ⎫
**croître** ⎭ =to grow (*of plants*)
**grandir**=to grow (*of persons*)
**devenir vieux**=to grow old
**cultiver**=to grow, to till, to cultivate
**planter**=to grow, to plant
**adulte**=grown up
**les adultes** ⎫
**les grands** ⎭ =the grown-ups

### THE FRENCH VERB

French verbs are divided into four groups, according to the ending of the Infinitive.  These groups are called Conjugations.

1st Conjugation, Infinitive in **-er,**
    like **donner**=to give.
2nd Conjugation, Infinitive in **-ir,**
    like **choisir**=to choose.
3rd Conjugation, Infinitive in **-re,**
    like **prendre**=to take.
4th Conjugation, Infinitive in **-oir,**
    like **avoir**=to have.

**Verbs in -er**

Most verbs terminate in **-er** and they are conjugated like **donner** (*see pages* 391-392) except **aller** (*see page* 394) and a few minor changes in verbs (*see page* 371).

**Verbs in -ir**

Many verbs end in **-ir**.  Some are conjugated like **finir**, others are irregular.

#### FINIR=TO FINISH

| Present | Imperfect |
|---|---|
| je finis | je finissais |
| tu finis | tu finissais |
| il finit | il finissait |
| nous finissons | nous finissions |
| vous finissez | vous finissiez |
| ils finissent | ils finissaient |

| Future | Conditional |
|---|---|
| je finirai | je finirais |
| tu finiras | tu finirais |
| il finira | il finirait |
| nous finirons | nous finirions |
| vous finirez | vous finiriez |
| ils finiront | ils finiraient |

(*Continued on page* 368)

### English

1. Foliage; 2. Trunk (of tree); 3. Branch; 4. Twig; 5. By-road; 6. Main road; 7. Grass; 8. Meadow; 9. Poplars; 10. Ass; 11. Panniers; 12. Hamlet; 13. Farm; 14. Ploughman; 15. Team of oxen; 16. Ploughed land; 17. Furrow; 18. "Spit" (of soil); 19. Fowls; 20. Fowl house; 21. Peasant (girl); 22. Hayricks; 23. Cattle chewing cud; 24. Hilly country; 25. Hill; 26. Mountain top; 27. Valley; 28. Vineyard; 29. Fallow land; 30. Chestnut tree; 31. Telegraph poles; 32. Spinney; 33. Man in shirtsleeves; 34. Woman knitting; 35. Thermos flask; 36. Hamper; 37. Man fishing; 38. Fishing rod; 39. Fishing-tackle; 40. Stream or brook.

### French

1. Feuillage (m.); 2. Tronc (m.); 3. Branche (f.); 4. Brindille (f.); 5. Chemin

| Further Useful Expressions | montagneux | accidenté | boisé |
|---|---|---|---|
| | mountainous | hilly | woody |

# À LA CAMPAGNE

(m.) vicinal; 6. Chaussée (f.); (route (f.) nationale); 7. Herbe (f.); 8. Prairie (f.); 9. Peupliers (m.); 10. Âne (m.), bourrique (f.); 11. Panier de bât (m.); 12. Hameau (m.); 13. Ferme (f.); 14. Laboureur (m.); 15. Attelage (m.) de bœufs; 16. Terre (f.) labourée; 17. Sillon (m.); 18. Bechée (f.) de terre; 19. Volaille (f.); 20. Poulailler (m.); 21. Paysanne (f.); 22. Meules (f. pl.) de foin (m.); 23. Bétail (m.) ruminant; 24. Terrain (m.) accidenté; 25. Colline (f.); 26. Cime (f.), sommet (m.); 27. Vallée (f.); 28. Clos (m.) de vigne (f.); 29. Terre (f.) en friche; 30. Châtaignier (m.); 31. Poteaux (m. pl.) télégraphiques; 32. Bosquet (m.); 33. Homme en bras de chemise; 34. Tricoteuse (f.); 35. Bouteille (f.) isolante (thermos); 36. Panier (m.) à provisions; 37. Pêcheur (m.); 38. Canne (f.) à pêche; 39. Attirail de pêche (m.); 40. Ruisseau (m.).

| escarpé | sauvage | boueux | marécageux |
|---|---|---|---|
| steep | wild | muddy | marshy |

Perfect: **j'ai fini, tu as fini, il a fini,** etc.
Imperative: **finis, finissons, finissez**

The verb **choisir** = to choose is conjugated like **finir.**

**sortir** is conjugated like **dormir, servir, partir** and **sentir** (see page 395).

**cueillir** = to pluck, to gather, to pick, is like **ouvrir,** to open, but Future is **je cueillerai,** Conditional is **je cueillerais,** and the Perfect is **j'ai cueilli.**

**j'ouvre, tu ouvres, il ouvre, nous ouvrons; j'ouvrais; j'ouvrirai; j'ai ouvert,** etc.

**couvrir** = to cover is like **ouvrir.**

**Verbs in -re**
There are a few dozen of them. Some are conjugated like **vendre** (see page 391), others are irregular.

Of the verbs occurring in this lesson, **faire** has been given on pages 105 and 149 and **mettre** on pages 122 and 149. New verbs are **battre** and **croître.**

### BATTRE = TO BEAT, TO THRASH
Present:

**je bats**
**tu bats**
**il bat**
**nous battons**
**vous battez**
**ils battent**

Imperfect: **je battais,** etc.
Future: **je battrai,** etc.
Conditional: **je battrais,** etc.
Perfect: **j'ai battu,** etc.
Imperative: **bats, battons, battez**

### CROÎTRE = TO GROW
Present:

**je croîs**
**tu croîs**
**il croît**
**nous croissons**
**vous croissez**
**ils croissent**

Imperfect: **je croissais,** etc.
Future: **je croîtrai,** etc.
Conditional: **je croîtrais,** etc.
Perfect: **j'ai crû** (f., **crûe**)

Note the circumflex which is used to distinguish it from forms of **croire.**

### CROIRE = TO BELIEVE
Present:

**je crois**
**tu crois**
**il croit**
**nous croyons**
**vous croyez**
**ils croient**

Imperfect: **je croyais,** etc.
Future: **je croirai,** etc.
Conditional: **je croirais,** etc.
Perfect: **j'ai cru,** etc.
Imperative: **crois, croyons, croyez**

**Verbs in -oir**
There are only a few of them, but they are all irregular. **Avoir** = to have, **voir** = to see, **vouloir** = to wish, and **pouvoir** = to be able, have already been given. A new verb in this lesson is:

### RECEVOIR = TO RECEIVE
Present:

**je reçois**
**tu reçois**
**il reçoit**
**nous recevons**
**vous recevez**
**ils reçoivent**

Imperfect: **je recevais,** etc.
Future: **je recevrai,** etc.
Conditional: **je recevrais,** etc.
Perfect: **j'ai reçu,** etc.
Imperative: **reçois, recevez, recevons**

## EXERCISES

### I Répondez en français aux questions suivantes

1. Fait-il chaud en été? 2. Restez-vous en ville en été? 3. Qu'y a-t-il dans les champs? 4. Qu'est-ce qui pousse dans le verger? 5. Où poussent les poires? 6. Y a-t-il des fruits aux arbres en hiver? 7. Où fait-il plus chaud, au soleil ou à l'ombre? 8. Que fait le laboureur en été? 9. Comment appelle-t-on les petits de la vache? 10. Où les Lesage vont-ils passer le dimanche? 11. Quand se lèvent-ils? 12. Qu'est-ce que Mme Lesage leur

prépare? 13. Que font-ils quand il fait chaud? 14. Que font-ils quand ils ont faim?

## II Traduisez en anglais

1. Au printemps les arbres portent des fleurs; en été ils sont couverts de feuilles et ils portent des fruits; en automne les feuilles tombent. 2. Quand il fait beau on préfère être en plein air. 3. Votre mère n'est-elle pas sortie? 4. Comme le cœur me bat! 5. Ne battez pas le chien! 6. Croyez-vous ce qu'elle a dit? 7. Qui est-ce qui croit tout ce qu'il lit? 8. Il laisse croître ses cheveux. 9. Il ne sait pas ce qu'il veut. 10. Je pourrai vous aider quand vous voudrez.

## III Traduisez en français

1. I shall finish my job on Saturday. 2. Haven't they finished yet? 3. You can have an apple tree or a plum tree: choose. 4. They are fighting (beat themselves) for nothing. 5. I never believe what he says. 6. Why don't you believe me? 7. I read it, but I did not believe it. 8. We get two pints (about a litre) of milk each morning. 9. He got ten pounds of apples. 10. You will get them tomorrow. (*Key on page* 370.)

# KEY TO THE EXERCISES

## Lesson Thirty-two

### I

1. Il est au centre de Paris. 2. M. Lesage en est le propriétaire. 3. Elle est dans la banlieue. 4. Il y a des tables, des chaises, des machines à écrire, etc. 5. La sténo-dactylo les écrit. 6. Le garçon de bureau. 7. J'en ai une (je n'en ai pas). 8. Il fait beau (mauvais). 9. En novembre. 10. Il (ne) fait (pas) chaud aujourd'hui. 11. C'est aujourd'hui le trois avril. 12. C'est à moi *or* c'est le mien.

### II

1. Le commis arrive au bureau à huit heures moins le quart. 2. Le patron dicte beaucoup de lettres. 3. La sténo les tape à la machine. 4. Le commis va au bureau à pied. 5. Quand il pleut il vient en autobus. 6. Il s'assied dans le métro. 7. Quand le train arrive il descend. 8. Elle habite la banlieue. 9. Ne soyez pas en retard. 10. À qui est cette machine à écrire? 11. À qui écrivez-vous? 12. Il est sept heures cinq. 13. Il est très tard. 14. Il fait beau. 15. À qui est cette montre? Elle est à moi *or* c'est la mienne.

### III

1. Mr. Lesage's factory is in the suburbs. 2. The boss employs many clerks. 3. The typist arrives at five to nine. 4. The clerk gets out of the bus. 5. He lives near here. 6. She does not want to stand. 7. The owner of the firm does not travel third class. 8. The station is not far from his house. 9. They get out on to the platform and wait for the train. 10. When the train arrives they get in.

## Lesson Thirty-three

### I

1. This game interests me more than any other. 2. He runs (or is running) faster than any of his opponents. 3. None of them has arrived in time. 4. None of the spectators has seen him. 5. There is another cycling track near here. 6. He never speaks of anything else. 7. I remained in the house alone; the others went to the swimming-bath. 8. He has the same handicap as I. 9. We play in the same team. 10. If you don't like these events we can see others. 11. You are asking me if I play both tennis and football? I play neither. 12. Will you be present at the distribution of prizes, which will take place to-morrow?

### II

1. Aucun de vos amis n'était sur le terrain de sports. 2. Je n'ai vu ni l'un ni

l'autre. 3. Ils sont plus rapides qu'aucun de leurs concurrents. 4. Avez-vous joué avec eux l'autre jour? 5. Il joue toujours sur le même court de tennis. 6. Cette partie l'intéresse plus qu'aucune autre. 7. Nous jouions une partie de tennis l'autre jour. 8. Êtes-vous membre de l'association sportive? 9. Êtes-vous le cousin de Charles? 10. Avez-vous assez chaud? 11. Venez-vous? 12. Allez-vous jouer?

## Lesson Thirty-four

### I

1. Come and help me. 2. She regrets not to be able to meet you to-night. 3. I have not the time to send you letters. 4. Allow me to give you advice. 5. I am glad to hear you speaking like this. 6. Will you please have me called at six? 7. I am going to have an afternoon frock made at my dressmaker's. 8. As it is cold we have made a fire. 9. I'll have your suitcase sent to you. 10. I believe that I have seen this man. 11. Tell the maid to come. 12. I am going to post these letters. 13. They are going to finish in a minute. 14. He seems to have forgotten his appointment. 15. He has just seen your father.

### II

1. Il vient de sortir. 2. Ils viennent d'arriver. 3. Je vais ouvrir la fenêtre. 4. Allez-vous jouer maintenant? 5. Je crois avoir vu votre tante au concert. 6. Ils (elles) vont partir ce soir. 7. Est-ce qu'il fait froid? 8. Est-ce qu'il faisait chaud hier? 9. Faites fermer les fenêtres; il fait trop froid. 10. Je le ferai travailler. 11. Faites bouillir ces œufs. 12. Je crois les connaître. 13. Au lieu de patiner nous irons nager. 14. Après avoir fini son travail il faisait une excursion à bicyclette dans les environs de la ville. 15. J'aime regarder les patineurs. 16. Il s'est égaré en rentrant du vélodrome. 17. Il m'a donné un bon tuyau. 18. Mon sport favori est le cyclisme. 19. L'autre jour il a perdu cinquante francs. 20. Ce n'était pas son jour de veine.

## Lesson Thirty-five

### I

1. Oui, il fait chaud en été. 2. Je n'y reste pas tout le temps. 3. Il y a du blé. 4. Des pommiers, des poiriers, des cerisiers, des pruniers, etc. 5. Elles poussent sur le poirier. 6. Il n'y en a pas. 7. Il fait plus chaud au soleil. 8. Il coupe le blé. 9. On les appelle des veaux. 10. À la campagne. 11. Ils se lèvent de bonne heure. 12. Elle leur prépare un bon déjeuner. 13. Ils vont dans la forêt. 14. Ils mangent leur déjeuner.

### II

1. In spring the trees have blossom; in summer they are covered with leaves and they bear fruit; in autumn the leaves fall. 2. When it is fine one prefers to be in the open air. 3. Hasn't your mother gone out? 4. How my heart beats! 5. Don't beat the dog! 6. Do you believe what she said? 7. Who believes all that he reads? 8. He lets his hair grow. 9. He does not know what he wants. 10. I shall be able to help you when you wish.

### III

1. Je finirai mon travail samedi. 2. N'ont-ils pas encore fini? 3. Vous pouvez avoir un pommier ou un prunier: choisissez! 4. Ils se battent pour rien. 5. Je ne crois jamais ce qu'il dit. 6. Pourquoi ne me croyez-vous pas? 7. Je l'ai lu, mais je ne le croyais pas. 8. Nous recevons un litre de lait chaque matin. 9. Il a reçu dix livres de pommes. 10. Vous les recevrez demain.

---

### ANOTHER TONGUE TWISTER

**Les soixante-six chemises fines de l'archiduchesse sont archi-sèches.**

The sixty-six fine shirts of the archduchess are bone-dry.

### ZOOLOGIE

Le maître: Citez-moi un quadrupède?
L'élève:    Une table, monsieur.

**Citer,** to name, point out (as an example).

# ROUNDING OFF YOUR KNOWLEDGE

AS the student has now reached a stage in the Course where he should be able to read French newspapers and even books, no further reading material is provided. The Study Guide at the end of the book gives a selection of reading for those who wish to acquire a knowledge of the best French literature, and also about France itself.

The purpose of the present section, which is divided into 20 items, with an Appendix on Irregular Verbs and one on Correspondence, is to round off the student's knowledge, especially of French Grammar, and to leave him in a position where he can undertake adequately any ordinary problem of speaking, reading or writing, in French.

## I

### PARTICULARS OF SOME VERBS IN -ER

1. envoyer = to send
Present: j'envoie, tu envoies, il envoie, nous envoyons, vous envoyez, ils envoient.
Imperfect: j'envoyais
Future: j'enverrai
Conditional: j'enverrais
Imperative: envoie, envoyons, envoyez
Perfect: j'ai envoyé
Similarly: nettoyer = to clean, il nettoie; essuyer = to wipe, il essuie. Verbs in -ayer may either make this change or keep the "y", e.g., payer, il paie or il paye.

2. manger = to eat
Present: see Lesson VIII.
Imperfect: je mangeais
Future: je mangerai
Conditional: je mangerais
Imperative: mange, mangeons, mangez
Perfect: j'ai mangé

3. appeler = to call
Present: see Lesson XXI.
Imperfect: j'appelais
Future: j'appellerai
Conditional: j'appellerais
Imperative: appelle, appelons, appelez
Perfect: j'ai appelé

4. acheter = to buy
Present: see Lesson XIV.
Imperfect: j'achetais
Future: j'achèterai
Conditional: j'achèterais
Imperative: achète, achetons, achetez
Perfect: j'ai acheté

5. espérer = to hope
Present: j'espère, tu espères, il espère, nous espérons, vous espérez, ils espèrent
Imperfect: j'espérais
Future: j'espérerai
Conditional: j'espérerais
Imperative: espère, espérons, espérez
Perfect: j'ai espéré

*Note:*

1. Verbs in -yer change y into i before e mute.
2. Verbs ending in -ger insert e after the g whenever the next letter is a or o. (so that the g remains soft throughout).
3. Verbs in -ler double the l before e mute.
4. e becomes è when the next syllable has e mute.
5. é becomes è when the final syllable contains e mute.

## II

### VERBS CONJUGATED WITH ÊTRE
Il est devenu vieux = He has become old
Elle est morte = She has died; she is dead
Ils sont restés chez nous = They have stayed with us

In addition to the verbs of motion (see Lesson XVII) the following are conjugated with être:

rester = to stay (je suis resté)

devenir=to become (je deviens, il devient, nous devenons, ils deviennent; je devenais; je deviendrai; je suis devenu)

mourir=to die (je meurs, il meurt, nous mourons, ils meurent; je mourrai; je suis mort)

### VERBS OF MOTION NOT CONJUGATED WITH ÊTRE

J'ai sauté=I have jumped.
Avez-vous nagé?=Have you been swimming?

Il n'a pas couru=He did not run.

A few verbs of motion are conjugated with **avoir**. The most frequent of these are:

sauter=to jump (j'ai sauté)
nager=to swim (nous nageons, je nageais, etc., like **manger**)
courir=to run (je cours, il court, nous courons, ils courent; je courais; je courrai; j'ai couru)

Certain verbs of motion may be used either with **avoir** or **être**. Such verbs are:

rentrer=to go (*or* come) home
sortir=to go out
monter=to go up (*or* upstairs)
descendre=to go down (*or* downstairs)

These verbs are conjugated with **avoir** when they have a direct object. Compare the following:

**Il a monté les chaises**=He took the chairs upstairs.
**Il est monté**=He went upstairs.
**Elle a descendu vos malles**=She took your trunks downstairs.
**Elle est descendue**=She went downstairs.
**Il a sorti les enfants**=He took the children out.
**Il est sorti**=He went out.
**Ils ont rentré les enfants**=They brought the children home.
**Ils sont rentrés**=They went (have come) home.

## III

### AGREEMENT OF PAST PARTICIPLE

1. When used with **avoir**:

(a)

| | |
|---|---|
| **j'ai acheté** | I have bought |
| **un chapeau** | a hat |
| **une cravate** | a tie |
| **des chapeaux** | hats |
| **des cravates** | ties |

When the object follows, the Past Participle is invariable.

(b) **Le chapeau que j'ai acheté**=The hat that I bought.
**La cravate que j'ai achetée**=The tie that I bought.
**Les chapeaux que j'ai achetés**=The hats that I bought.
**Les cravates que j'ai achetées**=The ties that I bought.

If the direct object precedes the Past Participle, the Participle must agree with that direct object in number and gender (i.e., -e is added in f. sing., -s in m. pl., -es in f. pl.).

2. Used with **être** the Participle agrees with the Subject in number and gender (except in the case of reflexive verbs):

**Il est arrivé**=He has arrived
**Elle est arrivée**=She has arrived
**Ils sont arrivés**=They (m.) have arrived
**Elles sont arrivées**=They (f.) have arrived

*Note:*

1. This question of agreement concerns chiefly the spelling, as the forms are pronounced alike except when the past participle ends in a consonant. E.g., **allé, allée, allés, allées** are all pronounced alike (ah-lay); **dit** (dee), **dite** (deet), **dits** (dee), **dites** (deet).

2. When the object preceding a verb conjugated with **avoir** is an indirect object the Past Participle remains invariable, e.g., **je leur ai écrit**=I wrote to them.

3. When the Past Participle ends in -s, it remains unchanged in masculine plural, e.g., **pris** (pree)=taken, m. pl., **pris**; f., **prise**; f. pl., **prises**.

# IV

## REFLEXIVE VERBS

**Va te coucher!**=Go to bed!

**Dites-leur de se dépêcher!**=Tell them to hurry!

**Elle s'est acheté une robe**=She bought a dress for herself.

**Est-ce que vous vous êtes blessé?**=Did you hurt yourself?

**Je me suis fait mal au pied**=I hurt my foot.

**Il s'intéresse à la musique**=He is interested in music.

**Il s'est marié avec une jeune Française**=He got married to a young Frenchwoman.

**Elle se trompe**=She is making a mistake, she is mistaken.

**Dites-lui de se taire!**=Tell him to keep quiet!

**Ils s'aiment beaucoup**=They love each other very much.

**Nous nous connaissons depuis longtemps**=We have known each other for a long time.

**Ils se sont reconnus**=They recognised each other.

**Nous ne nous sommes pas compris**=We did not understand each other

**Nous nous manquons beaucoup**=We miss each other very much.

**Quand nous reverrons-nous?**=When shall we see each other again?

**Elle s'est couchée à neuf heures**=She went to bed at nine o'clock.

Note from the above examples that some reflexives may also be reciprocal, naturally only in the plural. In that case **nous, vous** or **se**="each other," "one another."

Compound tenses of reflexive verbs are formed with **être**. The Past Participle agrees with the reflexive object if it is direct.

# V

## VERBAL FORMS TERMINATING IN -ANT
### (Present Participle)

The French Present Participle, corresponding to English verbal forms in "*-ing*", has the termination **-ant,** the same for all verbs; it can easily be formed from the 1st person plural of the Present Tense by replacing **-ant** for **-ons; nous parlons**=

we speak; **parlant**=speaking; **nous man-geons**=we eat; **mangeant**=eating, etc.

The only exceptions are: **ayant**=having; **étant**=being; **sachant**=knowing.

The Present Participle is often merely descriptive and therefore treated as an adjective, i.e., it agrees in gender and number with the noun it qualifies.

e.g., **le mois suivant**=next month
    **la semaine suivante**=next week
    **les chapitres suivants**=the following chapters
    **les personnes suivantes**=the following persons

If the Present Participle has the function of a verb, i.e., if it expresses an action, it is invariable.

**Ne voulant pas l'offenser, j'ai accepté son invitation**=Not wishing to offend him, I have accepted his invitation.

**Croyant que l'autre restaurant serait meilleur marché, nous y allâmes**=Thinking that the other restaurant would be cheaper, we went there.

**Étant fatigué, il s'est couché de bonne heure**=Being tired, he went to bed early.

**Ayant déjeuné très tard, je n'ai pas encore faim**=Having lunched very late I am not hungry yet.

**En voyageant on apprend beaucoup de choses**=By travelling one learns a great many things.

**En le faisant maintenant, vous gagnerez du temps**=By doing it now you will save time.

**En lui écrivant n'oubliez pas de e mentionner**=When writing to him don't forget to mention it.

**Il est tombé en traversant la rue**=He fell while crossing the street.

Note in the last four examples the use of **en** to denote that one action is going on at the same time as another.

The French verbal form in **-ant** is much less frequently used in French than the corresponding form in "*-ing*" is in English. On the other hand the Infinitive is most widely used in French.

# VI

### THE INFINITIVE

In French the Infinitive is used:

(*a*) As Subject:

**Voir c'est croire**=Seeing is believing.

**Il avoue avoir dit cela**=He admits having said it.

**Jouer n'est pas travailler**=Playing is not working.

(*b*) After prepositions (except after **en**, which is followed by the Present Participle):

**Après avoir vu le cadeau**=After having seen the present.

**Le plaisir de vous voir**=The pleasure of seeing you.

Sans tourner la tête=Without turning his head.
Avant de commencer=Before starting.
Il passe son temps à lire=he spends his time reading.

(c) In public notices, posters, etc., the Infinitive is used instead of the Imperative:

Pousser—Tirer=(on doors) Push—Pull
Se méfier des contrefaçons=Beware of imitations
Prière de faire suivre=Please forward
Prière de ne pas marcher sur le gazon= Please do not walk on the grass
Défense d'afficher sous peine d'amende= Billposters will be prosecuted
Défense de fumer=Smoking forbidden

(d) As in the above examples the Infinitive, which is really a noun, is very often governed by à or de:

une machine à coudre=a sewing machine
une machine à écrire=a typewriter
continuer à chanter=to continue to sing; to go on singing

refuser de payer=to refuse to pay

(e) The Infinitive is preferred to a subordinate clause when the subject does not change:

Je crois connaître votre cousin=I think (that) I know your cousin.
Il pense avoir raison=He thinks (that) he is right.

Je crois avoir vu votre femme=I think (that) I saw your wife.

(f) aller chercher=to call for, to go and fetch
envoyer chercher=to send for

# VII

## COMPLEMENTS OF VERBS

1. Je l'ai rencontré hier=I met him yesterday.

2. Ne leur parlez pas=Don't speak to them.

3. Il a payé cent francs à mon père=He paid my father a hundred francs.

4. Dites à votre mère qu'il viendra à midi= Tell your mother that he will come at noon.

5. Elle a acheté une robe à sa fille=She bought a dress for her daughter.

6. J'ai emprunté cet argent à mon ami= I borrowed this money from my friend.

7. Il pense à elle=He thinks of her.

French verbs with direct or indirect complements correspond to a great extent to English verbs with the same kind of complements (examples 1 and 2). Whereas English verbs often have the appearance of having two direct objects (example 3), in French one is direct and the other indirect. The preposition before an indirect complement cannot be omitted as in English (example 4). The preposition indicating the indirect complement is usually à, which not only translates "to" but also "for", "from", "of", etc. (examples 5-7).

The following are some of the most frequent verbs which take indirect complements in French but direct in English:

apprendre qch.[1] à qqn.[2]=to teach smn.[3] smth.[4]
conseiller à qqn. de faire qch.=to advise smn. to do smth.
commander à qqn. de faire qch.=to command smn. to do smth.
coûter à qqn.=to cost smn.

---

[1]quelque chose          [3]someone
[2]quelqu'un              [4]something

dire à qqn. de faire qch.=to tell smn. to do smth.

défendre à qqn. de faire qch.=to forbid smn. to do smth.

demander à qqn. de faire qch.=to ask smn. to do smth.

ouvrir à qqn.=to let smn. in

ordonner à qqn. de faire qch.=to order smn. to do smth.

obéir à qqn.=to obey smn.

permettre à qqn. de faire qch.=to allow smn. to do smth.

promettre à qqn. de faire qch.=to promise smn. to do smth.

pardonner à qqn. d'avoir fait qch.=to forgive smn. for having done smth.

plaire à qqn.=to please smn.

rappeler qch. à qqn.=to remind smn. of smth.

répondre à qqn.=to answer smn.

recommander à qqn. de faire qch.=to recommend smn. to do smth.

souhaiter qch. à qqn.=to wish smn. smth.

faire peur à qqn.=to frighten smn.

faire plaisir à qqn.=to please smn.

faire savoir qch. à qqn.=to let smn. know smth.

faire du bien à qqn.=to do smn. good

faire du mal à qqn.=to harm, hurt smn.

faire croire qch. à qqn.=to make smn. believe smth.

demander pardon à qqn.=to ask (to beg) smn.'s pardon

penser à qqn.=to think of smn.

Direct in French, but indirect in English, are the following:

aimer qqn. ou qch.=to be fond of smn. or smth.

attendre qqn. ou qch.=to wait for smn. or smth.

chercher qqn. ou qch.=to look for smn. or smth.

aller chercher qqn. ou qch.=to call for smn. or smth.

envoyer chercher qqn. ou qch.=to send for smn. or smth.

demander qqn. ou qch.=to ask for smn. or smth.

écouter qqn. ou qch.=to listen to smn. or smth.

regarder qqn. ou qch.=to look at smn. or smth.

sentir qch.=to smell of smth.

payer qch.=to pay for smth.

# VIII

### THE SUBJUNCTIVE

1. Je sais qu'il est parti=I know that he has left.

2. Il est possible qu'il soit parti=It is possible that he has (may have) left.

3. Je doute qu'il soit parti=I doubt if he has left.

4. Pensez-vous qu'il soit parti?=Do you think that he has (may have) left?

In sentence No. 1 (I know that he has left) the dependent clause expresses a plain statement of fact.

But when the statement in a dependent clause (as in sentences 2-4) is considered by the speaker as uncertain or doubtful, a different form of the verb is used in French: the Subjunctive Mood (plain statements are said to be in the Indicative Mood).

There are only two simple tenses of the Subjunctive, viz., Present and Imperfect, but the latter has become almost obsolete in modern spoken French, its place being taken by the Present Subjunctive.

The Present of the Subjunctive is formed from the Present Participle by changing the ending -ant into -e, -es, -e; -ions, iez, -ent.

|  | give | end, finish | lose | have | be |
|---|---|---|---|---|---|
| That I may | que je donne | finisse | perde | aie | sois |
| That you may | que tu donnes | finisses | perdes | aies | sois |
| That he may | qu'il donne | finisse | perde | ait | soit |
| That we may | que nous donnions | finissions | perdions | ayons | soyons |
| That you may | que vous donniez | finissiez | perdiez | ayez | soyez |
| That they may | qu'ils donnent | finissent | perdent | aient | soient |

Note that both **avoir** and **être** have irregular Present Subjunctives which bear a close resemblance to the Imperative (see page 391).

Irregular Present Subjunctives are:

| aller | venir | boire | prendre | faire |
|---|---|---|---|---|
| que j'aille | vienne | boive | prenne | fasse |
| que tu ailles | viennes | boives | prennes | fasses |
| qu'il aille | vienne | boive | prenne | fasse |
| que nous allions | venions | buvions | prenions | fassions |
| que vous alliez | veniez | buviez | preniez | fassiez |
| qu'ils aillent | viennent | boivent | prennent | fassent |

|  | vouloir | pouvoir | savoir | recevoir |
|---|---|---|---|---|
| que je | veuille | puisse | sache | reçoive |
| que tu | veuilles | puisses | saches | reçoives |
| qu'il | veuille | puisse | sache | reçoive |
| que nous | voulions | puissions | sachions | recevions |
| que vous | vouliez | puissiez | sachiez | receviez |
| qu'ils | veuillent | puissent | sachent | reçoivent |

The Subjunctive is used in the following cases:

(a) After verbs expressing some emotion, such as fear, joy, sorrow, surprise, regret, etc.

Such are:

    **craindre**=to fear
    **avoir peur**=to be afraid
    **être charmé**=to be delighted
    **être surpris**=to be surprised
    **s'étonner**=to be astonished
    **être bien aise**=to be glad
    **être fâché**=to be sorry
    **se réjouir**=to rejoice
    **c'est dommage**=it is a pity

(b) After verbs expressing a wish, will or desire, such as:

**aimer**=to like
**désirer**=to desire
**vouloir**=to be willing, to want
**préférer**=to prefer
**souhaiter**=to wish
**avoir envie**=to wish

Exception: **espérer**=to hope, which never takes the Subjunctive.

(c) After expressions of doubt and uncertainty:

**douter**=to doubt
**nier**=to deny
**il est douteux**=it is doubtful
**il est invraisemblable**=it is unlikely
**je ne crois pas**=I don't believe

**Il n'est pas sûr**=it is not certain and others.

(d) After the following:

**il faut que**=it is necessary that
**il est possible que**=it is possible that
**afin que** ⎫
**pour que** ⎭ so that
**à moins que**=unless
**avant que**=before
**quoique** ⎫
**bien que** ⎭ although
**en cas que**=in case that
**de peur que**=for fear that
**il est temps que**=it is time that

(e) In certain exclamations:
**Vive le Président!**=Long live the President!
**Dieu soit loué!**=God be praised!

# IX

### THE PASSIVE VOICE

(a) **Son père a été tué dans un accident**=His father has been killed in an accident.
**Elle a été transportée à l'hôpital**=She has been taken to hospital.
**Ils sont très alarmés par la maladie de leur mère**=They are very much alarmed by the illness of their mother.
**Elles ont été reçues par votre ami**=They have been received by your friend.

(b) **Comment s'appelle-t-il?**=What is he called?
**Ces oranges se vendent quatre francs la douzaine**=These oranges are sold at four francs a dozen.
**Vous vous trompez**=You are mistaken.

(c) **Je n'en connais pas les détails**=I am not acquainted with the details.
**On me dérange tout le temps**=I am being disturbed all the time.
**On appelle cela une fermeture éclair**=That is called a zip fastener.
**On lui a dit de partir**=He was told to go.

(a) The passive voice is made up of the verb **être** and the Past Participle, which must agree in number and gender with the subject. In many cases the French passive corresponds to the English passive. Note from the examples under (a) that **été** corresponds to the "*been*" of the English passive voice, and that **par** translates English "*by*" after a passive.

(b) Some reflexive verbs are translated into English by passives, e.g.,
**se vendre**=to be sold
**s'appeler**=to be called
**se tromper**=to be mistaken
**s'étonner**=to be astonished

(c) An active construction in French often corresponds to the English Passive (see also Lesson XXIX).

### HOW TO TRANSLATE DO, DID

(a) **Fume-t-elle?**=Does she smoke?
**Elle ne fume pas**=She does not smoke.
**Si, elle fume**=Yes, she does.

(b) 1. **Avez-vous commencé?** = Did you begin?
**Je n'ai pas regardé**=I didn't look.
**L'avez-vous fait?**=Did you do it?
**Il n'a pas oublié**=He did not forget.
**Pourquoi ne l'avez-vous pas fait?**=Why didn't you do it?
**Lui avez-vous parlé?**=Did you speak to him (*or* her)?
**Y avez-vous pensé?**=Did you think of it?

Je ne l'ai pas payé = I didn't pay for it.

2. Êtes-vous sorti? = Did you go out?
Êtes-vous parti de bonne heure? = Did you leave early?
Pourquoi n'y êtes-vous pas resté? = Why didn't you stay there?

3. Vous êtes-vous amusé? = Did you enjoy yourself?
Vous êtes-vous fait mal? = Did you hurt yourself?
S'est-il trompé? = Did he make a mistake?
Se sont-ils brulés? = Did they burn themselves?

Nous ne nous sommes pas trompés = We didn't make a mistake.

(a) "Do" or "does" cannot be translated in questions or replies. "Does she smoke?" (the same as "Is she smoking?") = Fume-t-elle?

(b) There are three ways of translating "Did you . . .?" and "I didn't . . ."

1. Avez-vous . . .? Je n'ai pas . . . This is the usual translation.
2. Êtes-vous . . .? Je ne suis pas . . . When the verb denotes motion.
3. Vous êtes-vous . . .? Je ne me suis pas . . . With all reflexive verbs.

Questions can also be made:

1. By a rising inflexion of the voice without change of word order (as in English): Vous avez fumé? = You have smoked (been smoking)?
2. By est-ce que, where the subject retains its place before the verb: Est-ce qu'il a fumé? = Did he smoke? Has he smoked (been smoking)?
3. When the subject of the question is a noun it precedes the verb, which must be followed by a personal pronoun of the same person, gender and number as the noun subject: Votre frère fume-t-il? = Does your brother smoke? Is your brother smoking?

## X

### MUST, OUGHT

Tu dois dire la vérité = You must tell the truth.
Tu devrais dire la vérité = You should (ought to) tell the truth.
Le train doit être en retard = The train must be late.
Vous devez venir me voir = You must come and see me.
Il doit tenir sa parole = He ought to keep his word.
Les enfants doivent obéir à leurs parents = Children ought to obey their parents.
Elle doit y être maintenant = She must be there now.
S'il n'est pas chez lui il a dû sortir = If he is not at home he has had to go out.

Nous devons faire ceci = We have to do this.
Il doit arriver de meilleure heure = He is to arrive earlier.

The verb devoir (of which the ordinary meaning is "to owe") is used in translating "must," "ought to," "should," "have to," "am to," "is to," "are to".

The forms of the verb devoir are:

Present: je dois, tu dois, il doit, nous devons, vous devez, ils doivent.
Imperfect: je devais, etc.
Preterite: je dus, etc.
Future: je devrai, etc.
Perfect: j'ai dû, f. due

The difference between devoir and falloir

(see Lesson XXII) is that **falloir** denotes absolute necessity, whereas **devoir** implies obligation or certainty. Another difference is that **devoir** can take a personal subject (**je, tu, vous, mon ami,** etc.), whereas **falloir** is always used impersonally, i.e., it can only have **il** as subject.

The forms of the verb **falloir** are:

Present: **il faut**
Imperfect: **il fallait**
Perfect: **il a fallu**
Preterite: **il fallut**
Future: **il faudra**
Conditional: **il faudrait**

**Il me faut y aller**=I must go there
   (it is necessary for me to go there)

**Je dois y aller**=I must go there
   (I am obliged to go there)

# XI

**THE ONE WHO, THOSE WHO (WHICH)**

**Lequel est le chef d'orchestre?**=Which one is the conductor?

**Celui qui est debout en avant**=The one who is standing in front.

**Lesquels sont les violonistes?**=Which are the violinists?

**Ceux qui sont à gauche**=Those who are on the left.

**Laquelle est la harpiste?**=Which one is the harpist?

**Celle qui est assise à droite**=The one who is sitting on the right.

**Lesquelles sont les cantatrices?**=Which are the singers?

**Celles qui sont debout en arrière**=Those who are standing at the rear.

Celui qui conduit l'orchestre est le chef d'orchestre.    Celle qui joue de la harpe est la harpiste.
Ceux qui jouent du violon sont les violonistes.      Celles qui chantent sont les cantatrices.
Celle qui joue du piano est la pianiste.

**Lequel est votre sac à main?**=Which is your handbag?

**Celui qui est sur la table**=The one which is on the table.

**Lesquels sont vos gants?**=Which are your gloves?

**Ceux qui sont un peu déchirés**=Those which are a bit torn.

**Laquelle est sa chaise?**=Which is his chair?

**Celle qui est au jardin**=The one which is in the garden.

**Celui qui** =the one who, he who (referring to a masculine noun)
the one which, that which (referring to a masculine noun)

**Celle qui**=the one who, she who (referring to a feminine noun)
the one who, that which (referring to a feminine noun)

**Ceux qui**=those who *or* which (referring to masculine nouns)

**Celles qui**=those who *or* which (referring to feminine nouns)

**Laquelle de ses peintures préférez-vous?**= Which of his paintings do you prefer?

**A laquelle de ses sœurs pensez-vous?**= Which of his sisters are you thinking of?

**Auquel de mes frères avez-vous écrit?**= To which of my brothers did you write?

**Duquel parlez-vous?**=Of which one (masc.) are you speaking?

**De laquelle parlez-vous?**=Of which one (fem.) are you speaking?

**Desquels parlez-vous?**=Of which (masc. pl.) are you speaking?

**Desquelles parlez-vous?**=Of which (fem. pl.) are you speaking?

# XII

## QUELQUE

**Ne voulez-vous pas acheter quelques fleurs?** = Won't you buy some flowers?

**J'ai quelques livres pour vous**= I have got some books for you.

**Il l'a trouvé quelque part**= He found it somewhere.

**Quelqu'un m'a dit**= Someone told me.

**Quelqu'une de ses amies** = One of his girl-friends.

**Quelques-unes de ses amies**= Some (plural) of his girl friends.

**Quelque jour**= Some day or other.

**Ces quelques lignes**= These few lines.

**Il y a quelques années**= Some years ago.

**Quelques amis**= A few friends.

**quelque**= some, any, a few

**quelqu'un, quelqu'une** (plur. m. **quelques- uns**; plur. f. **quelques-unes**)= somebody, someone, anybody, anyone

**quelque chose** (m.)= something

**quelque part**= somewhere

**quelquefois**= sometimes

**quelconque**= whatever, any

N.B.—**quelque chose de bon**=something good
**rien de nouveau**=nothing new
**Rien** and **quelque chose**, followed by an adjective, require **de.**

# XIII

### TOUT, TOUS, TOUTE, TOUTES

1. **Tout le temps il est occupé**=All the time he is busy.

**Toute la famille est partie**=All the family (the whole family) has left.

**J'ai travaillé tout le dimanche**=I worked all Sunday.

**Il n'a pas travaillé toute la semaine**=He did not work the whole week.

**Tous les hommes ne sont pas les mêmes**=All men are not the same.

**Il a mangé tout le gâteau**=He has eaten all the cake.

**Il a bu toute la bière**=He has drunk all the beer.

**Il a fumé tous mes cigares**=He has smoked all my cigars.

**Voici toutes mes cigarettes**=Here are all my cigarettes.

**Elle n'a pas dormi toute la nuit**=She did not sleep all night.

**Je n'ai pas mangé toute la journée**=I have not eaten all day.

**Tout le monde est content**=Everybody is pleased.

2. **Nous voulons tout voir**=We want to see everything.

**Tout est perdu**=All is lost.

**Ils ont tout perdu**=They lost everything.

**J'ai vu tout cela**=I have seen all that.

3. **C'est tout autre chose**=That is quite another thing.

**Je suis tout prêt**=I am quite ready.

**Elle est tout heureuse**=She is completely happy.

1. "All" as an adjective=**tout, toute, tous, toutes.**

2. "All" (=everything) as a pronoun=**tout.**

3. **tout** as an adverb=quite, completely.

Pronunciation:

   **tout**—*too* except in liaison where **t** is pronounced.

   **toute, toutes**—*toot.*

   **tous**—usually *too*, but when stressed, *toos.*

E.g.,

Unstressed: **Où sont tous vos livres?**=Where are all your books?

Stressed: **Je les ai tous vendus**=I sold them all.

Unstressed: **J'ai vu tous vos enfants**=I have seen all your children.

Stressed: **Je les ai vus tous**=I have seen them all.

Note also the following expressions:

tout de suite=at once
tout à fait=entirely
tout à coup=suddenly
tout à l'heure=a moment ago; just now; in a moment
tout au plus=at most
tout à vous (in closing a letter)=yours sincerely

tout de même=all the same
pas du tout or du tout=not at all
rien du tout=nothing at all
tout le monde=everybody

### LA DAME ET LE MENDIANT
Mais vous ne me racontez pas du tout la même histoire qu'hier!
Naturellement, Madame: vous n'avez pas cru celle d'hier.

# XIV

### PEOPLE
1. La nation=nation
   la nation irlandaise=the Irish people

2. le peuple=nation, the masses
   le roi et son peuple=the king and his people
   la volonté du peuple=the will of the people

3. gens; le monde=persons

les jeunes gens=young people
les vieilles gens=old people
beaucoup de gens ⎱
beaucoup de monde ⎰ =many people
la plupart des gens ⎱
la plupart du monde ⎰ =most people
quels sont ces gens?=who are these people?
peu de monde=few people

4. on dit=people say

# XV

### UN COUP DE . . . ETC.

un coup=a blow, a stroke, a knock, is very frequently used in combination with other words. Some of the most common are:

un coup de pied=a kick

un coup d'œil=a glance, a view

un coup de téléphone=a "ring"
un coup de tonnerre=a clap of thunder
un coup de poing=a blow (with the fist)
un coup de coude=a nudge
un coup de fusil=a rifle shot
un coup de bâton=a blow with a stick
un coup de brosse=a brushing
un coup de canon=a gun shot
un coup de théâtre=an unexpected incident
un coup de main=a helping hand
boire un coup=to have a drink
boire à petits coups=to sip
tout à coup=suddenly
tout d'un coup=all at once; at one blow
coup-sur-coup=in quick succession

# XVI

### WHO, WHOSE, WHOM, WHICH
#### (Relative Pronouns)

L'homme qui parle est mon père=The man who is speaking is my father.

C'est la jeune fille qui vous a écrit=It's the girl who wrote to you.

C'est la jeune fille à qui vous avez écrit=It's the girl to whom you wrote.

Les bateaux qui venaient du nord=The ships which came from the north.

L'homme que vous avez entendu parler= The man whom you heard speaking.

C'est une chos edont je ne suis pas surpris= That is a thing (something) I am not surprised at (at which I am not surprised)

Les bateaux que vous avez vus=The boats which you saw.

C'est la dame que vous avez vue l'autre jour =That is the lady whom you saw the other day.

Voici le livre que vous cherchez=Here is the book you are looking for.

Je ne connais pas le monsieur dont il parle=I don't know the man of whom he is speaking.

C'est la dame dont nous avons reçu la lettre=That is the lady from whom we have received the letter.

Le monsieur dont vous connaissez la fille=The man whose daughter you know.

**Qui**=who, which, that—when Subject.

**Que**=whom, which, that— when the Direct Object.

**Dont**=whose, of whom, of which, from whom, from which.

*Note.* (1) Relative pronouns are always expressed in French, whereas in English they are frequently understood, e.g., **la dame que j'ai vue**=the lady I saw.

(2) When **dont** is used the word order must invariably be:

| 1. | 2. | 3. |
|---|---|---|
| Antecedent | Dont | Subject |
| **Le monsieur** | **dont** | **vous** |

| 4. | 5. |
|---|---|
| Verb | Direct Object |
| **connaissez** | **le fils** |

(3) **Dont** can never be preceded by a preposition; if the relative pronoun is governed by a preposition, or depends on a noun which is itself governed by a preposition, **qui** is used when referring to persons, or some form of **lequel** (compare Lesson XXXI) when referring to things.

L'homme dans la maison de qui je demeurais =The man in whose house I lived . . .

Voilà le monsieur avec qui nous avons joué= This is the man with whom we have played.

C'est l'hôtel dans lequel nous avons demeuré =This is the hotel in which we lived.

Ce n'est pas le restaurant auquel je pense= This is not the restaurant I am thinking of.

C'est le garçon à qui j'ai payé l'addition=
This is the waiter to whom I paid the
bill.

La maison, à laquelle je vais vous conduire=
The house to which I am going to take
you.

C'est le jardin dans lequel nous étions l'année
dernière=This is the garden in which we
were last year.

Les gens avec qui nous avons joué=The
people we played with (with whom).

Les cartes avec lesquelles nous avons joué=
The cards we played with (with which).

# XVII

**WHO, WHOSE, WHOM, WHAT, WHICH**
**(Interrogative Pronouns)**

**Qui, que, lequel, laquelle,** etc. (but not
"**dont**") are used as both relative pronouns
and interrogative pronouns (i.e., for asking
questions).

**Qui est arrivé?**
**Qui est-ce qui est arrivé?**
　　　　Who has arrived?

**Qu'est ce qui s'est passé?**
　　　　What has happened?

**Que faites-vous?**
**Qu'est-ce que vous faites?**
　　　　What are you doing?

**Qui voyez-vous?**
**Qui est-ce que vous voyez?**
　　　　Whom do you see?

**Que voyez-vous?**
**Qu'est-ce que vous voyez?**
　　　　What do you see?

**qui est-ce qui?**
**or qui?** ⎫ who?

**qui est-ce que?**
**or qui?** ⎬ whom?

**qu'est-ce qui?**
**or quoi?** ⎫ what? (Subject)

**qu'est-ce que?**
**or que?** ⎬ what? (Object)

**À qui parlez-vous?**=Whom are you speaking to?

**De qui parlez-vous?**=Whom are you speaking of?

**À quoi pensez-vous?**=What are you thinking of?

**De quoi parlez-vous?**=What are you speaking of?

*Note.*—Prepositions are followed by **qui**
when referring to persons, and by **quoi**
when referring to things.

**Quoi** as the subject is used when the verb
is omitted:

**Quoi de nouveau?**=What is the news?

**Quoi** is also used as a kind of noun
equivalent in the following expressions:

**Il a de quoi vivre**=He has enough to live on.

**Donnez-moi de quoi écrire**=Give me
something to write with.

**Il n'y a pas de quoi**=Don't mention it (in
answer to apologies).

**Un je ne sais quoi**=An indefinable something.

**Lequel, laquelle, lesquels, lesquelles,**
**auquel, à laquelle, auxquels, auxquelles,**
etc., are used in the sense of which (one)?
(Compare Lesson XXXI.)

**Lequel de vos livres est le plus intéressant?**
=Which of your books is the most
interesting?

# XVIII

### USE OF DE AND À

(a) un salon de thé=a tea-room
une lanterne de papier=a paper lantern
une table de bois=a wooden table
la lune de miel=honeymoon

un cadeau de noces=a wedding present
un bateau de pêche=a fishing boat
un voyage d'agrément=a pleasure trip
une maison de campagne=a country house
un chapeau de paille=a straw hat
un timbre d'un franc=a one franc stamp
le train de minuit=the midnight train
une leçon de français=a French lesson
un professeur de français=a teacher of French

(b) un bateau à voiles=a sailing boat

un moulin à vent=a windmill
une brosse à dents=a tooth-brush
une cuiller à thé=a teaspoon
un verre à vin=a wine-glass

Note from the above examples the use of de and à to translate English nouns used as adjectives.

(a) When the English adjective means "made of", "composed of", "belonging to", the French equivalent is a noun preceded by de.

(b) When the English adjective means "for the purpose of", "by means of", a noun preceded by à is used in French.

(c) Sometimes when definite things are referred to or are used with nouns which usually take the definite article in French (although not in English), the definite article is used in connection with de or à:

la boîte aux lettres=the letter-box
la tour de l'église=the church tower
le prix du café=the price of coffee
aller à l'église=to go to church
être à l'école=to be in school
du nord au sud=from north to south
de l'est à l'ouest=from east to west
du matin au soir=from morning to night

(d) After rien, quoi, personne, quelqu'un and quelque chose, de is inserted before an adjective:

e.g., quelque chose d'intéressant=something interesting

rien de nouveau=nothing new
il n'y avait personne d'important=there was no one important there

est-ce qu'il y avait quelqu'un de tué dans l'accident?=was anybody killed in the accident?

quoi de si pressé?=what is the hurry about?

(e) For de used after expressions of quantity see Lesson XXIX.

(f) **Jouer**=to play; (1) with **de** when applying to a musical instrument: **jouer du piano**=to play the piano; **jouer de la harpe**=to play the harp, etc.; (2) with **à** when referring to games: **jouer au tennis**= to play tennis; **jouer aux cartes**=to play cards, etc.

Quoi de si pressé?

# XIX

### DE OR À BEFORE INFINITIVE

(a)
**Essayez de travailler un peu**=Try to work a little.

**Avez-vous fini de le lire?**=Have you finished reading it?

**Elle a oublié de me réveiller**=She forgot to wake me up.

**J'ai offert de le lui prêter**=I offered to lend it to him (or her).

**Il refuse de nous aider**=He refuses to help us.

**Tâchez d'être ici à neuf heures**=Try to be here at nine o'clock.

**Il n'a pas besoin de travailler**=He does not need to work.

**J'ai envie d'aller au théâtre demain**=I should like to go to the theatre tomorrow.

**Il a honte de ne pas l'avoir fait**=He is ashamed of not having done it.

**Il a peur de vous le dire**=He is afraid to tell you.

**Vous avez eu raison de ne pas le leur dire**= You were right in not telling them.

**Nous n'avons pas le temps d'aller le voir**= We have not time to go and see him.

**Il n'a pas l'air d'être très intelligent**=He does not seem to be very intelligent.

**Je suis content de vous avoir vu**=I am glad to have seen you.

**Il est difficile d'apprendre cette langue**=It is difficult to learn that language.

C'est aimable de la part de votre sœur de me prêter son parapluie=It is kind of your sister to lend me her umbrella.

(b)

Il aime à manger des huîtres=He likes to eat oysters.

Vous a-t-il aidé à faire cela?=Did he help you to do this?

J'ai beaucoup à faire aujourd'hui=I have much to do to-day.

Elle apprend à chanter=She is learning to sing.

Je suis prêt à sortir=I am ready to go out.

Je n'ai rien à lui dire=I have nothing to tell him (or her).

Cherchez à le comprendre=Try to understand him.

Commençons à jouer=Let us begin to play.

Elle demande à vous parler=She wants to speak to you.

Elle demande à voir le directeur=She asks to see the director.

J'ai du travail à faire=I have some work to do.

Cette règle est facile à comprendre=This rule is easy to understand.

The usual translation of "to" before an infinitive is **de.** If "to" denotes the aim or end in view **à** is used.

Specially note the following:

With de:

il s'agit de=it is a question of

finir de=to finish

avoir besoin de=to need to

avoir envie de=to wish, want, desire

avoir honte de=to be ashamed to

avoir peur de=to be afraid to

avoir raison de=to be right to

avoir tort de=to be wrong to

avoir l'amabilité de=to have the kindness to

avoir l'air de=to seem, to appear

avoir l'obligeance de=to be good enough to

de la part de (de ma part, de sa part, etc.)=on behalf of, on the part of

With à:

prendre plaisir à=to take pleasure in

passer le temps à=to pass the time in

être habitué à=to be accustomed to

prêt à=ready to

habitué à=accustomed to

acheter à tempérament=to buy on instalments

être à la mode=to be in fashion

filer à l'anglaise=to take French leave

*Note.*—1. **Il est,** followed by an Infinitive, requires **de;** c'est requires **à.**

Il est difficile de faire cela

C'est difficile à faire

        That's difficult to do

2. Verbs or adjectives take **pour** (i.e., in order to) before Infinitive, when cause, reason or motive is stated.

E.g. **Il fait trop chaud pour rester au soleil**
= It is too hot to remain in the sun.
**Il fait trop sombre pour lire** = It is too dark to read.

3. The Infinitive is used without a preposition after the following verbs:
**pouvoir** = to be able
**savoir** = to know how to
**vouloir** = to wish
**falloir** = to be necessary
**devoir** = to owe
**aller** = to go ⎫ and all other verbs of
**venir** = to come ⎭ motion
**faire** = to make
**laisser** = to let
**oser** = to dare
**voir** = to see
**entendre** = to hear
**sentir** = to feel
**désirer** = to desire
**préférer** ⎫
**aimer mieux** ⎭ = to prefer
**croire** = to believe
and other verbs of thinking, wishing and declaring.

E.g. **Il me fallait le quitter ce matin** = I had to leave him this morning.
**Savez-vous jouer du piano?** = Can you play the piano?
**Je l'ai vue sortir** = I saw her go out.
**Il voulut dîner tard** = He wanted to dine late.
**Allez-vous me donner l'argent?** = Are you going to give me the money?
**J'espère revenir bientôt** = I hope to return soon.
**Nous préférons rester chez nous** = We prefer to stay at home.

# XX

## RULES FOR GENDERS

Unfortunately no rules can be given for determining the gender of every noun. The following rules, however, will be found useful as they cover a considerable number of them:

**Masculine are:**

1. Men and male animals—**un homme, le chat, le chien, le tigre.**
2. Seasons, months, days—**le printemps, le mois de janvier, le lundi.**
3. Winds, cardinal points—**le nord, le sud, l'est, l'ouest.**
4. Mountains, metals, trees—**le Mont Blanc, le fer, le rosier.**
5. Adjectives and infinitives used as nouns—**le bleu, le manger, le boire.**
6. Most nouns ending in a consonant—**le prix, le rat, le bras, le fort, le bout.**

7. Most nouns ending in a sounded vowel—**le café, un opéra, le bateau, le pneu.**
8. Nouns ending in -ment—**le département, le gouvernement, le régiment.** (Exception: **la jument,** mare.)
9. Nouns ending in -age—**le village, le langage, le garage.** (Exceptions: **la cage, une image, la nage, la page** (of a book), **la plage, la rage.**)

**Feminine are:**

1. Women and female animals—**la femme, la chatte, la chienne, la tigresse.**
2. Most countries ending in -e mute—**La France, La Belgique, La Russie.**
3. Words ending in -tion—**la nation, la révolution.** (Exception: **le bastion.**)
4. Most nouns ending in -ie, -te, -tie—**la boulangerie, la clarté, l'amitié** (friendship). (Exceptions: **le parapluie, le génie, un incendie, le foie**).

5. Abstract nouns ending in -eur—**la peur, la chaleur, la douleur.** (Exceptions: **l'honneur, le labeur, l'heur** (luck, chance), **le bonheur, le malheur.**)

6. Abstract nouns ending in -té—**la majesté, la qualité, la liberté, l'égalité, la fraternité.**

Some nouns whether masculine or feminine apply to either sex: **le professeur** = the teacher (man or woman); **la brute** = the brute (man or animal); **la recrue** = the recruit; **la connaissance** = acquaintance; **la personne** = person.

Some nouns are either masculine or feminine according to the sex of the person referred to: **le** or **la concierge**; **un** or **une enfant, élève** (pupil), **artiste.**

A few nouns have two genders with change of meaning. The most frequently used of them are:

**le livre** = book; **la livre** = pound
**le page** = page-boy; **la page** = page (of a book)
**le tour** = turn, trick; **la tour** = tower
**le critique** = critic; **la critique** = criticism
**le manche** = handle; **la manche** = sleeve;
**La Manche** = English Channel
**le poêle** = stove; **la poêle** = frying pan
**le mousse** = cabin boy; **la mousse** = froth, moss
**le voile** = veil; **la voile** = sail

# APPENDIX I

### Synopsis of Conjugations (Regular and Irregular Verbs)

## THE AUXILIARY VERBS

### AVOIR (to have) ÊTRE (to be)

#### Present Participle

ayant = having      étant = being

#### Past Participle

eu = had      été = been

#### Compound (Perfect) Participle

ayant eu =      ayant été =
    having had      having been

### Indicative Mood

#### Present

J'ai = I have      Je suis = I am
tu as = thou hast      tu es = thou art
il a = he has      il est = he is
elle a = she has      elle est = she is
nous avons = we have      nous sommes = we are
vous avez = you have      vous êtes = you are
ils ont = they have      ils sont = they are
elles ont = they have      elles sont = they are

#### Imperfect

j'avais      j'étais
tu avais   I was    tu étais   I was
il avait   having   il était   being
nous avions   I had,   nous étions   I was,
vous aviez   etc.    vous étiez   etc.
ils avaient      ils étaient

#### Preterite

j'eus      je fus
tu eus      tu fus
il eut   I had,   il fut   I was,
nous eûmes   etc.   nous fûmes   etc.
vous eûtes      vous fûtes
ils eurent      ils furent

#### Future

j'aurai      je serai
tu auras   I shall   tu seras   I shall
il aura   have,   il sera   be, etc.
nous aurons   etc.   nous serons
vous aurez      vous serez
ils auront      ils seront

#### Conditional

j'aurais      je serais
tu aurais   I   tu serais   I
il aurait   should   il serait   should
nous aurions   have,   nous serions   be,
vous auriez   etc.   vous seriez   etc.
ils auraient      ils seraient

Compound Forms, see page 392

#### Imperative

aie       } = have      sois      } = be
ayez               soyez
ayons = let us have      soyons = let us be

## Subjunctive Mood

**Present**

| | |
|---|---|
| que j'aie | |
| que tu aies | |
| qu'il ait | that I may have, etc. |
| que nous ayons | |
| que vous ayez | |
| qu'ils aient | |

**Imperfect**

| | |
|---|---|
| que j'eusse | |
| que tu eusses | |
| qu'il eût | that I might have, etc. |
| que nous eussions | |
| que vous eussiez | |
| qu'ils eussent | |

| | |
|---|---|
| que je sois | |
| que tu sois | |
| qu'il soit | that I may be, etc. |
| que nous soyons | |
| que vous soyez | |
| qu'ils soient | |

| | |
|---|---|
| que je fusse | |
| que tu fusses | |
| qu'il fût | that I might be, etc. |
| que nous fussions | |
| que vous fussiez | |
| qu'ils fussent | |

## THE REGULAR VERBS

| I | II | III |
|---|---|---|
| donner=to give | finir=to finish | vendre=to sell |

**Present Participle**

| | | |
|---|---|---|
| donnant=giving | finissant=finishing | vendant=selling |

**Past Participle**

| | | |
|---|---|---|
| donné=given | fini=finished | vendu=sold |

**Compound (Perfect) Participle**

| | | |
|---|---|---|
| ayant donné=having given | ayant fini=having finished | ayant vendu=having sold |

## Indicative Mood

**Present**

| | | | | | |
|---|---|---|---|---|---|
| je donne | | je finis | | je vends | |
| tu donnes | I give, I am giving, etc. | tu finis | I finish, I am finishing, etc. | tu vends | I sell, I am selling, etc. |
| il donne | | il finit | | il vend | |
| nous donnons | | nous finissons | | nous vendons | |
| vous donnez | | vous finissez | | vous vendez | |
| ils donnent | | ils finissent | | ils vendent | |

**Imperfect**

| | | | | | |
|---|---|---|---|---|---|
| je donnais | | je finissais | | je vendais | |
| tu donnais | I was giving, etc. | tu finissais | I was finishing, etc. | tu vendais | I was selling, etc. |
| il donnait | | il finissait | | il vendait | |
| nous donnions | | nous finissions | | nous vendions | |
| vous donniez | | vous finissiez | | vous vendiez | |
| ils donnaient | | ils finissaient | | ils vendaient | |

**Preterite**

| | | | | | |
|---|---|---|---|---|---|
| je donnai | | je finis | | je vendis | |
| tu donnas | I gave, etc. | tu finis | I finished, etc. | tu vendis | I sold, etc. |
| il donna | | il finit | | il vendit | |
| nous donnâmes | | nous finîmes | | nous vendîmes | |
| vous donnâtes | | vous finîtes | | vous vendîtes | |
| ils donnèrent | | ils finirent | | ils vendirent | |

## Future

| je donnerai | | | je finirai | | | je vendrai | | |
|---|---|---|---|---|---|---|---|---|
| tu donneras | | I | tu finiras | | I | tu vendras | | I |
| il donnera | | shall | il finira | | shall | il vendra | | shall |
| nous donnerons | | give, | nous finirons | | finish, | nous vendrons | | sell, |
| vous donnerez | | etc. | vous finirez | | etc. | vous vendrez | | etc. |
| ils donneront | | | ils finiront | | | ils vendront | | |

## Conditional

| je donnerais | | | je finirais | | | je vendrais | | |
|---|---|---|---|---|---|---|---|---|
| tu donnerais | | I | tu finirais | | I | tu vendrais | | I |
| il donnerait | | should | il finirait | | should | il vendrait | | should |
| nous donnerions | | give, | nous finirions | | finish, | nous vendrions | | sell, |
| vous donneriez | | etc. | vous finiriez | | etc. | vous vendriez | | etc. |
| ils donneraient | | | ils finiraient | | | ils vendraient | | |

## Imperative

donne
donnez } = give
donnons = let us give

finis
finissez } = finish
finissons = let us finish

vends
vendez } = sell
vendons = let us sell

## Subjunctive Mood

### Present

| que je donne | | | que je finisse | | | que je vende | | |
|---|---|---|---|---|---|---|---|---|
| que tu donnes | | that | que tu finisses | | that | que tu vendes | | that |
| qu'il donne | | I | qu'il finisse | | I | qu'il vende | | I |
| que nous donnions | | may | que nous finissions | | may | que nous vendions | | may |
| que vous donniez | | give, | que vous finissiez | | finish, | que vous vendiez | | sell, |
| qu'ils donnent | | etc. | qu'ils finissent | | etc. | qu'ils vendent | | etc. |

### Imperfect

| que je donnasse | | | que je finisse | | | que je vendisse | | |
|---|---|---|---|---|---|---|---|---|
| que tu donnasses | | that | que tu finisses | | that | que tu vendisses | | that |
| qu'il donnât | | I | qu'il finît | | I | qu'il vendît | | I |
| que nous donnassions | | might | que nous finissions | | might | que nous vendissions | | might |
| que vous donnassiez | | give, | que vous finissiez | | finish, | que vous vendissiez | | sell, |
| qu'ils donnassent | | etc. | qu'ils finissent | | etc. | qu'ils vendissent | | etc. |

## Compound Forms

| I have, etc. | j'ai | I shall | j'aurai | that I | que j'aie | |
|---|---|---|---|---|---|---|
| | tu as | have, etc. | tu auras | may have, etc. | que tu aies | eu had |
| | il a | | il aura | | qu'il ait | été been |
| | nous avons | | nous aurons | | que nous ayons | |
| | vous avez | | vous aurez | | que vous ayez | |
| | ils ont | | ils auront | | qu'ils aient | donné given |

| I had, etc. | j'avais | I should | j'aurais | that I | que j'eusse | fini finished |
|---|---|---|---|---|---|---|
| | tu avais | have, etc. | tu aurais | might have, etc. | que tu eusses | |
| | il avait | | il aurait | | qu'il eût | vendu sold |
| | nous avions | | nous aurions | | que nous eussions | |
| | vous aviez | | vous auriez | | que vous eussiez | |
| | ils avaient | | ils auraient | | qu'ils eussent | |

## REFLEXIVE VERBS

Reflexive verbs have two pronouns of the same person—one is the subject, the other the object. They form their compound tenses with **être**.

The past participle of reflexive verbs agrees in number and gender with the reflexive pronoun if it is the direct object. If the pronoun is the indirect object, the past participle agrees only when preceded by the direct object.

Conjugation of the Reflexive Verb **se reposer**=to rest.

Present Participle: **se reposant**=resting.
Past Participle: **reposé**=rested.

### Indicative Mood

| Present | Preterite | Imperfect |
|---|---|---|
| I rest, I am resting | I rested | I rested, I was resting |
| je me repose | je me reposai | je me reposais |
| tu te reposes | tu te reposas | tu te reposais |
| il se repose | il se reposa | il se reposait |
| nous nous reposons | nous nous reposâmes | nous nous reposions |
| vous vous reposez | vous vous reposâtes | vous vous reposiez |
| ils se reposent | ils se reposèrent | ils se reposaient |

| Future | Conditional | Imperative |
|---|---|---|
| I shall rest | I should rest | |
| je me reposerai | je me reposerais | repose-toi |
| tu te reposeras | tu te reposerais | reposez-vous } =have a rest |
| il se reposera | il se reposerait | reposons-nous=let us have a rest |
| nous nous reposerons | nous nous reposerions | |
| vous vous reposerez | vous vous reposeriez | |
| ils se reposeront | ils se reposeraient | |

### Subjunctive Mood

| Present | Imperfect |
|---|---|
| that I may rest | that I might rest |
| que je me repose | que je me reposasse |
| que tu te reposes | que tu te reposasses |
| qu'il se repose | qu'il se reposât |
| que nous nous reposions | que nous nous reposassions |
| que vous vous reposiez | que vous vous reposassiez |
| qu'ils se reposent | qu'ils se reposassent |

### Compound Tenses

| I have rested | | I shall have rested | |
|---|---|---|---|
| je me suis | reposé | je me serai | reposé |
| tu t'es | or | tu te seras | or |
| il or elle s'est | reposée | il or elle se sera | reposée |
| nous nous sommes | reposés | nous nous serons | reposés |
| vous vous êtes | or | vous vous serez | or |
| ils or elles se sont | reposées | ils or elles se seront | reposées |

| I had rested | | I should have rested | |
|---|---|---|---|
| je m'étais | reposé | je me serais | reposé |
| tu t'étais | or | tu te serais | or |
| il or elle s'était | reposée | il or elle se serait | reposée |
| nous nous étions | reposés | nous nous serions | reposés |
| vous vous étiez | or | vous vous seriez | or |
| ils or elles s'étaient | reposées | ils or elles se seraient | reposées |

| That I may have rested | | That I might have rested | |
|---|---|---|---|
| que je me sois | ⎫ reposé | que je me fusse | ⎫ reposé |
| que tu te sois | ⎪ or | que tu te fusses | ⎪ or |
| qu'il or qu'elle se soit | ⎬ reposée | qu'il or qu'elle se fût | ⎬ reposée |
| que nous nous soyons | ⎪ reposés | que nous nous fûssions | ⎪ reposés |
| que vous vous soyez | ⎪ or | que vous vous fussiez | ⎪ or |
| qu'ils or qu'elles se soient | ⎭ reposées | qu'ils or qu'elles se fussent | ⎭ reposées |

### Conjugated Negatively

je ne me repose pas
tu ne te reposes pas
il ne se repose pas, etc.

je ne me reposais pas, etc.

je ne me suis pas reposé
tu ne t'es pas reposé
il ne s'est pas reposé

je ne me reposerai pas, etc.

### Conjugated Interrogatively

est-ce que je me repose?
te reposes-tu?
se repose-t-il? etc.

me reposais-je? etc.

me suis-je reposé?
t'es-tu reposé?
s'est-il reposé? etc.

me reposerai-je? etc.

### Conjugated Negatively-Interrogatively

est-ce que je ne me repose pas?
ne te reposes-tu pas?
ne se repose-t-il pas?

ne me reposais-je pas? etc.

ne me suis-je pas reposé?
ne t'es-tu pas reposé?
ne s'est-il pas reposé?

ne me reposerais-je pas? etc.

### Imperative Conjugated Negatively

ne te repose pas, ne vous reposez pas, ne nous reposons pas

## IRREGULAR VERBS IN COMMON USE

(a) The verbs are arranged in alpha-betical order.

(b) Compound forms are not given; when nothing is said to the contrary they are formed with avoir+the past participle.

(c) The pronouns are omitted in the following tables. If at first confusing write on a loose slip of paper: je, tu, il (elle), nous, vous, ils (elles).

(d) Since the endings of the Imperfect, Preterite, Future, Conditional and Subjunctive are always regular they can be ascertained from the preceding tables. Only the 1st person singular (je . . .) is given below.

(e) Only the familiar form of the Imperative is given. The other forms are identical with the plural forms of the Present Indicative ending in -ez and -ons.

| Infinitive | Participles | Present Indicative | Imperfect, Preterite | Future, Conditional | Imperative | Subjunctive |
|---|---|---|---|---|---|---|
| Aller[1] go (aux. être) | allant allé | vais, vas, va allons, -ez, vont | allais allai | irai irais | va (vas-y) | que j'aille que j'allasse |
| Boire drink | buvant bu | bois, -s, -t buvons, -ez, boivent | buvais bus | boirai boirais | bois | que je boive que je busse |
| Conduire conduct | conduisant conduit | conduis, -s, -t conduisons, -ez, -ent | conduisais conduisis | conduirai conduirais | conduis | que je conduise que je conduisisse |

[1] Like aller is conjugated: s'en aller=to go away (je m'en vais, tu t'en vas, il s'en va, etc.).

| Infinitive | Participles | Present Indicative | Imperfect, Preterite | Future, Conditional | Imperative | Subjunctive |
|---|---|---|---|---|---|---|
| **Connaître** *know* | connaissant connu | connais, -s, aît connaissons, -ez, -ent | connaissais connus | connaîtrai connaîtrais | connais | que je connaisse que je connusse |
| **Courir** *run* | courant couru | cours, -s, -t courons, -ez, -ent | courais courus | courrai courrais | cours | que je coure que je courusse |
| **Craindre** *fear* | craignant craint | crains, -s, -t craignons, -ez, -ent | craignais craignis | craindrai craindrais | crains | que je craigne que je craignisse |
| **Croire** *believe* | croyant cru | crois, -s, -t croyons, -ez, croient | croyais crus | croirai croirais | crois | que je croie que je crusse |
| **Devoir** *owe* | devant dû, (f.) due | dois, -s, -t devons, -ez, doivent | devais dus | devrai devrais | — | que je doive que je dusse |
| **Dire** *say* | disant dit | dis, -s, -t disons, dites, disent | disais dis | dirai dirais | dis | que je dise que je disse |
| **Dormir**[1] *sleep* | dormant dormi | dors, -s, -t dormons, -ez, -ent | dormais dormis | dormirai dormirais | dors | que je dorme que je dormisse |
| **Écrire** *write* | écrivant écrit | écris, -s, -t écrivons, -ez, -ent | écrivais écrivis | écrirai écrirais | écris | que j'écrive que j'écrivisse |
| **Envoyer**[2] *send* | envoyant envoyé | envoie, -es, -e envoyons, -ez, envoient | envoyais envoyai | enverrai enverrais | envoie | que j'envoie que j'envoyasse |
| **Faire** *do, make* | faisant fait | fais, -s, -t faisons, faites, font | faisais fis | ferai ferais | fais | que je fasse que je fisse |
| **Falloir** *be necessary* | fallu | il faut | il fallait il fallut | il faudra il faudrait | — | qu'il faille qu'il fallût |
| **Lire** *read* | lisant lu | lis, -s, -t lisons, -ez, -ent | lisais lus | lirai lirais | lis | que je lise que je lusse |
| **Mettre** *put* | mettant mis | mets, mets, met mettons, -ez, mettent | mettais mis | mettrai mettrais | mets | que je mette que je misse |
| **Mourir** *die* (*aux.* être) | mourant mort | meurs, meurs, meurt mourons, -ez, meurent | mourais mourus | mourrai mourrais | meurs | que je meure que je mourusse |
| **Ouvrir**[3] *open* | ouvrant ouvert | ouvre, -s, -e ouvrons, -ez, -ent | ouvrais ouvris | ouvrirai ouvrirais | ouvre | que j'ouvre que j'ouvrisse |
| **Pleuvoir** *rain* | pleuvant plu | il pleut | il pleuvait il plut | il pleuvra il pleuvrait | — | qu'il pleuve qu'il plût |
| **Pouvoir** *be able* | pouvant pu | peux (or puis), -x, -t pouvons, -ez, peuvent | pouvais pus | pourrai pourrais | — | que je puisse que je pusse |
| **Prendre**[4] *take* | prenant pris | prends, -s, prend prenons, -ez, prennent | prenais pris | prendrai prendrais | prends | que je prenne que je prisse |
| **Recevoir** *receive* | recevant reçu | reçois, -s, -t recevons, -ez, reçoivent | recevais reçus | recevrai recevrais | reçois | que je reçoive que je reçusse |
| **Rire**[5] *laugh* | riant ri | ris, -s, -t rions, -ez, -ent | riais ris | rirai rirais | ris | que je rie que je risse |
| **Savoir** *know* | sachant su | sais, -s, -t savons, -ez, savent | savais sus | saurai saurais | sache | que je sache que je susse |

[1] Like **dormir** are conjugated: **partir** = to set out, to start; **mentir** = to lie; **servir** = to serve; **sentir** = to feel.
[2] All verbs ending in -yer change y into i before e mute.
[3] Like **ouvrir** are conjugated: **couvrir** = to cover; **découvrir** = to discover; **offrir** = to offer; **souffrir** = to suffer.
[4] Like **prendre** are conjugated: **apprendre** = to learn; **comprendre** = to understand; **entreprendre** = to undertake.
[5] Like **rire** is conjugated: **sourire** = to smile

| Infinitive | Participles | Present Indicative | Imperfect, Preterite | Future, Conditional | Imperative | Subjunctive |
|---|---|---|---|---|---|---|
| **Suivre** *follow* | suivant suivi | suis, -s,*-t suivons, -ez, -ent | suivais suivis | suivrai suivrais | suis | que je suive que je suivisse |
| **Tenir**[1] *hold* | tenant tenu | tiens, -s, -t tenons, -ez, tiennent | tenais tins | tiendrai tiendrais | tiens | que je tienne que je tinsse |
| **Venir**[2] *come* (aux. être) | venant venu | viens, -s, -t venons, -ez, viennent | venais vins | viendrai viendrais | viens | que je vienne que je vinsse |
| **Vivre** *live* | vivant vécu | vis, -s, -t vivons, -ez, -ent | vivais vécus | vivrai vivrais | vis | que je vive que je vécusse |
| **Voir** *see* | voyant vu | vois, -s, -t voyons, -ez, voient | voyais vis | verrai verrais | vois | que je voie que je visse |
| **Vouloir** *wish* | voulant voulu | veux, x, -t voulons, -ez, veulent | voulais voulus | voudrai voudrais | veuille veuillez | que je veuille que je voulusse |

[1] Like **tenir** are conjugated: **appartenir** = to belong; **contenir** = to contain; **obtenir** = to obtain; **retenir** = to retain.
[2] Like **venir** are conjugated: **devenir** = to become; **revenir** = to return; **se souvenir (de)** = to remember.

# APPENDIX II
## LA CORRESPONDANCE

### 1. Cartes d'invitation

Monsieur et Madame Dupont prient Madame x . . . de leur faire le plaisir de venir dîner avec eux lundi prochain le 23 avril à 7 heures 30.

Monsieur et Madame Dupont prient Monsieur x . . . . de leur faire l'honneur de venir passer la soirée chez eux samedi le 4 décembre.

**prier** = to ask
**faire plaisir** = to give pleasure
**prochain** = next
**la soirée** = the evening

### 2. On accepte l'invitation

Madame x . . . . remercie Monsieur et Madame Dupont de leur aimable invitation à laquelle elle se rendra avec le plus vif plaisir.

**remercier** = to thank
**se rendre** = to go
**vif** = great

### 3. On décline l'invitation

(*a*) Monsieur x . . . remercie Monsieur et Madame Dupont de leur aimable invitation. Il regrette vivement qu'un engagement antérieur le prive du plaisir de s'y rendre et les prie d'agréer ses hommages respectueux.

(*b*) Madame,
Je vous remercie infiniment de votre aimable invitation. Des affaires urgentes me forçant à quitter Paris, je devrai malheureusement me priver du plaisir de me présenter chez vous lundi. Je vous prie, Madame, de croire à mon vif regret.

J'ai l'honneur d'être, Madame,

votre très dévoué,

x . . . .

**vivement** = extremely
**antérieur** = previous
**priver** = to deprive
**agréer** = to receive, to accept
**infiniment** = infinitely
**les affaires** (f. pl.) = business
**je devrai** = I shall have to
**malheureusement** = unfortunately
**croire** = believe
**l'honneur d'être** = the honour of being
**dévoué** = devoted

## 4. Renseignement

Monsieur,

Le 18 de ce mois (du mois prochain), j'arriverai à . . . (accompagné de ma famille); je compte rester quinze jours.

Veuillez donc m'informer si vous tenez à ma disposition une chambre à un lit (deux lits) et à quel prix, tous frais compris.

Dans l'attente d'une prompte et affirmative réponse, veuillez agréer, Monsieur, mes salutations.

Jules Lambert.

le renseignement = enquiry
compter = to count, to expect
quinze jours = a fortnight
veuillez m'informer = please inform me
la disposition = disposal
les frais (m. pl.) = costs
dans l'attente = awaiting

## 5. Réponse à No. 4

Monsieur,

En réponse à votre lettre j'ai le plaisir de vous faire savoir que j'aurai une chambre à deux lits à votre disposition le 18 juillet.

faire savoir = to let know

Le prix de la pension, chambre et taxes comprises est de 50 frs. par personne.

comprendre = to include

La pension comprend:
Petit déjeuner—Café au lait ou thé, pain et beurre.
Déjeuner—Poisson, plat de viande, légumes, dessert et café.
Dîner—Potage, plat de viande, légumes, dessert.
La boisson n'est pas comprise.

le potage = soup
la boisson = drinks
la nourriture = food

Nous vous garantissons une nourriture soignée et une belle et grande chambre avec tout confort.

soigné = first rate

Espérant l'honneur de votre visite, veuillez agréer, Monsieur, l'assurance de ma considération dévouée.

espérer = to hope

(Mme) H. Picard

## 6. Réponse à No. 5

Madame,

Veuillez me réserver une grande chambre à deux lits, de préférence avec salle de bain. Nous arriverons samedi soir à neuf heures.

de préférence = preferably
la salle de bain = bathroom

Sincères salutations,<br>Jules Lambert.

## 7. Lettre privée

Mademoiselle,

Vous serez sans doute surprise de recevoir cette lettre, puisque nous ne nous connaissons pas.

Un ami d'affaires de mon père, Monsieur Pernot de Toulon, nous a écrit qu'une dame française avait exprimé le désir d'entrer en correspondance avec une Anglaise. Ayant l'intention depuis longtemps de rafraîchir mes connaissances de français acquises à l'école, je me permets de venir vous faire la proposition suivante:

Nous nous écrirons tous les quinze jours—vous en anglais

puisque = since
connaître = to know
exprimer = to express
ayant = having, as I have
depuis longtemps = for a long time past
rafraîchir = to brush up
la connaissance = knowledge
suivant = following
tous les quinze jours = every fortnight

et moi en français—en nous retournant chaque fois les lettres corrigées. Qu'en pensez-vous?

Je vais donc commencer par vous dire qui je suis. Mon nom est Florence May. J'ai vingt ans et j'étudie les langues modernes (français, allemand, italien) à une des écoles polytechniques à Londres.

Je suis une fervente du ski et du tennis. Le mois prochain je prendrai part à un voyage organisé par un des bureaux de voyages dans les montagnes d'Écosse pour y faire du ski. Je vous écrirai plus longuement encore à ce sujet.

J'espère recevoir bientôt de vos nouvelles et vous salue cordialement entretemps.

Votre amie inconnue,

Florence May.

corriger=to correct
le nom=name
étudier=to study
la langue=language
allemand=German
je suis une fervente de=
  I am keen on
prendre part=to take
  part
l'Écosse=Scotland
à ce sujet=about this
recevoir de vos nouvelles
  =to hear from you
bientôt=soon
entretemps=meanwhile
inconnu=unknown

## 8. Lettres d'affaires

Monsieur,

Ayant appris votre adresse par M. Georges Durant je me permets de vous écrire bien que je n'aie pas encore eu l'honneur de faire votre connaissance.

J'ai le vif désir d'entrer en relations avec la maison que vous représentez. Veuillez avoir l'obligeance de m'indiquer l'heure à laquelle vous pourriez me recevoir.

Agréez, Monsieur, avec mes remercîments l'expression de ma considération distinguée.

Charles Maurois.

appris=learned (from apprendre)
je me permets=I take the liberty
bien que (subj.)= although
avoir l'obligeance de=to be so kind as
indiquer=to indicate
recevoir=receive

Monsieur,

En possession de votre honorée du 3 ct. (=courant) je m'empresse de vous dire que j'aurai grand plaisir à faire votre connaissance et, si possible, à entrer en rapport avec votre maison si renommée. Vous me trouverez tous les jours, dans l'après-midi, entre les quatre et six heures à l'Hôtel Majestic.

Agréez, Monsieur, l'expression de toute ma considération.

M. Smith.

honorée=esteemed favour
courant=instant
le rapport=relation
la maison=firm
renommé=renowned

## 9. Demande de prix courant (carte-postale)

Messieurs,

Je vous prie de bien vouloir m'envoyer votre dernier tarif.

Agréez, Messieurs, mes salutations empressées,

Julien Herriot.

prier=to ask, to beg
de bien vouloir=to be kind enough to
dernier=last, latest
le tarif=price-list

## 10. Envoi de tarif

Monsieur,

Nous vous accusons réception de votre carte-postale d'hier. Ci-inclus vous trouverez notre dernier tarif.

Dans l'espoir d'être favorisés de vos ordres nous vous prions d'agréer, Monsieur, nos salutations empressées.

A. Legrand et Fils.

accuser=to acknowledge
ci-inclus=enclosed
trouver=to find
favoriser=to favour

| | |
|---|---|
| The date: | **Paris, le 21 juillet 194-**<br>**le 1er mars 194-**<br>**lundi, le 17 avril, 194-** |
| Business Letters: | Opening: **Messieurs (Monsieur, Madame)**<br>Ending: **Agréez, Messieurs, mes salutations empressées**<br>or: **Veuillez agréer l'expression de mes sentiments distingués**<br>or: **Agréez, monsieur, mes salutations les plus distinguées** |
| Moderately familiar: | Opening: **Cher Monsieur (Chère Madame, Chère Mademoiselle)**<br>Ending: **Croyez à mes sentiments distingués**<br>or: **Votre dévoué** |
| Familiar: | Opening: **Mon cher Dubois (Chère Madame Dubois)**<br>Ending: **Je vous envoie mes meilleurs souvenirs**<br>or: **Bien à vous** |

| Intimate: | Love Letters: |
|---|---|
| Opening: **Cher Jules (Chère Marianne)**<br>Ending: **Affectueusement à toi**<br>or: **Bien à toi** | To him: **Mon ami** or **Chéri**<br>To her: **Mon amie** or **Chérie**<br>Ending: **Ton Georges (Ta Marie)** |

The address is as in English, but no abbreviations are used for **Monsieur, Madame, Mademoiselle.**

Printed Matter: **Imprimés (pl.)**

Sample Without Value: **Échantillon sans valeur**

Please forward: **Prière de faire suivre**

C/o: **aux bons soins de . . .**

(The expression **Poste Restante**, for letters addressed to a Post Office to be left till called for, is more or less international.)

### EXPRESSIONS IN COMMERCIAL CORRESPONDENCE

**J'ai l'avantage de vous faire savoir** ⎱ I have pleasure in

**J'ai l'honneur de vous informer** ⎰ informing you

**En réponse à votre lettre**=In reply to your letter

**Recevant à l'instant votre lettre du . . .**= Having just received your letter of the . . .

**Faire savoir**=To let (someone) know

**J'ai l'honneur, l'avantage**—I have the honour, the pleasure

**Ayez la bonté (l'obligeance) de**=Be so kind as to

**Dans l'attente de votre réponse**=Awaiting your reply

**Espérant être favorisé de votre clientèle**= Hoping to be favoured with your kind orders

**Je vous suis très obligé de ce service**=I am much obliged to you for this (service)

**Je suis redevable de votre adresse à**=I am indebted to . . . for your address

**Ayant appris que vous avez besoin d'un**= Having been informed that you require the services of a

**J'ai l'honneur de vous offrir mes services**= I beg to offer my services

**À votre honorée du**=to your letter of

Je connais parfaitement ce genre d'affaires = I am perfectly conversant with this (kind of) business

Nous regrettons qu'il nous soit impossible de faire l'expédition le . . . = We regret that we are unable to despatch the goods by the . . .

Nous regrettons de ne pouvoir profiter de votre offre obligeante = We regret that we are unable to avail ourselves of your kind offer

Nous regrettons qu'il nous ait été impossible de répondre plus tôt = We regret that it was impossible for us to reply earlier

La livraison aura lieu le mois prochain = Delivery will be made next month

Nous vous prions d'avoir l'obligeance d'envoyer = We beg you to be good enough to forward

UNE RUE DU VIEUX MARSEILLE

Les maisons s'entretouchaient presque dans ce quartier pittoresque où la lumière du jour y pénétrait à peine.   Ce quartier à été détruit pendant la guerre.

| s'entretoucher | la lumière du jour | à peine | détruire | guerre (f.) |
|---|---|---|---|---|
| to touch together, meet | daylight | hardly | destroy | war |

## SEWING AND MENDING
*(Key to illustration on page 106)*

| | | | | |
|---|---|---|---|---|
| **Aiguille (f.)** needle | **ciseaux (m.pl.)** scissors | **machine (f.) à coudre** sewing machine | **dé (m.)** thimble | **épingle (f.)** pin |
| **épingle de sûreté** safety-pin | **mannequin (m.)** dressmaker's dummy | **coudre** to sew | **raccommoder** to mend | **repriser** to darn |

## RESTAURANT
*(Key to illustration on page 165)*

| | | |
|---|---|---|
| **Garçon, apportez moi . . .** Waiter, bring me . . . | **le menu** bill of fare | **la carte des vins** wine-list |
| **la carte du jour** menu of the day | **dîner à la table d'hôte** to take the set dinner | **l'addition, s'il vous plaît** bill, please |

For further expressions see page 197. Fish, page 169. Meat, pages 186-187. Vegetables, page 171. Fruit, pages 183-185. Drink, pages 70-71. Menu, page 168.

## CHARACTER

| | | | | | |
|---|---|---|---|---|---|
| **Aimable** kind | **amusant** amusing | **bête** stupid | **bizarre** odd | **entêté** obstinate | **fidèle** faithful |
| **gai** bright | **gentil** nice | **honnête** honest | **intelligent** clever | **paresseux** lazy | **ravissant** charming |
| **sage**[1] wise | **sensé** sensible | **sensible** sensitive | **sérieux** earnest | **sympathique** likeable | **timide** shy | **triste** sad |

## SPEECH

| | | |
|---|---|---|
| **Parler à haute voix (à voix basse)** to speak loudly (in a low voice) | **faire savoir à quelqu'un** to let someone know | **répéter** to repeat |
| **faire une gaffe** to put one's foot in it; to drop a brick | **causer avec** to converse with | **bavarder** to chatter | **chuchoter** to whisper | **discuter** to discuss |
| **expliquer** to explain | **raconter** to tell to, to relate | **répliquer** to reply | **bégayer** to stutter | **zézayer** to lisp | **se taire** to be silent |

## AMUSEMENTS
*(See also pages 282-287)*

| | | | | |
|---|---|---|---|---|
| **Cinéma (m.)** cinema | **cirque (m.)** circus | **salle (f.) de concert** concert hall | **opéra (m.)** opera, opera house | **opéra-comique** comic opera |
| **revue (f.)** revue | **casino (m.)** casino | **bal costumé (m.)** fancy dress ball | **palais (m.) de danse** dance hall | **guignol**[2] **(m.)** Punch and Judy |

## TREES

| | | | | |
|---|---|---|---|---|
| **Bouleau (m.)** birch | **cerisier (m.)** cherry tree | **chêne (m.)** oak | **frêne (m.)** ash | **hêtre (m.)** beech |
| **if (m.)** yew | **orme (m.)** elm | **peuplier (m.)** poplar | **pommier (m.)** apple tree | **sapin (m.)** fir tree |
| **saule (m.)** willow | **verger (m.)** orchard | **bois (m.)** wood | **forêt (f.)** forest | **bosquet (m.)** grove; thicket |

[1] "Well behaved" when referring to children.  [2] Pronounced *geen-yol*.

**MONT ST. MICHEL: LA GRANDE RUE**

Generations of pilgrims and tourists have worn smooth the flagstones of the main street of the little island of Mont St. Michel, historic Norman fortress-shrine which forms the background to Roger Vercel's novel *Sous les Pieds de l'Archange*.

# STUDY GUIDE TO FRENCH LITERATURE

*by*

## L. E. GENISSIEUX

IN the French course which the student has now completed, he or she has been led easily and pleasantly to a knowledge of elementary French. Many will wish to use this knowledge as a stepping-stone to a more profound study of French literature. They will also wish to become better acquainted with the life and culture of the French nation. A course of private reading is here mapped out and a number of interesting books will be mentioned. Most of these books are obtainable in cheap or very cheap editions. Any good bookseller will readily supply all necessary particulars regarding publishers and price, and will obtain the required works for the student. Others can be borrowed from public lending libraries or consulted in their reference departments.

### A Good Accent

It has been observed that the English and French languages have, after all, only a limited number of speech-sounds in common. In other words, only a small proportion of the letters of their common alphabet can be said to be pronounced alike by English and French speakers. This is due to what are called "habits of articulation" or, more familiarly, "a French or an English accent". Now, there are two very different approaches to the task of acquiring a good French accent, that is to say to form French habits of articulation, and both approaches should be resorted to.

Babies learn their native tongue by ear. They unconsciously echo the speech-sounds heard by them. Older children and adults who go and live in a foreign country enjoy much the same facilities as a baby. If they take care to turn themselves (in this respect only) into faithful parrots, their ears train themselves to hear, and their vocal organs

to utter, those foreign-sounding noises. The student of French who is unable to spend some time—a fairly long time—in a French-speaking country should seek contacts with French people (or Swiss, or Belgian, or French-Canadians), or at least with French voices. Mention will be made later of some ways in which this can be achieved. A passing reference need only be made here to some text-books intended to be studied in connection with gramophone records. Such courses are useful, but they are expensive, even when they can be found second-hand.

The other approach to a good French accent is the scientific study of language sounds. This is called phonetics. A very good introduction to the study of French phonetics is André Classe's *Handbook of French Pronunciation*. Here will be learned "the mechanics of speech" and how to make the organs of speech produce the required sounds. Exercises in ear-training and speech-training are suggested by the author, who also deals briefly but adequately with stress, rhythm and intonation.

### How to Learn Words

The student should endeavour to form a good stock of readily available French words. To this end there is no better plan than to enter all new words in a pocket note-book. The French words and their English equivalents should be listed in parallel columns, learned and constantly revised until the English word immediately calls forth its French counterpart. French nouns should always be preceded by the article *le* or *la* indicating their gender. When a sufficient number of words has been collected, they should be grouped according to subjects, as, for example, animals, parts of the human body, colours, moral qualities, etc., Always carry your note-book with you, and occupy an idle moment by revising your words.

A good English-French and French-English dictionary will soon become a necessary help to the understanding of new reading matter. Several good ones are on the market. All scholars are agreed that the best is *Harrap's Standard French and English Dictionary*, whose editor, J. E. Mansion, devoted half a life-time to its compilation. Advanced students will consult it in public libraries. Those who are no longer beginners will want to possess its abridgement, the *Shorter French and English Dictionary*, which is published in two volumes, French-English and English-French.

A handy, up-to-date and cheap volume containing both parts, French-English and English-French, is Kettridge's *Dictionary of the French and English Languages*. When the student is fairly advanced, he should begin to use an all-French dictionary, such as French people use, in which the meaning of French words is accurately defined in French, which is better than having more or less exact English equivalents. The famous *Petit Larousse*, with its copious illustrations and maps, rightly enjoys universal popularity.

Let the student beware of such words as have the same or nearly the same form in both languages and yet carry entirely different meanings. A French *casserole* is an ordinary saucepan; in English, *casserole* denotes a certain method of cooking. English *loyalty* is faithfulness; French *loyauté* is frankness, openness. *To control* is to be master of; *contrôler* is merely to supervise and check up. Such words are called "false friends" because their apparent similarity is deceitful. They are so numerous as to fill two useful French books, *Les Faux Amis* by Koessler and Derocquigny, and Professor Félix Boillot's *Le Vrai Ami du Traducteur Anglais-Français et Français-Anglais*.

Finally as to words, it should be borne in mind that, apart from isolated words,

VILLAGE SCENE IN ALSACE

This Alsatian village, with its vegetable seller announcing by bugle the wares in his quaint equipage, has a character of its own. Alsace is the scene of Maurice Barrès' *Colette Baudoche*, which deals with the period when this region was under German rule.

there are also ready-made groups of words forming idiomatic phrases. Being mostly based on some quaint conceit, they are picturesque and vivid. Skill in using them shows in a foreign speaker his intimate knowledge of a language. The student can learn them out of Kettridge's *French Idioms and Figurative Phrases*, and in *French for English Idioms* by the same author.

## Concerning Grammar

"*La grammaire est l'art de parler et d'écrire correctement*". Old French grammar-books began with this definition. To speak and write correctly means to observe and obey the grammatical rules of the language. French people have always treated their language with great reverence. One of their greatest political leaders, the Cardinal de Richelieu, founded the French Academy in 1635 for the express purpose of "fixing" the language, that is to say of defining the exact meaning of French words and of setting down the grammatical rules, infringement of which would be considered as grave "incorrections". The *Dictionnaire de l'Académie* has had many editions and is constantly kept up to date, because new words are introduced, denoting new objects or ideas. As for the *Grammaire*, the Academicians took so much care over it that its first edition did not come out till some twenty years ago.

The English student who wants to have a good French grammar for the sake of reference, and indeed he cannot refer to it too often, will find in *A School Grammar of Present-day French*, by J. E. Mansion, a safe, up-to-date and clear guide.

## A Useful Exercise

Most text-books contain exercises. Indeed there is an excellent volume of *Exercises in French Syntax*, based on the above-mentioned *Grammar of Present-day French* and published as a companion volume. But exercises are not much use to the student who teaches himself unless he is supplied with a key enabling him to correct his work. He can, however, make his own exercises by a judicious use of J. E. Mansion's convenient *Bilingual Series*, in which short literary works are published with the French text and an English translation on opposite pages. The exercise here recommended is a two-way process. Let the student read and translate at sight a page of French text, and check up his translation by referring to the English version. After an interval of a few days, he should attempt what is called a back-translation. This consists in taking the English printed version as a basis and trying to reproduce in writing the very words and turns of phrase of the French author. Not only language, but a good literary style will be learned in this way.

## Literature of France

The same conscientious care that the French have always lavished on their language has been exercised by their writers in their literary compositions. France has thus produced one of the greatest literatures of the world. "If", says Lytton Strachey, "we would seek for the essential spirit of French literature, where shall we discover it? In its devotion to truth? In its love of rhetoric? In its clarity? In its generalising power? All these qualities are peculiarly its own, but, beyond and above them, there is another which controls and animates the rest. The one high principle which, through so many generations, has guided like a star the writers of France is the principle of deliberation, of intention, of a conscious search for ordered beauty; an unwavering, an indomitable pursuit of the endless glories of art".

In this masterly appreciation the eminent critic rightly laid stress on the French taste for formal beauty, for what is to-day called technique. French prose-writers and poets have been fond of experimenting in literary forms, and often they have led writers of other nations, and particularly English writers, to experiment likewise in their own native languages.

Two other characteristics of French literature, also mentioned by Strachey, deserve to be more fully set forth. They are *clarity* and *generalising power.*

As to clarity, it is an essential requirement of the French reader that he should understand what he reads. *"Ce qui n'est pas clair n'est pas français"*. And this is true not only of the language, but of the orderly, logical, eminently reasonable presentment of the subject matter in a literary composition, whatever its nature. This clarity, demanded by Frenchmen and appreciated by readers from other countries, has been another cause of the world-wide influence of French literature. It is again a formal quality, but one intimately bound up with the very substance of thought. For the habit of clear speaking and clear writing necessarily springs from clear thinking.

And what is the chief object of thought for the great writers of France? Is it the material universe? Is it the varied aspects of Nature? These, indeed, are not absent from their preoccupations, but they do not constitute their principal or "proper" study. It was from his French models that Pope learnt that "the proper study of mankind is man". How the human mind works, what the true motives of human actions are, what makes men and women feel what they feel and behave as they do, those are the problems that French writers have chiefly attempted to solve, and the greatest of them have achieved their end with signal success. This is what one means when one speaks of their "psychological genius". Now when the French author searches the depths of a character,

ST. EMILION, IN THE BORDEAUX REGION

Here we see the grape harvest being gathered in, at a centre known by name to all drinkers of claret. This is the country so well described in François Mauriac's novels.

although he may have a Frenchman in view, the observations he makes are valid for any member of the human species, whatever his colour, creed or country. The French author's incisive, deliberate analysis leads him to the same general truths that Shakespeare discovered by his unique gift of intuition. This is the *generalising power* of French literature, the third, the chief factor in France's influence upon the literatures of other nations. For, just as Shakespeare has become universally popular, so have the French literary master-pieces become the common possessions of all civilized men.

It would be most attractive to sketch out an outline of the history of French litera-ture by watching, so to speak, its mirrored reflection, from period to period, in the stream of English literary output. One would see French influences—those of the allegorical *Roman de la Rose* and of the French versifiers of the XIVth century— preside over the very birth of English literature in the poetry of Chaucer. One would find in Jehan Froissart, the chronicler of the Hundred Years War, whom Lord Berners translated, a writer as popular with the English reading public as with that of France. Later, one would note how the spirit of the Italian Renaissance was transmitted to England largely through French channels. Spenser and Shakespeare himself owed not a little to French prose-writers and poets, while at least one French source can be mentioned for Milton's *Paradise Lost*. The greatest glory of French literature is probably its "classical period", the XVIIth century; and so one sees the great writers of tragedy, Corneille and Racine, taken as models by Dryden, while Wycherley adapts Molière's comedies. Likewise, in the early XVIIIth century, Pope's ambition is to be the English Boileau. Voltaire is mirrored in Gibbon—and, with peculiar originality and lyrical beauty, in Shelley. Swinburne borrows more than one splendour from the great Hugo and the greater Baudelaire. The more recent authors, Flaubert, Maupassant, Zola, Verlaine, Anatole

France, Marcel Proust, have all brought their indirect contribution to the develop-ment of English literature.

The full story of the literary relations between France and Britain is yet to be written. But French literature can be studied for its own sake in Dowden's *History of French Literature* (a library book), or in two excellent and cheap little volumes, G. Lytton Strachey's *Landmarks in French Literature* (Home University Library), already quoted above, and Laurence Bisson's *Short History of French Literature* (Penguin Books).

## What to Read in French

However useful, and indeed indispen-sable, the last named critical and historical studies may be, they cannot take the place of direct contact with the actual works they deal with. They are only books about books. As soon as the student can read French more or less off-hand, he should start on a course of reading based on the best writings in the language. Out of the accumulated wealth of nine centuries, and out of the considerable number of French books re-printed and available in Great Britain to-day, it is no easy task to select those works which are most suitable to the new student. The list given in the follow-ing pages is not exclusive, and the omission of many very good books implies no adverse criticism of them.[1]

## Step by Step

Apart from its linguistic value as material for translation from and into French, the *Bilingual Series* that has been mentioned before may well provide the learner with his first literary reading matter. Insomuch as the short stories included in the series are of real literary value, and are com-petently translated into English, they constitute ideal material at the initiation stage.

Several educational publishers have

---

[1] Some of the books listed may be out of print. Second-hand copies can often be obtained through the usual channels.

reprinted short French texts. These French "readers" are generally edited with suitable care and provided with glossaries and sometimes explanatory notes. Among them will be found French tales, one-act plays, short stories, etc. As they are graded with reference to the age of the scholars and their standard of attainment, it is possible for the adult student to work his way through a selection of some of them from the elementary to the more advanced stage.

Of these easy reading books, the following, originally written by some of the best French writers, are old favourites, and particularly to be recommended.

*La Tulipe Noire* is an entrancing short story by Alexandre Dumas, the famous author of *The Three Musketeers*. Its style is simple. The tale is told with ease, in a lively manner, and contains much conversational dialogue.

More thoughtful in manner, but equally vivid in the telling, is *La Canne de Jonc*, one of the three short stories that make up *Servitude et Grandeur Militaires*, by the great poet and prose-writer of the French Romantic school, Alfred de Vigny.

Immensely popular with readers of all nations has always been the collection of tales from the South of France published by Alphonse Daudet under the title of *Lettres de mon Moulin*.

The greatest French master of the short story, however, is Guy de Maupassant. His tales rise to the maximum of dramatic pitch with the minimum of effort. The acuteness of his psychological insight is only matched by the minute accuracy of his descriptions.

One more book may be mentioned here, a full-length novel this time, but one which generations of English people have enjoyed. It is Edmond About's *Le Roi des Montagnes*, an absorbing tale, half humorous, half dramatic, of wild adventures in modern Greece.

### Reading Course for Advanced Students

We will now assume that the student has reached a standard of proficiency sufficient to enable him to read and enjoy in the original text the chief masterpieces of French literature. In the following list the works are arranged according to the various chronological periods, beginning with the XVIth century, because Old French requires a special study. Only those works are mentioned which can easily be procured.

### Renaissance Period

Ronsard, *Poèmes Choisis*. Du Bellay, *La Défense et Illustration de la Langue Française; Poésies; Les Chefs ,d'Œuvre Lyriques de Ronsard et de son École* (ed. A. Dorchain); J. Amyot, *Les "Vies des Hommes Illustres" de Plutarque*. (North's translation of this work was used by Shakespeare.)

### Classical Period

Corneille, *Théâtre Choisi*. Molière, *Théâtre complet* (comedies). Racine, *Théâtre complet* (tragedies, and one comedy). Pascal, *Pensées*. Fénelon, *Dialogues des Morts*. La Bruyère, *Les Caractères*.

*The Eighteenth Century.*—The greatest names are those of the fore-runners of the French Revolution of 1789: Montesquieu, *Lettres Persanes; Grandeur et Décadence des Romains*. Voltaire, *Contes; Poésies*. Rousseau, *Émile*. Dramatic works: Marivaux, *Le Jeu de l'Amour et du Hasard*. Beaumarchais, *Le Barbier de Séville; Le Mariage de Figaro*. Novels: Le Sage, *Gil Blas*. Bernardin de Saint-Pierre, *Paul et Virginie*.

### Romantic Period

This is ushered in by the great prose-writer Chateaubriand (*Atala, René, Le dernier Abencérage*). The chief glory of French romanticism is its lyrical poetry, with Lamartine, Vigny, Musset and Victor Hugo.

Next comes the romantic drama, enriched by the influence of Shakespeare: Vigny, *Chatterton;* Musset, *Comédies et Proverbes, Lorenzaccio;* and again Hugo.

The same period produced also several great novelists, who are among the world's greatest: Vigny, *Servitude et Grandeur Militaires;* Balzac, *Les Chouans, Le Père Goriot, Le Médecin de Campagne,* and many more works; George Sand, the gifted woman who wrote *La Mare au Diable*, *Le Meunier d'Angibault*, and a great number of other novels. She is also remembered for her short and unhappy affaire with Alfred de Musset, her own version of which she gave in *Elle et Lui*. Other novelists of the Romantic period who are well worth reading are: Théophile Gautier, *Le Capitaine Fracasse*, *Le Roman de la Momie;* Eugène Fromentin, *Dominique;* Mérimée, *Chronique du Règne de Charles IX*, *Colomba*, and various short stories in the purest French prose style; Stendhal, a writer of genius, who was as he himself proclaimed, fifty years ahead of his generation, and whose masterpieces are *Le Rouge et le Noir* and *La Chartreuse de Parme*. Alexandre Dumas is known in translations all over the world. His *Trois Mousquetaires*, *Vingt Ans après*, *Le Vicomte de Bragelonne*, *Le Comte de Monte-Cristo*, etc., must be read in the French original for the vividness of their narrative and conversational style. His more recent imitators also deserve to be mentioned here: Amédée Achard, *La Cape et l'Epée*, etc.; Jules Lermina, *Le Fils de Monte-Cristo*. And once more there are Victor Hugo's novels.

But Hugo deserves a paragraph to himself. By the abundance and variety of his production, by the vigour of his literary temperament and the splendour of his artistry he towers above his contemporaries and his · figure dominates the whole century. There is no literary form which he did not attempt. Reference has already been made to his lyrics, to his dramas, and to his novels. His chief works may be conveniently listed here:

Lyrical poems: *Les Feuilles d'Automne*, *Les Voix Intérieures*, *Les Contemplations*, *Les Chansons des Rues et des Bois*, *L'Art d'être Grand-père*.

Satirical poetry: *Les Châtiments*.

Epic poetry: *La Légende des Siècles*.

Philosophical poetry: *Dieu*, *Les quatre Vents de l'Esprit*.

Dramatic works: *Cromwell*, the long preface of which was one of the chief

AVIGNON: PALACE OF THE POPES

Avignon sheltered the Popes for centuries during the Middle Ages, when they were driven out of Rome. Here is the Palace which they occupied during their exile. Avignon is the centre of the country described in Alphonse Daudet's *Lettres de Mon Moulin*.

### FALAISE : BIRTHPLACE OF WILLIAM THE CONQUEROR

From a window in this castle Robert, father of William the Conqueror, sighted Arletta, daughter of Fulbert the tanner, washing clothes in a stream. Their romantic story can be read in Augustin Thierry's *Histoire de la Conquête de l'Angleterre par les Normands.*

### MARKET DAY IN SAVOY

These farmers and townsmen of Mégève, Savoy, discussing the day's business at the conclusion of the livestock fair, might have been taken from one of the novels of Henri Bordeaux. Many of his works have the mountains of Savoy as their background.

manifestoes of the Romantic school; *Hernani; Ruy Blas.*

Novels: *Notre-Dame de Paris* (known to English readers as *The Hunchback of Notre-Dame*), *Les Misérables, Les Travailleurs de la Mer, Quatre-vingt-treize.*

### Nineteenth Century Historians

A remarkable school of historians flourished in France during last century. The greatest of them is Michelet. His *Jeanne d'Arc* was originally published as part of his monumental *Histoire de France.* Mignet is the author of *La Révolution Française*, also a fragment from a general history of France. By Renan we have the admirably written *Vie de Jésus* and his *Souvenirs d'Enfance et de Jeunesse*; and by Augustin Thierry the picturesque *Récits des Temps Mérovingiens.* The fascinating story of Napoleon may be read in Albert Vandal's *L'Avènement de Bonaparte* and in the *Mémoires* of the Duchesse d'Abrantès.

### Post-Romantic Period

The poet of this period is Charles Baudelaire, whose best known collection is *Les Fleurs du Mal.* His small poetical output will live as long as Hugo's numerous tomes. Three masters of the novel belong to the "naturalist" and "realist" schools, whose influence has been world-wide: Flaubert, *Madame Bovary, Salammbô, L'Education Sentimentale*; Maupassant, *Contes;* Zola, *Une page d'Amour*, etc.

There is plenty of fun and humour in the light comedies of Eugène Labiche, *Le Voyage de M. Perrichon*, etc. Readers who like books of travel will enjoy Pierre Loti's *Jérusalem;* and those whose hobby is natural history will relish two admirable studies of insect life, J. H. Fabre's *Scènes de la Vie des Insectes* and Maeterlinck's *La Vie des Abeilles.*

### Late Nineteenth Century, and Contemporary Novelists

The following alphabetical list of authors is given for reference and should by used in conjunction with publishers' catalogues. Space forbids the inclusion of the titles of the books themselves except in the case of outstanding works: Edmond About, Jean Aicard (*Maurin des Maures*), Maurice Barrès (*Colette Baudoche*), René Bazin, Henri Bordeaux, Paul Bourget (*Le Disciple*), René Boylesve, Jean de la Brète (*Mon Oncle et mon Curé*), Albéric Cahuet, Madame Caro, Gaston Chérau, Victor Cherbuliez (*L'Aventure de Ladislas Bolski*), Jules Claretie (*Le petit Jacques*), Maurice Constantin-Weyer (*Un homme se penche sur son Passé*), Pierre de Coulevain (*L'Île inconnue*), Alphonse Daudet (*Lettres de mon Moulin, Contes du Lundi, Le Petit Chose, Jack*), Georges Duhamel (*Confession de Minuit*), Erckmann-Chatrian (*L'Ami Fritz*), Octave Feuillet (*Le Roman d'un jeune homme pauvre*), Anatole France, the great stylist (*Sur la Pierre blanche*, etc.), Léon Frapié, Emile Gebhart, Maurice Genevoix, Gyp, Ludovic Halévy (*L'Abbé Constantin*), Louis Hémon (*Maria Chapdelaine*), Emile Henriot, Anatole Le Braz, Marie le Franc, Eugène Le Roy (*Le Moulin du Frau*), Hector Malot, François Mauriac, André Maurois (*Les Silences du colonel Bramble, Les Discours du Dr. O'Grady*), Louis Pergaud, Ernest Pérochon, J. H. Rosny, Jérôme et Jean Tharaud (*L'Ombre de la Croix*), André Theuriet, Marcel Tinayre, E. M. de Vogüé (*Les Morts qui parlent*).

To complete this bibliography of French literature, students are strongly recommended to acquire and have always at their side a good book of selections from the best French authors, chiefly the poets. The *Oxford Book of French Verse* is a standard work, but omits the more recent poets. Very convenient for the pocket (in more than one sense) are *The Hundred Best Poems in the French Language* (lyrics only), F. M. Forrest's *French Poetry*, Victor Cohen's *Modern French Verse*, and the more recently published Penguin book *Des Vers de France*, selected by Laurence Bisson, with a masterly introduction giving the characteristics of French poetry and showing how it differs from English. Also to be recommended are the small annotated volumes by H. E. Berthon, *Specimens of Modern French Verse* and *Specimens of Modern French Prose*, and his more scholarly *Nine French Poets* (of the XIXth century). Add also *Je t'Aime*, an anthology of love poems selected by the present writer.

### Pleasant Land of France

There are several reasons why one may wish to learn a foreign language. To read in their original text the great authors who have written in that language is only one of them. Another reason is surely to get an insight into the people who speak that language, to know the country they live in and their ways of life. To achieve these ends there is, of course, no better way than to live in the country or to visit it. But it is not given to everyone to be able to travel abroad: for their instruction some will have to rely on books. On the other hand, a visit to France, especially if it is to be a short one, should be carefully prepared. Thus it will be both more profitable and more enjoyable. Whoever contemplates a journey to France must therefore "get up his subject", in other words, read some good books about the country, its past history and present condition. Students will, it is hoped, be grateful for the mention in the following pages of a few such books.

The soundest basis for a knowledge of France is a good geography text-book, such as *France* (in English) by Estyn Evans. That is the scientific approach. It should be supplemented by some chatty narrative of a journey to France. Fletcher's *Tour de France en Auto* is a pleasant and easy narrative of such a journey. The book contains good photographic illustrations and is provided with a vocabulary. It takes the reader through the chief French provinces and depicts that striking variety of natural aspect, customs and habits, which make up and enrich the unity of the French nation. For France is extremely varied. Its Eastern provinces have some characteristics of Central Europe; the South gives one a foretaste of Italy and Spain; a fishing village in Brittany is almost like a village in Cornwall; while French Flanders is really a part of the Dutch and Belgian geographical area.

Within this frontier zone of mountains and sea-coasts France has other high mountains: the volcanic summits of Auvergne; great rivers and rich valleys, such as those of the Seine, the Loire, the Garonne, the Rhône; forests, cornfields, vineyards and many towns and cities, each with its peculiar individuality.

### Paris

Of all French cities one has the distinction of being at the same time the metropolis of a great country and one of the capital cities of the world.

Paris is both the heart and brains of France. Paris alone confers national recognition on provincial talent. Paris is the goal of each gifted and ambitious Frenchman. It is from Paris that the country and the empire are governed. It is not only the seat of government, but France's chief seat of learning, with its University, its museums and libraries, its academies, its schools for higher study, and its science laboratories covering all fields of human knowledge. But Paris is more than this. It is the meeting-place of whatever is distinguished in all walks of life throughout the world, a centre of new ideas and of artistic creation. Not only do good Americans, as the proverbial saying is, go to Paris when they die, but thousands of live men and women come to Paris from all lands under the sun for its charm and the opportunities it offers.

A popular introduction to French everyday life as it is concentrated in Paris will be found in an easy and attractive form in Dr. W. G. Hartog's *Le Voyage des Dupont*, a series of seventy-five conversations that originally appeared in the *Daily Mail* under the title *Brush up your French*. M. and Mme Dupont are a French couple who live in London and go back to their native country for a holiday. They spend most of their time in Paris, visit all sorts of shops, fall ill and recover, and finally go for a short spell at the seaside. The book has witty illustrations and a helpful vocabulary. Those who would prefer a similar work in English are advised to read *Discovering France*, by Maurice and Eithne Thiéry, one of the series called "Discovery Books". This discovery of France is made by an English boy and his sister who go to live with a French family in Paris, explore the capital and ultimately finish their holiday in Normandy and Brittany: a good book to read as a preparation for a visit to France or as a substitute for such a visit.

## French · Characteristics

There are curious contrasts in the psychological make-up of the French man or woman. They are intensely individualist and impatient of state regulations, yet they are very sociable and, without forcing themselves in the least, are ready to sympathise with any human being, whatever his race, creed or class. Their chief passion is liberty. They are realists, as is to be expected of a race of peasants, yet they have given the world sublime examples of patriotic and religious idealism. They like to live well, paying great attention to their food and the elegance of their clothes, and at the same time their chief interests lie in things of the mind. Their gifts are intellectual and artistic more than practical, yet they have achieved great feats of engineering. They are supposed to be light-hearted and care-free, but can be profoundly serious when they are clearly convinced of the righteousness of a course of action. They are also found excitable and believed erratic, yet their chief intellectual virtue is that they distrust sentimentalism and insist on having clear notions of whatever they consider. They are fond of reasoning, of building up logical systems and of arguing about them. Some of these characteristics are explained in English and in very simple language in Hebe Spaull's *France*. The author wrote her book for English school-children, but adults may read it with profit. Written for American school-children, but widely used in English schools, François Denoeu's recent *Petit Miroir de la Civilisation Française* treats the same subject in fuller detail and in a very attractive form.

In the same book Miss Spaull shows how the France of to-day has been shaped and her present characteristics determined not only by her geographical conditions, but also by the course of her long history. The political institutions which a country has given to itself fashion in their turn the outlook of the people. The France that we know at present cannot be fully understood unless one follows her destinies through the ages.

How France grew from a loosely joined assemblage of feudal territories into a powerful kingdom whose national consciousness was for ever embodied in the heroic figure of Joan of Arc; how the kings of France consolidated their power and set up the political framework which was to make of France under the Revolution and during the reign of the first Napoleon the most highly centralised of European states; what a Louis XI, a Richelieu, a Louis XIV contributed to the formation of French unity and to the concentration of power in the hands of governments that were by turns royalist, imperial and republican, all this fascinating story can be studied in the usual history books. Let it suffice here to mention two little volumes written in easy French and dealing with the history of France chiefly from a picturesque and anecdotic point of view. They are Maurice Thiéry's *Histoire de France* (from the early Middle Ages to the French Revolution) and the same author's *Légendes et Mystères de l'Histoire de France* (from Joan of Arc to the ill-fated son of Louis XVI and Queen Marie-Antoinette).

## Development of Modern France

It is, however, the development of modern France that is chiefly important in view of the part she has played and will play again in world affairs. The modern period begins with the Revolution of 1789. In that period France has known, first a Republican government, then successively an Empire, two monarchic régimes, a Second Republic, another Empire and then the Third Republic, which temporarily collapsed in June 1940. Contrary to the views commonly held on the supposed inherent instability of French governments, it is worthy of note that out of that period of roughly 150 years the whole latter half (1870-1940) was one of peaceful and prosperous internal development under the democratic institutions of the republican régime proclaimed on September 4, 1870.

In *La France et sa Civilisation de la Révolution à nos Jours*, by Professors René Lanson and Jules Desseignet, French institutions are described against their geographical and historical background. The chief points treated are the French social structure, so different from that of England, the parliamentary system, the organization of the various branches of public administration, law-courts, schools and universities, the fighting services, the Church in its relation with the State, and France's colonial policy. It must not be forgotten that France possesses a colonial empire second only in extent to the British Empire, nor that it was almost entirely an achievement of the Third Republic.

More limited in scope, since it covers only the crucial period 1919-1933, Professor Vaucher's *Post-war France* (Home University Library) deals competently with the country's domestic and foreign policies after the first world war had been won and before the system of collective security had collapsed.

The story is taken up and brought down to the second world war, to the French armistice of 1940 and to the German occupation in the remarkable volume on *France* by Pierre Maillaud, published in 1942 in the Oxford University Press cheap series, "The World To-day". The small book is a marvel of condensation.

Many books, perhaps too many, have been written on the crushing military defeat suffered by France in May and June

A BASQUE "BULLFIGHT"

This somewhat comic bullfight, with ample means of escape provided for the amateur "toreadors," takes place in a village in the Basque country, in the south-west corner of France. This is the country described in Pierre Loti's work *Ramuntcho*.

1940. The first one to appear still retains a great value as the testimony of an eye-witness who noted down in his diary the momentous events as they occurred from May 10th to June 21st. It is *The Last Days of Paris*, by Alexander Werth, the well-known journalist, who was at the time Paris correspondent of the *Manchester Guardian*. The story of French resistance against the German conqueror, in Paris as well as in the non-occupied zone, is told in simple, vivid, moving terms by a lady who escaped to England in 1942, Madame Madeleine Gex Le Verrier, in *Une Française dans la Tourmente*. Both these books are obtainable in English as well as in French, the former having been trans-lated into French by the writer of this guide as *Les Derniers Jours de Paris*, and the latter into English as *France in Torment*.

### Additional Helps

To the foregoing bibliography, which has been drawn up especially for the benefit of students, an appendix is now added in which will be mentioned a number of other important helps to study.

The student will need a French song-book. A cheap and convenient one is *Chansons de France*, edited by Marcel Vigneras.

The chief periodical publications pub-lished in French in Great Britain are: *La France*, a weekly illustrated paper for schools; the beginner will find it easy to read; *France*, another weekly contain-ing general news, articles, classified adver-tisements, etc.; it was established in London in 1940; the monthly periodical *Entente*, published in French and English on parallel pages; it is copiously illustrated and is devoted to the promotion of mutual understanding between the two countries; and finally, the admirable monthly review *La France Libre*, also founded in 1940, which has always maintained a very high literary standard.

Besides the written word, there is the spoken word. Needless to say, students should use every opportunity to form acquaintances and friendships with French-speaking people. But, in the privacy of their homes, they have a simple means of hearing the best French spoken. They need only tune in to the French broadcasts. Several times a day the news is given in French by the B.B.C. French news section. At other times may be heard French programmes of music, short talks on current topics and school broadcasts in French.

Frequently a good French talking film—and most French films are excellent—is shown in London and in the larger provin-cial towns. The British Film Institute has a special section of foreign films, which are lent to educational bodies under certain conditions.

We welcome the resumption of a scheme which functioned before World War II. It provides for the exchange of letters between British and French school-children. It is part of a world-wide service, the *Correspondance Scolaire Inter-nationale*, officially sponsored by the League of Nations through its Institute for In-tellectual Co-operation. It works mainly through the schools, but applications coming from adults seeking correspondents in foreign countries are also dealt with.

Finally, attention is directed to some French centres in London and the pro-vinces where contacts may be made and maintained with French people and French things. There are Anglo-French societies or French circles in many towns, and one large association, *Les Français de Grande-Bretagne*, which welcomes British "sym-pathizers". London is, of course, fortunate in having the French Institute in South Kensington (*Institut Français du Royaume-Uni*) whose dual purpose is the education of French children living in Britain and the promotion among English people of the study of French and all matters concerning France. The Institute holds classes and lectures, mainly for advanced students who read for the University of London certifi-cate of proficiency in French or for a French University degree. There are also lectures for the general public, film shows and dramatic performances. The Institute also has a very ample French library.

# ALPHABETICAL GUIDE TO MAIN CONTENTS

# WORD-BUILDING PICTURES AND DIAGRAMS

*Published 1947*

Copyright S. 147 T.   Printed in Gt. Britain by Keliher, Hudson & Kearns, Ltd., Hatfields, S.E.1